UNDERGROUND CATHOLICISM
IN SCOTLAND

UNDERGROUND
CATHOLICISM IN SCOTLAND
1622-1878

by
PETER F. ANSON
Illustrations by the Author

MONTROSE:
STANDARD PRESS
1970

TO

THE REV. WILLIAM JAMES ANDERSON, M.A.
Archivist of Columba House, Edinburgh
(Scottish Catholic Archives)

Printed in Scotland at the
Standard Press, Montrose

CONTENTS

ILLUSTRATIONS

ILLUSTRATIONS contd.

FOREWORD

AGAIN AND AGAIN in recent years, people have asked me where they could pick up second-hand copies of *The Catholic Church in Modern Scotland,* which was published by Burns, Oates and Washbourne in 1937 and is long since out of print. Others enquired whether a second edition was ever going to appear. They pointed out that my book, whatever its defects, remained the only source of reference to the history of post-Reformation Catholicism in Scotland and they were not far wrong. In 1883 Alfons Bellesheim, a canon of Cologne Cathedral, published his *Geschichte der katholische Kirche in Schottland.* Four years later Dom Oswald Hunter-Blair, a monk of Fort Augustus Abbey, brought out the first of the four-volumes translation of this monumental work, with additional notes, entitled *History of the Catholic Church in Scotland from the Introduction of Christianity to the Present Day.* Eighty-three years have elapsed and, although several Catholic authors have had books published covering specific periods, there is nothing to put against the array of Scottish ecclesiastical histories produced by Protestant writers.

Shortly after the second world-war came the realisation that little serious research had been done by Catholics on the history of religion in Scotland for well over half a century. This resulted in the formation of a Scottish Catholic Historical Committee composed of priests and layfolk, and the publication of the first issue of *The Innes Review* in 1950, under the editorship of the Rev. David McRoberts, S.T.L. The purpose of this periodical was to print serious articles on Scottish Catholic history, and it has continued to encourage students in this direction. The name given to the Review was a tribute to Thomas Innes (1662-1744), in the hope that the title would serve to keep alive something of the patience in research, the impartiality of judgment, and the kindliness towards all men which characterised all the work of this historian and missionary priest. More recently the archives of Blairs College, Aberdeen, have been transferred to Edinburgh, where they are under the charge of the Rev. William James Anderson, M.A., as resident archivist.

Having sought the advice of both Fr. McRoberts and Fr. Anderson, I was assured that no other author, as far as they were aware, was working on a book covering the same period as my *Catholic Church in Modern Scotland*. So I decided to revise the text. These two priests made it clear enough that it would be a long time before the researches of the Scottish Catholic Historical Committee would reach the stage of a really authoritative survey of post-Reformation Catholic life in this country. The work is difficult and involves much expense, since the history of Scottish Catholicism lies buried, for the most part, in archives at home and abroad.

By far the most important source for the history of the post-Reformation Catholic Mission to Scotland, in so far as it was staffed by secular clergy and members of religious orders other than the Society of Jesus, is to be found in Roman archives, chiefly but by no means exclusively those of *Congregation de Propaganda Fide*. These can be supplemented in important ways by the material in Catholic hands in Scotland but the former is the central source. How extensive it is can be gathered from an article by Fr. Cathaldus Giblin, O.F.M., published in *The Innes Review*, Volume V (1954). Of these 'Proceedings' or 'Acts' alone there are 275 volumes for the period 1622-1900, in which all volumes from the beginning to 1878 (and to a lesser degree after that year) contain material essential to this story. In addition there is the series of *Scritture riferite'* (Documents submitted) copied either verbatim or in summary. In this series, for example, there are seven large volumes for the period 1623 to 1878 devoted wholly to Scotland. Very little of all this material filed at Rome has been made available so far. Only very few selected documents were included by Bellesheim in his four-volume history, first published in Germany eighty-three years ago. Since then no serious attempt has been made to investigate the Roman sources of information. All historians will appreciate at once that at the present time, and for a long time to come, any survey of Scottish Catholicism must be provisional in character. So the present book can be regarded merely as a stimulus to historians better qualified than myself. I have merely scraped the surface.

I imagined that the revision of my *Catholic Church in Modern Scotland* would be completed within a few months, but I had not reckoned with Fr. Anderson. Each chapter was sent to him and returned to me covered with red pencil comments, corrections and criticisms. More often than not, valuable new material was enclosed, throwing light on this or that incident or controversial point. Not content with this collaboration, Fr. Anderson was generous enough to lend me rare seventeenth and eighteenth century books and pamphlets, so that I could quote direct from them. The MS grew longer and longer, until I realised that limits must be put on the period covered. Such is the reason for confining the present work to the years between the re-organisation of the Catholic Mission in Scotland under the care of the Congregation of Propaganda, which began in 1622 to send secular priests to Scotland, and the restoration of the Hierarchy in 1878.

The original version of the book had to be condensed to about half its length, and I have been working on this job for nearly eight years. My thanks are due not only to Fr. Anderson but to many others who have helped me, including Mr Allan W. Campbell, Dr Gordon Donaldson, the Right Rev. Mgr David McRoberts, the Rev. S. G. A. Luff, the Rev. G. Mark Dilworth, O.S.B., the Rev. James K. Robertson, also the Librarians of Fort Augustus Abbey and Pluscarden Priory.

On one subject, the story of the Scots Colleges abroad, this work will be found inadequate. It is quite impossible to write briefly about Paris, Douai, Rome, Madrid and Valladolid — even more so about Ratisbon, which was both a Benedictine abbey and a seminary for secular clergy. The history of these overseas institu-tions is fascinating, but difficult and in part highly controversial. For these reasons it had to be excluded, and must wait an oppor-tunity for fuller treatment.

Sometimes truth is stranger than fiction, and I have no doubt that some readers will find passages in this book both unwelcome and even offensive. Although I have tried to avoid controversial matters, the history of Scotland at all periods has been marked by them. It has never ceased to be melodramatic and often it has been characterised by violent contrasts of black and white, with few half-tones. Whatever may be the religious standpoint of a historian, it is difficult for him to be impartial in his judgments, or for that matter to feel kindly towards all men. The history of the restoration of the Catholic Church of Scotland, which covers a period of roughly 300 years, is far from peaceful — to make an understate-ment.

PETER F. ANSON

Caldey Island,
off Tenby,
Pembrokeshire.

INTRODUCTION *

WHEN ELIZABETH became Queen of England and Ireland on the death of her Catholic half-sister Mary I, in November 1558, she realised at once that not only the political security of her nations but also the restoration of the Anglican *via media* of Protestantism, depended first on breaking Scotland's 'Auld Alliance' with France, which was stronger than it had been for centuries. Her cousin Mary Stuart had been sent to France at an early age, and in her marriage treaty with the Dauphin, Francis, conveyed the crown of Scotland to the King of France, making him her heir if she died without issue. Mary's mother, Queen Mary of Guise, had been acting as Regent of Scotland since 1554. Henry II died in July 1559 and this meant that Mary was Queen-Consort of France as well as Queen of Scotland. She was also the rightful Queen of England if the divorce of Henry VIII and Catherine of Aragon was invalid. In actual fact Scotland had ceased to exist as an independent nation for nearly five years, and had become an overseas province of France held together by French troops until a French king came in person to deal with his new province.

Acting on the advice of her wise and prudent Secretary of State, William Cecil (later Baron Burleigh), Elizabeth resolved to sponsor a revolution in Scotland by making use of a ruthless but skilful minority. This was composed of an alliance of unscrupulous nobles who were opposed to this French alliance that was in imminent danger of becoming a French annexation. Hungry to enrich themselves with yet more church lands and benefices, they were quite willing, as the old enemies of national unity, to support the Protestant daughter of Henry VIII if she would help them.

The lords could also rely on the backing of a comparatively small group of Protestant reformers, who firmly believed that God had called them to purge the Kirk of papistical idolatry and superstition. Most of these men had come under English influence and

---

* This necessarily brief introduction understates reasons other than political which helped to bring a change of religion in Scotland. The period is given much fuller treatment in the 496 pages of *Essays on the Scottish Reformation*, 1513-1625, edited by David Roberts (Glasgow, 1962). These fifteen essays by scholars working independently present a picture of sixteenth-century life which is much more involved, much more human, exciting and real, and therefore much more credible than the uncomplicated and ingenuous tales of our grandfathers, whether Protestant or Papist.

their leader, John Knox, had spent five years in England (1549-54), with a later spell among English Protestant refugees at Frankfurt and Geneva. They had no clear-cut doctrinal standpoint, only a negative anti-Catholic 'front', and were not agreed among themselves. Knox too had greatly offended Elizabeth by his pamphlet entitled *The First Blast of the Trumpet against the Monstrous Regiment of Women* (1558), which stated that government by a woman is contrary to the law of nature and to Divine ordinance. The Queen never forgave him for this diatribe, even though it was applied primarily to Mary Tudor and Mary of Guise. No matter, when Knox ultimately returned to Scotland in 1559 and became the recognised leader of the reforming party, his first effort was to procure money and troops from England to enable the lords to drive the French out of the country.

The Scottish Church had become as corrupt as in most continental countries, much more so than in England, and for over a decade it had been trying to reform itself. Three Provincial Councils had passed innumerable and detailed statutes more or less on the lines of the Decrees of the Council of Trent (1543-63) for the reformation of morals and the extirpation of heresy. Heretical books, mostly Lutheran at first, had been smuggled into Scotland in spite of an Act of Parliament in 1525 forbidding their importation. The execution of several Protestant reformers helped to make the Church unpopular and led to the murder of Cardinal Beaton in May 1546, following on the burning of George Wishart. The delay in enforcing the Statutes of the Provincial Councils was due largely to the unsettled political state of the country and all this time propaganda for a revolutionary change and a complete overthrow of the old religion and its institutions was going on unchecked. The Queen Regent herself hoped that, when a French Catholic King took control of Scotland, heresy would be stamped out and the Church would regain its former power.

By February 1560 Elizabeth felt that the moment had come to interfere in the religious and political affairs of her northern neighbour, although Cecil still advised caution. A pact was made between the English Government and the Scottish 'Lords of the Congregation' by which Elizabeth would become the Protector of Scotland. An English fleet appeared in the Firth of Forth. Troops were landed and helped the Scots insurgents to besiege Leith. The Queen-Regent was deposed, and power transferred to a 'Great Council of the Realm'. She died in June, and a few weeks later a treaty was signed at Berwick, followed on July 6 by another treaty at Edinburgh providing for the withdrawal of foreign forces from Scotland. The English armies of Elizabeth had put the Protestant barons into power, and all was now ready for a *coup d'état*.

In August Parliament accepted the reformed *Confession of Faith*, drawn up in four days (so Knox says) by himself and five other preachers. This typically Calvinist document of twenty-five articles was a direct attack on papal authority as prejudicial to Scotland. Civil magistrates were declared to be lieutenants of God and it was their duty to conserve and purge the Kirk when necessary, although supreme authority was ascribed to the Word of God. Incidentally, the acts passed by the 'Reformation Parliament' of August 1560 contravened the terms of the 'Concessions' granted to the Scots by the Treaty of Edinburgh, which was signed only a month before. There it was stated explicitly that all religious questions should be submitted to the "intention and pleasure" of the King and Queen.

This legal flaw did not worry Elizabeth. With the help of men and money, she had achieved an almost bloodless and astonishingly rapid revolution, which transformed Scotland within two months from a Catholic nation into a Protestant one. But what *kind* of Protestantism it was to be was still not settled. All that mattered to Elizabeth and her Secretary of State was that they had broken the 'Auld Alliance' of Scotland and France, and forged a new alliance with her southern neighbour, which for centuries had been the 'Auld Enemy'.

Francis II of France died in December that same year and his young Scots Queen was left a widow. In January 1561 some of the Lords of the Congregation finally agreed with reservations to subscribe to the *Book of Discipline*, which had been drawn up by John Knox and five of his fellow reformers, and was completed by the end of May 1560. It was a comprehensive plan for the ordering and maintenance of the reformed Kirk, based on the Genevan 'Ordonnances' of Calvin, but adapted to Scottish requirements. Parts of this book were not welcomed by the nobles, because they indicated a loss of church lands and revenues for the benefit of a national system of education. For lack of civil authority, the book remained a dead letter and was not enforced.

By the time when Queen Mary returned to her native land in August 1561, after an absence of thirteen years, the Protestant Lords of the Congregation had already acquired supreme control of the nation. All she could do was try to re-assert the normal power of the crown, and even in this she failed. There was no immediate prospect of seeking to re-establish Catholicism, as her cousin Mary I had done in England after her accession in 1553. On the other hand, Fr. Nicolas of Gouda, S.J., who had been sent to Scotland as papal envoy in 1561, returned to the continent the following year, quite optimistic that the medieval church would eventually be resurrected with a Catholic sovereign using the royal prerogative, Catholic bishops, councillors, colleges, and a Spanish alliance.

From first to last, the Scottish Reformation, unlike that of England and most continental countries, took the form of a political revolution in defiance of the reigning sovereign. Although it was so drastic, at first it involved much less disturbance of existing institutions and officials. Most of the Bishops were related to the pro-English Lords of the Congregation—better described as wealthy lairds rather than shepherds of souls. With other dignitaries, the bishops retained their offices and continued to be members of the Privy Council, alongside whole-hearted supporters of Calvinism. One of the thirteen sees was vacant and only one of the remaining twelve prelates took a definite line against the reformers. This was James Beaton, Archbishop of Glasgow, who had gone on diplomatic business to France in 1560 and did not see fit to return. Four of the hierarchy gave unqualified support to the revolution, the Bishops of Caithness, Galloway and Orkney becoming militant followers of Knox. Three more bishops went on administering their dioceses and, directly or indirectly, helped to infiltrate the doctrines and policy of Calvinism in Scotland. The rest played for safety, hoping that the hurricane would blow itself out.

Though a certain number of monasteries were looted by Protestant mobs, none were suppressed as *legal corporations*. It was no longer possible, however, to celebrate Mass within their walls. Their superiors, many of them commendatory abbots or priors, continued to draw their revenues. Five of Queen Mary's bastard brothers had held great monasteries in this fashion since they were boys.* A considerable number of religious were left undisturbed and were still paid the stipends to which they had been entitled before 1560, though how far they continued to observe their rules is another matter. In most places too the canons-regular, monks and friars were not turned adrift. If they stopped saying or assisting at Mass, they were able to stay on in their houses. Many took advantage of this. As all popish ceremonies were now forbidden under the familiar triple penalty of death for the third offence, anything like regular observance of the religious life was rendered impossible.

The beneficed secular clergy had at least two thirds of their income secured to them for life. Like not a few of the regular clergy, some took the chance to contract matrimony, which was now legal for them. The new parochial ministry, quite insufficient for the spiritual needs of the laity, was recruited mainly from the former parish priests, canons-regular, monks and friars. Only a handful of these refused to accept the tenets of the reformed religion and retired to live with relations or sought safety abroad.

The whole system of enforcing the new form of religion was much more subtle than in England. Every kind of direct persecution, cruelty and bloodshed was absent at first. None of the bishops,

* By 1539 three of the natural sons of James V, all minors, were abbots of Holyrood, Kelso and St Andrews. Later on one of these boys became Abbot of Melrose as well as of Kelso. Another royal bastard was Prior of Coldingham, and his half-brother became Prior of the Charterhouse at Perth. All these appointments are made with dispensations from the Holy See; the later ones by Paul III, who had already made cardinals his teenaged grandsons, Alessandro Farnese and Guido Sforza.

clergy or laity (except schoolmasters) were compelled to subscribe to the 1560 *Confession of Faith*. It was not until 1573 that subscription was made an obligatory condition for holding a benefice. Although the laity at first were not forced to partake of the Lord's Supper, the centuries-old spiritual life of the country faded out, mainly because the celebration of Mass was prohibited under the pain of death. The general attitude of people towards the Reformation is indicated by the absence of any armed Catholic rebellions in Scotland. There was never anything like the English 'Pilgrimage of Grace', Wyatt's Rebellion or the Northern Rising. In Scotland there was nothing to compare with the wholesale execution of Papist priests and layfolk during the later years of the reign of Elizabeth. It is doubtful if more than one Scottish priest suffered the death penalty for saying Mass in the last forty years of the sixteenth century. In fact, organised opposition to the Reformation was on a very small scale, and so the Calvinist reformed Episcopal Kirk very nearly became the undisputed church of the nation.

It took a hundred and thirty years for the Church of Scotland as it exists today to become securely entrenched. Not until after the death of Knox in 1572 and the return of Andrew Melville to Scotland from Geneva in 1574 did the last traces of medieval prelacy disappear, with the drawing up of a second *Book of Discipline* in 1578. This manifesto of Presbyterian polity was endorsed by the General Assembly in 1581, though it never obtained complete civil recognition. What eventually turned the bishops for a time into nothing more than superintendents, for administering the business of the Kirk, were the so-called 'Black Acts' of 1584, which also defined the supremacy of the sovereign in ecclesiastical affairs. Yet it must not be forgotten that different forms of episcopacy persisted until 1638, and that bishops were restored in 1660 after the Covenanting interlude. They were finally abolished in 1690. So it is true enough to say that from 1560 to 1690, except for the years 1638-60, the established Church of Scotland remained a reformed Episcopal Church.

What is most significant about the Scottish Reformation is that the withdrawal of public recognition of the Catholic Church — as it had existed from the time of St Margaret in the eleventh century — was followed immediately by its collapse as an *institution* almost as completely as in Denmark, Norway and Sweden. But this need not have happened. Public recognition merely gives obvious practical advantages to the Church. In certain countries, at different periods of history, an established Catholic Church which has degenerated into little more than a state department has often been a grave danger to both faith and morals. In its essential nature the Church is utterly independent of Caesar. If the fairly strong Catholic minority had been able to gain control and remain united, it is conceivable that *Ecclesia Scoticana* might have been restored to communion with the Holy See, but this was frustrated by the failure of the Jesuits to make a convert of the young King James VI.

Facts are facts, and there is little doubt that the foundation of *Ecclesia Scoticana,* which Celestine III had declared in 1192 was the 'special daughter' of the Holy See, subject to it without the intermediary of York, had been so undermined that the top-heavy medieval superstructure collapsed suddenly with the force of an earthquake. Only the ruins remained, though bits and pieces of them were incorporated in the structure of the reformed Church.

The Bishops died off one by one, most of them having accepted the new religion either openly or tacitly. By 1596 only James Beaton, Archbishop of Glasgow, was left. Two more of the old hierarchy ended their days overseas. William Chisholm (II), the unconsecrated coadjutor Bishop of Dunblane, eventually became a Carthusian monk and died at Rome in 1593. John Leslie, appointed Bishop of Ross in 1566, became Mary's ambassador to Elizabeth three years later. After imprisonment in England from 1571 to 1573, he was released on condition that he retired abroad. In 1579 he was appointed suffragan bishop and vicar-general of Rouen. He was translated to the see of Coutances in 1593, but he never administered this diocese. He spent his last years with the Austin Canons at Guirtenburg, near Brussels, where he died in 1596.

After the execution of his mother in 1587, James VI found it convenient to regard the elderly Archbishop Beaton as his personal ambassador in Paris. Though what we call 'tulchan'* bishops were appointed to Glasgow after 1571, the see was not regarded as vacant by the King himself and no true successor was appointed until after Beaton's death on April 15, 1603. Indeed he was restored to the temporalities of his see on June 19, 1598, for his services as ambassador, though the amount of income he derived from his Scottish regality is not certain. But the appointment of John Spottiswoode as the first true Protestant Archbishop of Glasgow was not made until July 20, 1603, and this minister of the reformed Kirk did not receive Anglican consecration until 1610.

Beaton never lost theoretical jurisdiction over Catholics in the Glasgow archdiocese. As the last surviving Scottish Catholic bishop, he is likely to have had some authority over missionary work. He was consulted when Catholic envoys were sent to Scotland, but he was in no position to exert any jurisdiction over the few priests left in the country who had not conformed to the new religion. They really had no superior except the Pope himself as 'universal ordinary', whose jurisdiction never fails if that of a local ordinary is impeded.

---

* A tulchan is a stuffed calf-skin, placed under a cow that withholds her milk. 'Tulchan bishops' in fact, though not in name, existed before the Reformation and implied the holder of a see who drew its revenues for the benefit of others.

With the death of Archbishop Beaton, the Catholic Church in Scotland, as it had been understood for five centuries, came to an end. Not more than about half a dozen priests remained, and in 1605 it was reported that there was only one, but this may have been painting too black a picture. No serious attempt was made to start excavating the foundations of a new Church until twenty years later, and it was not until 1653 that what might be called the foundation stone was laid. The building of this new Church took 225 years, and it was not completed until 1878.

Even before it was clear that the old Church could not be re-built and refurnished, colleges had been founded abroad for training missionaries destined to work in Scotland. The first two were at Douai (1576-1612) and Rome (1600). The Scots College at Paris originated in the fourteenth century as a small group of endowed scholarships or bursaries in the gift of the Bishop of Moray. It was refounded by Archbishop Beaton's will. For reasons which will be explained, none of these colleges managed to send a regular succession of secular priests to the Scottish Mission for at least the first fifty years after their foundation. This was due partly to the apparent indifference of the Roman authorities to Scotland's spiritual welfare.

From 1603 to 1653 the few remaining Catholics in Scotland were left without even a rudimentary organised Church. They lacked any visible unity, and they hardly realised that they were still under the remote jurisdiction of the Vicar of Christ. The long and complex story of the building of a new *Ecclesia Scoticana* in communion with the Holy See (the subject matter of this book) is made up of an almost never ending series of hold-ups and set-backs, disappointments and frustrations. In one sense we may be thankful that there is no material continuity between the medieval Catholic Church, whose structure fell to pieces before the impact of the movement sponsored by Elizabeth of England in 1560, and the new organisation which has been created to occupy the place of the Church of the Middle Ages.*

* In 1969 the estimated Catholic population of Scotland was 818,930, i.e. roughly 16% of the total population of 5,187,500 in 1968.

CHAPTER ONE

CATHOLIC LIFE IN SCOTLAND
1622-1653

The break-up of Catholic Europe after the Reformation and missionary work in other continents.

THOUGH THE CATHOLIC CHURCH was always a missionary church, until 1622 it never worked out a strategic plan to convert the whole world. This date is important also for Scotland, because it was only then that the Roman authorities faced the fact that the pre-Reformation Scottish Church could not be brought back to life, and that henceforth Scotland must be treated as a missionary country.

By the second decade of the seventeenth century the whole world was known and mapped, imperfectly no doubt, but the great discoveries were over. Theologians were perturbed at the unexpected number of heathen and were estimating their prospects of hell and heaven. By 1622 it was also clear that Protestant countries were not going to listen to the invitations of the Council of Trent (1545-1563), and intended to remain out of communion with Rome. There were therefore non-Catholic nations to be re-converted, which had formerly been part of the Western Patriarchate.

The Council of Trent realised that complete reconciliation of countries which had lapsed into heresy and schism might be a slow process, but hoped to maintain contact with them by diplomatic methods. If the reigning sovereign were a Protestant, a papal nuncio or even what we would now call a personal envoy might be acceptable. This had been done in England, with a succession of somewhat tenuous relations between the Papacy and the Government. But where the break had been drastic it was the papal practice to entrust the nearest Nuncio with a kind of watching brief to supervise Catholic interests in a 100 per cent. Protestant country so far as he could. The Nuncio in Brussels, then the capital of the Spanish Netherlands, had such a duty for Scotland.

Foundation of the Congregation for the Propagation of the Faith, 1622

This Roman Congregation originated in a commission of Cardinals, set up by Gregory XIII primarily to promote the reconciliation of the schismatic oriental Churches. The Commission was expanded by Clement VIII, and was erected into a permanent Congregation by Gregory XV in the Constitution *Inscrutabili,* on June 22, 1622. Its specific task was to spread the faith throughout the world, and more especially to meet the spiritual needs of the newly discovered heathens in America, Africa and Asia. From 1622 to 1878 Catholic life in Scotland remained under the direct supervision of the Congregation *de Propaganda Fide,* which from 1627 maintained a missionary training seminary in Rome — the *Collegio Urbano de Propaganda Fide.*

In regard to Protestant countries, Propaganda had a new idea which took some time to work out. Contrary to previous practice, attempts were made to send duly consecrated bishops into countries, without permission of the civic rulers, often without their knowledge. Of necessity, such bishops would not do many things which till then had been regarded by the civil authorities as part of their functions. Roman Canon Law was no longer recognised by Protestant nations, so a bishop's judgment concerning, *e.g.* marriage, or will and inheritance, had no legal effect at all. A bishop could ordain and confirm, he could rely on the obedience of his clergy, but his sanctions were purely spiritual. He acted as a delegate of the Pope, and in countries where a local episcopate had been suppressed or died out, or lapsed into heresy and schism, then as now he became automatically the Bishop or Ordinary of any Christian. That is why such bishops are styled 'Vicars-Apostolic'. They have what powers the Pope gives them, no more and no less. Scotland had to wait until 1694 before it obtained its first Vicar-Apostolic.

The religious state of Scotland at the time of the erection of the Congregation de Propaganda Fide.

James VI had been resident in England for nineteen years when the Congregation for the Propagation of the Faith was erected in 1622. He governed the northern sister-kingdom from London, with a small group of men of his own choosing on the various bodies forming the Scottish legislature, executive and judiciary. Scotland still had its own Cabinet or Privy Council, directly subject to the King. The nobles, however, were the intermediate rulers of the nation, and it paid them to keep on the right side of James, knowing that he was quite ready to bribe them with favours or pensions.

After long drawn-out negotiations, the General Assembly of the Established Church agreed in 1610 to a new form of administrative episcopate which gave the bishops certain rights over the admission, deposition and supervision of parish ministers. On October 21 in the same year, the King arranged for three ministers —John Spottiswoode, Andrew Lamb and Gavin Hamilton, who occupied the sees of Glasgow, Brechin and Galloway respectively

—to receive episcopal consecration in London. The ceremony was performed by the Bishops of London (George Abbot), Ely (Lancelot Andrews), Rochester (Richard Neile), and Worcester (Henry Parry).

According to one version of the story, Dr Bancroft, Archbishop of Canterbury, had stated that he saw no need for making the three ministers deacons and priests according to the form and manner printed in the *Book of Common Prayer*. Ordination by a presbytery, he maintained, was lawful when bishops could be had, and not to recognise their orders would be casting aspersions on those of the Reformed Churches abroad.

On their return to Scotland the three prelates consecrated the remainder of those appointed to be bishops. No attempt was made to re-ordain ministers in presbyterian orders, so the result was the recognition by the Church of England of a church with a ministry composed of pastors who had not received episcopal ordination, and in which the rite of confirmation was practically unknown.

This moderate variant of episcopal government was accepted in Scotland with few protests. The majority of layfolk could not see that it made much difference to the Kirk, because the bishops were still subject to the General Assembly if occasion arose. It was a compromise, but it worked fairly well for the short time it lasted. The Catholic remnant saw no reasons for entering into what we should now call ecumenical relations with the Establishment. It was a body with a policy best described as 'bishop-in-presbytery'— neither strictly presbyterian nor episcopalian as now understood— which confronted Propaganda when considering how the reconversion of the Scottish nation could best be attempted.

The Scottish Reformers had abolished the official observance of the traditional Christian seasons, but in 1614 the King was bold enough to order the re-introduction of Christmas and Easter. Four years later he went a step further and put forward certain ritual and ceremonial requirements which became known as the Five Articles of Perth. These, however, were bitterly opposed by the more Presbyterian-minded clergy and laity. The royal attempt to infiltrate Anglican customs into Scotland met with so little response that the ever-astute James VI promised to make no further changes in his lifetime. The Bishops did not enforce the Five Articles. Public worship remained virtually the same as it had been when the Established Kirk was ruled by presbyters. Papists were not encouraged to believe that it was even a purged version of pre-Reformation Catholic worship.

English Archpriests given nominal jurisdiction over Catholics in Scotland (1598 and 1625)

In 1598 the few remaining secular priests in Scotland had been put under the jurisdiction of George Blackwell, the first of the three so-called 'Archpriests' nominated for England. None of them, however, appears to have concerned himself with the religious affairs of the Sister Kingdom, where there were seldom more than two or three secular priests working simultaneously. The last of the three Archpriests was William Harrison. Appointed in 1615, he was given faculties, confirmed by Paul V, which covered 'the kingdoms of England, Scotland, Ireland, Man and other places subject to the King of Great Britain, and for persons belonging to those places exclusively.'*

On March 23, 1623, two years after the death of William Harrison, William Bishop was appointed Vicar-Apostolic for England and Scotland, with the style of Bishop of Chalcedon. A handful of Scottish secular priests on the continent felt obliged to protest against the nomination of an Englishman to rule over what was left of the Church in Scotland. One of their number, David Chalmers (Chambers, *'Camerarius'* or *'Camerinus'*) addressed a memorial to the Pope in which he stressed the ancient enmity between the two nations.†

He reminded the Roman authorities of the disastrous results in the past of trying to subject the Church in Scotland to prelates, and explained that the English had no knowledge of the domestic affairs of this adjacent country. If priests had to apply to a bishop in England for rulings on reserved cases and similar matters, he would be at a loss to know how to deal with them—Scots Law then, as now, being different from English Law. Mr Chalmers doubted whether a bishop was required in Scotland. Priests would still have to be educated overseas in colleges and religious houses, and ordained there. As Catholics in Scotland had been deprived of the sacrament of Confirmation for nearly half a century, so God would continue to supply its special grace, at least until the situation seemed more propitious.

Apparently Gregory XV paid no attention to this protest. He died about a month after the consecration of William Bishop. When Urban VIII nominated Richard Smith as the second Vicar-Apostolic in January 1625, he gave him the same status as his predecessor, but Bishop Smith's stay in England was brief and unhappy, and he retired to France in 1631.‡

---

*Cf. Tierney, Dodd's *Church of England* (ed. 1839), Vol. V. Appendix, no. xxvii.

† Apparently ordained in France, Chalmers visited Scotland in 1631, and acted as Principal of the Scots College, Paris, from 1637 to 1641.

‡ It has sometimes been stated that William Ogilvie, Abbot of Wurzburg, was appointed "Prefect of the Scottish Mission" by Urban VIII in 1629. The actual documents make it quite clear that he was given jurisdiction only over the very few Benedictine missionaries in Scotland. (Cf. Alphons Bellesheim, *History of the Catholic Church in Scotland*, translated by D. Oswald Hunter-Blair, O.S.B. (1890), Vol. IV, p. 41.

Catholics in the Lowlands of Scotland remained under the purely nominal jurisdiction of English Vicars-Apostolic for twenty-eight years. To all intents and purposes, the layfolk were sheep without shepherds, for Scotland never had crowds of 'seminary priests', like those who flocked to England from abroad during the reigns of Elizabeth and James.*

Very little is known of the activities of the few secular priests who worked in Scotland between 1613 and 1624.† None seems to have remained long in the country. They either left on their own initiative or were banished.‡ Two years after the erection of the Congregation of Propaganda five secular missionaries began work in their native country—James Rollock, Archibald Hegat, David Tyrie, Thomas Beattie and William Stewart. In 1625 Andrew Leslie turned up, but soon he realised it would be to his material and spiritual advantage to return to the continent and join the Society of Jesus.§ The following year Patrick Gordon, brother to the laird of Letterfourie, Banffshire, had the courage to come back to Scotland as a priest but, like the rest, he soon departed.**

The Society of Jesus in Scotland

If a young Scots Catholic in the first quarter of the seventeenth century felt called to devote his life to the reconversion of his country, the obvious thing for him to do was to seek admission to the Society of Jesus. Unless he had private means or relatives to maintain him, the hazardous life of a secular priest was virtually impossible.

Founded in 1534 by St Ignatius Loyola, this new and novel

* So far as is known, the first secular priest ordained abroad, who returned to Scotland, was Robert Philip of Sanquhar, Dumfriesshire, who arrived in 1612. He had been educated at the Scots Colleges in Paris and Rome. He was arrested, tried in Edinburgh, and banished from the kingdom. Soon after his return to France he joined the Oratorians, and was one of the chaplains who accompanied Queen Henrietta Maria to England after her marriage (by proxy) to Charles I in 1625. He went back to France, and died at Paris in 1647. His name was put forward as a bishop for Scotland in 1637.

† In the course of this book secular priests are always given the title of 'Mister', because until about a hundred years ago the style of 'Father' was reserved to members of religious orders. It was not until well after the middle of the 19th century that secular priests in England began to be addressed as 'Father', a custom introduced apparently from Ireland. In Scotland the secular clergy continued to be addressed as 'Mr' until after the restoration of the hierarchy in 1878. This was in accordance with the custom in most countries of Europe, e.g. 'Monsieur le Curé' (or 'Monsieur le Vicaire) in French; 'Signore' or 'Don' in Italian.

‡ Among their numbers were Andrew Crichton, William Thomson, James Seaton, George Ashlown, and Robert Crichton.

§ He became a Jesuit in Flanders in 1627, and later on became an active missionary in Scotland.

** A list of secular priests who were in Scotland between 1612 and 1637 will be found in Appendix V of M.V. Hay's The Blairs Papers (1603-1660), (1929), pp. 247-9.

type of religious institute had grown by the close of the century into a vast world-wide 'army', under the supreme command of a Father-General resident in Rome, with more than 14,000 men owing him allegiance. Like the Communist Party in our day, the Society had 'cells' in every Catholic country in Europe, all equipped with colleges, not only for training its own members but also for the general education of boys and youths. The Jesuits had also gained control of several universities. Their 'commando' troops had infiltrated into almost all the now Protestant nations in Europe, and were engaged in an underground warfare against Anglicanism, Calvinism and Lutheranism. Foreign mission work on a big scale was being carried out in India, China, Japan and Central and South America, and soon it was to be extended to North America. To all intents and purposes the Society of Jesus was Christ's Church militant here on earth from the point of view of the Papacy, even if this would not have been admitted.

Every 'recruit', no matter whether he was destined for the priesthood or as a lay-brother, was given a long and arduous training, and it was seldom that anyone was considered ready to engage in any sort of apostolic work within ten years of the start of his training. No pecuniary means were required for admission to this international Papist 'Salvation Army'. Men were accepted at almost any age, so long as they had reasonably good health and showed signs of that spirit of obedience which was the hall-mark of a true Jesuit.

Almost as soon as the Congregation of Propaganda was erected, trouble arose between it and the Society. Was the Society controlled by Propaganda or was it not? That question, which was of world-wide importance, was not finally settled so far as the Society was concerned, until its suppression by Clement XIV in 1773.

The Jesuit 'invasion' of England had started in 1580 and no time was wasted in forming a separate mission to Scotland, because it was realised that this country "was, in fact, a key-piece in the conversion of England, and so in the conversion of Europe".[*]

Fr. Persons, who was in command of the Jesuit missionaries in England, stressed this when he wrote to the fifth General, Fr. Claude Acquaviva: "On the conversion of Scotland depends every hope, humanly speaking, of the conversion of England." Gregory XIII gave his approval for a separate Scottish Mission. He also got in touch with Archbishop Beaton of Glasgow, then living in Paris, and decided to send two Jesuits to spy out the land.

Early in 1582 Fr. William Crichton, formerly Vice-Provincial of Aquitaine, and Brother Emerson, who had been a close friend of Fr Edmund Campion, left for Scotland, but the Mission was not

---

[*] James Quinn, S.J., 'The Jesuits in Scotland', in *The Tablet*, January 30, 1960, p. 106.

The Chapel, Scots College, Rome (1656).

14

formally erected until 1584, when Fr. Crichton and Fr. James Gordon returned to their home country. Later, Fr. Edmund Hay, a Scotsman who had been Provincial of France, was put in charge of the Mission, and from then onwards there were usually at least half-a-dozen Jesuits leading lives of extreme danger and often heroism. They went about in disguise and generally lived with members of the aristocracy who had remained loyal to the Catholic religion.

Their method of apostolate was political as well as spiritual, for they firmly believed that the chief thing to do was to win over the nobility and landed gentry. Fr. Robert Abercromby went one better and somehow managed to obtain the official rank of Keeper of the King's Falcons at Holyrood Palace. At one time he was optimistic of reconciling James VI with the Church, and though he failed in this he later managed to persuade James's Lutheran Queen, Anne of Denmark, to 'go over to Rome'.

So, when all was said and done, the secular clergy hardly counted in Scotland during the first quarter of the seventeenth century. They were so few in number that they could not have provided teachers for three of the Scots Colleges overseas and, as a result, Douai (1612), Rome (from 1615) and Madrid (1627) were controlled by the Jesuits.* Paris remained the only college staffed by secular priests.

In 1615 Fr. John Ogilvie suffered martyrdom at Glasgow—the only post-Reformation Scottish Catholic who has been beatified. Ten years later Propaganda introduced what was called 'The Mission Oath'. Every student, admitted to a college and supported by its funds, had to promise not to enter a religious order or congregation until he had served at least three years in Scotland as a secular priest. This oath was intended to prevent the Jesuit professors using undue influence to persuade students to join the Society.

More than once the Scottish Jesuits tried without success to get this oath abolished. It seemed quite unreasonable to them. Many students, having lived with Jesuits, undoubtedly did not feel drawn to the secular priesthood. While the highly centralized organisation of the Society gave them a sense of security and *esprit de corps*, as secular priests they found themselves more or less isolated individuals, once they arrived on the Scottish Mission. In theory the Scottish Mission was subject to an Archpriest in England, but in

---

* The Douai College started at Tournai in 1576, then moved to Pont-à-Mousson, when its associations with the Jesuits began, thence to Douai. After a series of moves to Louvain and Antwerp it was re-established at Douai in 1612.

For the history of the Roman College, see *The Scots College, Rome* (Edinburgh, 1930); and ' Abbé Paul Macpherson's History of the Scots College, Rome ', in *Innes Review* (Vol. XII, 1961), ed. by W. J. Anderson.

practice it was dependent on the Pope alone or, in a vague way, on the papal nuncios at Paris or Brussels. If a priest's health broke down, there was no place to which he could retire. If he was banished, as happened not infrequently, he could not demand a refuge in France, Italy or the Spanish Netherlands. To all intents and purposes he was an itinerant, free-lance evangelist, even after the erection of the Congregation of Propaganda in 1622. The priests were supposed to be maintained by the Congregation, but, as will be repeated again and again in this story, very often the money promised failed to arrive and they were reduced to dire poverty, even to starvation. The wonder is that any young Scots Catholic, knowing what difficulties and obstacles he would have to face once he went on the Mission, ever had the courage to become a secular priest at all. From every point of view there was everything to be said in favour of joining the Society of Jesus.

Members of other religious orders working in the Lowlands of Scotland.

During the first quarter of the seventeenth century other religious orders had priests working on the Scottish Mission, but there were seldom more than half-a-dozen of them all told. Little had been recorded about their apostolate.

Throughout this period the three Scottish Benedictine monasteries in Bavaria — Ratisbon, Würzburg and Erfurt — were more in the nature of refuges overseas, where Scotsmen could dedicate their lives to the service of God among their compatriots, than centres for training and sending forth missionaries. They never fulfilled quite the same purpose as did the four monasteries of the English Benedictine Congregation which were founded on the continent between 1607 and 1643.*

The first Capuchin Franciscan — Fr. Epiphanius Lindsay — arrived in Scotland about 1620. At first he acted as chaplain to the nobility, but later his apostolate took on a more Franciscan character. For more than thirty years he wandered around the country, disguised as a shepherd. He used to play the pipes at fairs, or at other occasions where he was likely to meet Catholics. Three times he was betrayed by false friends but he always managed to escape. He died in 1666, aged eighty-four.

George Leslie, who was given the religious name of Archangel when he joined the Capuchins, was the son of James Leslie of Peterstone, an Aberdeenshire laird. Having been reconciled with the Church, he left Scotland and entered the Scots College at Rome, in 1608, but soon decided that he had a vocation for the religious state. In the Marches of Ancona he endured the rigours of a Capuchin Franciscan novitiate and then he was professed and

---

* Douai (1607), Dieuluard Lorraine (1608), Paris (1611), and Lambspring, Hanover (1643).

ordained priest. In 1617, stationed at Bologna, he was hearing the confessions of English, Scots and Irish exiles, and six years later the Minister-General allowed him to return to Scotland, as a missionary. His apostolate extended from Galloway in the south to Aberdeenshire in the north-east, and he appears to have made many converts. In 1630, cited by Propaganda to answer charges made against him by some of his fellow missionaries, Fr. Archangel was forced to return to Italy. There he was acquitted and became Guardian of the friary of Monte-Giorgio, hidden away among the mountains in the Marches of Ancona. He was allowed to go back to Scotland in 1634, and died three years later at his mother's home near Aboyne.* Several other Scotsmen joined the Capuchins, including John, ninth Lord Forbes (Brother Archangel the second) who succeeded to the title in 1616 and died the same year.

The reconversion of Scotland to Catholicism was not checked only by persecution from without, as is often taken for granted. Untold harm was also done by internal dissentions largely bound up with disputes over jurisdiction and strife between the secular and regular clergy, over a long period. This all too important lack of unity in the Mission may have led to many layfolk lapsing into heresy and schism. But the strife, from first to last, was between the secular priests and members of the Society of Jesus. Other religious orders hardly counted.

There was, in fact, no possibility of a co-ordinated nation-wide apostolate, for there were really two Scotlands—the Highlands and the Lowlands. They had never been properly fused at any period of history.

The Highlands and Islands.

When the Congregation for the Propagation of the Faith began to investigate the re-conversion of Scotland, its predominantly Italian officials must have found it difficult to grasp the fact that the spiritual campaign could not be conducted as a united front— that this small and far-off nation was divided into two distinct entities, kept apart not only geographically, but even more by language, customs and social structure. The Lowlanders, descended mainly from Teutonic tribes which invaded Britain in the fifth and sixth centuries, and who first settled along the eastern seaboard, spoke what was called 'Inglis', a northern form of primitive

---

* He became famous throughout Europe by reason of a romance written by Mgr. Rinuccini, Archbishop of Fermo, first published in 1644, and entitled *Il Cappucino Scozzese*. The author's object was to arouse interest among Continental Catholics in the Scottish Mission. The book was translated into French and went through many editions. Cf. *The Blairs Papers*, p. 213. For a scholarly examination of this Capuchin romance, see Thomas G. Law, ' The Legend of Archangel Leslie ' and ' Archangel Leslie of Scotland, a sequel ', in *Collected Essays and Reviews* (1904).

C

English.* This language had its roots in the Anglican tongue of ancient Northumbria. It was due to the Protestant Reformers, who looked for sympathy to their co-religionists in England, that the influence of the South upon Lowland speech was first felt. The Catholic party actually taunted their opponents for their anglicizing tendencies.

Westward of a rough line drawn north and south between Inverness and Glasgow, Gaelic was spoken by all classes of society. In this largely mountainous area, with no towns west of Stirling, Perth and Inverness, life at the time of the Reformation still went on in much the same way as it had done for centuries. The people were ruled by their chiefs and utterly dependent on them. It was still a wild and barbaric world, hardly touched at all by the political and religious tensions which affected the Lowlands so acutely in the fifteenth and early sixteenth centuries. There were no roads, and a journey to Edinburgh might take weeks or even months in bad weather. Catholic life in the Highlands had never at any time been thoroughly organised. There were very few monasteries, schools, collegiate churches or hospitals. And though the Highlands and Islands were all included in the Kingdom of Scotland before the end of the Middle Ages, and though their bishops formed part of the hierarchy, they remained more or less a world apart. Even after 1560 they still continued to be so, hardly conscious that Parliament by a stroke of the pen had changed the religion of the nation, and that now it was no longer the religion of the Catholic and Roman Church.

At first no general or systematic attempt was made to convert the Highlanders and Islanders to Calvinism.† There was a lack of Gaelic-speaking priests to minister to them and so they drifted into a state of semi-paganism, though retaining many Catholic traditions. The faith just faded out; it was never suppressed.

First attempts to provide Gaelic-speaking priests for the Highlands and Islands

Credit must be given to the Society of Jesus for trying to provide spiritual ministrations for the Highlands and Islands after the Reformation. The pioneer was Fr. Claude Acquaviva, fifth General of the Society. Having heard from the Fathers working in the Lowlands how the Highlands had been utterly abandoned, he wrote in 1610 to the Jesuit Superior in Ireland, asking if he could spare some of his forty priests, but nothing came of this appeal.‡

---

* Gavin Douglas (c. 1475-1522) is the first writer of importance to use the word ' Scottis ' for his native language. Just as in England, so too in Scotland, there were many different dialects in use by the 16th century.

† It was John Carswell, appointed titular Bishop of the Isles in 1566, who translated John Knox's *Forme of Prayers* or *Book of Common Order* into Gaelic—the first book to be printed in this language (1576).

‡ Cf. W. Forbes-Leith, S.J., *Narrative of Scottish Catholics under Mary Stuart and James VI* (Edinburgh 1885)), p.291.

In November 1611, Fr. Patrick Anderson, S.J., Rector of the Scots College in Rome, pointed out to Paul V that the islands off the west coast of Scotland had never seen a priest since the death of the last of the pre-Reformation clergy. The Gaelic-speaking people, he pointed out, had no knowledge of God except faint memories of the Catholic religion handed down by their parents. Mgr. Guido Bentivoglio, papal nuncio at Brussels, had already informed Cardinal Borghese that the only way to help the Islanders was to send Irish priests to them. Even if priests could have been spared from the Lowlands, few if any of them spoke Gaelic.*

James VI, by that time, had managed to subdue the unruly Highland chiefs, largely with the help of Bishop Andrew Knox of the Isles, and though no attempt was made to alter the social structure of the clans, a reformation through religion and education was now approaching. Two years later, acting on orders from the Father-General in Rome, Fr. Christian Holywood, Superior of the Irish Jesuit mission, sent Fr. Galway from Cork "to visit and console or convert" the inhabitants of Islay, Oronsay, Colonsay, Gigha, Arran and other islands off the south-west coast of Scotland. This priest also landed on the Mull of Kintyre, where a minister and his beadle got soldiers, armed with swords, pikes and long knives, to arrest him while he was hearing confessions, but he managed to escape. On his return to Ireland, Fr. Galway reported many conversions "from atheism and heresy" on every island he visited. But this brief mission, the exact date of which is uncertain, was not followed up.†

Realising that his brothers in Ireland were unable to help, Fr. Anderson appealed to the Irish Friars Minor. Then followed much correspondence with the papal nuncio at Brussels, and after a delay of several years, an approach was made to St Anthony's College, Louvain.‡

But neither here, nor at St Isidore's, Rome (another community of Irish Friars Minor), were any volunteers for the Scottish Mission forthcoming. On October 16, 1618, Fr. MacCaughwell, Guardian of the Louvain College, informed the nuncio at Brussels that there were not enough Gaelic-speaking friars even for the needs of the

---

* Cf. Cathaldus Giblin, O.F.M., 'The Irish Mission to Scotland in the 17th century (till 1647)', in *Franciscan College Annual* (Multifarnham, 1952, p. 9). Fr. Giblin's subsequent researches were incorporated into ' The Irish Franciscan Mission to Scotland, 1619-1647 ' (*Proceedings of the Irish Catholic Historical Committee, 1957* (Dublin 1957), pp. 15-24. Further details will be found in his Irish *Franciscan Mission to Scotland, 1619-1648* (Dublin, 1664.) See also John Lorne Campbell, 'Some Notes and Comments on 'The Irish Mission to Scotland' in *The Innes Review*, Vol. IV (1953), pp. 42-8.

† Cf. Edmund Hogan, S.J., *Distinguished Irishmen of the 16th Century* (1894), pp. 493-5.

‡ Founded by Florence Conry, O.F.M., Archbishop of Tuam from 1609 to 1629. He spent these twenty years mainly in Flanders and Spain, but appointed vicars-general who administered diocesan affairs.

Irish mission, and the College benefactors would give no more financial help if they heard that Scotland was stealing some of the friars. He also hinted that it would be a waste of men and money to send priests to the Highlands and Islands, because they would probably end up in prison or be executed.*

Next followed the suggestion that the Roman authorities should pay for the training at Louvain of a certain number of friars for the Scottish mission. But Paul V was spending vast sums on finishing St Peter's and other building-schemes, and it was doubtful if he could spare any cash. Negotiations dragged on throughout the year 1618. By the end of that year the so-called Thirty Years War had begun between the Catholic Emperor Ferdinand II and the Protestants of Bohemia. Soon it was to involve France and Spain as well.

The first Franciscan missionaries to the Highlands and Islands

Even if the Jesuits realised how greatly the Highlanders and Islanders were in need of re-conversion, they were shrewd enough to be aware that the chiefs of the various clans had no political importance. They did not mix with court circles. In comparison with most of the nobility and landed gentry in the Lowlands they were uncultured. So perhaps it was better that some other religious order should be found to minister to them and their peoples.

At long last, after yet more correspondence between Rome, Brussels and Louvain, Fr. MacCaughwell agreed to spare two priests and a laybrother from St Anthony's College. On January 4, 1619, Fr. Edmund McCann (sometimes called Cone), Fr. Patrick Brady and Br. John Stuart (a Scotsman) — all disguised as soldiers —left Louvain, sailed across the North Sea and landed at Leith. Each friar had been given a small sum of money and everything necessary for the celebration of Mass. While Fr. McCann made his way west to the Islands, Fr. Brady remained on the mainland. Br. Stuart acted as their messenger and during the next three years he made several voyages between Scotland and the Netherlands without being arrested.

News of the arrival of two Papist priests soon reached the ears of the Bishops of Argyll and the Isles, and it was with no small alarm that they heard of the 'perversions' being made by Fr. McCann. He was arrested in October 1620 and taken to Glasgow, where he was tried by Archbishop Spottiswood. Imprisoned in Stirling Castle for two years, he was then banished from the kingdom, under pain of death should he return. Fr. Brady was more fortunate, for he managed to continue his apostolate on the mainland without being arrested.

Early in 1623 a new Guardian of the Louvain College informed

* Cf. Giblin in *Franciscan College Annual*, p. 10.

the recently erected Congregation of Propaganda that he had twelve friars who spoke Gaelic and appeared suitable for the Scottish mission.* The following year Br. Stuart was arrested on his way to Ireland, and banished from the three kingdoms.†

On September 4, 1623, instructions from Propaganda reached Louvain, giving full details of the behaviour expected from the friars sent to Scotland. Each priest was to record in a notebook the names of persons baptized or converted. The missionaries were all to keep in close touch with each other, and each had to compile a report on the state of religion in his district. They were urged to acquire a thorough knowledge of Scots Gaelic, and to make friends with the leading chiefs, so that 'histories' could be written.

Mgr. Ingoli, the secretary of the Congregation, must have had a very vague idea about social conditions in the Highlands and Islands. He cannot have realised that a priest marooned on some remote island in the Outer Hebrides might have to wait weeks if not months before he could get a letter across the Minch; that if the letter reached the mainland, there was no regular postal service to transport it to Edinburgh; and that even then there was no certainty when the correspondence could be entrusted to the care of a captain of a ship bound for the continent.‡ If he had realised that, he would not have stipulated, as he did, that the missionaries must write to Propaganda each week, using a cypher to prevent the letter being read en route to Italy.

In the late autumn of 1623 four priests left Louvain — Fr. Edmund McCann (prepared to face death by defying his previous banishment), Fr. Paul O'Neill, Fr. Patrick Hegarty and Fr. Cornelius Ward. This second group of Franciscan missionaries reached Scotland by way of Ireland and the North Channel, and after battling with the open sea for twenty miles in a small rowing boat they landed exhausted on the little island of Sanda off the Mull of Kintyre. It is recorded that Fr. Hegarty preached, heard confessions, celebrated Mass and administered Holy Communion to forty persons. He remained in Kintyre, while Fathers Ward, McCann and O'Neill set off for the Hebrides.

Fr. Hegarty reported to Louvain that during the first eight weeks he had reconciled 206 persons with the Church. Usually he lay hidden in caves, venturing forth only after dark. From Kintyre he was rowed across Kilbrennan Sound to Arran, where he made eighteen converts. Fearing arrest, he returned to Kintyre, took a boat to the island of Gigha and thence to Islay. During a fortnight on this large island he baptized nineteen persons, exorcised four,

* This indicates that the papal nuncio at Brussels had already been relieved of the responsibility for finding priests for the Highlands and Islands.

† He died at Louvain in 1625.

‡ Most of the letters addressed to Louvain were written in Irish Gaelic and there translated into Latin before being sent on to Rome.

*St. Brendan, Craigston, Barra (1858). Franciscan
missionaries worked on this island from about 1626
to 1640.*

22

and reconciled 119. Then, hearing that a party had been sent out to arrest him, he crossed the narrow Sound of Islay and landed on Jura, where he reconciled 102 men and women within a fortnight. Another voyage of about ten miles in a small open boat brought him to Colonsay. Here 133 persons were absolved from heresy and schism. By this time the altar wine and hosts had been used up, so a man was sent across to Ireland for a further supply. After about a year Fr. Hegarty returned to the mainland of Kintyre, and reported to his Superiors at Louvain that over 600 people had resumed the practice of their religion.

It is not known how Fr. Con Ward found his way from the southern tip of the Mull of Kintyre to the Isle of Eigg, about eight miles west of the mainland of Inverness-shire, but he risked including his brown Franciscan habit in his scanty luggage and wore it under his Mass vestments. The inhabitants said they had not seen a priest for seventy years and during the eight days he remained on Eigg people came in hundreds to be baptized, or reconciled with the Church. Only one family stood out. Here we seem to have an example, not unparalleled, of mass conversions resulting, so far as human agency is concerned, from the impact of a zealous missionary visiting for the first time a primitive people, speaking their own language and of their own race. The other Franciscans were able to report similar results.

From Eigg Fr. Ward sailed the forty or fifty miles across the Minch to South Uist, where he remained three months. Next followed what seems to have been his second visit to the Isle of Barra in February 1626. This time he reconciled 117 persons including "a man of noble birth and lawful heir of the island", whom he "joined in marriage".* On returning to the mainland Fr. Ward presented himself to Sir John Campbell of Calder in the disguise of an Irish bard, carrying a harp, and not until three days after arriving at Muckairn Castle on the south side of Loch Etive did the 'bard' dare to reveal that he was a priest. The laird, his family and servants were soon reconciled with the Church.†

Urban VII and the officials of Propaganda must have found it hard to believe the figures of conversion given by Fr. Ward in his report dated 1626. Within eight months, he stated, 2,773 persons in

* This was a MacNeill, whose younger brother had seized Kishmuil Castle by force and imprisoned his father until his death. He released his older brother only after the latter had sworn not to claim his lawful inheritance. This rebellious MacNeill refused to be reconciled with the Church, fearing that he would be compelled to release his father, and hand over the estates to his elder brother (Cf. John Lorne Campbell, 'The Macneills of Barra and the Irish Franciscans', in *The Innes Review*, Vol. V (1954), pp. 33-8.

† In February 1631 Calder was arrested for having made "shameful apostacie and defection from the trew religion", and for sheltering Jesuits and "mass priests". (*Register of the Privy Council of Scotland*, Vol. IV. p. 147).

the Highlands and Islands had been brought back into communion with the Roman Church. He had baptized 383, and the numbers would have been greater had he been able to remain longer in each district. The 1625 tour included the reconciliation of the whole population of North Uist, except fourteen persons, mostly of the minister's household. It was also in 1626 that the Friars Minor at Louvain were informed that 2,070 persons had abjured heresy within a year, and the four missionaries had brought about 6000 men and women back into communion with the Church.

James VI may not have been aware how many of his Scottish subjects were following the example of his queen-consort, Anne of Denmark. He had never visited the Highlands and Islands of Scotland.

Fr. Ward insisted that Propaganda must pay a definite annual salary to each missionary. He explained that he himself refused all financial help from the people, not wanting to give the smallest scandal to the flocks, or to have the Protestants accusing him of robbing the poor. He also asked for special faculties to dispense from canonical impediments; powers to reconcile chapels which had been used for heretical worship; and permission to celebrate Mass without a server or lighted candles.*

In the spring of 1626 Fr. Ward sailed across to Ireland, where he met Archbishop Thomas Fleming — also a Friar Minor — in Dublin. Then he set off for Rome, taking with him Ranald MacDonald, son of the chief of the Clanranald branch of the Macdonald clan. This young man had been the first Presbyterian minister in South Uist but he was converted by Fr. Ward and after studying at Louvain was ordained at Douai in 1628. He was the first secular priest to work in the Hebrides since the death of the last of the pre-Reformation clergy.†

Charles I was dead by that time. Cromwell had invaded Scotland and Charles II was trying to gain possession of the throne. Fr. Ward got no further than Paris and Brussels, where the nuncio advised him to return to Scotland with a promise that faculties and dispensations would be forwarded as soon as they

---

* Anyone with a contemporary knowledge of war and persecution cannot fail to be surprised at the rigidity of the Roman authorities in the early seventeenth century. Priests in our time would regard the conditions in the Highlands and Islands of Scotland then as fully justifying the saying of Mass with inadequate vestments, no server and no lights. Permission would be presumed, not only in details of ritual and ceremonial, but also as regards fasting and abstinence.

† Ranald MacDonald was arrested in London with Fr. Ward in 1630 but managed to return to Scotland. He was captured in 1642 and taken to Edinburgh, where he convinced the authorities that he had been coerced into becoming a priest, which was untrue, and so he was allowed to go back to the Hebrides. Part of the teinds of Snizort in Skye were granted him for maintenance. Eight years later he was excommunicated by the Synod of Argyll, for having at diverse times juggled with his religion and profession. By 1650 he had openly proclaimed himself a priest.

had been received from Propaganda. At Paris Fr. Ward wrote to the Archbishop of Armagh that about half-a-dozen of the leading chieftains were demanding that a bishop should be appointed to the Highlands and Islands to preserve the faith of their people.* Few Scottish historians have noticed that in the first year of the reign of Charles I, most of the leading chiefs, together with all their clansmen, from Harris to the Mull of Kintyre including the lesser isles, appealed to the Pope to give them a vicar-apostolic.

Catholic life in the Lowlands during the first years of the reign of Charles I

Life for a Catholic in the non-Gaelic-speaking parts of Scotland was utterly different from that in the Highlands and Islands. Since the Reformation the old religion had been kept alive by a few great families, but only in certain areas, for there were large districts in the Lowlands where Catholicism had completely disappeared within half-a-century. It is never safe to label this or that family as 'Catholic', because the religious practice of individuals was seldom consistent. A handful might be pious Papists but the majority were little more than crypto-Catholics, who did not dare to practice their religion. Owing to the lack of priests it was only on rare occasions that Mass was celebrated in castles and mansions whose owners were rich and powerful enough to defy the law. Normally the children of professedly Catholic parents were baptized by the parish minister. Weddings took place in the parish kirk. Funerals—sometimes quite stately functions— were also conducted by the ministers of the Established Church.

It became quite common for a nobleman or country gentleman, who regarded himself as a good Catholic, to attend the services in his parish kirk on Sundays, accompanied by his family, servants and tenants. Families which might have remained loyal to the faith often drifted into indifference. Some gave up the struggle altogether. Overwhelming pressure from without proved too strong for powers of resistance. The situation, taken as a whole, had something in common with what prevails today in countries behind the iron curtain.

South of Edinburgh and Glasgow the whole country was strongly Protestant, except for about half-a-dozen small Papist 'pockets' represented by certain families of the House of Douglas, two branches of the House of Hamilton, and the more militant Maxwells and Setons. The Earls of Abercorn, Angus, Nithsdale and Winton were the heads of these families, which were closely related by marriage.

The Maxwells — turbulent as they were styled, because of frequent feuds among themselves—were entrenched mainly around

* Cf. J. L. Campbell, 'The Letter sent by Iain Murideartach, 12th chief of Clanranald, to Pope Urban VIII in 1626', in *The Innes Review*, Vol. iV (1953), pp. 110-16.

*The chancel of Terregles Kirk, Kirkcudbrightshire,
built in 1583, has served as the mortuary chapel of
the Herries and Maxwell families since the Reformation. Mass has been celebrated here on certain
anniversaries during the past 400 years.*

Dumfries.* Catholic customs and traditions lingered on among the people on both sides of the estuary of the Nith. It was safe enough to light bonfires on saints' days and to have children baptized by priests. Boys were smuggled out of the country to the Scots colleges abroad, Douai in particular, because it was most accessible. Usually there was a Jesuit chaplain in one or other of the Maxwell households. From time to time the ministers, backed up by the civil authorities, tried to check this Popish activity, even imprisoning men and women who had heard Mass or gone to confession. The eastern corner of Galloway was very much cut off from the rest of the Lowlands and formed a little world of its own, as it still is. The Stewarts of Traquair House, Peebles-shire, were another powerful Catholic family, but less aggressive than the Maxwells to whom they were closely related by marriage. The first and second Earls of Abercorn, who inherited the rich lands of Paisley Abbey, were seldom more than nominal Catholics, but the Countess Marion (wife of the first Earl), herself a convert, openly proclaimed her religion. Also lukewarm in the defence of his faith was the first Marquis of Douglas, who succeeded his father as eleventh Earl of Angus in 1611. His chamberlain, Patrick Douglas, was later denounced by the Lanark presbytery for encouraging Popery around Douglas Castle.

At Seton Palace, a splendid mansion nine miles east of Edinburgh, George, third Earl of Winton, lived in great state. Both his first and second wives belonged to influential Catholic families, the first a daughter of the Earl of Erroll, the second a daughter of the Earl of Nithsdale. It was seldom that a Jesuit chaplain was not in residence at Seton Palace and often it was the hiding place for priests and layfolk on their way to and from the continent, for it was situated within a mile of the Firth of Forth. The presbytery of Haddington was finding it very difficult to repress Popery in this district, for the Earl was a member of the Privy Council.

In Edinburgh Catholic life had gone underground but some of the nobility still kept priests in their town houses, where they celebrated Mass in secret.†

Between the Forth and the Tay lay the entirely Protestant county of Fife, where the old religion had been uprooted after 1560. North of the Tay, throughout Angus and the Mearns, the presbyteries were all-powerful, though here and there an isolated Catholic family managed to survive. Perthshire was another

---

* Caerlaverock Castle, five and a half miles east of Dumfries, had belonged to the Maxwells since the 13th century. Kirkconnell, near New Abbey, and Terregles were other strongholds of the family.

† Among other apparently Catholic families in the Lothians during the first half of the 17th century were the Wauchopes of Niddrie, a fair number of Setons, and a sprinkling of Cockburns, Hamiltons, Maitlands and Semples. There were also crypto-Catholic Hamilton households in Clydesdale.

Protestant area, but Mass was celebrated occasionally in the chapel at Stobhall, built by the Drummond family in 1578.

"In some ways it is surprising how Catholicism both survived and re-emerged among the great families in the Lowlands whose estates were sometimes placed in the very heart of the country most closely mastered by the Presbyterians. The degree of their independent authority was often greater than that of their English counterparts, but the final pressure brought to bear on them was more formidable. They had against them the power of the Kirk and its unremitting hostility. Society in Scotland was more egalitarian . . . In England there was a privileged Catholic grouping which at least in the reign of Charles I secured a measure of immunity. In Scotland south of the Firth of Tay there was no such provision. The families of the Auld Kirk were isolated in a world that was preparing for the Solemn League and Covenant." *

As has already been explained, there were two Scotlands—the English-speaking Lowlands and the Gaelic-speaking Highlands and Islands. Actually there was a sub-section of the Lowlands made up of the counties of Aberdeen, Banff and Moray, where variants of the so-called Buchan dialect were spoken. It was a remote and different world, dominated by the Gordons of Huntly and a number of other Catholic lairds, represented by members of the families of Abercromby, Dunbar, Forbes, Fraser, Hay, Innes, Leslie, and Ogilvie. Like the Maxwells in Galloway, most of them were turbulent, often engaged in family feuds, and entangled in inter-marriages. Not only were their castles dotted over the countryside; Aberdeen, Banff and Elgin had splendid town houses which were occupied mainly during the winter months. Except at times of definite persecution it was safe enough for people of all classes to profess the Catholic religion in these north-eastern counties.

The Gordons were the most powerful of all these professedly Papist families and regarded the Marquis of Huntly as their chief. But as Archbishop David Mathew points out: "An attachment to Rome was common enough among those who had some form of dependence on or connection with the House of Huntly. As far as the men of the Gordon main line are concerned it is difficult to disentangle religious interests from a general preference for the old traditions. It was rather the women who were fervent."†

In the reigns of James VI and Charles I a Catholic traveller making the seventy-mile journey from Aberdeen to Elgin could take his choice of households where he could spend the night without danger of being molested. There was no other part of Scotland where such comparative freedom existed. Nevertheless the ministers from time to time did try to exert their authority. As far back as 1604 complaints had been made to the General

* David Mathew, *Scotland under Charles I* (1955), p. 207.
† Ibid, p. 152.

Assembly of " the erection of the adolatrie of the Masse in diverse quarters of the land . . . in the Earl of Huntly's house in Strathbogy, and Auld Aberdeene, in the Earl of Erroll's at Logyamont and Slaines." It was primarily *esprit de corps*, a closely-knit relationship between most of the leading families, together with a pride in and regard for traditions, that kept the faith alive in the North-East.

After Queen Henrietta Maria and her twelve French chaplains arrived in London in the summer of 1625, Catholics throughout Britain enjoyed greater freedom than they had done for many years. Charles I, although he himself was quite satisfied with the sacramental Anglicanism in which he had been brought up, was not inclined to persecute those of his subjects who had the same religion as his wife. Quite a number of conversions took place in court circles. In 1629 eight bearded Capuchin friars landed in England. Mass was celebrated openly in chapels, not only in London but in the country. Two papal agents were sent from Rome and accredited to the Queen.

Writing from Antwerp in April 1628, Fr. John Macbreck, S.J., informed his Father-General that everything was going on in Scotland "sufficiently prosperously". There were eight Jesuit missionaries in the Lowlands, and two more were expected shortly. Fr. William Leslie, the Superior of the mission, generally resided at Slains Castle on the coast of Aberdeenshire with the Earl of Erroll, High Constable of Scotland. Fr. Patrick Stickel, who had his permanent quarters at Gordon Castle with the Marquis of Huntly, was bringing many influential people back to the Church. He had even managed to arrange a marriage between Erroll's daughter and Huntly's son, though these two families, among the most powerful in the kingdom, had hitherto been " divided by fierce and mortal hatred." When gossip of this matrimonial alliance reached the ears of Patrick Forbes (described as " the pseudo-Bishop of Aberdeen"), he protested strongly, and said that " one Jesuit had effected what the King, what the Council of the Kingdom, what the ministers and bishops themselves, had been unable to bring about."

Indeed the situation could not have been more promising. Fr. William Christie had reconciled within two-and-a-half years more than 400 persons, most of them belonging to the upper classes and resident in the North-East. Fr. James Seton and Fr. John Stephen had been able to gain a footing in several castles, even in the strongly Protestant counties of Angus and Fife. The latter hoped to bring back the seventh Baron Ogilvy (later created first Earl of Airlie) to the faith of his ancestors, whose lineage could be traced to the eleventh century. But this priest was here, there and everywhere promoting the greater glory of God. Some time he served the "tolerably large mission much attached to our Society" in Aberdeen. Then he was off to Douai with ten young students, next in Spain, but soon back in Scotland. Fr. James Macbreck lived at Seton Palace with the Earl of Winton, and acted as tutor to his sons. His cousin, exiled at Antwerp, reported that "he works with much fruit, though like a new athlete he has not yet come forward publicly in the arena, nor does he as yet go out much". Fr. Christie "the elder" was hidden in the house of the Countess of Linlithgow, because her husband was still "a most obstinate heretic". Fr. Robert Valens was more fortunate, since he enjoyed the hospitality of either the Earl of Abercorn or the Earl of Angus. Fr. John Macbreck, who was imprisoned for a time and forced to retire to the continent after being apprehended by the Bishop of Brechin at Dundee in 1626, wrote that: "On the whole, praise be to God, the number both of workers and of Catholics increases daily, so that there is a visible change, both in the temper of the people generally, and in the zeal and fervour of the Catholics, compared with some years back." *

Two things, however, were urgently needed — more money to support the Jesuit missionaries; and some fixed place in France or the Spanish Netherlands where they could retire from their labours and recover their strength, and where "the new ones may be instructed for two whole years at least in their final studies, before they descend into the area." That same year the number of Jesuits in Scotland was increased to nine with the arrival of two more priests from Rome — Fathers Robert Mortimer and John Leslie. So many peers, peeresses and other members of the aristocracy bearing Ensigns Armorial were being reconciled with the Roman Church that it almost looked as if the re-conversion of the nation was well on the way. These three years, however, were merely a lull before another storm.

Renewal of persecution in the Lowlands in 1629.

The persecution of Papists was renewed with vigour in 1629, and encouraged by the bishops. It took the form, as in the past, of lists being drawn up of the names, residences and properties of all persons who absented themselves from Episcopalian public worship. More oppressive measures were soon adopted. Catholics were compelled under penalty of high treason to abandon their houses, and to hand over the keys within one day of receiving notice. Even women and children were driven to the hills and forests, where they often took shelter in huts or lived in the open air.

Most of the bishops had no doubt that militant methods were demanded to divert idolaters from Communion with Rome. Convinced that they were carrying out the Will of God they commanded all persons to attend the kirks, receive the sacrament of the Lord's Supper according to some form of Protestant rite, and subscribe to

* Forbes-Leith, op. cit. Vol I, pp. 5-13.

the Confession of Faith (1581) under pain of excommunication, loss of all offices and confiscation of goods. Even this was a lenient way to treat " Babylon the Great, the Mother of Harlots, and Abominations of the Earth " alluded to in the seventeenth and eighteenth chapters of *Revelation*. For with this ' woman ', so it was related in God's Word, the kings of the earth had committed fornication, and the inhabitants of the earth had been made drunk with the wine of her fornication. In 1629 it was only too clear that the woman, " arrayed in purple and scarlet colour, decked with gold and precious stones " was " that great city [of Rome] which reignest over the kings of the earth."

Neither could the bodies of Papist idolaters be buried with those of Christians, for did not the prophet Jeremiah say " they shall be for dung upon the face of the earth"? Their servants must be dismissed. No debts owing to those who associated with ' the Mother of Harlots ' need be paid, and no intercourse with them could be tolerated. Soldiers were ordered to tramp down the crops of all those who had ' committed fornication ' with ' the great whore '.

In spite of this bitter persecution, no priests suffered the death penalty. Queen Henrietta Maria tried to intercede on behalf of Scottish Catholics, but she was usually told that repressive methods were necessary for the maintenance, honour and prosperity of the whole realm. The Papist nobility were singled out by the bishops for attack. Both the Marquis of Huntly and Lord Lovat were proclaimed rebels. The Earls of Angus, Argyll and Nithsdale, and the Countess of Abercorn, were among others accused of high treason. Some Catholic lairds went into voluntary exile to find peace and quiet overseas. Others abjured their religion, not from conviction but from sheer weariness.

The situation became worse in 1630. Fr. William Christie, S.J., informed his Father-General on September 3 that: "the evil increases daily, and in human judgment the game is well-nigh played out. New laws are made every day against Catholics, old edicts revived, judgments of unheard of cruelty pronounced. . . Truth and justice are thrown to the winds . . . We have nowhere to go, nowhere to hide . . . I need not tell you, most illustrious Sir, of the rest of our troubles, which you very well know; I merely supplicate you in my own name and that of all our friends, to get help from the Lord Urban [Pope Urban VIII], and others who are in a position to give it." *

It would have been difficult for Urban VIII to intervene in the domestic affairs of the kingdom of Scotland. The Thirty Years' War was then at its height. The Pope had to remain strictly neutral from fear of offending the Emperor Ferdinand and the

---

* Forbes-Leith, op.cit. Vol. I, pp. 80-1.

League of Catholic Estates on the one hand, and Louis XIII and Cardinal Richelieu on the other.   Allied with France were the Lutheran German princedoms and Gustavus Adolphus of Sweden. Their object was to break the power of the Catholic Hapsburgs, not only in Austria, but also in Spain and the Netherlands. Charles I was on friendly terms with Louis XIII, who was his wife's brother. Urban VIII was busy fortifying the frontiers of the Papal States and of the city of Rome itself.

While a considerable part of the continent of Europe was being ravaged by war, the Episcopalian bishops and ministers in Scotland kept on reminding the civil authorities that if they ceased persecuting Papists they would be failing in their duty to the King, and would be charged with neglect. From time to time Charles I did try, ineffectively in most cases, to check the zeal of the clergy in stamping out Popery with methods almost evocative of the Spanish Inquisition.   In 1632 an order was obtained from the Privy Council forbidding Scots youths being sent to seminaries overseas.

The Coronation of Charles I in Edinburgh 1633

On June 1, 1633, Charles I was crowned King of Scotland in Edinburgh, with ritual and ceremonial that shocked most of the congregation in St Giles' Cathedral.* Fr. John Leslie, S.J. reported to his General in Rome that after the coronation: "a sermon followed, and the communion was celebrated according to the Anglican rite. The English call it 'service', the Scots, and especially the Puritans, a Mass turned upside down, English superstition, Romish idolatry, stage plays, etc. It appeared to me an imitation of the Mass. The altar was laid out with great costliness and splendour, there was an introit with collects, oblation of bread and wine, and a form of consecration; on the altar were books, candles, crucifix, images of the Apostles, etc., music of chant and organ, and many other things . . ."†

Two years later Fr. Andrew Leslie wrote that the King had stopped persecution of Catholics by law, and that the ministers and presbyters, who were mainly responsible for the persecution, were now considering themselves the persecuted party. He added: "I have already stated that His Majesty wants to introduce the Anglican ritual into the Scottish synagogue. Altars are erected, organs being built, matins and evensongs sung daily, the surplice worn at the altar and in the pulpit, the communion received kneeling, the festivals of our Lord and the Apostles observed. All these things are redolent of popish idolatry, in the opinion of the Puritans, who have said so in a book they have lately published, notwithstanding the addition which the King made to their revenues

* The see of Edinburgh was founded by Charles I in 1633.
† Forbes-Leith, Vol. I, p. 164.

and benefices. "The Protestant bishops have applied for the abbacies, in order to have the ritual celebrated with greater splendour in their cathedrals." *

Fr. Leslie doubted if this 'Catholic Crusade' in the Established Kirk would gain many adherents. He went on to say: "The new Episcopal sect considers that they have added to the element of splendour which was wanting in their Church, so that the pomp of Roman ceremonial will no longer attract. The Puritans, if ever they abandon their obstinate opinions, will be more likely to embrace the truth than imitate these apings of Roman piety. A few people, perplexed by these changes of worship, have fallen in love with the constancy and completeness of the Catholic system, but the greater number suspend their judgment and attach themselves to no particular religion. The most serene King hopes notwithstanding to secure unity of religious belief by means of the State bishops, though he acknowledges himself that it will take some time, owing to the resistance of the Puritans; so that the Calvinists are not only separated from the Catholics, but divided among themselves as well."†

No wonder the Calvinists were alarmed. Orders were issued that copes were to be worn during the administration of the Holy Communion in the Chapel Royal and in all cathedrals.

The Scottish Liturgy of 1637

Catholics in the Lowlands, above all the Jesuit missionaries, wondered what would happen next. In May 1634 they heard that the King had given permission to the bishops to "draw up a liturgy as near to that of England as might be". The book was not published until May 1637, when the Privy Council recommended its use throughout the kingdom. Neither the General Assembly nor Parliament was consulted. Few of the ministers had ever seen the liturgy in its final form. The Jesuits informed their brethren in Rome that the new Scottish Prayer Book, though "spurious and corrupt, is not greatly opposed to the Catholic faith, as well as the rites, canons, and ceremonies of the English Protestants."‡

It was the reading of Mattins from this new Prayer Book in St Giles' Cathedral, Edinburgh, on July 23, 1637, that "set the heather ablaze." The Jesuits in Rome were informed that: "the liturgy was trodden under foot, the powers of the Protestant bishops and sectarian ministers were thown into the dust; the Puritans tore up the falsely so-called liturgy, and trampled upon it. The deacons, who attempted to read it in public, were maltreated with clubs and

* ibid, pp. 171-2.
† ibid, p. 173.
‡ ibid, p. 203. For details of the 1637 Scottish rite, see W. Jardine Grisbrooke, *Anglican Liturgies of the 17th and 18th centuries* (1958), pp. 1-18, 163-82; also Gordon Donaldson, *The History of the Scottish Prayer Book of 1937* (Edinburgh, 1954).

fists, and hustled out of the churches. Then they turned their arms against the State bishops, who were everywhere stoned by the women and boys, and several of them narrowly escaped with their lives. But their wild fury did not stop here, for they rose in insurrection against the King and the great officers of state."*

A National Covenant was drawn up, a long and abstruse document which set forth in legal phraseology the constitutional rights of parliaments and assemblies as opposed to those of the sovereign, proving that the Confession of Faith of the Established Kirk, first subscribed in 1581, could not be discarded either by the King or by bishops. Certain paragraphs were sufficiently clear in their meaning that all ' idolatry', whether propagated by Episcopalians or by Papists, was illegal and must be rooted out. On the other hand, the National Covenant carefully refrained from explicit condemnation of episcopal government; it was essentially a constitutional, not a theological document. What the Covenant did achieve was to unite almost the entire nation, even if " it may possibly be regarded as a formula which produced a deceptive appearance of unanimity."†

The National Covenant and its effects on the Catholic minority in Scotland

This document was first signed in the Greyfriars Kirk at Edinburgh in February 1638, amid scenes of wild enthusiasm. The General Assembly met in Glasgow in November, and in defiance of the Marquis of Hamilton, the Royal Commissioner, deposed and excommunicated all the bishops. On December 8 it was decreed that episcopacy was to be "removed out of this Kirk". Most of the prelates were accused of specific offences, including playing cards on the Sabbath, using crucifixes, bowing to the holy table and committing adultery.‡

Everybody was made to sign the Covenant — even the King himself, though he may have agreed with Fr. James Macbreck, S.J., who described it as "devilish", in a letter written to the Father-General on June 13, 1641. "It is offered to all without exception," he explained, "and those who refuse it are set down as enemies of their country, and of the godless heresy which they call the Reformed religion, and prosecuted with the utmost rigour."§ Covenanters roamed around the countryside, forcing an entry into the houses of both Papists and Episcopalians, often during the night. There was no safety anywhere for persons suspected of popery and prelacy. Fr. Macbreck wrote: "The enemy are mad with fury, in

---

* ibid, p. 204.

† *A Source Book of Scottish History*, Vol. III (ed. 1960), p. 104.

‡ An apostate priest, one Thomas Abernethy, formerly a Jesuit, denounced John Guthrie, Bishop of Ross, for having danced in his shirt at his daughter's wedding.

§ Forbes-Leith, op.cit. p. 216.

full strength, and able to do just what they please." At the same time Pope Urban VIII had allowed his nephews to involve him in an unjustifiable and very costly war with the Duke of Parma, who was backed up by the Republic of Venice and other Italian states. The persecuted Catholics in Scotland could not look for any help from the papacy in their hour of need.

On September 10, 1641, the General Assembly ordained "all idolatrous images, crucifixes, pictures of Christ to be demolished and removed forth from all kirks, colleges, chapels and other public places."

The civil authorities were warned of the penalties which would be inflicted if they did not ensure that all "monuments of idolatry" were removed within three months. For God had said to Moses: "Thou shalt not make unto thee any graven image, or any likeness of anything that is in heaven above or that is in the earth beneath, or that is in the water under the earth."* God's orders on Mount Sinai, issued with thunders and lightnings, and with "the voice of a trumpet exceeding loud", must be enforced in both the Lowlands and Highlands of Scotland — "Ye shall make you no idols nor graven images, neither rear you up a standing image, neither shall ye set up any image of stone in your land, to bow down unto it: for I am the Lord your God. Ye shall keep my sabbaths, and reverence my sanctuary."†

Throughout the year 1642 the Covenanters enjoyed an orgy of iconoclasm, purging temples of everything they regarded as idolatrous and superstitious.‡ Catholics and Episcopalians in Scotland were certainly being harassed, but what they were having to endure was little in comparison with what was going on all over Europe between the North Sea and the Carpathian Mountains. Swedish, French and Spanish troops were causing untold suffering among the civil population, few of whom had any interest in the alleged reasons for starting the Thirty Years' War. Countless towns and villages were laid waste. Reprisals followed bitter reprisals. Famine set in and cannibalism broke out in several parts of Germany. In 1637 Cardinal Richelieu sent the Abbé Chambers to Scotland to enlist troops for service in French regiments and this secular priest gradually became more and more involved in the intrigues of politicians. In the service of Richelieu he even took the side of the Covenanters.§ So it was that, indirectly, Scotland

---

* *Exodus*, xx, 4.
† *Leviticus*, xxvi, 1-2.
‡ At Elgin Cathedral the great rood-screen was demolished in December 1640. The reredos in St. Machar's Cathedral, Aberdeen, was hauled down in June 1642. Much carved stonework in St. Nicholas's, Aberdeen, was smashed to bits. Similar acts of vandalism went on all over the Lowlands. Even the Synod of Argyll went to endless trouble in destroying 'idolatrous monuments' in remote parts of the Highlands.
§ See M. V. Hay, *The Blairs Papers*, pp. 126-9.

Aboyne Castle
(See p. 37)

Gordon Castle
(See p. 55)

might have been committed to actual participation in the long
drawn-out war on the continent of Europe.

There still remained a few remote castles in the North-East
where life went on quietly enough. Among them was Aboyne,
where from 1637 to 1642 a secular priest named Gilbert Blackhall
(often spelt Blakhal) acted as chaplain, having superseded several
Jesuits.* His hostess was the Viscountess of Aboyne.

The castle was an ideal centre for mission work and Mr
Blackhall covered a wide district—usually on horse-back and in all
weathers—from Deeside in the south to Buchan in the north-east,
and north-west to Strathbogie. He kept a diary, which was later
printed with the title *A Brief narration of the services done to
Three Noble Ladies.*†

Lord Aboyne kept open house, with hospitality on a generous
scale. Poor kinsfolk were welcomed and employment was found
for them if possible. Fr. James Macbreck described the castle as
" a sort of asylum for Catholics for the celebration of divine
worship". Lent was kept very strictly. Fr. Blackhall recorded
that he " made exhortations every Sunday, Tuesday and Friday
upon the Passion of our Saviour, which did please Lady Aboyne
and her domestics, especially her master cook, Alexander Lamb,
who thereafter abjured his heresy, and died some two years after
a devout Catholic." Every year, usually during the octave of the
feast of the Assumption, Lady Aboyne went to stay with her
mother-in-law, the Marchioness of Huntly, at Gordon Castle.
Thence she made a pilgrimage to the holy well of Our Lady of
Grace on Speyside.

Mr Blackhall had many adventures when visiting Catholic
households. On one occasion he had a narrow escape from
drowning, when his hat and a little valise of red Spanish leather,
containing his vestments, chalice, altar-stone, etc., were carried
away by the flood. So great was the social status of Lady Aboyne
in the North East, that no ministers dared molest her chaplains
while she was alive.

Mr Blackhall did not confine himself to the spiritual welfare of
his hostess and her household. Finding that there were only two
pistolets for defending the Castle, he procured double-muskets,
light guns and other weapons. It was invaded twice between 1637
and 1642, on the first occasion by a band of men from Badenoch,
and on the other by Camerons from distant Lochaber. The
chaplain relates that his room was right above the butler's pantry,

* Ordained priest at the Scots College, Rome, in 1630, he engaged in
mission work, but owing to difficulties with the Jesuits, he retired to France
for five years. He returned to Scotland in 1637. From 1651 to 1653 he
was Principal of the Scots College, Paris, and died there in 1671.

† Ed. by John Stuart (Spalding Club, Aberdeen, 1844). The other two
'noble ladies' were the Lady Isabella Hay, eldest daughter of the 9th Earl
of Erroll, and the Lady Henrietta Gordon, the daughter of Lady Aboyne.

which "was open to all that would keep him company till midnight."

Before Lady Aboyne died on March 12, 1642, she begged Mr Blackhall to ensure that her young daughter, Henrietta, was brought up a Catholic. So he took her to France, where the Queen-Regent, Anne of Austria, appointed her a lady-in-waiting at court. *

Catholic life in the Highlands and Islands (1628-1644)

The Irish Friars Minor, who continued their mission work in the Highlands and Islands throughout the reign of Charles I, were affected only remotely by the political events recorded in the preceding four sections of this chapter. Fr. Paul O'Neill retired in 1627 and Fr. Francis MacDonnell took his place. Fr. Con Ward twice went to Flanders to procure supplies and discuss business with the Nuncio at Brussels. He was arrested in 1630, imprisoned in London, and finally released through the intervention of the Polish ambassador. He went abroad, got as far as Prague, intending to reach Rome, but eventually received orders from Propaganda in 1633 to return to Scotland, unless he felt it would be too dangerous.

Fr. Hegarty was nearly captured on Iona in September 1630, when John Leslie, Bishop of the Isles, was making a visitation of his diocese. The Bishop followed this priest, who was perverting "the simple, ignorant people of the isles by saying Mass and otherwise," and Fr. Hegarty was arrested on South Uist. But some of the islanders, tenants of the Captain of Clanranald, "accompanied by about thirty persons armed with bows, darlochs [sheafs of arrows], hagbuts and pistols, at the direction of and hounding out of Ranald McAllane McEane [Macdonald of Benbecula], uncle to the said Captain, followed the said Bishop and his company, presented their arms at them, and forcibly took the said priest out of their hands."†

Boarding a small boat, Fr. Hegarty sailed across the open Atlantic, and after a voyage of about 140 miles, landed on the coast of Antrim, where he retired to the friary at Bunamargy. Beside Ballycastle Bay and facing Rathlin Island, it had been founded by the Third Order Regular of St Francis in 1500 and early in 1626 Propaganda handed it over to the Friars Minor of the Irish Province, because it seemed a convenient base for directing mission work in the Gaelic-speaking parts of Scotland. From Fair Head only fifteen miles of water separated Ballycastle Bay

---

* Louis XIV had succeeded his father, Louis XIII, in 1643. The Scots priest, Mr Thomas Chalmers, mentioned already, was Almoner, first to Cardinal Richelieu and afterwards to Cardinal Mazarin, who after the death of the former in 1642, became Prime Minister of France. It appears to have been Chalmers who introduced Lady Henrietta Gordon to Anne of Austria.

† Register of the Privy Council of Scotland, 2nd series, Vol. IV (1630-2) (Edinburgh, 1902).

from the Mull of Kintyre, the nearest point on the mainland of Scotland.

Bunamargy soon became a refuge for those Scotsmen and women who were prepared to face an often dangerous sea voyage in order to be baptized or confirmed. In 1639 Bonaventure Magennis, the Franciscan Bishop of Down and Connor, confirmed about 700 persons from Scotland. Fr. Hegarty acted as Guardian of the friary and Definitor of the Irish Province between 1631 and 1637. He informed Propaganda in 1640 that within four months over 1000 men and women had been reconciled with the Church at Bunamargy; and that during each of the eight previous years roughly 500 had come over from Scotland for this purpose. *

Bunamargy became a veritable spiritual oasis. There was no place in Scotland during the reign of Charles I where priests dared to carry out the rites and ceremonies of the liturgy. At this friary beside the sea, however, there were opportunities to assist at the daily Masses celebrated at the ' privileged altar', and so to gain rich indulgences. Scots Catholics, for the first time in their lives, were able to enjoy Benediction of the Blessed Sacrament, and to make the popular Franciscan devotion of the Stations of the Cross.

Not only Gaelic-speaking Scots folk, but also a few Lowland lairds found their way there. Fr. Andrew Leslie, S.J., wrote in 1633: "Some of the highest character, both men and women, have resolved to emigrate to Ireland, and some have already gone . . . Sir Alexander Gordon [of Cluny, Aberdeenshire] has crossed the Sodorian sea, and is living quietly at Derry, among the Irish. He did not expect to find the natives very civilised, but he has found them at any rate good Catholics, and although there are many Calvinists among them, they are accustomed to restrain the rude bitterness of controversy, and are not perpetually giving utterance to it. Others are likely to follow him soon, after they have made their peace with God and the Church by penance, for fear they should be shipwrecked on the voyage. Conscious of their own weakness they go in search of a safer shore, where tempests do not always blow, and where they will not be in perpetual terror of the raging of a stormy sea."†

Meanwhile Propaganda was granting more faculties and issuing detailed instructions to the Irish Friars Minor for their mission work in the Highlands and Islands of Scotland. On September 16, 1633, three Dominicans were ordered to go to those parts of the north-west of Scotland where the Franciscans had not been able to

---

* What was known as the 'Plantation of Ulster, to a large extent by Presbyterian farmers from the Scottish Lowlands, had begun in 1609, after the escheatment of lands on the 'Flight of the Earls'. But the glens of Antrim still remained largely Catholic. It was not until later in the same century that Ulster became a haven of refuge to the harassed Covenanters from the south-west of Scotland.

† Forbes-Leith, op.cit. Vol. 1 pp. 129-30.

penetrate, and Propaganda promised to pay them a salary. So far little has been discovered about the Irish Dominican mission.*

It was not only lack of missionaries but also lack of money that hindered the re-conversion of the Gaelic-speaking parts of Scotland. Fr. Hegarty on one occasion stated quite bluntly that he had been forced to retire to Ireland because the stipends promised by Propaganda had not reached him. Then followed much correspondence between Rome and Brussels about these claims. In 1634 only three Irish Franciscans were working on the Scottish mission.

Fr. Con Ward returned to Scotland in February 1633, having travelled from Prague by way of Barcelona, Madrid and Ireland. He wrote that within two months he had reconciled about fifty persons on the Isle of Skye, and administered the sacraments to many more. Reports of these perversions to Popery greatly alarmed Neil Campbell, who succeeded John Leslie as Bishop of the Isles in 1634.

Two years later Fr. Ward brought 203 men and women on the islands of Benbecula and Uist into communion with 'The Beast' within three months. Sailing on, he made a perilous voyage to Berneray, the most southerly of the Outer Hebrides, fourteen miles beyond Barra.† He appears to have landed also on the islet of Fieray at the north end of Barra. During the course of one month over 200 persons received the sacraments and fifty were reconciled with the Church. On the orders of Bishop Campbell, a minister tried to arrest this Irish priest, but he managed to escape to the mainland, and for about two months he continued his apostolate in Moidart, around Loch Arkaig. Then, having used up his supply of wine and white flour (to make hosts), and being unable to say Mass, he set off on the 150-mile journey to Edinburgh to renew his supplies. On his return to the Highlands he fell ill, with neither a doctor nor a priest to minister to him, but he recovered. Until the spring of 1637 Glenelg, Lochaber and Moidart appear to have been the districts in which he spent most of his time.

In a report sent to Propaganda, Fr. Ward stressed the dire poverty of the people. They were forced to pay teinds for the support of the few Episcopalian ministers, most of whose parishes were very large. Simple-minded folk, they " did not consider that priests required any means of support from them, as they looked on a priest as a servant of God who did everything for his Master's glory without any expectation of a reward."‡

In fact, the example of priests working without visible means of support was the reason why not a few Protestants felt called to

* Cf. D. C. Pechin Mould, *The Irish Dominicans* (Dublin, 1957), p. 154.
† Barra Head Lighthouse now stands on the highest part of this lonely island in the Atlantic.
‡ Cf. Giblin, op.cit. p. 20.

St Michael's, Ardkenneth, South Uist (1820). There have been resident priests on this outer Hebridean island since 1716.

St Michael's, Eriskay (1903). The inhabitants of this small Hebridean island have remained Catholics since 1630.

become Catholics. In Lochaber alone there were said to be at least one thousand people prepared to be reconciled with the Roman Church. Neither the Bishop of Argyll nor the Bishop of the Isles had managed so far to make many converts to their some-what arid form of Episcopalianism.

In August 1637 Fr. Ward was rowed from one of the Hebridean islands to the coast of Antrim and when he found that the Roman officials refused to accept his former reports to Propaganda at their face value, he got the Scottish crew of the boat to testify that the statements were true. Two of the Lords of the Isles also confirmed what he had written. So did the Guardians of the friaries at Buna-margy and Carrickfergus. *

Bishop Magennis of Down and Connor then informed Propaganda that Fr. Ward had been obliged to leave Scotland for health reasons, and that he deserved to retire; also that a payment of 100 scudi should be made annually to each Irish friar working in the Highlands and Islands. This was agreed the following year but fifteen months later Fr. Hegarty had to notify Propaganda that so far no money had reached the missionaries, who in the meantime had reconciled with the Church at least one hundred of the leading families in the Gaelic-speaking parts of Scotland. As has been pointed out already, neither Urban VIII nor his cardinals can be blamed for their apparent indifference to the spiritual welfare of Catholics in a remote part of an island kingdom that none of them had ever visited, and about which they had only the vaguest of ideas. During the 1630s they were far too alarmed by closer contacts with plague, war and famine over a large part of the continent of Europe.

By the winter of 1639-40 the situation had become desperate. Fr. Hegarty recommended that Fr. John Gormley and Fr. Anthony Gerlon should replace Fr. Brady and Fr. Ward, both of whom had now retired. Fr. Luke Wadding, the famous Franciscan historian, then living at the College of St Isidore in Rome, was consulted by Propaganda about the appointment of these two missionaries and Cardinal Barberini gave his approval on September 14, 1640. But it is not known if Fr. Gormley and Fr. Gerlon ever went to Scotland.

Once again there was talk of appointing a Vicar-Apostolic for the Highlands and Islands and various names were put forward. In 1640 Propaganda discussed the possibility of reviving the ancient diocese of Sodor, which at one time, like the diocese of Orkney, was under the jurisdiction of the Norwegian Metropolitan of Nidaros. It embraced the western islands of Scotland as well as the Isle of Man. Bishop Magennis advised that F. Hegarty should be made the first bishop, but nothing happened.

* ibid, p. 20.

That same year the Second Bishops' War broke out in the Lowlands and the signing of the Covenant was made compulsory on every person in Scotland. Irishmen crossed the sea and joined the royalist forces. Priests went with them as chaplains. Fr. Hegarty wrote to Propaganda, asking that special faculties should be granted them. He himself was still waiting for money from Rome, and complained about its non-arrival.

Driven to desperation by more than a decade of injustice and persecution, the Irish Catholics massacred many of the Protestant settlers in 1641. Fr. Hegarty was captured and imprisoned for five years. He obtained his release in 1646 and died soon after, having spent more than eighteen years on or in service for the Scottish mission.

The question of reviving the Franciscan mission to the Highlands and Islands was discussed by Propaganda in 1644. Ample faculties were granted to the four friars who were chosen, but it seems that they never reached Scotland. It was not until 1668 that the Irish Friars Minor resumed their missionary work in the Highlands and Islands.*

Persecution of both Papists and Episcopalians after the Solemn League and Covenant (1643)

Once the Solemn League and Covenant had been accepted by the Scots and English Parliaments in 1643, the same time as the one-year-old Louis XIV succeeded his father, Louis XIII, as King of France, Catholics and Episcopalians in Scotland found themselves in the same boat, so to say. An interdenominational gathering of about 130 Protestant ministers and laymen met in London, with the object of setting up a British and Irish Church with complete uniformity of doctrine and worship on an Anglo-Saxon model. The form of government would be Presbyterian. Four years were spent on drawing up a Confession of Faith, which was ratified by this so-called Westminster Assembly on August 27, 1647, and finally approved by Parliament on June 20, 1648.†

A *Directory of Worship*, composed for this projected new British and Irish Calvinist Church, repudiated all traditional liturgical formulae and dismissed them as "old rotten wheelbarrows to carry souls to hell." Scotsmen were assured that if they accepted all that had been drawn up and approved by the Westminster Assembly, they and their posterity would "as brethren, live in Faith and Love," and that the Lord would delight to dwell in the midst of them.‡ No provision, however, was made for either

* See p. 70.
† The Church of Scotland still adheres somewhat vaguely to this exposition of the Christian religion as the final statement of its doctrine.
‡ Cf. *A Source Book of Scottish History* (revised 1960), Vol. III, pp. 180-1.

Papists or Prelatists. Both minorities would be treated without mercy as idolaters.

Although the leaders of the Established Kirk never ceased to harass, heckle, maltreat and persecute both Catholics and Episcopalians between 1643 and 1661, never once did a Scots Samuel hew his popish or prelatist Agag to pieces before the Lord in Gilgal. There was nothing in Scotland resembling what happened in England during the reign of Mary I (1553-8) when at least 300 Protestants were killed, most of them burned alive. Between 1535 and 1681 more than 600 Papists were put to death in England. The result is that the only Episcopalian martyr who finds a place in the Scottish Book of Common Prayer is King Charles I, whose beheading in London is commemorated on January 30. The only Catholic martyr whose feast is kept by twentieth-century Papists in Scotland is the Jesuit, John Ogilvie, who was beatified in 1929, and whose special Mass is celebrated annually on March 10.

Many pages of the letters written by the Scottish Jesuits to their Father-General in Rome are taken up with stories of the sufferings endured by Catholics in the Lowlands at this time. In one letter Fr. Macbreck mentions priests, most of them Irish, who were attached to the royalist forces under James, Marquis of Montrose. Mass was usually celebrated in most primitive conditions.   The soldiers, many of them Irish, insisted on holy water being blessed before every Mass, because there were no vessels suitable for conveying it on the march. A scarcity of salt added to the value of the holy water. Guards and sentinels were posted at the entrances of these improvised chapels to prevent the priest being disturbed while celebrating Mass. More often than not the buildings were burnt after the service to prevent desecration by the Presbyterians.*
Montrose, with very much reduced forces after his defeat at the battle of Philiphaugh, near Stirling, retired to Loch Lomond, where the feast of All Saints, 1645, was spent.   On All Souls Day a requiem Mass was celebrated for the repose of the slain. Many men went to confession, and gave alms as generously as their means would allow. †

Charles I surrendered to the Scots in September 1646, was handed over to the English army in January the following year, and imprisoned at Carisbrooke Castle in the Isle of Wight.   Montrose fled to Norway. The Covenanters, now in supreme power, renewed their efforts to stamp out both popery and prelacy in Scotland.

---

* Cf. Forbes-Leith, op.cit., Vol. I, pp. 179, 310.
† ibid, pp. 335-6. It is difficult to understand what were Montrose's religious convictions. He took a practical interest in the welfare of his Catholic soldiers, was highly educated, but dismissed the book of *Common Prayer* as " a dead service book, the brood of the bowles of the whore of Babel."

Fr. Andrew Leslie, S.J., was arrested in May 1647. He was charged with having said Mass for the royalist soldiers, and imprisoned at Aberdeen, where he remained until January 1648, plague having broken out. Writing from Douai in March 1649, after the French ambassador had obtained his reprieve, he informed the Father-General that: "never was there so much excitement witnessed at Aberdeen. The entire population of the town turned out to see me quit my dungeon, and the preachers and the magistrates prohibited my leaving on that day. My departure was put off from day to day, and the people kept continually in suspense. Market-place, streets, lanes were crowded every day with multitudes eager to see my exit."

Finally it was decided to allow this notorious Jesuit to travel south under armed guards. The road lay through the Mearns. The under-sheriff of the county accompanied the prisoner most of the way. Fr. Leslie continued:

"I was a strange spectacle to the people of this portion of the coast, where there is now not a single Catholic resident; a priest being regarded as being of different species from other mortal men. Young and old crowded out of the town of Drumlithie to look at me, so that I was conducted on my way by a procession of young girls and boys. I saluted them all, and at first they were taken by surprise, and hesitated, but after a time they returned my greeting, wishing me a pleasant journey and good luck, and continued to reiterate their kindly good wishes, the people glanced at one another, as if remarking among themselves that I was not very dreadful to look at, that my words were friendly, and my manners civil, and that I exhibited some marks of vigour in my form and bearing." *

Quite likely the inhabitants of this village, seven miles southwest of Stonehaven, were disappointed, expecting that a priest would have seven heads and ten horns, like the scarlet-covered beast, on which rode the Whore of Babylon. Their parish minister at Glenbervie may well have preached on this particular vision of John the Evangelist.

The guards feared there might be demonstrations in Angus, where there still remained a few scattered Catholic families, so Fr. Leslie was transferred to the custody of soldiers, after the authorities in one town had rivalled one another in showing him attention, even entertaining him handsomely at an inn instead of lodging him in the local gaol. Friends in Aberdeen had warned Fr. Leslie that the Calvinists in Dundee might rouse the inhabitants to stone him. What happened was just the opposite; he was treated with the utmost respect. After three days the magistrate accompanied him to the vessel on which he was to embark, supplied him with provisions at the public expense, and assured him that he would do

* Co. Forbes-Leith, op.cit. Vol. I, pp. 179, 310.

all he could for the sake of the Leslie family. The letter continued: "Many people predicted that I should be torn into pieces in the province of Fife, to which I now proceeded. It turned out, however, quite differently. The assistant judge threw me into the worst dungeon in the prison, to the great disgust of the gaoler, but I was soon removed to a better lodging."

Here he was visited by the "tutor of the young Earl, who is the hereditary chief of the county, but is many years under age," wanting to discuss religion. The rest of the journey to Edinburgh was a succession of hospitable receptions by all classes of society. At Burntisland some sailors greeted the Jesuit "with great marks of kindness and affection." When he landed at Leith the magistrates received him courteously. Having reached Edinburgh, one of the magistrates remarked he was glad a priest had come, for he would be able to say Mass for the Catholics who had gone underground. Nevertheless Fr. Leslie was confined in the common prison amid all classes of criminals. Daily prayers were said by order of the head-keeper, consisting of a short psalm and five chapters of the Bible, during which the priest used to recite his breviary—the only time he was sure of not having to listen to "blasphemous language and profane swearing." The French envoy was allowed to visit the prison, and his chaplain frequently heard the Jesuit's confession. Even Fr. James Macbreck, who was in Edinburgh, came in. To end a long story, thanks to the intervention of the French ambassador, Fr. Leslie finally obtained his freedom and was allowed to leave Scotland. The whole thing looked like a miracle and he wrote that "the blood of our zealous and illustrious martyr [Fr. John Ogilvie] may have quenched the cruel thirst of the persecutors." *

Two months before Fr. Leslie related his adventures in the long letter written from Douai, Charles I was beheaded in London. Montrose, having returned from Norway, gathered a small army and was routed on the shores of Dornoch Firth on April 17, 1650. Twelve days later Prince Charles, who had been proclaimed King of the Scots, sailed from Holland, and landed at Speymouth in Morayshire on June 23. He travelled south to Edinburgh, where he was forced to listen to long controversial sermons. He had no choice but to sign a declaration stating that he was "deeply humbled and afflicted because of his father's opposition to the work of God and to the Solemn League and Covenant, by which so much of the blood of the Lord's people had been shed, and for the idolatry of his mother." He was crowned at Scone on January 1, 1651, after taking part in a solemn fast to atone for the sins of his prelatist father and popish mother. The small army he had raised,

---

* ibid, p. 44. Fr. Leslie went to Rome where he became Rector of the Scots College. Then he returned to the Mission and died in 1654.

mostly composed of Scotsmen, was defeated at Worcester on September 3. After many adventures Charles was smuggled across to France, and remained nine years in exile.

Many of his Catholic followers in Scotland had to suffer for their loyalty rather than their religion. The Earl of Abercorn, the Marquis of Douglas, Lord Gray and Lord Linton were excommunicated and heavily fined. Also in 1649 the second Marquis of Huntly, like the Marquis of Montrose, was beheaded at Edinburgh. Seton Palace, the chief home of the Earl of Winton, was plundered and turned into a tavern.

A Roman Agent appointed for the Scottish Mission (1650).

In the summer of 1650 Charles II was forced to sign the Covenant before he was allowed to come ashore in Spey Bay, and about the same time six secular priests found themselves together in Paris, discussing the affairs of the Scottish Mission. * All were uncertain as to their future. They agreed that to give the Mission a permanent character it must have a resident superior endowed with full canonical authority. Equally important was some provision for definite stipends to maintain the missionaries. Their first idea, it seems, was to keep in touch with Propaganda by procurators in Paris, who could communicate with Rome through the papal Nuncio to France. Then they realised that this would be a complicated way of doing business. It would be more practical to have a prudent and energetic Scots priest, resident in Rome as Agent for the Mission, and able to act directly with Propaganda.

The group of priests chose William Leslie as their representative with the Holy See. Catholicism in Scotland owes much to this son of Alexander Leslie of Conrack. This junior branch of the famous Aberdeenshire family gave many priests, including several Jesuits, and more than one bishop to the Church. William, who was born in 1620, entered the Scots College, Rome, at the age of twenty-one. After his ordination to the priesthood in 1647, he left Rome for Paris to prepare for mission work in Scotland, but because of the troublous state of the country he remained in France for the next three years. Staying in Paris in 1650 was Carlo Barberini, who three years later was to become one of the many Barberini cardinals. He was about to return to Rome, and offered to take Mr Leslie with him to act as tutor to one of his young nephews. Although Leslie was most unwilling to give up the idea of apostolic work in Scotland, Mr Ballantyne managed to convince him that his presence in Rome as Agent would greatly benefit the Mission and having a secure position with the Barberini family would relieve him of financial worries. So Leslie left Paris in company with the

* William Ballantyne, James Crichton, Thomas Lumsden, John Walker, John Smith, and William Leslie.

future Cardinal and his suite. He lived in Rome until his death in 1707, never appears to have taken a holiday, and never ventured beyond the Papal States.

Later on he obtained official work as Archivist to Propaganda, in which Congregation Barberini cardinals had a predominating influence during its earlier days. This gave him a first-hand knowledge of foreign mission work all over the world, including the vast areas then staffed by the Society of Jesus. Leslie never concealed his antipathy to the Jesuits and, whenever he had the chance, tried to undermine their activities, not only in Europe but also in the Far East. He was utterly convinced that the Society was obstructing his own ruling ambition—the appointment of a secular priest as bishop for Scotland. He went on fighting the Jesuits until his death bed, when he tried to excuse himself for all he had written and done against them in countless ways. * There is no doubt that he was brutally outspoken and made many enemies. On the other hand he must be regarded as one of the chief builders of the reconstructed Catholic Church in Scotland. He was the one priest above all others who was responsible for forming a handful of secular clergy into a Mission under a Prefect-Apostolic, and finally under a Vicar-Apostolic, out of which evolved the present Scottish hierarchy.

The Society of Jesus tries to secure possession of the Scots College, Paris (1650)

By 1650 the Society of Jesus could claim that it had maintained a succession of priests in the Lowlands of Scotland for nearly sixty years and their number had seldom dropped below half-a-dozen at any period. Considering that the Society also had to staff vast mission fields in India, China and North, Central and South America not to mention colleges and universities in Italy, Spain, Portugal, France, Germany, Austria, Poland and the Spanish Netherlands, it could not be said that Scotland was being neglected. The Society was also helping to keep the faith alive in both England and Ireland, each country with its own Province. Just because the few secular priests who had worked in Scotland during the first half of the seventeenth century had never been properly organised, it was almost inevitable that most of the Jesuits on the Scottish mission should regard them as interlopers and trespassers on their preserves. They did not fit into the pattern. It was hoped that sooner or later Scotland would be made an exclusively Jesuit mission field ruled over either by Vicars-Apostolic drawn from the Society or, if this were impossible, with Jesuit-nominated bishops. Whether Propaganda would ever have agreed is doubtful.

What stood in the way of the Society acquiring absolute control of Scotland was the Paris College, the only one of the Scots Colleges

* For a somewhat hostile account of William Leslie, see M. V. Hay, *Failure in the Far East* (1957).

abroad which was not staffed by members of the Society. There was a verbal tradition, handed down by Michel Christie, a Canon of Saint-Quentin, who had been secretary and chaplain to Archbishop James Beaton of Glasgow, that the Archbishop had intended to entrust the direction of the Paris College to the Jesuits. In 1624 the Nuncio at Paris, at the request of Propaganda, had investigated the affairs of the College and reported unfavourably to Rome. The Society would have been put in charge at that date, if the Principal (Mr Alexander Pendrick) had not managed to convince the Nuncio that the wording of Beaton's will prevented this. *

In November 1649—nine months after the execution of Charles I and the establishment of a republican form of government in Britain—Fr. Robert Gall informed the Rector of the Scots College, Rome, that steps were being taken by the Jesuits in Paris to get hold of Archbishop Beaton's will. He expected opposition, not only from the Principal of the College, but also from the Carthusians who claimed to be legal owners of the property. No matter; the Queen Mother, Anne of Austria, and her Prime Minister, Cardinal Mazarin, both friendly towards the Society, would be able to use their influence.

Fr. Gall hinted that discreet use for the same object would be made also of the Marquise de Sécencé, niece of Cardinal de Rochfoucauld, first Lady of Honour to the Queen-Regent, whose spiritual directors were Jesuits.† More than this: Fr. Gall recommended that Innocent X should be persuaded to order the Priors of the Grande Chartreuse and the Paris Charterhouse to hand over the Scots College to the Society, on the plea that it was incompatible with the spirit of strictly enclosed monks that they should be indirectly responsible for the care of youths being trained for missionary work—not that the Carthusians had ever attempted to meddle in the domestic affairs of the College, so far as is known.

Fr. Christie succeeded in procuring Beaton's will — it is not recorded whether this was due to the influence of either the Queen-Regent, Cardinal Mazarin, or the Marquise de Sécencé—and great was his disappointment to find that it contained no reference to the Society of Jesus. Meanwhile both the Carthusians and the staff of the College were united in opposition to Jesuit diplomacy, and gained the support of the University of Paris.

Public and private espionage were a profitable form of business in Paris at that date, so it is not surprising that in August 1650 Fr. Christie wrote in strict confidence to Fr. Gall of rumours that Mr Ballantyne was trying to persuade Scots Catholics to petition the Pope to give them a bishop. Only direct intervention with Innocent

---

* Cf. *The Blairs Papers*, p. 75, note 1.
† Cf. *The Blairs Papers*, p. 76.
‡ Saint-Beuve described the Marquise as "dévote, emportée et capricieuse" (Port-Royal, Paris (ed. 1861), Vol. III, p. 162). In 1653 she sold her place at court to Cardinal Mazarin for 100,000 livres. He gave it to one of his many nieces.

X could ensure that the Paris College was handed over to the Society. Considering that Gallican principles were already being held by more and more of the French clergy and statesmen— including the doctrine that the Pope had no dominion over things temporal and that kings were not subject to the authority of the Church in temporal and civil matters — the Jesuits could have requested the omnipotent Cardinal Mazarin, already a dictator and virtual ruler of France, to declare that the *Collège des Ecossais* was under royal patronage and outside papal jurisdiction. He could in fact have handed over the property to his former schoolmasters. * He had been putting pressure on Innocent X since 1646.

By the late autumn of 1652 the Jesuits were growing really alarmed by reports of secret negotiations by the Agent of the secular clergy in Rome, now employed by Propaganda. Having failed to gain control of the Scots College, Paris, they were prepared to do almost anything. Fr. Gall wrote from Douai warning Fr. Adam Gordon, the recently appointed Rector of the Scots College at Rome, of imminent danger: "Sundry secular priests are to repair hence to Scotland, where they intend to live well by the pension of 100 crowns which the congregation of Propaganda is said to bestow upon each of them yearly: their drift is to have a Bishop and by his authority to derogate our privileges and thus frustrate the fruit of our labours. Of this I write to our Reverend Father and this is all the good we reap of such secular priests as are bred in your College. Ponder this maturely, I pray you, and see how you and our Father-General may impede this, or prevent such hindrance to the advancing of the Catholic faith in our country."†

Fr. Gall and Fr. Christie may have expected the re-conversion of Scotland to be brought about sooner or later by the reconciliation of Charles II with the Church of Rome. Since his escape to France after the battle of Worcester on September 3, 1651, he had been in close touch with many prominent French Catholics. In fact, rumours of the exiled King's reception into the Church had already been spread by English spies in Paris. One of them wrote to John Thurloe, Secretary to the Council of State, early in 1652: "On Thursday last Charles Stuart and his fraternity went to pass away the afternoon at the Jesuits of St Antony's Street, and under pretence of the feast of New Year's Day he did begin to

---

* Jules Mazarin (1602-61), of an old Sicilian family, had been educated by the Jesuits in Italy. At the instigation of Louis XIII he was made a Cardinal in 1641, and the following year he succeeded Richelieu as prime minister. Though never raised to the priesthood, he held the see of Metz and at least twenty-seven abbacies, using their revenues as the basis of a vast fortune. He was said to be "as powerful as God the Father was when the world began".

† ibid. p. 186 (spelling modernised).

contribute to the service of idols, which discovers more the baseness of their hearts." *

Then before long there was gossip among the Jesuits that Charles was again toying with the idea of a marriage with Anne Marie Louise de Monpensier, cousin of Louis XIV. Known as a *Grande Mademoiselle,* she was one of the richest women in Europe. Queen Henrietta Maria was reported to be trying to raise money with the help of some friars to enable her son to promote the Catholic religion should he regain the throne. On March 8, 1652, Fr. Gall wrote to Fr. Adam Gordon in Rome that the King, who had been living on credit for some months, had left Paris for an unknown destination, and it might well be Rome, where he hoped for financial assistance from Innocent X.†

About the same time Fr. Francis Spreul (often called Murray) wrote to Fr. Adam Gordon, asking him to try to procure for the Jesuit missionaries in Scotland, whose situation had become much easier, a share of the stipends which Propaganda was alleged to be paying the secular clergy in the Lowlands. He hinted that the dangerous Mr Ballantyne was busily engaged in persuading young men to join the secular priesthood, and diverting them from the Society of Jesus. Something had to be done to stop this. Fr. Gall had already informed Rome that if the present calm continued in Scotland there was likely to be " a greater store of Catholics than ever since the heretical rupture and schism, for the Puritans were disgusted at their minister's treachery and perjury."

There were warnings of dangers to the Society's control of missionary work in Scotland if the secular clergy managed to persuade Propaganda to appoint a bishop. Fr. Goswin Nickel, a seventy-year-old German Jesuit who had been elected General in March 1652, must have found it difficult to deal with this. He had many more important matters to consider, e.g., the long drawn-out controversy over the so-called ' Chinese Rites,' and the spread of Jansenism in France during the past twenty years.

In any case, he did not see his way to ask Propaganda to pay

---

* Thurloe. *State Papers,* Vol. I, p. 622. Lord Acton in ' Secret History of Charles II' (*Historical Essays and Studies,* 1907) stated that there is little doubt that the King secretly became a Catholic while he was in exile though the general opinion is that he was not received into the Church until shortly before his death on February 6, 1685 (See p. 78.).

† In 1665 Charles II acknowledged that the eldest of his several natural sons was James Stuart, whose mother was Marguerite de Cartaret of Jersey. There is a story that in 1668 Fr. John Paul Oliva, General of the Society of Jesus, informed the King secretly that his son had entered the novitiate at Rome, having been received into the Catholic Church at Hamburg shortly before this in the presence of the ex-Queen Christina of Sweden. The novice went under the name of Cloche du Bourg. The King replied that he hoped his son would be ordained priest and come to England. It is possible that this royal Jesuit did turn up in London, arrangements for his journey having been made by his father, but what happened to him remains an unsolved mystery.

annual pensions to the regular clergy, including Jesuits, working in Scotland. *

It was the Society of Jesus which was largely responsible for the constitution ' Cum occasione ' issued by Innocent X on May 31, 1653, which condemned five propositions embodied in the dogmatic substance of Jansenism.   Cardinal Mazarin, wanting for political reasons to keep the right side of the Pope, decided to enforce this papal pronouncement, even at the risk of offending a considerable number of the French bishops.

On October 13 that same year the Jesuits won another victory. Innocent X, probably on the advice of Propaganda, formed the opinion that the time was not yet ripe to give Scotland a bishop. He compromised, however, by making William Ballantyne a prefect-apostolic.   Although to all intents and purposes this merely gave him canonical authority over the ten secular priests working in the Lowlands, they were promised annual stipends of 500 crowns each. Half a loaf was better than none so far as they were concerned at the moment.

William Ballantyne (otherwise known as Bellenden or Bannan-tyne), born in 1618, was the son of the parish minister at North Berwick.   His boyhood was spent at Douglas, Lanarkshire, to which parish his father was translated in 1621.   He grew up in a world of crypto-Catholicism, because the Marquis of Douglas was at least sympathetic towards the old religion.   After studying at the University of Edinburgh, where he took no degree, William appears to have become a Catholic during a visit to France.   He entered the Scots College at Rome in 1641, was ordained priest there five years later, and then moved to France.   Until 1649 he continued his studies at the Scots College, Paris, and then he returned to Scotland. Not long after his arrival he was arrested and imprisoned, but when he resumed mission work he managed to reconcile several distinguished people with the Church.† It is recorded that "the weight of his arguments in reasoning with his Protestant friends and acquaintances was much increased by meekness and sweetness of temper, unusual among the theological disputants."

Mr Ballantyne was back in France again in the summer of 1650, when he discussed the future of the Mission with other secular priests. All but Mr Leslie returned with him to Scotland. From the frequent references to 'Banantin' or 'Banandin' in letters written by the Jesuits, it looks as if they suspected that he would be made a bishop, for the secular clergy obviously regarded him

---

* It was discovered that the aged Capuchin, Fr. Epiphanius Lindsay, had been receiving an allowance since 1647. He died in 1666, having worked on the Mission for nearly half-a-century (See p. 16.).

† Among them was his younger brother, Archibald, who having started as a page to Frederick, Elector Palatine of the Rhineland (titular King of Bohemia) whose wife, Elizabeth, was the daughter of James VI, rose to the rank of Major in the Covenanting forces.

as their unofficial leader.   Hence the warnings to the Father General in Rome, mentioned already.   It may well be that they feared Mr Ballantyne more than the other seculars, because of his influence over 'people of quality'.

Nevertheless some of the Scottish Jesuits were still hopeful that it would not be long before Charles II was reconciled with the Church.   It was reported that he had been conferring with Jean-Jacque Olier, the saintly founder of the Society and seminary of Saint-Sulpice.* Given a Catholic sovereign, the re-conversion of Scotland would be easy.

* Cf. E. M. Faillon, *Vie de M. Olier* (Paris 1841), Vol. II, pp. 320, 334. Bishop Burnet in his *History of My Own Times* was almost certain that the exiled King was secretly received in 1655 (ed. M. J. Routh, Oxford, 1823), Vol. I, p. 126.

CHAPTER TWO

PREFECTS-APOSTOLIC
1653-1694

Scotland during the Commonwealth (1649-1659)

ON DECEMBER 16, 1653—two months after William Ballantyne was nominated Prefect-Apostolic of the non-Gaelic-speaking parts of Scotland—Oliver Cromwell dismissed the Long Parliament and was made Lord Protector of Britain. For the next seven years he ruled the nation as a dictator, with the help of the army. English garrisons were stationed in Ayr, Inverlochy, Inverness, Leith and Perth. Scotland, in the last stages of exhaustion, was helplessly prostrate before a foreign enemy. The Commonwealth government may have given justice and security, but the actual state of the country was worse than it had been during the previous sixteen years of war. Cromwell, as an English Independent, i.e. a Congregationalist, had no use for Presbyterianism. One of his first acts was to grant toleration to all who worshipped God in any " Gospel Way". Under the Commonwealth there was no official persecution of Papists, but they never ceased to be harassed by the Kirk. The eight commissioners, representing the government in London, did not interfere.

The duties entrusted to the Prefect-Apostolic were:—(1) General supervision of the handful of clergy; (2) Distribution of their allowances when they arrived from Propaganda; (3) Correspondence with Paris and Rome; (4) Selection and transmission of students to colleges abroad; and (5) Presiding at meetings of the priests. Mr Ballantyne found the Mission in a very disorganised state. So was the Kirk, for the General Assembly had been suppressed by the Government in 1653. Each secular priest used his own judgment in almost everything. He stayed where he fancied, or roamed around the country, as inclination or necessity disposed him. The regular clergy, mostly Jesuits and Benedictines, were better off because they could appeal to their local or major superiors, keeping in touch with them by letters.

It is recorded that the first Prefect-Apostolic was " a tall stately person, of brown complexion, well proportioned, very comely and well bred . . . a gentleman of excellent parts. He had an excellent way with Protestants, whom he gained not only with the solidarity of his Reasons, but also by the Meekness and Sweetness of his spirit. He was also a good and zealous preacher, which does much with them."*

Great prudence as well as zeal was needed to carry on his duties. The half-dozen or so secular clergy had their own masters for so long, that it was not easy to make them conform to even a minimum of discipline. We are told that after 1653 they began to act in consort with new ardour. They worked mainly among the poorer classes, allowing the regular clergy to concentrate their efforts in towns or with the nobility and landed gentry. In some parts of Scotland Presbyterians began to attend their instructions. Some were converted, and others reconciled with the Church if they had lapsed. Among the latter was the third Marchioness of Huntly. She provided a refuge for Mr Ballantyne at Gordon Castle, hitherto usually served by Jesuit chaplains. Then known as 'The Bog o' Gight', it stood on windswept marshes near the mouth of the Spey. Meanwhile the Kirk Sessions went on hunting down Papists, and spying on all who kept company with them. From time to time sentences of excommunication were issued against converts for their "defection from the true Protestant reformed religion".

The Jesuit reaction to the appointment of a Prefect-Apostolic.

The Jesuits had been opposed to the appointment of a Prefect-Apostolic from the moment that the plan was suggested. After Mr Ballantyne assumed his duties they did not make things any easier for him, as is proved by some of the letters sent to the Father-General at Rome. They regarded him as an interloper and were not prepared to accept him as temporary substitute for a bishop. They grew alarmed when they heard that he was sending youths to colleges abroad to be trained for the secular priesthood. They were shocked by what we should now call the ecumenical relations between Catholics and Protestants, allowed by the secular clergy, which included permission to attend Presbyterian services for special reasons. They tried hard to make Propaganda stop this abuse, for they felt it might result in the ruin of the Catholic religion in Scotland. In some of the reports sent to Rome it was hinted that the seculars were not doing as much as they claimed— that their converts came solely from the 'lower orders', and not from the aristocracy. An increase in the number of seculars might well mean the end of a system which had worked well enough for half-a-century. Nearly every Report conveyed the impression that, thanks to the Jesuit missionaries, the re-conversion of Scotland was making rapid strides, especially because of their influence among the landed gentry. Year after year the Father-General was informed of the sedulous manner in which his sons were adminis-

* Preface to the first edition of *A Preparation for Death*, by William Ballantyne, quoted by Hay in *The Blairs Papers*, p. 183.

tering the sacraments, and making many remarkable conversions. The happy state of affairs recorded in 1649 continued, with an increase of piety among the gentlefolk converts.

"It was a joyful sight to see men of rank and their ladies, some of them women with child, travelling immense distances to keep their Easter as prescribed by the Church, that their courage might be confirmed and strengthened by the Sacraments of Confession and Holy Communion. The houses of the Catholic nobility, in which our Fathers are accustomed to find a refuge, resemble religious houses at these seasons . . . All make a general confession once a year, many once or twice a month. For some days in Holy Week they piously entertain their minds with the Spiritual Exercises . . . Women of high rank minister with perfect humility to the sick and dying, and wrap the dead poor in winding sheets, and lay them out for burial; and these and similar spiritual and corporal works of mercy, all make it a practice to observe." *

From time to time a Jesuit missionary, having been too bold, found himself in prison, after which he was usually banished from Scotland. Taken as a whole, they were a courageous band, just as they had been in the past. They were more successful than the secular clergy because they acted as a united force and also because they were generally certain of financial support. They travelled around from castle to castle, or from mansion to mansion, usually carrying vestments, an altar-stone, chalice, paten and missal. Very often they had to be lodged in a remote part of the building for reasons of safety. Nearly always they took the precaution of changing their names from time to time.

Mr John Walker's Report to Propaganda, 1655

The secular clergy also changed their names. There was a Mr John Walker, otherwise known as Ross, one of the four priests who had accompanied Mr Ballantyne to Scotland five years previously. In 1655 he drew up a Report which was sent to Propaganda and in it he explained that although there was no persecution of Papists by the Commonwealth government, nevertheless the Presbyterian ministers had " girded themselves up to write books, not for the building up of their own religion, but for the pulling down of ours." One of the most virulent of these publications was Dr. William Guild's *Noveltie of Poperie,* issued at Aberdeen in 1655. Apparently in collaboration with Sir Alexander Irvine of Drum, Mr Walker replied to the many attacks on the Catholic religion which appeared about this time. His book was entitled *The Presbyterie's Trial,* and was printed at Paris in 1657. That same year Mr Walker was imprisoned at Edinburgh. After his release he went to France, where he remained until 1660. †

---

* W. Forbes-Leith, S.J., op.-cit. vol. ii, pp. 56-8.

† See p. 72.

Vincentian missionaries in the Highlands and Islands, 1651–1657

Two years before Mr Ballantyne's appointment as first Prefect-Apostolic of the non-Gaelic parts of Scotland in 1653, there had been correspondence between Propaganda and St Vincent de Paul about sending missionaries to the Highlands and Islands. *

In 1645 Innocent X asked St. Vincent to spare some of his priests for Ireland. Of the eight who went there the following year, one was Dermot Duggan, a native of Limerick, who became the first Lazarist missionary in Scotland. Having returned to France from Ireland in 1651, he left Paris with Mr Thomas Lumsden and, disguised as merchants, they reached Holland. Here they met the newly converted son of the eighth Chief of Glengarry, with whom they crossed the North Sea. By slow stages the two priests made their way north from Edinburgh, and after a walk of 200 miles they reached Lochaber where they reconciled Macdonnell of Glengarry, the ninety-year-old father of the young laird, with the Church.

Mr Lumsden belonged to Aberdeenshire and spoke little or no Gaelic. Probably because of this he moved north-east, hoping to make converts among the Lallans or Scots-speaking natives. Mr Duggan remained in the west and later he crossed the Minch to some of the Outer Hebridean islands.

Another Lazarist missionary—Mr Francis White — came to Scotland in 1652 and that same year Mr Duggan wrote a long letter to St Vincent, reporting on the work done. He explained that there was little or no contact with the rest of Scotland, but far more with Ireland. Most of the islanders had "welcomed him as an angel from heaven" and between 800 and 900 persons had been converted on the islands of Canna, Eigg and Islay. They were virtual pagans. Although some called themselves Catholics, having memories of the Irish Friars Minor who had visited them, few of them had been baptized and " these people were so little instructed that they did not know how to make the sign of the Cross." He went on to say: "Money is very scarce in these parts; nevertheless everything is very dear here, and what increases my poverty is that I need two men; one assists me on my journeys and in passing from one island to the other, and when I travel by land he helps me to carry the vestments for Mass and my few other effects, I myself having quite sufficient difficulty in walking on foot over bad roads as much as fourteen or fifteen miles before saying Mass. The other attendant, whom I have instructed to that end, assists me to teach the *Pater, Ave* and *Credo,* and serves Mass, there not being any one except him who can do so."

It was the lack of money to buy even a small open boat for crossing from one island to another that prevented Mr Duggan from extending his missionary labours. Accustomed as he was to

---

* St. Vincent had founded the Congregation of the Mission, first known as Lazarists, in 1625, with its main object to preach the Gospel to the poor, and to convert heathens and heretics.

the decent living conditions at the College of Saint-Lazare, the headquarters of the Congregation of the Mission in Paris, the squalor of life in the Outer Hebrides must have been a real penance. He informed St Vincent that: " ordinarily we only take one meal a day which for the most part consists of nothing else but barley bread or oatcake, with cheese or salt and butter, and we pass sometimes whole days without being able to find anything but what we have carried with us. Our drink in summer is plain water, and in winter we have a little meal boiled in it, which is indeed very injurious to my health, being as your Reverence knows, of a phlegmatic temperament. It is true that in some places we find a little beer or whisky, but this is of rare occurrence. Anyone who wishes to have meat must buy a whole beast, a stirk or an ox, because there are no butchers in the country. This meat which the Islanders do sometimes eat, makes one disgusted, for they are content to half cook it on the embers, and then they throw it on the ground on the straw, which with them serves for the table, tablecloth and plate, so that we scarcely ever eat it". *

Travelling around the Hebrides three hundred years ago, even in summer, was no pleasure trip. Mr Duggan and his two companions usually slept in the open air and on the ground. Where they were able to gather heather or brushwood they made a sort of hut in which to pass the night, covering themselves with their cloaks. When they were made welcome in a primitive cottage it was seldom that there was straw to lie on. There were no roads in the islands, only rough paths among the rocks and heather.

Not only did the missionary's luggage contain everything needed to celebrating Mass; it also included two folio volumes of the Scripture commentary of Tirinus, printed in Antwerp in 1645.†

Mr Duggan ended his long letter to St Vincent with an appeal for both men and money. He insisted that teachers were badly needed who could speak Gaelic, and who were prepared to "suffer hunger and thirst and to sleep on the ground." Nothing was said about what Mr White was doing on the mainland, and he hoped that his fellow-Lazarist would be writing direct to Paris.

During the five years that this missionary was sailing in

* Considering that herring fishing was being carried on off the Outer Hebrides, mainly by Dutch vessels; and that white fish of many species were waiting to be caught in these same waters, and that lobsters—then as now — abounded around these islands. Mr Duggan could not blame nature for this spartan diet—merely the lack of initiative on the part of the natives.

† In one of these volumes, now preserved in the Blairs College archives, is the inscription in Mr Duggan's writing: " Ce livre appartienne aux prêtres de la mission de S. Lazare de Paris en France, acheté en Anvrope par les premiers missioners de la ditte compagnie de S. Lazare envoyés en Ecosse par l'ordre de Sa Sainteté, nommés François le Blanc et Germain Duguin, les x novembre, et arrivés en Ecosse le premier de mars 1651. Fait dans l'Ile de Huiste, le 25 de mars. D. Duguin (prêtre) indigne de la Mission." A smaller Vulgate Bible, which belonged to Francis White, has also survived.

open boats across the often stormy waters of the Minch, Admiral
Blake was attacking the Dutch fleets off the coasts of England and
Holland.   Mr Duggan returned to Barra in the spring of 1653,
about the same time that Blake gained a victory over Van Tromp's
men-of-war off Portsmouth.   When St Vincent received a letter
from Mr Duggan, relating how the people were most devout and
eager for further instruction in the faith, the bull of Innocent X
which had just been promulgated in condemnation of Jansenism
must have seemed very remote.   The simple piety of the natives
of the Outer Hebrides was not tainted by heresy, even if they tended
to be superstitious.   For as Mr Duggan reported: "It is enough to
teach one child in the village the *Pater, Ave* and *Credo;* in two
days the whole village knew them—children and adults."   For
reasons of prudence he usually deferred giving them Communion
for some time after a general Confession.   Some of the Barra folk
were much troubled and annoyed by ghosts and evil spirits, but
were generally delivered from them after Baptism.

The success of this lonely missionary's labours was phenomenal.
On South Uist, for instance, there was hardly one practising Catholic
before 1651, but three years later they had increased to roughly
1,200.

It was when staying on South Uist in the spring of 1637 that
Mr Duggan decided to visit Pabbay, an island six-and-a-half miles
south of Barra, between Sandray and Mingulay. This would have
involved a voyage of nearly twenty miles, exposed to the full force
of the Atlantic most of the way. He described this remote island
as a "strange and terrible place" and so it remains. But he never
got there, for he fell ill and died on May 17. There was no priest
to give him the last Sacraments, and his body was buried by the
people amongst whom he had ministered.   They revered him as a
saint, and gave his name to a chapel where his remains were laid
to rest.

St Vincent did not send another Lazarist to replace Mr Duggan,
so the thousands of converts he had made were abandoned for
several years.   Mr Francis White, whose labours were confined to
the mainland, made his headquarters at Invergarry Castle on Loch
Oich, about half-way between Fort William and Inverness. In
February 1655 he set off on a seventy mile walk to Gordon Castle,
hoping to find there a priest to hear his confession. On Ash Wednes-
day he was arrested, along with Fr. Grant, S.J., and a secular priest.
They were taken to Aberdeen and imprisoned, but obtained their
release after six months. 'Francois Le Blanc' (to give Mr White
the name by which he was known to St Vincent and his fellow
Lazarists) then returned to Glengarry and resumed his apostolate.
For the next twenty years he endured poverty and privations,
often in danger of being molested by the parish ministers or their
accomplices. * It is related that the crofter-fishermen on the west

* See p. 69.

coast put great trust in his prayers, and that on one occasion, after he had sprinkled holy water on the sea, the weather changed and their nets were filled.

Little is recorded of Mr Lumsden's mission work in the northern Highlands, among people who showed little or no desire to be reconciled with the Church. He was probably the first priest to visit Orkney since the death of the last of the pre-Reformation clergy. On Easter Sunday 1654 he celebrated Mass in the house of a laird on one of the islands and gave Communion to fifty persons, of whom twenty were his converts. Although some of the ministers grew alarmed by this infiltration of popery, he managed to escape imprisonment.

Mr Ballantyne's imprisonment and exile in France, 1656–1660

In the summer of 1656 Mr Ballantyne left Scotland, planning to pay a business visit to France. The ship he boarded at Rye in Sussex was captured by a Spanish vessel in the Channel, and he was put ashore at Ostend, where the Government liberated him on discovering that he was a priest. For some reason Mr Ballantyne decided to sail back to Rye, where he was arrested and taken to London on suspicion of being an agent of the Spanish Government. He was lodged in the Tower, where he had to pay the cost of his keep. But he soon won the esteem of John Thurloe, Cromwell's secretary, who released him. For the next year the Prefect-Apostolic was kept in a house at Westminster, under custody, and then he was given funds by Cromwell and was shipped to France. He found a refuge at the Scots College in Paris. In May 1659 Patrick Con, son of the laird of Auchry, Aberdeenshire, met him and wrote to Propaganda: "I have found here Mr Ballantyne, the Superior of the poor Scottish mission; he is still weak from the hardships of his recent imprisonment. But for all that he keeps a stout heart and is not wanting in good will to carry out the duties of his vocation. I beseech your Excellence not to hinder by delays his pious designs. The poor man has incurred so many expenses in prison that he does not know how to satisfy his creditors, unless the congregation comes to his assistance. It will be urgent to do quickly what is to be done, because many will suffer from his absence . . . I fear, that in the end, those poor men will be obliged to change their condition [i.e. become regulars] if things go on in the future as they have done in the past." *

The Papal Nuncio in Paris was then acting as financial agent for the Scottish Mission, and received all funds sent from Rome by Propaganda. Very often the money was held up in France. In September 1659 Patrick Con wrote another letter to Propaganda, stating that the missionaries had been complaining bitterly about not receiving their small subsidies, as they were reduced to abject

* *The Blairs Papers*, p.200.

poverty. He added that the Vincentian priests in the Highlands were being paid regularly, and received far more than the secular clergy, whose stipends as a rule only reached them "after a thousand delays, and about half was deducted by the cost of the transport of letter, which they could not get without great expense and extreme danger."*

Having nothing else to do in Paris, Mr Ballantyne drew up a very long and detailed report on the state of religion in Scotland for the benefit of Propaganda, whose knowledge of this remote country was extremely vague. †

The exiled Prefect-Apostolic did not attempt to tone down the reasons for the sudden collapse of the Catholic Church in Scotland as an organisation, and wrote: "For the most part the abbots and priors were the sons of the nobles or bastard sons of the kings; moreover, as there was not yet any accommodation in inns, travellers generally received hospitality in the monasteries, so the religious grew fat through banquets and revelling, while welcoming guests in a style suited to their rank, and the religious life was greatly relaxed. Very many of the abbots and priors took to hunting and hawking, and interested themselves in breeding hawks and hounds; numbers of them openly kept concubines; the bishops did the same, and as they have their bastard children, especially their daughters in marriage, many of our more distinguished noble families have that origin . . . Finally, in the space of a few years the Catholic faith was completely destroyed . . . and one thing is noteworthy, very, very few of the churchmen resisted that apostasy, but almost all fell into it." ‡

The fullest possible details were given about the doctrines and modes of worship of Presbyterians and Prelatists, i.e. Episcopalians. Mr Ballantyne informed Propaganda that some of the latter maintained that "the Roman and Anglican Churches are to be

---

* ibid, p. 192.

† Divided into 13 sections the Report deals with the origin of heresy and its effects; the authority and number of the ministers; their methods of preaching; the administration of the Lord's Supper; baptism and visitation of the sick; the doctrines of various sects; the Courts of Justice and their decrees; divination and witchcraft; the chief Catholic families; the number of missionaries; and the difficulties facing the Mission. (Cf. 'Narratives of the Scottish Reformation III. Prefect Ballantyne's Report, c. 1660', ed. by Rev. W. J. Anderson, in *Innes Review*.

‡ Clerical concubinage was more or less taken for granted. The Statutes of the 1549 Provincial Council merely stated that the clergy were not to keep their bastard bairns with them in their houses, to promote them to benefices, nor to enrich them from the patrimony of the Church. Clerics who could afford it, often had their natural sons legitimated so that they could hold and inherit property. The Provincial Councils of 1552 and 1559 drew up more Statutes in a desperate effort to purge the Kirk, but it was too late. In 1556 Cardinal Sermoneta, Protector of the kingdom of Scotland, urged Paul IV to stop the scandalous alienation of church property, benefices and goods, besides many more abuses.

compared to two sister churches, and as sound members (though members in a more general sense) of the same Catholic Church, whose frontiers they extend so far as to be able to include in its bosom the schismatic Greeks, nay even any heretic whatever who admits the unity of the Godhead and trinity of persons . . . But when you get to close grips with them, they abandon the conclusion from universal tradition and the fathers, say goodbye to them and take refuge in the normal shelter of heretics, the pure word of God as expounded in their own opinion."

George Fox (1624-91), the founder of the Society of Friends, otherwise known as Quakers, formed several groups of his disciples in Scotland after 1652. Mr Ballantyne felt it worth while to inform Propaganda that they "feign inspired raptures and divine exstasies and tremble with a horrible and often involuntary stiffening of the body." He also mentioned extraordinary examples of divination and witchcraft in the Highlands, and even in parts of the Lowlands. *

From the list of houses at which it was safe for the missionaries to stay, it is clear that the writer had travelled over the greater part of the non-Gaelic-speaking Scotland. He mentions the roof-less cathedral at Elgin, and the " two very famous abbeys, Kinloss and Pluscarden," recording how the former was still fairly complete, only the church lacking its roof. The gardens and orchard were full of unusual and very fine fruits. Then pilgrims still worshipped at the Morayshire shrine, known as Our Lady of Grace. He had never been there without finding people kneeling in prayer beside the holy well. †

Yet what could only sixteen priests in the whole of Scotland do to win back the inhabitants to the faith of their fathers? Eight of them were Jesuits. Of the secular clergy, three Irish were working in the Highlands. ‡ Two Dominicans and one Capuchin Franciscan roamed around the countryside. Owing to constant harassing by the Kirk, little progress was being made "except among the common people," whose poverty was such that loss of fortune was less to be feared. The nobility and landed gentry were afraid to be reconciled with the Church, lest they should be reduced to poverty. This Report sent to Propaganda conveyed a somewhat different impression from the annual letters written by the Scottish Jesuits to their General in Rome.

Mr Ballantyne summed up Presbyterian worship as "wholly Pharisaic". He informed the cardinals and monsignori that

* Mr Ballantyne must have been familiar with the alleged witches and warlocks who abounded in the counties of Banff, Moray and Aberdeen, all within access of Gordon Castle where he usually resided. Some of the Jesuit reports sent to Rome refer to witchcraft, especially in Galloway.

† See p. 69.

‡ The Vincentians are secular priests under simple vows, not religious in the strict sense.

sermons and meetings were frequent both on Sundays and week-days. They began and ended with "long extempore prayers, lasting an hour each." The Presbyterians strictly abstained from all servile work on Sundays. No food or drink was allowed to be sold. The streets in towns were silent. Nobody dared to appear out of doors, except to go to the kirks. Watchmen prowled around and arrested Sabbath breakers.

The exiled Prefect-Apostolic stressed that priests sent on the Scottish Mission must be "really learned", and that great care must be taken before faculties were granted to them. They must be men "with no thought for their own advantage but only for the glory of Christ". Another point: it was almost impossible for a stranger to remain in a town for long without arousing suspicion. The situation was no better in the country, because even well-to-do Catholic families had Protestant servants. Any man whose identity was not confirmed was suspected of being a priest. English soldiers were stationed in some parts of Scotland, but more danger-ous were the ministers and elders of the Kirk. Innkeepers and landladies of lodging houses had to submit the names of their guests. Persons who could not give a satisfactory account of themselves were arrested as vagrants.

Propaganda officials must have rubbed their eyes and wondered if the Prefect-Apostolic was crazy when they read his recommen-dation for the missionaries to become what we should now call "Worker-Priests". He wrote: "Each missionary might be taught some mechanical craft, or might have some honourable profession, for example, he might be a portrait-painter or a glazier or a watch-maker, or he might be able to profess some knowledge of medicine, and so he would escape the danger of investigation. The result would be the Catholics would be more safe to welcome him into their houses, if when the officials came round to search, the priest could show even a minimum skill in trades or professions of this kind."

These revolutionary suggestions must have shocked the cardinals and monsignori, for they were altogether contrary to canon law. Mr Ballantyne explained that the handful of priests in Scotland was quite insufficient to administer the sacraments to the widely scattered Catholics. Again, there was no inducement to a young priest to lead a roving life, because he knew that if obliged to retire from the Mission for reasons of persecution or ill health, there was no certain refuge for him on the continent of Europe, and no funds available to maintain him. It was a scandal that some of the priests who had been sent to Scotland were utterly ignorant of preaching, catechising, or even administering the sacraments. Mr Ballantyne informed Propaganda that these priests "did not know how to undertake the care of souls, or to lead men from their conversion to a life of virtue."

St Margaret's, Mulroy, Lochaber (1826). A succession of priests began to work here about 1650.

St Cumin's, Loch Morar (1889). Both regular and secular priests have served this district since 1658.

The long Report ended with the Congregation being told that only a change in the whole system of training priests could prevent the Catholic religion in Scotland soon dying out, "while the young men turn aside, as they have continually done in the past, some to Civil Law, some to Medicine, some to Trade or Military service". In the thirty years since 1629, hardly twenty secular priests had been sent to Scotland from the three seminaries abroad which had been founded specifically for this purpose. The concluding words were: "Your Eminences, this is the report, written in a plainer style than it ought to have been, of the present state of Scotland which I make to your Holy Congregation. It is my hope that your Holy Congregation will interpret my simplicity as a sign of my gratitude and respect, and take in good part any slips I have made in writing it. One thing I can venture to assert: there is nothing in the Report which any fair critics would not admit to be absolutely true. Meanwhile I, who am on the point of setting out to risk my life for the Gospel, pray that you, Most Holy and Eminent Princes of the Church, may enjoy all prosperity".

It is not known if the Report was read by Alexander VII, who was elected Pope in 1655, but if so he may have felt that the affairs of Scotland were not nearly so important as building the colonnade in front of St Peter's, draining the Bracciano marshes, endowing the Sapienza college with a valuable library or writing Latin verses when he was on holiday at Castelgandolfo. Moreover he was being pestered with tiresome business from France all the time, where both Gallicanism and Jansenism were a menace, disturbing his promotion of literature and the fine arts. He preferred to leave administrative affairs in the hands of his brother and nephews.

Mr Alexander Dunbar acts as Vice-Prefect, 1657–1660

During the years that Mr Ballantyne was in exile at Paris, Mr Alexander Dunbar acted as Vice-Prefect of the Scottish Mission. * He was an astute diplomat, and it is recorded that he had made " such close study of the art of wrapping up his meaning in terms of such ambiguity and obscurity, as to defy the interpretation of anyone but the persons for whom the information was intended." † Much younger than most of his brethren, he soon won their confidence. His first step was an attempt to bring about happier relations between the secular and regular clergy, and he drew up instructions to this end.

When he arrived in Scotland in 1658 he found that in some parts of the country, especially in Galloway, Catholics were still being harassed and even bitterly persecuted. Armed horsemen

---

* Born in Moray, he went to the Scots College, Rome, in 1651, where he was ordained in 1657. The following year he returned to Scotland after a long stay in Paris. He used several aliases, and was often referred to as Winchester or Winster.

† *Scotichronicon*, pp. x-xi.

raided the castles and mansions of the nobility and carried away vestments and altar furnishings for profane uses. The Countess of Nithsdale, though arrested, had refused to abandon her religion. Several Jesuits were in prison.

Oliver Cromwell died on September 3, 1658, and was succeeded as Protector by his son Richard, who resigned on April 22 the following year.   On May 8, the monarchy was re-established, mainly through the efforts of General Monk, and Charles II proclaimed King. On the 29th of that same month he entered London amid scenes of wild enthusiasm.

Mr Ballantyne resumes his duties as Prefect-Apostolic

It was now safe for Mr Ballantyne to return to Scotland from France. On June 29, 1660, he reached Elgin, where he stayed with his former benefactress, the dowager Marchioness of Huntly. One of his first actions was to reconcile with the Church a former student of the Scots College, Rome, named James Crichton. Ordained about 1650, Crichton had apostasised and married. A letter was sent to the Papal Nuncio at Paris in which the Prefect-Apostolic said: "I set out to find my other colleagues, who have pleased me much by their diligence and the consequent results which have really exceeded my expectation. By the grace of God there is no persecution for the moment, yet it is necessary to proceed with the usual caution so as not to give occasion to our enemies to complain to Parliament of our too great presumption during the present period of toleration.   We expect from this Parliament some sort of Edict against us like the laws against Catholics in the days of Queen Elizabeth: for this reason those who have some considerable property stand aloof, fear to lose temporal goods prevailing over the salvation, and the affection which, for the most part, they have for following the Catholic faith. But at the same time a good number of people, of those who have few temporal goods to lose, join us every day, but we are so few in number that it will be quite impossible to help all as it ought to be done . . . I beg you, moreover, to deal with the Congregation [of Propaganda] so that in the future they will provide punctually the usual pension, for I cannot describe the difficulty there is to live in this miserable country, being reduced to extreme poverty and the costliness of everything." *

The Act Recissory (March 1661) stated that the King would maintain the doctrine and discipline of the Established Church of Scotland as they had been under his father and grandfather; also that he would settle its form of government in the manner most agreeable to the Word of God, most suitable to monarchial government, and most consistent with public peace and quiet.   For the time being kirk sessions, presbyteries and synods were allowed to

* The Blairs Papers, p. 200.

function.   The tiny Catholic minority was not sure how it would
be treated by Charles II.

Four months after the passing of this Act of Parliament Mr
Ballantyne was taken seriously ill at Elgin, where he died on
September 2.   The following morning a requiem Mass was celebrated in Lady Huntly's private chapel, so Mr Alexander Dunbar
and Mr Thomas Lumsden informed Propaganda in a joint letter.
So strong was the sympathy for the old religion in Moray, even a
hundred years after the Reformation, that the coffin was taken to
the Great Hall, where it remained surrounded by a great number
of torches and tapers until three hours after sunset, when it was
borne through the streets to the Cathedral.   The Magistrates and
leading citizens walked in the procession; also some of the local
lairds, although most of them were Protestants. It must have been
an impressive sight, for more than fifty torches lit up the darkness.
The body of Scotland's first Prefect-Apostolic was laid to rest in the
Gordon vault in St. Mary's south choir-aisle of the Cathedral.

Mr Alexander Dunbar appointed second Prefect-Apostolic, 1662

It was not until the year after the death of Mr Ballantyne that
Mr Alexander Dunbar—Winchester, Winster, whichever name one
prefers to call him—was nominated by Propaganda as the second
Prefect-Apostolic.   As has been stated already, he was a very
different type of man from his predecessor.   A shrewd organiser
and an astute diplomat, he was as wise as a serpent and as harm-
less as a dove.

Such qualities were needed by the Superior of the Scottish
Mission in 1662.   That same year episcopal government was
restored to the Established Church. Only one member of the old
hierarchy survived — Dr Thomas Syderf of Brechin. James Sharp
and Robert Leighton were privately ordained deacon and priest
before being made bishops, while Andrew Fairfoud and James
Hamilton had been episcopally ordained ministers by Scottish
bishops of the first Anglican line of succession. These four men
were consecrated by Dr Gilbert Sheldon, Bishop of London, on
December 15. Sharp was nominated to the see of St Andrews
and Fairfoud to Glasgow. From then onwards Sharp especially
did all in his power to suppress Presbyterianism.

All ministers in the United Kingdom who were not episcopally
ordained were to be deprived of their livings.   They were also
obliged to make a declaration of the illegality of taking up arms
against the King, and in Scotland had to repudiate the National
Covenant of 1638. The result was that a large number of
ministers, with their wives and children, were driven out of their
parishes. The Covenanters broke into open rebellion, and were
persecuted with greater ferocity than the papists had ever been.
The gaols were crammed with prisoners, some of whom were
deported to Barbados as slaves.   So convinced were the majority

of the Bishops of the divine revelation of prelacy that they believed they were promoting the Christian religion by allowing the torture and even the slaughter of all who refused to abjure the Covenant.

It is estimated that about 17,000 persons of both sexes were outlawed and persecuted for attending illegal conventicles. On the other hand, about two-thirds of the former Presbyterian ministers took the line of least resistance and became Episcopalian clergymen. The Bishops did not try to enforce any version of the *Book of Common Prayer* in their dioceses. There was no obligatory form of public worship. It was only seldom that the Lord's Supper was administered more than once or twice a year. The ritual and ceremonial at all services hardly differed from what it had been during the previous Presbyterian interlude.

Rather later an English army chaplain, Thomas Morer, stationed in Scotland, wondered why the Episcopalians and Presbyterians "should so much disagree between themselves when they appear to the world like brethren . . . Truly their difference is hardly discernible; for their singing of psalms, praying, preaching, and collection are the same, and 'tis the whole of their worship in both congregations." *   The state of affairs in the North East was slightly different. In Bishop Patrick Scougal's time (1664-82) there were daily morning and evening prayers in St Machar's Cathedral, Aberdeen, but they were mainly extemporary utterances. Episcopalians were as unfamiliar with Confirmation as the Papists—the former because "the laying on of hands upon those that are baptized and come to years of discretion" had never been introduced into the post-Reformation policy of prelacy; the latter because there were as yet no bishops to confer the sacrament.

So when Mr Dunbar took on his duties as second Prefect-Apostolic, he was not faced with competition by what we should now call Anglo-Catholicism. Externally, at least, there was little or no difference between Presbyterians and Episcopalians. He made Gordon Castle his base of operations. Here still resided the widowed Marchioness of Huntly and her children, the eldest son, George, being the fourth Marquis. †

Jesuit reports on the state of the Scottish Mission during the first years of the reign of Charles II.

As in the past, the annual reports sent to Rome by the Jesuit missionaries were invariably filled with variations on the same theme — edifying stories of individual conversions, exciting adventures and miraculous occurrences. In 1663 the Father-

---

* *Ecclesiastical Records.* Spalding Club, lxix. In Glasgow under six successive archbishops, and with parochial clergy, communion was administered only twice during the 28 years of the second episcopate; once under Alexander Burnet and once under Robert Leighton. (Cf. W. D. Maxwell, *A History of Worship in the Church of Scotland* (Oxford, 1955), p. 119.

† He was created 1st Duke of Gordon in 1684.

General was informed that the Catholic aristocracy was keeping up its high standard of piety. There were noblemen who wore hair-shirts, even when hunting. Delicate maidens often scourged their bodies with 'disciplines'. Young men stripped themselves of their clothes to clothe Christ in His poor. Alms were given generously to all who were reduced to poverty. There was one titled lady who provided entirely for five paupers every year in honour of the Five Wounds of Christ. Daily meditation and examination of conscience were the rule in many a castle and mansion. The writer added: "We have no monasteries or religious houses in this land, but religious hearts are not wanting, of either sex. I could give many instances of all these things, but in fact they are so frequent that I need not dwell on individual cases. Many do not even take fish on Fridays, some only dried bread and cold water." *

The state of Catholics in the Highlands and Islands

Mr Dunbar felt he had a spiritual responsibility towards the Gaelic-speaking parts of Scotland as well as the Lowlands, for the Vincentian missionaries, except Mr White, had returned to France, and there was only one secular priest, Mr Horan, working in this vast area.

On March 28, 1664, Mr Dunbar wrote to Mr Leslie in Rome, begging him to ask Propaganda to find a few priests for the Highlands and Islands. He lamented the fact that there were more Jesuits on the Mission than secular priests; also that the colleges in Rome and Paris were sending no priests to Scotland. He felt that the only solution at the moment was to get Irish priests, especially for the Gaelic-speaking districts, where there were between three and four thousand Catholics without any spiritual ministrations, with no priest available except Mr White of Glengarry. Ewan MacAllister, who acted as schoolmaster under Mr White, had written to the Prefect-Apostolic blaming him for not finding an assistant teacher. The appeal ended with the words: "It is pitiful to hear these poor people of the Highlands complaining to us frequently, as if we had abandoned them after having drawn them into the light of faith. It would have been better, in a sense, if they had never known us, because if they had remained ignorant of the faith they would have been excused in some way. It is really terrible to hear their laments. I beseech you again, for the love of God and for the same of Jesus Christ, to beg for help for the Highlands and for an allowance for Mr White, who does the work of three; he is in great need, and I do what I can, but you know I can do but little." †

The following year Propaganda asked Mr John White to go to Scotland to assist his brother in the Highlands. It was also decided

---

* Forbes-Leith, op.cit. vol. ii, pp. 89-90.
† Cf. Cathaldus Giblin, O.F.M., 'Mission to the Highlands and Isles, c. 1670', in *Franciscan College Annual* (Multyfarnham, 1954).

to write to Edmund O'Reilly, Archbishop of Armagh, who had been driven out of Ireland and was staying in Paris, requesting him to find a priest for Scotland.   But nothing happened: Mr John White explained that, as he was not bound by the Mission Oath, he did not feel inclined to leave Ireland for Scotland.   On January 10, 1667, Mgr. Roberti, the papal nuncio at Paris, informed Propaganda that two Irish Friars Minor, Frs. Francis and Mark MacDonnell, were prepared to go to the Highlands.   They had been strongly recommended by the Guardian of the Irish Franciscan College of St Isidore at Rome and were willing to work under the jurisdiction of the Prefect-Apostolic.*   On hearing this, Propaganda agreed to forward the money for the cost of their journey to Scotland, and promised them the usual allowance paid to the secular clergy.

Meanwhile in Scotland there had been a rebellion in the West. The Covenanters had tried to capture Edinburgh and had been routed on the Pentland Hills. It was not until August 1667 that the two Franciscans managed to leave Paris. Their ship was wrecked on the east coast of England and they were stranded at Newcastle, where they were befriended by a Friar Minor missionary. Eventually, with all their possessions lost, they reached Edinburgh and were met by Mr Dunbar. On March 17, 1668, he informed Propaganda of their adventures and he appealed for more money for their support. Fr. Mark MacDonnell was too ill to move on to the Highlands. He joined his brother later.

Archbishop Oliver Plunket appointed Prefect of the Highlands and Islands, 1669

Propaganda now decided that the Irish Friars Minor in Scotland should have their own religious Superior, and recommended that six more should be sent to the Highlands and Islands. Nothing came of the latter suggestion and the two brothers MacDonnell, both in bad health, were left to minister to thousands of widely scattered Catholics. A Prefect was chosen, however. He was Oliver Plunket, the archbishop designate of Armagh, who for the past fifteen years had been professor of theology in the college *de Propaganda Fide* at Rome. His appointment was dated September 17, 1669, and his consecration took place in Ghent Cathedral on November 30. Clement XI, who had succeeded Alexander VII as Pope two years before, granted the Archbishop faculties for six priests to be chosen for mission work in the Gaelic-speaking parts of Scotland.

News of this appointment did not reach Fr. Francis MacDonnell until the summer of 1670, when he sailed from Scotland to Ireland to discuss matters with the Archbishop of Armagh. On December 6 that same year Propaganda wrote to the Irish Primate, asking

* Cf. Giblin, op.cit. pp 14-15.

why he had not yet made a Visitation of the Highlands and Islands, and though it has been said that Archbishop Plunket actually visited Scotland, it is fairly certain that he did not.   Apparently Fr. MacDonnell advised him that his appearance in Scotland might lead to further persecution of Catholics, and that it might be attributed to political reasons. On July 10, 1671, Fr. MacDonnell, still in Ireland, wrote that the best way to assist the Highlands and Islands was to select native youths and send them abroad for education at one or other of the Scots Colleges. For the time being, however, all that could be done was to spare a few Irish priests for work in Scotland. On September 1, the Archbishop sent off a Report to Propaganda, based on the facts given him by Fr. MacDonnell.

Although the Archbishop had more than enough to do restoring the Irish Church, which had been laid waste by continuous persecution, he appears to have been really anxious to make a Visitation of the Hebrides, for he wrote to the Marquis of Antrim: "It will be necessary for me to bring a priest and a servant with me, and to dress after the manner of these people, which is very different from that of every part of the globe".

Sir Compton Mackenzie comments on this letter: "There is something to beguile the fancy in the picture of the saintly Primate dressed in a belted plaid". *   It is fairly certain, however, that when mission priests travelled westwards beyond Inverness, nothing but Highland costume was ever worn. †

Had the Irish Archbishop made a Visitation he would have landed on South Uist, which was Fr. MacDonnell's usual base, and on the island of Barra he would probably have met Fr. George Fanning, an Irish Dominican, who carried on an active but more or less free-lance apostolate. ‡

In 1673 there was a renewed outburst of persecution in Ireland. Schools and chapels were closed, and for the next six years the Primate was kept on the run, usually hiding in the mountains. He was finally captured in December 1679, taken to London, and hanged at Tyburn on July 11, 1681. §

Little is known of Fr. MacDonnell's subsequent career, except that he took part in a raid of the Macdonalds against the Campbells, presumably as chaplain. He worked mainly on the mainland, and appears to have retired to Ireland about 1681.

Mr Francis White died on January 28th 1679, having worked in and around Glengarry since his release from prison twenty-four years previously. ** Again and again he appealed to his Vincentian superiors in Paris to send priests to the Highlands, or youths

* *The Book of Barra* (1938), p. 16.
† This was definitely stated later about Bishop Gordon.
‡ He died at Arisaig in 1678. About this time about three Irish Dominicans were working in Scotland.
§ His beatification took place on May 23, 1920.
** Cf. D. McRobert, 'The Death of Fr. Francis White', in *Innes Review* (Autumn, 1966), pp. 186-8.

who could be trained as schoolmasters, but to no purpose. In 1665 he said he could do with at least fifteen. In 1676 Mr Dunbar wrote to Mr David Burnet at Rome that Mr White was still gathering " a most abundant harvest of souls in the West Highlands; a truly Apostolic man, although broken down by hard work, his strength reduced by age and ill-health, greatly esteemed by all, even by the heretics, and much revered by them." After his death Mr Dunbar reported: "I went in fearful weather to visit the localities which he used to frequent in order to console as best I could the poor people he had served for so many years. God's peace be with him. If any of his countrymen would be sent to take his place, it would be a great help to me. Others, as you now are aware, are of no use to us, as they do not know the language." *

Mr John Walker acts as Prefect-Apostolic, 1668-71.

In 1668 — the year before Archbishop Plunket was appointed Prefect-Apostolic of the Highlands and Islands—Mr Dunbar (alias Winster) left Scotland for France where he remained three years. During this period Mr John Walker carried on his duties. †

Having arrived in Paris, Mr Dunbar drew up a Report, dated December 1668, which was forwarded to Propaganda. It was stated that among the Catholic nobles the young Marquis of Huntly was the most devout. As Catholic services in public were forbidden by law, Mass could only be celebrated in private houses. There was, however, much greater freedom in the Highlands and Islands. The Roman Rite was universally followed, except with regard to the calendar.‡ Catholics were ceasing to attend Presbyterian or Episcopalian services, a custom strongly disapproved of by the Jesuit missionaries. None of the laity, except those who had been abroad, had received the sacrament of Confirmation, for the lack of a bishop. The secular clergy still had no fixed places of residence. They moved around the country, not only to minister to their widely scattered flocks, but also to avoid

---

* Cf. Odo Blundell, O.S.B., *Catholic Highlands of Scotland: The Western Highlands and Islands*, p. 166.

† Born in Edinburgh, he graduated at the University there in 1635 with the degree of Doctor of Philosophy. Then he acted as secretary to Alexander, 2nd Lord Lindsay of Balcarres, and accompanied him on a journey to Portugal. Either before or after this he was reconciled with the Catholic Church. He studied at the Scots College, Rome, from 1643 to 1649 when he was ordained priest. On his way home he stayed at Paris, where he met Mr Ballantyne, and returned with him to Scotland. For the next five years he worked mainly in the North-East, making many converts, including Sir Alexander Irvine of Drum. He was arrested in 1655 and imprisoned in Edinburgh, after which he was allowed to go to France, where he remained until 1660. Little is known of his subsequent activities in Scotland. but in 1667 he was stationed in Edinburgh.

‡ Great Britain did not adopt the 'New Style', i.e., the calendar of Pope Gregory XIII (1582) until 1751, although it was adopted by most continental nations before 1587.

being arrested. All were miserably poor — some unable to support themselves—and they were always disguised as laymen. During the past five years five youths had been sent to the Scots College, Paris, but these were all from the Lowlands. There had been no vocations from the Highlands, partly because parents were unwilling to be separated from their sons. Nowhere in the Lowlands was there a Catholic school, though there were a few in the Highlands.

Mr Dunbar felt that the main obstacles to the progress of the Mission were the enforced Protestant education of children and the exclusion of Papists from every kind of civil office. The refusal of Parliament to carry out the policy of toleration wanted by Charles II and some of his ministers had encouraged the Episcopalian bishops to tyrannise over both Papists and Presbyterians. The Prefect-Apostolic drew attention to what he maintained were the defective conditions in the Scots Colleges at Rome, Douai, Paris and Madrid, all of which needed urgent reform. Up to that time only five priests had been sent to the Scottish Mission from the Madrid college since its foundation in 1633. As to the priests who were sent to Scotland, Mr Dunbar stated that the majority lacked the right preparation.

Like so many other reports nothing resulted from this one. When it reached Rome, Clement IX had far too many irons in the fire to think about Scotland. He was busy negotiating for the Treaty of Aix-la-Chapelle between France and Spain; advising Louis XIV about reconciling the Jansenist heretics with the Church and much else. Mr Dunbar might just as well have remained at home. Mr Walker, who had spent nearly twenty years on the Mission, and who had already asked permission to retire on account of ill-health, could not do much as acting Prefect-Apostolic, when the Episcopalian prelates with the support of the civil authorities began to molest both groups of dissenters in Scotland — Papists and Presbyterians. Among the priests arrested was Fr. Patrick Primrose, an Irish Dominican, who was roaming around the North-East.* He was imprisoned at Banff and died there, shortly after orders were received for his release and banishment from the kingdom. † The 'crimes' for which Fr. Primrose and about half-a-dozen more priests were imprisoned were baptising children, celebrating marriages, and saying Mass.

Although the numbers of Catholics in the North-East were slowly declining, even in such powerful families as the Gordons,

---

* A list of the Friars Preachers working in Scotland during the latter part of the 17th century and in the 18th Century is given in Pochin Mould's *The Irish Dominicans*, p. 242.

† As an excommunicated person he could not be buried in any graveyard of the Established Church, so his body was carried some 20 miles over the hills to the abandoned pre-Reformation church beside the Deveron, west of Huntly, where it was laid to rest. In 1672 orders were given that the stone erected there must be removed.

Inneses, Leslies and Lumsdens, whom it was safer for any sensible sheriff to leave alone, nevertheless Dr Patrick Scougal, Bishop of Aberdeen, ordered that lists of Papists were to be compiled, giving account of "any insolence committed by them in Churches against Ministers." He also wanted a record of "trafficking priests," together with baptisms and marriages alleged to have been performed by them. Lastly he insisted that he must have the names of those who had "sent their sons to popish universities, or their daughters to popish convents".

After Mr Dunbar returned to Scotland from Paris and Rome in 1671, Mr Walker was allowed to retire. His health had completely broken down after working on the Mission for nearly a quarter of a century. He died in Rome in April 1679 and Canon Clapperton wrote in his MS. *Lives of Missionary Priests*: "Thus passed away in poverty and obscurity one who had sacrificed an honourable position and brilliant prospects in the cause of charity, and whose good deeds are almost only recorded where they are recompensed." *

Jesuit Reports to Rome, 1672-1675.

Writing to their Father-General in 1672, the year after Mr Dunbar resumed his duties as Prefect-Apostolic, the Jesuit missionaries reported that an outcry against "the pest of Popery" was spreading over Scotland, but that the number of persons who had the courage to assist at Mass was increasing. On the other hand many, although sufficiently instructed, were "too lax or too cowardly" to declare themselves Catholics. They were waiting for more peaceful times to come out into the open. †

The position of Catholics throughout Britain was not made any easier by the "popish marriage" (by proxy) of James, Duke of York, to Princess Mary Beatrice of Modena in 1673. That same year the English Test Act was passed. It debarred all those who would not receive the Anglican sacrament from holding any public offices. In 1674 the Scots Parliament enacted new laws against Presbyterians who refused submission to the bishops. Had it not been for the opposition of the Duke of Hamilton, who was a crypto-Catholic, the penal laws against Papists would have been enforced more rigidly by Parliament.   Nevertheless, shortly after this the Privy Council ordered that the sons of Catholic nobles were to be handed over to the bishops or their friends and be brought up as Episcopalians.   The annual letter to Rome in 1675 stated that: "Some of them thereupon were actually taken away from their parents, in spite of all the efforts made by the latter to prevent their children falling into such hands in their tender years, at an age when they might easily be drawn into heresy, by flatteries

* Cf. *The Blairs Papers*, p. 231.
† Cf. Forbes-Leith, op.cit., vol. ii, p. 126.

and fair promises. A noble lady, the Countess of Traquair, fought
for her son with undaunted courage, like a lioness robbed of her
whelps, declaring that if he went to schools or academies, she
would accompany him, unless she were thrown into prison. If her
relations, who were some of the first men in the kingdom, had not
kept her at home, there was nothing she would not have endured
rather than have her son carried off, to the imminent peril of his
soul." *

Lord Sempill got into trouble for having sent his only son to
the Scots College at Douai. He informed the Privy Council that he
was prepared to recall the boy to Scotland, but he refused to have
him brought up as an Episcopalian. Then, removing his wig, he
said: "Take this, if this is what you want, but I never will consent
to have my son educated in any but the Catholic faith." †

Another story was told of an Episcopalian clergyman who had
been made tutor to the son of a Catholic laird. One day he took
him up in his arms, and tried to carry him to the kirk. The twelve-
year-old boy dug his heels into the minister's sides so vigorously
that the latter was forced to put him down. When reprimanded
for his misbehaviour, the boy replied: "You have nothing to
complain of, my master. If you make yourself my horse, it is only
fair that I should give you the spur." ‡

After more such edifying tales, the Annual Letter of 1675 ended
as follows: "Many years' experience has taught me that, in
missions as in military life, more result is gained by the choice of
instruments than by mere numbers. A few good and practised
warriors, who notice everything, choose their opportunities, and
avoid dangers hidden from other eyes will gain a victory with more
ease and better fortune than an unskilled multitude insufficiently
trained to war, whose rashness (to say no worse) will detract from
their reputation more than it can add to their real strength, or
contribute to their success. Our heretic countrymen are greatly
led by piety and gravity of manner, which their leaders specially
affect, and being acute and subtle in intelligence, and far from
illiterate, are well at home in controversies on matters of faith. We
therefore repeat, in all submission, the request which has already
been preferred in former Annual Letters, that none should be sent
on this mission except such as are well matured and fitted for it." §

It must be admitted that most of the Jesuits sent on the Scottish
Mission were far better equipped than the secular clergy. They
were an elite, whose probation usually lasted at least ten years.
Nearly all the priests had spent four or five years teaching in
colleges belonging to the Society before they were ordained. They

* ibid, pp. 131-2.
† ibid, pp. 134-5.
‡ ibid, p. 132.
§ ibid, p. 137.

had mixed with men of many nationalities, and they were in close contact with what was going on all over the world. It is not surprising that they tended to regard this secular clergy as amateurs.

Mr Alexander Leslie sent by Propaganda as Visitor to Scotland, 1677.

In 1677, the year when Princess Mary married Prince William of Orange and an Act was passed in Parliament requiring the Scottish lairds to control the often disorderly meetings in conventicles, Propaganda decided to send Mr Alexander Leslie to report on the state of the Mission. Instructions for his guidance were drawn up, containing no less than a hundred and four questions. Setting out from Rome, the priest-brother of the Scottish Agent crossed the continent and reached Scotland without being molested. In his Report, which was not delivered to Propaganda until January 1681, he stated that the number of Catholics in the country was estimated at 14,000, of whom roughly 12,000 were in the Highlands and Islands. * He praised the zeal and fidelity of the clergy and laity, but stressed that the latter could seldom assist at Mass more than two or three times a year, owing to the scarcity of priests. His recommendations were: (1) The allotment of fixed places of residence for the missionaries in different districts, notwithstanding the fact that the regular clergy, most of whom were Jesuits, opposed this and wished to continue the existing system; (2) The granting of universal faculties to both seculars and regulars, so that all occasion of jealousy would be removed and the laity would therefore not be encouraged to believe the secular clergy in any way inferior to members of religious orders, especially the Society of Jesus; (3) To appoint a general Superior for the whole of Scotland, with authority over seculars and regulars alike; (4) To ensure an equal distribution of the funds of the Mission, every priest to render a yearly account of his receipts; (5) Because the Scots colleges abroad had become little more than novitiates for the religious orders (the Society of Jesus in particular), no student should be admitted to any of them without a written testimonial from the Prefect of the Mission; and the mission oath should be taken as soon as possible after admission; (6) The Mission to receive an increased subsidy from Propaganda; (7) Missionaries—Irish priests if necessary—should be sent not only to the Highlands and Islands, but also to the Lowlands, even to districts where there were very few Catholics; (8) The Home for retired Scottish priests at Cadome in Normandy should be transferred to Paris.

The long Report ended with an urgent appeal to Propaganda to help with the establishment of schools in the Highlands and the supply of altar vessels, religious books and devotional objects.

* The distribution of Catholics in the Lowlands was as follows: Galloway 550; in and around Glasgow 50; Angus 72; Aberdeenshire 450; Banffshire 1000; Moray 28.

Mr Leslie also kept a sort of Diary, full of interest but very hostile to the Jesuits. No time was wasted by Propaganda, and within two months of the receipt of the Report directives were issued covering most of the points raised. The officials recommended that Mr Leslie should return as soon as possible to Scotland to ensure that the instructions were carried out. It would be the business of Cardinal Philip Howard, who had been made Protector of England and Scotland in 1679, to advise on the manner, time and plan of procedure. *

The effect of the 1678 'Popish Plot' on Scottish Catholics

It should be mentioned that in August 1678, shortly after Mr Alexander Leslie had started to collect information for the Report on the Scottish Mission, the discovery of an alleged ' Popish Plot ' by Titus Oates led to the re-enforcement of penal laws throughout Britain. Mr Alexander Dunbar, the Prefect-Apostolic, was not the only Catholic who decided to follow the example of the Duke of York and retire to Holland. Sermons were being preached in almost every cathedral and kirk by the Episcopalian bishops and ministers in thanksgiving for delivery from the machinations of the Pope and his minions. †

By the summer of 1679 the storm had died down. Both the Duke of York and the Scottish Prefect-Apostolic returned to Britain. Charles II then had the temerity to send his Catholic brother to Edinburgh as High Commissioner, where Mr Dunbar welcomed him as heir to the throne. Mass was celebrated in the Long Gallery at Holyrood House and the immediate result was a violent demonstration against Popery. The Duke, trying to pour oil on troubled waters, ordered that the persecution of the Covenanter remnant (known as the Cameronians) must cease. On August 13, 1681, the Scots Parliament ratified all acts in favour of the Protestant religion, and also secured the indefeasible hereditary succession to the throne. The royal supremacy over the Kirk was recognised, in spite of the probability that a Papist would become its supreme governor sooner or later. By this time Propaganda's instructions, dated March 4, 1681, had been received by the Prefect-Apostolic. With the support of the Duke of York and his Italian wife, Princess Mary of Modena, daughter of Duke Alfonso d'Este, he could begin reorganising the Scottish Mission.

* Grandson of the Earl of Arundel and Surrey, he joined the Dominicans in 1645, and came to England in 1662 as first chaplain to Queen Catherine of Braganza. He was forced to retire to Holland in 1664, and the following year he was made cardinal by Clement X.

† At the same time the Episcopalian clergy renewed their attacks on the Covenanters, who by way of revenge murdered the much hated Archbishop James Sharp of St. Andrews on May 3, 1679. The Covenanters were routed at the Battle of Bothwell Brig on June 22. The majority of the survivors were allowed to return home, but some continued to wage an underground war against prelates and prelacy, under the leadership of two preachers, named Cameron and Cargill.

Death of Charles II and succession of James VII in 1685

Believing that the 'Second Spring' might not be far off, Mr Dunbar, with his usual diplomacy, kept in touch with his handful of missionary priests scattered over the Lowlands.   Charles II died on February 6, 1685, having been reconciled with the Church the previous evening by a Benedictine monk, Fr. John Huddleston, who had saved his life after the Battle of Worcester in 1651. * Apart from the Cameronian minority, Scotland welcomed James VII with every expression of loyalty.   Shortly after this a good-looking, well-dressed papal nuncio, Count Ferdinand d'Adda, arrived in London, where he was much sought after by the court ladies.

In April 1686 the Scots Parliament rejected the King's offer of free trade with England, which was more or less a bribe for the relief of Papists from the penal laws. Feeling ran high when it was reported that the Duke of Gordon and the Earls of Seaforth and Traquair, who were Catholics, had been made members of the Privy Council. Then came the news that James, fourth Earl of Perth (Chancellor of the Kingdom), and his brother John, first Earl of Melfort (a Secretary of State), had been reconciled with the Roman Church. Other Scots nobles, lairds and leading citizens found convincing reasons for transferring themselves to what was known as "the King's religion". Several Protestants were deposed from high positions in the Government and replaced by Papists. The Duke of Gordon, regarded as the most devout Catholic among the nobility, was put in charge of Edinburgh Castle. Meantime the Episcopalian bishops, with but few exceptions, played for safety. They assured the King of their wholehearted allegiance on condition that he did not favour Presbyterians. Archbishop Rose of St Andrews and Bishop Paterson of Edinburgh forbade ministers and layfolk to speak of "Papists" and "Popery", lest it should offend His Majesty.

Increasing tension between Papists and Protestants, 1686.

Already on January 31, 1686, there had been a riot in Edinburgh when the prentice boys protested violently against the public celebration of Mass. The Earl of Perth and his Countess were saved from direct assault by being rushed away in disguise.

The King had given him £8,000 and bidden him order a supply of church furnishings and objects of piety from France.

In April that same year, George Sheill, minister of Prestonkirk, was reproved for " preaching rudely against Popery " in the Abbey Kirk of Holyrood.   He maintained that his sermon was in accord-

---

* After the Restoration in 1660, Fr. Huddleston lived at Somerset House, London, as one of Queen Henrietta Maria's chaplains. Following her death in 1669 he was appointed chaplain to Queen Catherine, with a salary and pension. He resided with the Queen Dowager until his death in 1698.

ance with " the Bishops' old instructions", and insisted that " such a ridiculous religion might be treated in ridicule". He was convinced that the Pope was " as little infallible as the Bishop of the Isles [Archibald Graham], who was one of the silliest bishops in the world". Mr Sheill stated that he " would believe the moon to be made of green cheese, and swallow Arthur's Seat, as soon as believe in transubstantiation." *

Pious Protestants, both Episcopalians and Presbyterians, were now certain that the prophesy of John the Evangelist had been fulfilled, for they "saw a beast rise up out of the sea, having seven heads and ten horns, and upon his horns ten crowns, and upon his heads the name of blasphemy." † They heard in September that Lord Perth had ordered that the keys of the Council Chamber at Holyroodhouse be handed over to him, so that it would be transformed into a temple of idolatry, where "the beast" would be worshipped. On November 23 the royal yacht arrived at Leith from London. The citizens of Edinburgh were horrified by the news that its cargo and passengers consisted of a "Popish altar, vestments, images, priests, and other dependers for the Popish Chapel in the Abbey." The Customs officers wanted to confiscate these symbols of superstition but dared not incur the wrath of the Chancellor. ‡

The King was living in a world of fantasy, quite out of touch with reality. Not satisfied with having furnished the Council Chamber at Holyrood as a Catholic chapel, he gave orders that the Abbey Church was to be repaired and redecorated. He was planning to revive the Order of the Thistle (of allegedly fabulous antiquity), and the Church would be used by the Knights. He told Lord Perth that the work must be completed with the least possible delay. On May 19, 1687, he nominated Mr Alexander Dunbar as Almoner of the Chapel Royal, and fixed his salary. At the same time the Privy Council was instructed to pay the musicians at the Chapel £100 annually.

A racy record of Catholic life in Edinburgh at this time is given in the memoirs of Fr. Richard Hay. § This twenty-five-year-old Canon Regular, quite at home in court circles and very much a man-of-the-world, recreates for us the exotic atmosphere of this brief revival of Catholicism in Scotland.

---

* Fountainhall, *Historical Observes of Memorable Documents*, ed. 1840, p. 717.

† *Revelation* xiii, 1 (Authorised Version).

‡ ibid, p. 763.

§ *Genealogie of the Hayes of Tweeddale, by Father George Hay, Prior of St. Pierremont, including Memoirs of his own Times.* (Edinburgh, 1835). George Hay, born in Edinburgh in 1661, joined the Canons Regular at Saint-Geneviève in Paris in 1678, and was ordained priest in 1685. To quote his own words: "longing to see the smoke of his own country, he returned home to enjoy himself among his friends." His Abbot gave permission on September 7, 1685. The ostensible purpose of his journey was to re-establish the Canons Regular in Scotland.

Meeting of the secular clergy at Gordon Castle, April 1687.

In February 1687 James VII granted toleration to Papists and Quakers under certain conditions. They were allowed to exercise their religious worship only in houses and chapels. Public processions in the streets of royal burghs were prohibited. Protestant churches were not to be invaded by force. There must be no preaching in the open fields. The King stated that from now onwards his Roman Catholic subjects would be "as free, in all respects, as any of our Protestant subjects whatsoever, not only in exercise of their religion, but to enjoy all offices, benefices and others which we shall think free to bestow upon them in all time coming." *

Two months after the proclamation of these so-called 'Indulgences' eight secular priests met at Gordon Castle for a conference. Mr David Burnet, the Vice-Prefect, acted as President. A report of their deliberations was forwarded to Cardinal Howard, who was still Protector of England and Scotland.

It was stated that there were only six priests working in the Highlands, nevertheless great progress was being made. Mr Alexander Leslie was resident chaplain at Gordon Castle, and serving the Enzie District, with 300 communicants. Mr John Irvine had charge of the eastern part of this area, with a larger flock. St Ninian's Chapel was being rebuilt. Mr Christie and Mr Jameson had Strathbogie under their care. An estimated 700 Catholics worshipped in a chapel at Huntly. Two Irish missionaries, Mr Carolan and Mr Trener, ministered in Glenlivet and Strathdon. The numerous Catholics in and around Aberdeen were served by three priests — Mr Robert Strachan, Fr. Fordyce, S.J., and a Benedictine. †

Cardinal Howard was asked to arrange for dispensations to be granted for those who wanted to contract marriages in the second degree of consanguinity and affinity. Guidance was requested as to the problem of Catholics who had their children brought up as Protestants, or who had been married by the ministers, and who were refused the sacraments. There was great difficulty in renewing the holy oils, for they were brought to Scotland from London after being consecrated by Bishop John Leyburn, who had been Vicar-Apostolic of England since 1685.

Now that almost complete toleration had been granted to Catholics in the practice of their religion, it was urgent that a bishop should be appointed, so that the faithful could receive the sacrament of Confirmation. A Vicar-Apostolic would be able to deal with the Government in regard to the affairs of the Mission‡ The

---

* James VII's Indulgences. Cf. *A Source Book of Scottish History* (Vol. III. 1954), pp. 194-7.
† In 1687 Abbot Marianus Irvine of Würzburg sent several of his monks to Scotland at the request of James VII.
‡ There had been three Vicars-Apostolic of England since 1623.

St Andrew's, Braemar (1839), replaced the first chapel (1795). Jesuits worked at the upper end of Deeside from 1688 to 1756.

names of David Burnet, Alexander Dunbar and Alexander Leslie were suggested as possible bishops.

Propaganda was given further details of the activities of the Scottish missionaries. Mr Nicol was travelling to and fro around the Buchan and Garioch Districts, lying north of Aberdeen. Mr David Guthrie and Sir George Innes covered a much larger area to the south, with widely scattered flocks in the Mearns and Angus, and even farther afield in Strathearn, beyond Perth. Mr Hugh Ryan (an Irish priest) looked after the Gaelic-speaking Catholics in Strathglass, west of Inverness. Mr Robert Munro had charge of Glengarry, farther south beyond Loch Ness and around Loch Oich. The numerous Catholics in Knoydart, between Loch Hourn and Loch Nevis on the sea coast, were under the care of two more Irish priests, Mr Devoir and Mr Cassie (Cahassy). Mr Lea and another priest were working on the islands of Barra and South Uist "where, blessed be God, the gentry do acknowledge the successor of St Peter, with a great deal of piety and devotion." Then there were a good number of regular clergy, mostly Jesuits, who, as in the past, acted as chaplains to the nobility and landed gentry in the Lowlands.*

'Papal Aggression' in Edinburgh between February 1687 and December 1688.

Having been granted what amounted almost to complete emancipation from the penal laws, the leading Catholics in Scotland felt that it was safe to ignore the prejudices of the majority of their fellow countrymen. The Jesuits persuaded the Chancellor to forbid the publication of any books against the Catholic religion. The King gave them permission to start a printing press at Holyroodhouse, which issued a number of books and pamphlets under royal patronage. The Edinburgh bookshops began to display Catholic literature and *objets de piété* imported from France. Then the Jesuits opened a 'Royal College' at Holyrood, and issued a prospectus, which stated that boys would be "taught gratis; nor shall there be any further charges or expense than the buying of pens, ink, paper and books." † Protestant parents were assured that there would be no proselytism. Their sons would not be forced to assist at Mass, catechisings or sermons. Every boy, no matter what his religion, would "be taught with equal diligence and care, and every one promoted according to his deserts." The curriculum included Latin and Greek, also Poetry, Rhetoric and Philosophy as the pupils rose to higher studies.

Fr. Hay's memoirs record all sorts of scandal and gossip and

* Cf. MS letter from Gordon Castle signed by the Prefect and eight priests, sent to Mr William Leslie, the Roman Agent. (Blairs College archives), quoted by Bishop Bennett in *St Peter's College Magazine,* June 1927.

† Cf. James Quinn, S.J., 'The Jesuits in Scotland', in *The Tablet,* January 30, 1960, pp. 106-7.

pious tittle-tattle. The Jesuits were amused because an over-rigid secular priest, Mr Robert Strachan, who was acting as the Chancellor's private secretary, refused to give absolution to some of the court ladies when they wanted to make their Easter Duties in 1687. They suspected that he was a Jansenist. Fr. Hay lost no time in discussing with Lord Perth the scheme for the Canons Regular taking over Holyrood. Meanwhile Mr Lewis Innes, Principal of the Scots College, Paris, had arrived in Edinburgh. He disclosed that the Benedictine monks of Ratisbon and Würzburg were also trying to get possession of the former abbey. On July 12 the King ordered the Provost of Edinburgh to arrange for the keys to be handed over, so that work could go ahead in rebuilding the Church for use by the noble Order of the Knights of the Thistle. John Paterson, recently translated from the see of Edinburgh to Glasgow, protested that the building was " a mensal and patrimonial church of the Bishopric of Edinburgh", and although the see was vacant at the moment, the Provost had no legal right to deliver the keys. Eventually the Chancellor secured them. Great was the indignation when it became known that the Papists had stolen a Protestant kirk. It was expected that St Giles' Cathedral would be seized next. *

The Canons Regular of Sainte-Geneviève, afraid that Lord Perth might advise the King to instal the Benedictines at Holyrood, wrote to Fr. Hay that the Abbot-General had made the Chancellor a *confrater,* promising him a share in all the spiritual privilege, prayers and good works of the Order.

Sir William Bruce (1630-1710), the most notable Scots architect of the period, had been instructed to design choir-stalls for the Knights of the Thistle, with a stately throne for the sovereign. There would be a large organ, marble pavements and some sculptures. The whole *décor* — classic in detail — did not attempt to harmonize with the Gothic setting.

Mr Alexander Dunbar celebrated the first Mass in the Chapel Royal on St Andrew's Day and on the feast of the Conception of Our Lady (December 8), a *Missa Cantata* was sung by the Jesuits, with the aid " of some few devout women brought over from France", so Fr. Hay related. His account of the midnight Mass, as given in the letter written to Mr Charles Whytford of the Scots College, Paris, is worth quoting verbatim: "On Christmas night High Mass was sung. I was under the impression that I was to officiate, at least the Chancellor said so to one of the Jesuits. However Father Abercrombie, a Benedictine, performed the function; he is a good honest man enough, but as nature has not favoured him with a good vocal organ, and he has been long away from his

---

* The immediate result of the King obtaining possession of the Chapel Royal was that work was started on building the present Canongate Kirk, intended for the people who had worshipped hitherto in the Abbey Kirk at Holyrood.

monastery (where I imagine there is not much in the way of singing), the poor Father acquitted himself very ill of his office. * There was no deacon nor sub-deacon—in Scotland they have not got so far as that. The choir was composed of a man who passes here for a musician, although he has neither voice nor any knowledge of plain-chant, of Mdlle. Alexandre and two girls she brought from France, with another woman of the same nation, the wife of a saddler here. Vespers were sung after dinner, but in a miserable style: I say nothing of the defects in the singing, but the rubrics were very ill-kept—the less said about them the better. The musician has twenty pounds a year stipend: his occupation consists in interrupting the devotion of the people by singing during Low Mass *Regina Coeli laetare, Alleluia,* or a verse or two of some hymn, chosen according to his own fancy. I forgot to mention that at the Christmas solemnity they sang a *Noel* in French. In churches where due reverence is shown to our Holy Mysteries, it is certainly not customary to sing in the sanctuary things written for the amusement of rustics and revellers. For my part I do not very often trouble the chapel. I have not said Mass there, and my devotion does not extend beyond our own walls, or the house of the Countess of Errol, or of other ladies who may ask me to say Mass in their chapels. I have no great desire to be letting it be thought that I have any wish of the kind." †

No matter, on Sunday January 22, 1688, Fr. Hay was bold enough to don his black biretta, white habit, surplice, rochet and almuce to perform the funeral of Agnes Irvine at Holyrood. On February 6, Protestants were horrified by the reports of the many litanies and masses said in the Abbey by the popish priests to deliver King Charles II from purgatory, for this was the third anniversary of his death. Fr. Hay was keeping the Abbot-General of the Canons Regular informed of his clandestine negotiations to obtain possession of Holyrood for the Order. He was sure that it would greatly benefit the Catholic revival in Scotland. There would be at least one church in which the liturgy was performed in a dignified manner. Meanwhile Queen Mary of Modena had presented silver altar vessels and other rich objects of piety for the adornment of the Chapel Royal. A clique of Edinburgh Catholics began to argue whether Easter ought to be celebrated according to the Gregorian kalendar, or to fit in with the Scots almanack, and

* Dom Christopher Abercromby was a monk of Würzburg. He died at Aberdeen in 1714, aged 73, in the 45th year of his religious profession, after spending 27 years outside his monastery on the Scottish mission. Other Benedictines who had come over from Germany at the King's request were James Bruce, Macarius Brown, Ambrose Cook, Augustine Bruce, Erhard Dunbar, and Boniface Mackie. With the exception of the last named, the rest appear to have returned to their Bavarian monasteries some time after 1689.

† Oswald Hunter-Blair, O.S.B., 'A Scotch Canon in France', in *The Month,* January 1890, pp. 74-6.

eventually it was decided to follow the former and ignore secular dates. So they went on building castles in the air, deluding themselves with golden dreams, shutting their eyes and ears to gangs of Protestants who roamed around the city, waiting for the moment to attack the papists. Some of these energetic Protestants were arrested and flogged, others were executed for high treason.

Catholics in England were deluding themselves in a similar manner. On January 30, 1688, Innocent XI had created four Districts or Vicariates, suggesting that it might not be long before the ancient hierarchy was restored. On June 8 seven Anglican bishops were imprisoned in the Tower of London, and a month later tried in Westminster Hall on a charge of seditious libel, but they were found 'Not Guilty'. Mr Alexander Dunbar, who was in London at the time, wrote home that there were " great rumours of war " and preparations being made for it. The people had had more than enough of a Papist monarch, yet few thought that the Dutch would dare to invade England and dethrone King James.

Efforts made to obtain the nomination of a bishop for Scotland.

Since the meeting of the secular clergy at Gordon Castle in April 1687, they had been scheming to get a bishop appointed for Scotland, while taking good care that the Jesuits did not hear of the project. The business was complicated by the fact that both James VII and Innocent XI had to be considered. The Pope would not venture to nominate a priest for the office of bishop unless the King had signified his approval of the candidate put forward. Mr William Leslie, the Roman Agent for the secular clergy, had been keeping in close touch with Mr Lewis Innes, Principal of the Scots College at Paris. Shortly after the Gordon Castle meeting the latter decided to go to England, so that he could have access to the King. It had been discovered that in February 1686, Bishop John Leyburn, Vicar Apostolic of England, had written to the Pope, recommending Mr Alexander Dunbar as eminently suitable as Vicar-Apostolic of Scotland. Leyburn also had under his jurisdiction the spiritual welfare of the British colonies in North America, and may have felt that he was indirectly responsible for Scotland as well. Both Leslie and Innes were determined that Dunbar should not be appointed. * On August 12, 1687, Mr Walter Leslie wrote from Rome to Mr Charles Whytford in Paris: "The Chancellor [Lord Perth] has written to the Cardinal [Howard] that there is great contentions with the Geometers [Jesuits]—God send us a man to remedy this, but I assure you that if it be Dunckan [Dunbar] that he be Bishop, every Geometer will be Vicar General." †

---

* Lewis Innes, the eldest of the six sons of James Innes of Drumgask, Aberdeenshire, was born in 1651. He was Principal of the Scots College, Paris, from 1682 to 1714. After James VII had fled to France, Innes became the special confidant of the exiled King. He died in Paris in 1738. (See pp. 133-4).

† M. V. Hay, *Failure in the Far East* (1957), p. 32.

The secular clergy became more alarmed when they heard that Fr. William Aloysius Leslie, S.J. was in the running. * They were convinced that the appointment of this Scottish Jesuit of high social standing would be a major disaster.

Meanwhile Abbot Placid Fleming † (1642-1720) had arrived in London from Ratisbon, hopeful of obtaining royal assistance for his monastery, its finances being at a low ebb. Innes felt that a Benedictine would be better than a Jesuit. Moreover the young Abbot had studied at the Scots College, Paris, and it was no secret that he had little love for the Society of Jesus. For this reason Innes strongly urged the King to nominate Fleming as bishop for Scotland. But the Abbot declined the offer, and later on gave his reasons for preferring to remain in his Bavarian monastery. He wrote: "I am of another body, of another profession, that stands in need both of dispensations and divorce, and besides having these twenty years past enjoyed the pleasures of a solitary life where a man can shut his doors, deny audience to everybody, and sweetly hug himself in his own laziness for some hours together, which surpasses all earthly contentment; to quit such a pleasant port and Elysian calm, and launch forth again into the ocean, and to be exposed to storms and tempests, to follow new modes and fashions, and begin in an old age to learn to steer a new course amongst a thousand rocks and sands, were a perfect madness." ‡

The one-time sailor, turned monk, had ' swallowed the anchor ' and was determined never to go to sea again, certainly not in command of a ship with an unreliable crew. He agreed with Leslie and his group that Innes was the right man for the bishopric, and wrote to Whytford that he was sure that Innes would " help much to animate the clergy and to confound the impudence of the

---

* Fourth son of Alexander Leslie of Tullos, who on the death of Count Walter Leslie in 1667 became 14th Baron of Balquhain. Having been ordained a secular priest, and been a Count and Canon of Breslau, William Aloysius joined the Society of Jesus in Rome. He was Rector of the Scots College there for two periods (1674-1683, and 1692-1695). After this he worked in Scotland.

† Thomas Fleming was descended from the Earls of Winton. Educated at Edinburgh, he went to Ireland in 1665, and later served in the English Navy under James Duke of York, then High Admiral. Captured by pirates, he sailed with them for a time. On regaining his freedom, he put in a year at the Scots College, Paris, before turning up at Ratisbon in 1669. On becoming a Benedictine novice he was given the religious name of Placid, and elected abbot at the age of 30, but his blessing was postponed until August 1692. He was one of the greatest abbots of the Schotten-klöster, and his monastery was in a flourishing state when he died on January 8, 1720. One of his achievements was the establishment in 1713 of a seminary for Scots boys. He set the Erfurt house in order, and obtained two university professorships for its monks, to be held always by Scots Benedictines.

‡ Walter R. Humphries, 'Abbot Placid', in Aberdeen University Review, vol. xxx (1944), p. 316 (Spelling modernised).

Padres [Jesuits] which really I think is come to an intolerable height". *

The nomination of a bishop for Scotland had now become a case of plot and counter plot. By this time it was certain that the King would appoint a Vicar-Apostolic, but nobody could be sure which of the rival candidates he would select. The chances of Innes and Dunbar were about fifty-fifty. William (Aloysius) Leslie (S.J.) and David Burnet were no longer in the running, the former too old and the latter apparently not a *person grata* with the King. † But there was still the possibility that a Jesuit might become the first bishop in Scotland since the death of the last of the pre-Reformation hierarchy.

About the time when the seven Anglican bishops were being tried for not reading the Indulgences and finally acquitted, the King nominated two secular priests for the episcopate and sent their names to Rome. They were Lewis Innes and Thomas Nicolson.‡ It is possible that the latter had been recommended by the Superior of the Scottish Jesuits. Cardinal Howard, having heard the news, wrote to Innes on August 30, 1688: "That no time be lost, I desire you to send us word which part of Scotland is to be your district, and which that of the other, your brother bishop."§ All that remained to be done was to get the royal nominations confirmed by the Pope, and for Propaganda to arrange when and where the bishops-elect were to be consecrated.

The abdication of James VII and his flight to France.

Man proposes but God disposes. On October 10, William Prince of Orange proclaimed at the Hague that he was going to take up arms for preserving of the Protestant religion, and for restoring the laws and liberties of the religion of Scotland. This declaration was read in all the chief Scottish burghs, amid wild rejoicings. The students at Edinburgh, Glasgow and Aberdeen made bonfires and burnt effigies of the Pope. The Dutch Calvinist Prince landed at Brixham in Devonshire on December 11 and proceeded to London.

James VII fled. Boarding a fishing boat at Dover, he landed on Christmas morning at Ambleteuse, a few miles north of Boulogne-sur-Mer. Louis XIV granted him the royal château of Saint-

* Hay, op.cit. p. 34.

† David Burnet, born in Aberdeenshire, was reconciled with the Church at Paris by Fr. Macbreck, S.J., in 1660. He studied at the Scots College, Rome, and after his ordination eventually returned to Scotland. In 1674 William Leslie asked him to act as assistant Agent in Rome, but he declined for health reasons. He became vice-Principal of the Scots College, Paris, in 1676, and remained there four years. He resumed work on the Scottish Mission in 1680, mainly in the Enzie District of Banffshire, where he acted as Vice-Prefect. James VII appointed him Dean of the Chapel Royal, Holyrood, in 1687.

‡ See p. 92.

§ Hay, op.cit., p. 37.

Germain-en-Laye, on the hills west of Paris. Many of the ex-King's former courtiers gathered round him, including some of the Catholic nobility and lairds who managed to escape to France. Bishop-elect Lewis Innes was appointed royal almoner.

When the news of the King's flight reached Edinburgh, a mob attacked Holyrood and desecrated the now restored and refurnished Chapel Royal. It was not only effigies of Pope Innocent XI which were burnt in the larger Scottish burghs. At Aberdeen were added those of the two Episcopalian archbishops — Arthur Rose of St Andrews and John Paterson of Glasgow.

Catholic priests and layfolk were now in peril of their lives. Some went into hiding, others managed to escape overseas, but many were arrested and imprisoned. The Earl of Perth and his Countess fled from Edinburgh on December 20, the very day when the Chapel Royal was desecrated. They tried to get away to France but their ship was boarded about three miles off the Bass Rock and they were taken to Stirling, where they were confined in the Castle for three years. After wandering around the Netherlands and Italy, they settled at Saint-Germain-en-Laye in 1695. *

Most of the secular priests were arrested. After being imprisoned for longer or shorter periods, they were usually banished from the kingdom, with the death penalty should they dare to set foot in Scotland again. The regular clergy fared no better. Half-a-dozen Jesuits landed up in gaol, as well as one Benedictine. Few of the leading Catholic layfolk got off without having their houses and castles invaded by popularly elected Protestant officials, who took what they fancied and often made bonfires of furniture. There was neither law nor order, because it was not until April 4, 1689, that it was resolved that James VII had forfeited the crown and the throne was vacant. The crown of Scotland was offered to and accepted by William and Mary. What was known as the Claim of Rights was adopted by the Scots Parliament, followed by the Articles of Grievances. This programme of a constitutional revolution included the abolition of prelacy and the restoration of presbyterian government to the Established Church. The King and Queen took an oath to " root out all heretics and enemies to the true worship of God" furth of Scotland. This meant the Papists and later the Episcopalians too.

For some reason or other Fr. Richard Hay managed to remain in Scotland until 1691, when he was allowed to return to France. †

* That same year he was created Duke of Perth. This Jacobite title was confirmed by Louis XIV in 1701, on the death of James VII, at the same time as the dukedoms of Berwick, Albemarle, Fitzjames and Melfort. The first Duke of Perth died at Saint-Germain in 1716 and was buried in the chapel of the Scots College, Paris. His eldest son, James, succeeded him, and married Lady Jane Gordon, daughter of the 1st Duke of Gordon. A militant Jansenist, he died at Paris in 1720.

† He came back some time after 1714 and devoted the rest of his life to antiquarian research, living either in Edinburgh or at Roslin Castle. He died in 1735 or 1736.

Mr Alexander Dunbar, still the Prefect-Apostolic, first took refuge in Edinburgh Castle when it was being defended by the Duke of Gordon. Then he escaped to the North where, it is so related, "he acted with so much circumspection as to elude all the endeavours of the Presbyterian parsons and soldiers, who, for a considerable time, were constantly on the watch to apprehend him." * Eventually he was arrested, released on bail, and allowed to stay at Gordon Castle. †

Mr David Burnet, Dean of the Chapel Royal, lost all his possessions but managed to save two chalices, a monstrance, a ciborium and small silver hand-bell. Taking them with him, he got away from Edinburgh after dark, but had to spend the night in a field, because there was no boat to cross the Forth until morning. Sailing from Newhaven, he took horse on landing on the coast of Fife. He was recognised when riding through Kirkcaldy, and a crowd chased him half a mile out of the town. Shortly after leaving Montrose, where he spent the night, the bailies were at his lodgings in search of him. Eventually he reached Speyside where he was reasonably safe. Mr Alexander Leslie joined him, and the two priests lay hidden in the heather for more than a month. Throughout the winter of 1688-9 they lived in a rough stone hut, which was often buried in snow. Their refuge appears to have been on the bleak hills of Aultmore, between Keith and the Moray Firth.

Realising that nothing would be gained by remaining in Scotland, Mr Burnet decided to join James VII, who was now in Ireland, hoping to regain possession of his two kingdoms with the help of French troops. Having borrowed money from friends, he travelled on foot through Strathdon, Speyside, Badenoch and Lochaber to Inverlochy. Then, after incredible adventures at sea in small boats, with landings on Iona and other Hebridean islands, Mr Burnet finally reached Sligo on the west coast of Ireland, and managed to find his way to Dublin, where he "kissed the King's hands." ‡

* *Scotichronicon*, p. 625.

† He resumed mission work a few years later, but as soon as Bishop Nicolson arrived in Scotland in 1697 his powers as Prefect ceased. (See p. 93). By this time he was living at Banff with the first Duchess of Gordon, who had left her somewhat dissolute husband. Mr Dunbar and the Duchess retired to Flanders, and in 1700 he was acting as her chaplain in Brussels. They returned to Scotland the following year and made their home at Gordon Castle. By 1704 they were back in Banff, where the Duchess nursed her chaplain, now confined to his bed with old age and infirmities. Here he died in January 1708. His body was laid to rest in St Ninian's cemetery in the Enzie District.

‡ The King ordered him to go to France on business, and after a brief stay in Paris, Mr Burnet moved north to Dunkirk, hoping to find a ship there to take him back to Scotland. His first attempt in a corsair (i.e. a licensed pirate ship) was unsuccessful, for she was attacked on the North Sea by a German vessel, and after a bloody battle, forced to sail back to

James VII was still optimistic of regaining the throne, especially after the Battle of Killiecrankie in July 1689, but shortly after this victory the Jacobite Highlanders were repulsed by the Cameronians at Dunkeld and that ended the Rising. The King's attempt to hold Ireland broke down when his troops were defeated at the Battle of the Boyne on July 1, 1690. Having returned to France, he hoped that with the aid of Louis XIV he would be able to dethrone his son-in-law, William III, but the naval battle off Saint-Vaast-la Hogue in August 1692 resulted in the loss of most of the French fleet and prevented the invasion of England.

Now that there was no immediate danger from Popish plotting to restore the Stewarts, the penal laws were slightly relaxed. Several priests were released from gaol, but usually confined within specific bounds. Some of the clergy, when offered their freedom by the Privy Council, refused and were cast into common prisons among thieves and prostitutes. Eventually most of them were set free and banished overseas. In 1691 a few Jacobite prisoners seized the Bass Rock in the Firth of Forth and maintained it for three years. From time to time a French ship landed ammunition and provisions. *

Several Irish priests managed to carry on a free-lance apostolate in the Highlands and Islands during these troubled times, but they were quite cut off from both Paris and Rome, and unable to obtain their subsidies.

Nomination of Mr Thomas Nicolson as first Vicar-Apostolic for Scotland, 1694.

From time to time reports reached Rome of the trials of Scottish Catholics since James VII abdicated and fled to France in December 1688, but Propaganda waited nearly six years before doing anything. Then, at long last, things began to move. In April, 1694, Innocent XII confirmed certain privileges granted by Urban VIII to the Scots College, Paris, in 1643. Shortly after this Propaganda decided that the moment had come to give Scotland a bishop, and chose Mr Thomas Nicolson. On August 24 the Pope confirmed the nomination. The news reached the bishop-elect at

---

Dunkirk. In November 1690 Mr Burnet managed to board another corsair. She was driven by the winds as far north as Fair Isle, between Orkney and Shetland, but eventually she managed to anchor off the mouth of the Ythan, twelve miles north of Aberdeen, where he got ashore. Resuming mission work in the Enzie District, the one time Dean of the Chapel Royal, Holyrood, died in 1696, worn out by his privations and sufferings. Some of his racy letters, giving detailed accounts of his adventures on land and sea, have been preserved in the Blairs College archives.

* Just before the garrison surrendered, Mr Nicolson, who had been nominated one of the two bishops for Scotland in 1688, and who was acting as chaplain to the English Benedictine nuns at Dunkirk, set sail with the intention of ministering to the Catholics on this small rocky island, but before his vessel reached the Firth of Forth it had been captured.

Dunkirk, where for the past five years he had been chaplain to the English Benedictine nuns. * He was informed that Propaganda would provide him with the requisite pontifical vestments and regalia, and the other essentials for his office as missionary bishop. The same faculties were granted to him as those already given to the Irish bishops. A yearly income of 200 scudi would be paid him, with an extra 50 scudi for travelling expenses. † His title would be Bishop of Peristachium *in partibus infidelium.* ‡

So it was that after an interval of ninety-one years since the death of the last member of the old hierarchy, Scottish Catholics found themselves again under the jurisdiction of a bishop. The first stage in the erection of a new *Ecclesia Scoticana* in communion with the Holy See was over.

---

* This community had been founded from Ghent in 1662, and was the first royal foundation since the Reformation, thanks to a donation of £3,000 from Charles II. The first Abbess was Dame Mary Caryll, grand-daughter of William, 2nd Lord Petre. Driven out of their convent at the French Revolution, the nuns reached England in 1795, after two years in prison. Until 1863 the community lived at St. Scholastica's Abbey, Teignmouth, South Devon.

† A scudo was an Italian silver coin, worth about 4s.

‡ Today the Turkish village of Sharkioi, about 20 miles north of the Dardanelles and the Gallipoli peninsula, facing the Sea of Marmara.

CHAPTER THREE

FIRST VICAR-APOSTOLIC
1694-1718

Thomas Nicolson's career previous to 1694

THOMAS JOSEPH NICOLSON was the second son of Sir Thomas Nicolson of Cluny, later of Kemnay, Aberdeenshire, and Elizabeth Abercromby. Their eldest son became Lord Kemnay. Thomas was born about 1642 at Birkenbog, the home of his mother's parents, between Cullen and Portsoy, in Banffshire. Educated at Aberdeen University, where he matriculated in 1660, he afterwards spent about fourteen years as Regent in Glasgow University. In 1682 he resigned his office and was reconciled with the Catholic Church. He left Scotland, spent a few months at the Scots College, Douai, and in 1685, after travelling in Holland and France, entered the Seminary at Padua (founded by St Gregory Barbarigo, 1616-97.) * He was ordained priest by the Cardinal Archbishop in 1686. † After spending a short time at the Seminary of Saint-Nicolas-du-Chardonnet in Paris, he returned to Scotland in 1687, making Glasgow his base. About six months later he was informed that James VII had chosen him as one of the two bishops for Scotland It was a surprising choice, for he cannot have had much contact with any important court officials, and as it was only two years since he was ordained priest, he would be almost unknown to the other secular missionaries. But his nomination may have been due to the social status of the Nicolson family.

In November 1688 the bishop-elect was arrested, apparently at Castlecary, near Falkirk, the home of the Catholic family of Baillie, to which Abbot Bernard Baillie of Ratisbon belonged. After imprisonment in Stirling Castle, he was released on bail and banished from Scotland. He sailed for France and, as related already, became chaplain to the English Benedictine Abbey at Dunkirk. He suffered much from ague, due to the effects of his confinement, and also to the damp climate of this low-lying seaport amongst the dunes and marshes. In August 1694 the Abbess

---

* Other Scotsmen found their way to this then famous seminary. Among them were John Paul Jameson, who was professor of theology there in 1685; Robert Strachan (another professor); and rather earlier, William Leslie, who held the chair of theology. He rose to be Prince-Bishop of Laibach (now Ljubljana in Yugoslavia), and Prince of the Holy Roman Empire.

† Gregory Barbarigo was beatified in 1761 and canonized by John xxiii in 1960.

allowed her chaplain to make a second voyage across the North Sea, in a ship which was to take some of the garrison of the Bass Rock back to France, and with him went three Jesuits. All the priests was made prisoners, taken to London and thence to Edinburgh, where they were shut up in the Tolbooth. On their release they were allowed to return to France, and Mr Nicolson resumed his duties at Dunkirk. Such, in brief, was the career of this convert-priest up to the time when he reached the age of fifty-two and heard that the Holy See had selected him to be Scotland's first Vicar-Apostolic.

The secret consecration and return to Scotland

War was still being waged by England and Holland against France and Spain, so Propaganda found it difficult to decide how and where to get Nicolson consecrated.* Eventually he received orders to proceed to Paris and there the ceremony took place on February 27, 1695, in the private chapel of Archbishop Francois de Harlay-Chanvallon. For fear of English spies, only a handful of Jacobite clergy and layfolk were admitted.† The consecrating prelate was Mgr. Mascaron, Bishop of Agen, who was assisted by Mgr. Barillon, Bishop of Lucon, and Mgr. de Ratabon, Bishop of Ypres. Acting as the new Bishop's almoner was Mr Thomas Innes, of whom more will be said later. He was then a recently ordained priest and tutor to the younger students at the Scots College. In the eyes of King William III, Nicolson was a rebel, who had been banished overseas.

James VII of Scotland and II of England had such a firm belief in the divine right of kings, and held such Gallican opinions of his own powers in ecclesiastical affairs that he would have regarded Nicolson's consecration as irregular if not invalid without his approval. He continued to nominate bishops until his death in 1701 and in 1693 he caused a flutter in Rome when he deposed certain Irish bishops appointed by Propaganda, destroyed their bulls, and intruded his own nominees. Still regarding himself as Supreme Governor of the Church of England, he also went on giving royal approval to the consecration of Non-juring bishops who refused to take the oath of allegiance to William and Mary.

So far as is known, Bishop Nicolson left Paris soon after his consecration. He intended to sail for Scotland from a port in

---

* Dunkirk, having been awarded to England after the defeat of the Spanish at the Battle of the Dunes in 1658, had been sold to France by Charles II in 1662.

† For similar political reasons the same secrecy had been observed the previous year, when the deprived Anglican Bishops of Norwich, Ely and Peterborough had consecrated George Hickes and Thomas Wagstaffe as titular Bishops of Thetford and Ipswich in a dwelling house at Southgate, Middlesex; having obtained a *congé d'élire* from the deposed Catholic sovereign at Saint-Germain-en-Laye.

Holland but it was none too easy, for he had no passport. Keeping on the move to elude English spies he received hospitality for a time in the Catholic parts of Germany, where he stayed at the Scots monasteries in Ratisbon, Nürnberg and Würzburg. Mgr. Giulio Piazza, the internuncio at Brussels, was in touch with Propaganda to find whether they could arrange his journey to Scotland. An appeal was also made to Maximilian Emmanuel, Duke of Bavaria, asking him to communicate with his ambassador in London to find whether Nicolson could be granted a passport. On January 27, 1696, Piazza informed Propaganda that King William had given permission for the titular Bishop of Peristachium to return to Scotland and the necessary documents were being forwarded to Holland.

A month later another attempt was made to restore King James to the throne, with the help of about 10,000 French soldiers, and although a storm off Calais scattered the ships before they could carry the troops across the Straits of Dover, it had the unfortunate result that King William and his Government intensified measures against the Jacobite rebels.

Bishop Nicolson decided to risk sailing from a Dutch port in spite of that. He was accompanied by a Mr William Stuart, a priest who had been ordained at Rome in 1694 and had spent two years at the Scots College, Paris, waiting to return to Scotland. As soon as they landed in England they were arrested. The Bishop was imprisoned in London until March 1697, when he was released on bail, and on May 25 he was allowed to travel to Edinburgh. Even there he was in danger of arrest, so he hurried north to Gordon Castle, where he remained in hiding.

On September 20 a treaty was signed at Ryswick between representatives of England, France, Spain and Holland. This brought a certain relief to Catholics, for the British Government now had an assurance that Louis XIV would not try to restore ' the King over the Water ', and that he recognised the sovereignty of William III and Mary. One point, however, was not gained. James, Queen Mary of Modena, and their court were allowed to remain at the palace of Saint-Germain-en-Laye, although William demanded that they should leave France.

Had the exiled King been willing to accept the situation, the position of Catholics in the British Isles would have been more peaceful, but this he refused to do. James felt that Innocent XII did not realise that the future of the Catholic religion in England, Wales, Scotland and Ireland depended on the restoration of the Stuarts. He instructed the Duke of Perth to send the Pope a strongly worded letter, urging him to communicate with the courts of Madrid and Vienna, and as a result of this the octogenarian Pontiff issued a memorial in favour of James II of England and VII of Scotland, which was circulated among the Catholic sovereigns of Europe. In it he pointed out the damage already done, not only to the pious King and his family, but to Catholics throughout his dominions. When the English Government got wind of this most undiplomatic papal interference, life was not made any easier for Bishop Nicolson, or priests and layfolk of Jacobite sympathies in Scotland.

The state of the Scottish Mission in the last years of the seventeenth-century

On September 21, 1697, the day after the signing of the Peace of Ryswick, Bishop Nicolson sent a brief report to Propaganda from Aberdeen. Explaining why it had taken him more than two and a half years to reach his Vicariate, he mentioned how the papal nuncios at Brussels and Cologne had helped him during the enforced hold-up in Germany and the Netherlands   The secular clergy were commended for their learning, piety and unanimity. So far the Bishop had met only a few of the regulars.   In recent years the laity had suffered more from contact with unbelievers than from direct persecution, for Protestants appeared to be lapsing into Socinianism, Deism and even Atheism.   Hence the importance of having priests on the Mission fully instructed in these " pestilential ideas ".   A knowledge of Scholastic philosophy and theology was not sufficient. The Bishop added that he hoped to visit the Highlands and Islands as soon as possible. He reminded the Roman officials that, on account of the novelty of his offices and for political reasons, he was "obnoxious to the Government" and was forced to live in the most absolute privacy. There was widespread poverty in Scotland, due largely to the general failure of the crops for two years, and the Mission had no funds to defray the travelling expenses of youths who felt called to study in the colleges abroad. The report ended with the words: "If one might judge . . . there would without doubt be hopes of a rich harvest if the state of things were restored which prevailed nine years ago. Meanwhile for what is left to us we owe thanks to Almighty God, who in His great mercy turns away the evil which our enemies plot against us." *

Bishop Nicolson's hide-out at Preshome

Any bishop in Britain, no matter whether he was a Papist, English Nonjuror or Scottish Episcopalian, had to lie low if he refused to take the oath of allegiance to William and Mary. Bishop Nicolson managed to find a retreat on the Duke of Gordon's estates in the heart of the Enzie district of Banffshire, roughly in the centre of the coastal parish of Rathven. He was Scotland's first Catholic bishop since the death of Archbishop James Beaton in 1603.

He took up his abode in a one-storied, heather-thatched cottage, a ' but-and-a-ben', at Preshome and for more than a century Preshome was to remain the strategic centre of Catholicism.   Later

* Cf. Bellesheim, op.cit. Vol. IV, appendix VI, pp. 364-7.

Vicars-Apostolic made it their headquarters too and its importance ended only with the death of Bishop James Kyle in 1869. For this reason it is worthwhile to describe the place in greater detail, for it will be mentioned again and again further on.

Preshome stands about 400 feet above the sea, fully exposed to the winds that blow from the north-west, north and north-east. Looking across the Moray Firth on a clear day, the Vicar-Apostolic could see the mountain ranges of Caithness and Sutherland, forty to fifty miles distant. Inland to the south were open moors, now broken up by small farms and crofts. Birkenbog, where the Bishop was born, lay east behind the Bin of Cullen, more than a thousand feet high. Glancing westwards, he gazed at the rolling hills of Moray, beyond Fochabers and Gordon Castle. The royal burgh of Elgin with a ruined Cathedral, and the ruins of Pluscarden Priory, lay hidden on lower ground twelve miles distant in the same direction. About half-way along the crescent-shaped coastline of Spey Bay, the white-harled houses of Garmouth, where the Spey flows into the sea, now catch the sun's rays, but this village had not been built at the close of the seventeenth century. The Bishop must have recalled that Charles II landed there in 1650, when he was forced to sign the two Covenants.* When he looked north there was still no sign of the half-a-dozen fishing villages which started to arise in the following century.

Just over a mile to the west beyond the Burn of Tynet, now the boundary between the counties of Banff and Moray, was a small church erected in 1687 by the first Duke of Gordon in St Ninian's cemetery, on the site of an older church dating from before the Reformation. Mass was celebrated there openly until the persecution of Papists started again after the accession of William and Mary two years later. Since then, when a priest was available, the scattered Catholics of the Enzie district had assisted at Mass in a barn or byre, hidden in a wooded gully about a quarter of a mile east of Preshome. Over the rising ground to the south-east stands Letterfourie House, which was still a Catholic stronghold, like the nearer mansion of Cairnfield. Most of the neighbouring lairds, Episcopalians as well as Papists, were still Jacobites in their loyalties and took good care that their tenants were equally loyal to the 'King over the Water'. The parish minister at Rathven, once he discovered that a Popish prelate had intruded into the Enzie district, would have hesitated to interfere with him.

Mr John Irvine's report to the papal nuncio at Paris on the state of the Scottish Mission (September, 1698)

In the summer of 1698 Bishop Nicolson decided to send one of his priests, Mr John Irvine, to assist Mr William Leslie, the Roman

* See p. 47.

Agent, who was growing old and infirm.* Having reached Paris, Mr Irvine submitted a long report dated September 5 to Mgr. Marco Delfino, then papal Nuncio, and explained that owing to renewed persecution of Catholics in Scotland the Vicar-Apostolic had been unable to write himself. The Nuncio was requested to recommend Mr Irvine as his procurator to the Holy See, and of the Scottish Mission, in consideration of the facts contained in the report.

The situation was alarming. Five months earlier the Privy Council had ordered that search must be made for priests, Jesuits, and masters of Catholic schools. They were to be imprisoned if found, and then to be taken under strong guard to prison in Edinburgh, until they were banished from the country. By the end of July 1698 every priest had fled to the mountains or some other lonely part of the country. None had been recaptured, and they were still ministering to their flocks by night. Mr Irvine stated that Bishop Nicolson felt he was better known than most of the priests and it might lessen further persecution if the Privy Council were informed that he had been driven out of the country. † Of the Bishop himself, Mr Irvine wrote that he was confirming men and women of all ages, preaching and instructing both clergy and layfolk, visiting the sick, taking them the sacraments and instructing converts. So far it had not been possible for him to go to the Highlands, where for three years in succession the people had been reduced to starvation for lack of oatmeal, due to the failure of the harvest. The report ended with an appeal to the Nuncio to use every effort with Propaganda on behalf of the Scottish Vicariate-Apostolic.‡

Persecution of priests and layfolk continued in the Lowlands. Many were arrested and imprisoned, including the Duke of Gordon who had tried to send his son, the Marquess of Huntly, to be educated in France.   The boy was detained in London, where Anglican bishops and clergymen did their best to win him over to communion with Canterbury, but without success.

Bishop Nicolson's Statutes, 1700

Contemporary writers make it clear enough that the social and moral condition of Scotland about 1700 could hardly have been worse. The total population was about one million, of whom 200,000 were beggars who roamed around the country. Many lived

---

* Irvine (often known as Cuttlebrae—a farm in the Enzie), like Nicolson, had been ordained at Cardinal Barbarigo's seminary at Padua in 1683. He soon returned to Scotland and worked on the Mission.

† There were 10 Jesuits and 4 Benedictines on the Mission. The secular priests mustered 23, of whom 10 were scattered in the Highlands, the rest working in different parts of the Lowlands.

‡ Irvine did not return to Scotland until 1705. He worked on the Mission until his death in 1717.

H

Our Lady Star of the Sea, Castlebay, Barra, was opened in 1888. The island has been served by a succession of priests since 1630; first Franciscans, then Vincentians, and from 1736 by secular clergy.

by robbery. Little or no encouragement was given by the Government to agriculture or manufactures, and there were no banks, no newspapers, no postal system, no stage-coaches, and no proper police force in any town or city. The judges were said to be corrupt, and most of them easily bribed. The simplest principles of toleration were unknown. Each group of Presbyterians persecuted the other, while all combined to harass Papists and Episcopalians. The general opinion was that the highest of earthly duties was to root out religious error.   This was promoting the greater glory of God, and saving men and women from eternal damnation.

Witchcraft, rampant in rural districts, caused the persecution of many innocent people. At Paisley, in 1697, six persons convicted of dealings with the devil were hanged, then cut down and their bodies burned. That same year a youth was hanged at Edinburgh for the alleged crime of blasphemy.

It was with this background in mind that Bishop Nicolson summoned his priests to Gordon Castle for a conference in 1700 and drew up a series of disciplinary regulations for them. Comment on these Statutes, and in particular on their apparent severity, will be found later on when Jansenism in Scotland is discussed. *

First Visitation of the Highlands, May-August 1700.

Accompanied by Mr Thomas Innes, a younger brother of Lewis Innes, who had been in the running for the bishopric in 1688, Bishop Nicolson made an extensive visitation of the Highlands and Islands between May and August, 1700. From Preshome they took the road westwards, and made their way on foot through the Great Glen to the shores of the Atlantic. Taking a boat at Arisaig in Morar, they landed on the Isle of Eigg, where they found three hundred Catholics "very constant in their faith and always loyal to their sovereigns." Then they sailed on by way of Rum and reached the Isle of Canna, where there lived 130 Catholics. Crossing the Minch, a distance of roughly twenty-five miles of open sea, the Bishop and Mr Innes arrived at South Uist.   About 1500 Catholics welcomed them, 900 of whom were confirmed at twelve different places. Benbecula was the next island visited. Here, as elsewhere, they found that many Catholics were away on the mainland with their flocks and herds. Sailing from South Uist the Bishop landed on Barra, where MacNeill, a very old man, acted as catechist and instructed his people every Sunday, in the absence of a priest. The Bishop, when reporting to Propaganda later on, wrote; "He proposed several remedies which might deliver the people from what he seems to have regarded as a dangerous influence, and referred the matter to 'the impartial judgment' of the Roman cardinals."

* See pp. 131-6.

On their return to the mainland, after a voyage of nearly sixty miles across the Minch in an open boat, the Bishop and his companion travelled on through Morar, Knoydart and Glengarry, to reach Banffshire by the end of August. During the three months roughly 3,000 persons received the sacrament of confirmation. *

Submission of the Jesuit missionaries to the authority of the Vicar-Apostolic, 1701.

The Jesuit missionaries in Scotland made a formal and complete submission to the authority of the Vicar-Apostolic on February 7, 1701. A document was drawn up and signed by Fr. Leslie at Aberdeen, in the presence of Mr Robert Strachan and Fr. Christian Abercrombie, O.S.B.†

No longer could anybody accuse the Jesuits of remaining in the houses of the nobility in the Lowlands, and of neglecting Catholics in the Highlands. Their manner of life by the first decade of the eighteenth century was virtually the same as that of the secular priests on the mission. The report sent to the Father-General in 1702 gives a vivid idea of the hardships endured by some of them when wandering around the country. For instance, there was Fr. John Innes, who disguised himself as master, servant, musician, painter, brass-worker, clock-maker and physician, trying to be all to all that he might save all. Fr Robert Strachan had managed to learn enough Gaelic to compose a controversial catechism in this language. He wrote: "The region I dwell in is steep and sterile, mountainous and rugged, and much hardship and inconvenience has to be put up with. The people are so poor that they keep their cattle in their own dwellings. We live as we can on butter, cheese and milk; rarely get flesh, fish hardly ever. We usually drink water, sometimes beer; wine we never taste but at the altar. We lie on the ground, or on a little straw or heather."‡

Formation of the Scottish Society for Propagating Christian Knowledge, 1701.

It was also in the year 1701 that a group of Presbyterians in Edinburgh, "reflecting upon the Ignorance, Atheism, Popery and Impiety that did so much abound in the Highlands and Isles of Scotland, did justly reckon that they flowed, in a great Measure, from the want of suitable means of Instruction." §

* Cf. Bellesheim, op.cit. Vol. IV, pp. 151-2.

† Cf. article by Bishop Bennett in *St Peter's College Magazine*, June 1927, p. 25. This Fr. Leslie was the same who was mentioned as a possible Vicar-Apostolic in 1688, and it was Fr. Abercromby who sang the midnight Mass at Holyrood in 1687 (See p. 83).

‡ Cf. Forbes-Leith, op.cit Vol. II, p. 200.

§ *An Account of the Rise, Constitution and Management of the Society in Scotland for Propagating Christian Knowledge.* (2nd. ed. Edinburgh, 1720, p. 6).

At first the Scottish S.P.C.K. was associated with the Anglican missionary organisation of the same name, which had been formally commended by Dr Tenison, Archbishop of Canterbury, in 1699. An 'outed' Episcopalian minister, James Kirkwood, was appointed by the English S.P.C.K. as its corresponding member in Scotland. From him the Edinburgh Presbyterians learned of the growing belief of the London committee that education of the children of the lower orders would prove to be "the panacea for social, religious and political ills." So it was resolved to open the first school in the parish of Abertarf, on the north-west side of Loch Ness, because it was " the centre of a country where Popery does much abound." The school, however, met with such opposition from mainly Papist parents that it had to be closed after a year and a half.

In 1706 the General Assembly decided that this admirable method of checking Popery must be given the full protection of the Established Kirk. Two years later Queen Anne granted letters-patent for erecting the organisation into The Society in Scotland for propagating Christian Knowledge. She signed the document at Kensington Palace on August 18, 1708. The teaching given in the schools was rigidly Calvinist, anti-Catholic and anti-Jacobite. At first the masters were forbidden to speak Gaelic, or allow the bairns to read books in their native language, but it was realised later that this did not help to win over either parents or their offspring from the errors of Romanism. Moreover the S.P.C.K. failed to gain the support of the Jacobite chiefs and lairds, the majority of whom were Episcopalians. By 1724, however, there were sixty schools in the Highlands and Islands, with 1733 boys and 591 girls.

The Society was able to inform its friends and benefactors that "the priests in some corners are losing their Credit, and in divers places where Popery and Superstition did abound, there is an earnest desire among the people after Christian Knowledge . . . Through the Diligence of the Masters, Barbarity and the Irish Language are almost rooted out."

Not content with trying to convert the 'Irish'-speaking High-landers from idolatry and superstition, the S.P.C.K. had the courage to launch a campaign in the mainly Catholic Enzie district of Banffshire, where two schools were opened. They had another school in Glenlivet but it was soon closed because the people showed no desire to become Presbyterians.

Queen Anne's efforts to suppress Popery in Scotland.

James VII died in exile on September 6, 1701, and his brother-in-law, William III, died of a fall from his horse on March 6 the following year. James's sister, Princess Anne, succeeded to the throne. As a devout Anglican, encouraged by her spiritual adviser, Dr Gilbert Burnet, Bishop of Salisbury, she lost no time in

H1

tightening up repressive measures against Romanism. In 1704 she ordered a solemn proclamation in the burghs of Scotland, calling upon "all sheriffs, bailies, magistrates, officers of the law, and justices of the peace; that they at once put the laws into force against Jesuits, priests, sayers of Mass, resetters, or harbourers of priests, and hearers of Mass; to seize and apprehend all priests or Jesuits, and to put down all mass meetings." The Lords of the Treasury and ministers of the Gospel were commanded to be diligent in carrying out this royal proclamation. It was their duty to take down carefully the names of men, women and even children who were suspected of Popery, or in any way assisting Papists. Robert Wodrow—the pious but credulous Presbyterian minister, well known as the historian of his Church — wrote at this time: "I cannot help wishing that there were some civil fund for the persecution of Papists, as enemies of the civil constitution and liberty." *

Fearful of Clement XI gaining control over Scotland, and picturing the Pope as the whore of Babylon, the General Assembly organised an impressive procession through the streets of Edinburgh. The public hangman and his men were dressed in priests' vestments. One carried a large crucifix, and another a chalice. At the close of this anti-Papist pageant the symbols of idolatry were solemnly burnt at the Mercat Cross.

Several priests were arrested and imprisoned, both in the Lowlands and in the Highlands. The widowed Countess of Seaforth had her fifteen-year-old son dragged away from her by force and handed over to Protestant kinsfolk. Many mansions and castles were attacked by armed mobs, in the hope of finding priests hidden within their walls. Bishop Nicolson had to remain in seclusion at Preshome. Visitations of the Southern parts of his Vicariate would have been too dangerous. The penal laws, however, were not enforced so strictly in the North-East, and he managed to make secret journeys through Buchan, Deeside and Strathbogie, where Catholics were fairly numerous. A few of them conformed to the Established Kirk, more from weariness of persecution than for religious convictions. More than a dozen members of the Scottish nobility were still practising Catholics, the majority loyal Jacobites.†

There were thirty-three priests working in the Vicariate during this period of renewed persecution. ‡ Bishop Nicolson did not know how to replace those who died off. In 1705 only four were left in the Highlands. He appealed to Ireland, Flanders, France and Germany for Missionaries, but none of these countries was

---

* *Analecta* (Maitland Club, 1842), Vol. III, p. 202.
† *Dukes*—Gordon and Perth; *Earls*—Aboyne, Huntly, Melfort, Nithsdale, Seaforth and Traquair; *Barons*—Banff, Drummond, Oliphant and Semple; and *Count* Leslie.
‡ 17 secular clergy (15 Scotsmen and 2 Irish), 9 Jesuits, 4 Benedictines and 5 Irish Franciscans.

able to help him. To add to his difficulties, all regular transport between Britain and France had ceased owing to war-time conditions.

Proposal to erect a Chapter in Scotland, 1704.

Scotland's first Vicar-Apostolic, now in his sixties, realised that he needed a coadjutor, but he took no immediate steps to obtain one. Meanwhile some of his clergy felt that a Chapter would secure greater stability in the Vicariate. This was first proposed at Paris, by the brothers Lewis and Thomas Innes, and two other secular priests. A document was drawn up in 1704, and forwarded to Rome.* The proposal, however, was turned down by Propaganda, which replied that what was needed was a coadjutor Vicar-Apostolic with right of succession.

James Gordon nominated Coadjutor to Bishop Nicolson, 1705.

Propaganda then began to think of a suitable coadjutor for Bishop Nicolson. Great secrecy was essential, because the new 'King over the Water' also believed that only he had the right to nominate both Catholic and Episcopalian bishops for Britain. After the death of James VII on September 16, 1701, the Pope, anxious to keep the right side of Louis XIV, had virtually recognised the 'Old Pretender' as de jure King of England, Scotland and Ireland.

William Leslie, the Roman Agent for the Scottish Mission, favoured George Adamson as coadjutor. His name was twice put forward and twice turned down. Another candidate was Thomas Innes, already mentioned. His appointment would have had catastrophic consequences, because he was in close sympathy with the Jansenists. †

Living in Rome at this time, and acting as assistant to William Leslie was a secular priest named James Gordon. One of the Gordons of Letterfourie, he was a cousin of the Duke of Gordon and of the Roman Agent. Born at Glastirum in the Enzie district on January 31, 1665, he had been educated at Louvain and Paris. Having been ordained priest he returned to Scotland in 1692, working mainly in his native Banffshire and acting as procurator to the Mission. After he went to Rome, Mr Gordon worked on the Statutes which had been drawn up by Bishop Nicolson. They were submitted to Propaganda in 1703.

In the summer of 1705 the Cardinals informed Bishop Nicolson of their choice—apparently without reference to King James VIII. Owing to the War of the Spanish Succession, in which most European countries were involved, letters took a longer time than

---

* William Bishop, appointed Vicar-Apostolic for England in 1623, set up a Chapter, but it served little useful purpose as a corporate body.
† See pp. 131-3.

usual between Italy and Scotland. It was not until November that same year that the Bishop replied to Propaganda, thanking them for the nomination of Mr Gordon. A delay of six months occurred between his appointment and consecration, due partly to troubles in connection with the Scots College at Rome, which was being mis-managed by the Italian Jesuits.*

It was decided that the consecration should take place at Montefiascone on the shores of Lake Bolsena, about fifty miles north of Rome. Its Bishop, Cardinal Marcantonio Barbarigo, had made a visitation of the Scots College, Rome, in 1693, and was a friend of Mr William Leslie, the Agent for the Mission. †   For political reasons the ceremony had to be done with the utmost secrecy, lest English spies got word of it, for the bishop-elect was closely related to some of the leading Jacobite lairds in Scotland. So Cardinal Barbarigo performed the consecration in his private chapel on Low Sunday, April 11, 1708, when Mr Gordon became the titular Bishop of Nicopolis. ‡

Before leaving Rome, Bishop Gordon obtained from Propaganda some liturgical books for the use of the missionary priests, also catechisms printed in Irish Gaelic for the benefit of laity in the Highlands and Islands.   He was accompanied on his homeward journey by Fr. Augustine Mulligan, an Irish Austin Friar, whom he had met in Rome and at Montefiascone.§ They stopped at Genoa, where the Bishop secured the services of two Irish Dominicans—Frs. Peter Cluan and John Gusman. Having reached Paris, the Bishop went to Saint-Germain-en-Laye to pay his respects to the exiled royal family. Then, by way of Holland and a voyage across the North Sea, the travellers landed at Leith. Towards the end of July Bishop Nicolson met his coadjutor at Aberdeen. The former had been much depressed by troubles with some of his clergy, and the apparent impossibility of finding others to take the place of those who had recently died.

The titular Bishop of Nicopolis was able to give the Vicar-

---

* Mr Gordon, in the name of Scottish Catholic clergy and laity, petitioned that the College should be restored to Jesuits of Scottish nationality. (See 'Abbé Paul Macpherson's History of the Scots College, Rome', ed. by W. J. Anderson, in Innes Review (Vol. XII, 1961), pp. 101-4).

† The Cardinal was a cousin of St Gregory Barbarigo, the founder of the seminary at Padua, where Bishop Nicolson had made his studies (See p. 92).

‡ Whether this particular Nicopolis was in Bulgaria or Greece is not certain, because there are three titular sees of this name.

§ He worked on the Scottish Mission for sixteen years, apparently to the great satisfaction of Bishop Gordon. It is difficult to identify him, as he seems to have used another surname. but he was seriously proposed as a Vicar Apostolic for the Highlands. This office could hardly have been filled by any but a native Scot. In 1730 he was provided to the Diocese of Armagh in Ireland, but was not briefed until 1732. He died on July 23, 1739.

Apostolic full details of the reconciliation with the Roman Church in 1704 of John Gordon, Episcopalian Bishop of Galloway. *

The Statutes of 1706

The last Scots Parliament had been elected in 1703. The appointment of a Commission two years later, to discuss Union between the kingdoms of England and Scotland, led to riots and petitions throughout the latter country in 1706. That same year Bishop Nicolson had copies made for his clergy of the Statutes which had finally been approved by Propaganda. † They remained in force for eighty years until they were modified by Bishop Hay in 1780. ‡ These Statutes throw a great deal of light on Catholic life in Scotland during the early years of the eighteenth century; they also contain certain regulations which would surprise a twentieth century Catholic. Though they have often been misunderstood and used as a support for accusations of Jansenist heresy, they must not be used as an argument: their authority is absolutely papal and Roman.

They lay down that fasting is obligatory on all the forty days of Lent, on fourteen Vigils and twelve Ember Days, making a total of sixty-six days in the year when only one full meal was allowed. Moreover the principal meal in Lent has to be taken after sunset, and on other fasting days after 3 p.m. All this may seem over-penitential to present-day Catholics, but such was the normal universal law at that time.

It is interesting that, in accordance with Early Christian custom, the Statutes forbade the presence at Mass of those under instruction, until they had made their Profession of Faith. Moreover, those under Church censures were excluded from the *missa fidelium* until they had been reconciled. A very long period of

---

* Born in 1645, John Gordon had served as an English naval chaplain in the North American colonies for about ten years. He was a close friend of James, Duke of York, and after the latter succeeded to the throne in 1685, Gordon returned to Scotland. In 1687 he became the last Bishop of the independent see of Galloway. Ten months later prelacy was abolished in Scotland, so Gordon moved to Ireland, where King James appointed him Chancellor of the Protestant Diocese of Dublin. He followed his sovereign to France. Eventually he was received into the Church, and abjured his errors at Rome before Cardinal Sacrapenti, then Protector of the Scottish Mission. An enquiry into his ordination was begun and in 1704 the Holy Office pronounced his orders null and void. But he was given the tonsure, and Clement XI granted him an annual pension, chargeable on a Portuguese benefice. So far as is known, Gordon spent the rest of his life at Rome, where he died in 1726. Full details of his career will be found in *A Profest Papist, Bishop John Gordon*, by T. F. Taylor (1958).

† Bellesheim included the full Latin text in the German edition of his *Catholic Church in Scotland* (Cologne, 1883), but Hunter-Blair's translation (1890) only gives a summary of them (Vol. IV, pp. 168-74). It appears that they were never printed, but circulated in manuscript copies among the clergy, and never put into English.

‡ See p. 182.

instruction was required before a convert could be received into
the Church, and with good reason at that date. It is sometimes
forgotten that there were no *public* Papist places of worship in
Scotland during the eighteenth century. All meetings for Mass
were secret. Strangers were rightly suspect; they might be
informers. Would-be converts were sometimes not in good
faith; for instance there were paupers who hoped for alms or
more generous benefactions if they expressed a desire to become
Papists.

The discipline for public penance was a far cry from present-
day mentality. In the eighteenth century a member of a congregation, who was a delinquent possibly for some sexual offence, or for
having got married before a minister, would be called forward to
the altar or made to stand up in the room which served as a chapel,
and there to receive public rebuke.

After the service the man or woman was dismissed, and
ordered to return the following Sunday for further public denuncia-
tion. The penitents were not allowed to be present at the main
part of the Mass, i.e. the Liturgy of the Upper Room. There was
nothing ' Protestant ' about this practice; it was common in the
Early Church and survived until the Middle Ages. The Calvinists
merely retained a Catholic form of discipline and made it more
rigid. Scottish Presbyterian penitents, i.e. persons condemned for
alleged grave offences, were sentenced to stand at the kirk door
in sackcloth for many Lord's Days in succession, at least half-an-
hour before public worship. During the long service they were
exposed to the public gaze at the 'pillar' or 'stool of repentance'.
In some places they were not allowed to enter the kirk, and
remained outside in the pillory.

The Roman revisers of the 1706 Statutes added to the draft
the reason given for public penance — "lest the discipline of the
Church seem too lax, if penitents are received back on easier
conditions among Catholics than they would find among heretics".
It may have surprised some of the officials at Propaganda that such
discipline was possible in Scotland, but they accepted the explanation that it was even more severe among Protestants.

A modern reader cannot fail to notice the absence of any stress
on the desirability of more frequent communion than at Easter.
while the need for precaution against unworthy reception of the
Sacrament is emphasised. One phrase says that even at the hour
of death communion must not be given "unless the dying person
seems to understand something of the truth about so august a
sacrament". This wording was struck out by the Roman revisers
and replaced by a directive that persons were to be admitted to the
"necessary sacraments" which they were judged fit to receive.
This left wider discretion to priests.

Section three of the first title recalls a curious link between
Scotland and France at this period, because the faithful were

warned against the errors of the Bourignonites.* Bishop
Nicolson must have been in touch with Lord Deskford at Cullen
House, about seven miles east of Preshome, who corresponded
with Madame Guyon and other French Quietists. At Rosehearty,
on the north coast of Buchan, lived George Garden, another
Quietist, formerly minister at St Machar's Cathedral, Aberdeen. In
1710 he was attacked by the synod of Aberdeen for having retired
"unto a corner of the country where he is flocked unto from all
parts of the Kingdom, and there to erect a mixed-mongrel, monas-
terial-nunnery, whence with large commendations he dispenses
the books of Antoinette Bourignon." It was reported that a community of unmarried men and women were living in this fishing
village, propagating the doctrines of this mystic, and others of a
pernicious nature. The majority of these Quietists were Episcopalians, but it is significant that Bishop Nicolson felt obliged to
warn his priests against the spread of this heresy in the North-East
of Scotland. †

Living in France was Andrew Michael Ramsay (c.1686-1743),
another Scotsman who in his earlier years had been a disciple of
Madame Bourignon. After being received into the Catholic Church
by Archbishop Fénelon at Cambrai, he became private secretary
to Madame Guyon, later tutor to the boy Prince Charles at Rome.
By 1734 Ramsay (now knighted) was Grand Chancellor of the
Freemasons of France. The range of his interests was wide,
embracing education, politics, economics and metaphysics—even
the transmigration of souls and the ultimate salvation of demons.‡
Had this son of a master-baker and burgess at Ayr remained in his
own country, and not been associated with the Bourignonites, it is
improbable that his name would have become famous in most
cultured circles in Europe.

*The religious condition of Scotland at the time of the passing of
the Act of Union, 1707.*

The so-called Articles of Union between the Kingdoms of
England and Scotland were ratified by the Scots Parliament on
January 16, 1707, and received royal assent on May 1. This Act
safeguarded the established Kirk, Scots Law and the law courts,
but it contained no reference to greater toleration for Papists. At

---

* Antoinette Bourignon (1616-80) was a Flemish mystic, who after
1662 drifted away from orthodox Catholic doctrine, believing herself to
be the ' woman clothed with the sun '. (Rev. xii, 1). Her spirituality was
a species of Quietism, of which the fundamental principle is its condemnation of all human effort.

† Cf. G. D. Henderson, *Mystics of the North-East* (Third Spalding Club,
Aberdeen, 1934); and *Religious Life in 17th Century Scotland* (Cambridge,
1937). See also A. R. MacEwen, *Antoinette Bourignon, Quietist* (1910);
and R. A. Knox, *Enthusiasm* (Oxford, 1950), 66. 352-5.

‡ Cf. G. D. Henderson, *Chevalier Ramsay* (1952); also Albert Cherel,
Un aventurier religieux au XVIIe siècle (Paris, 1926), and *Fénelon au
XVIIe siècle en France* (Paris, 1917).

that date Bishop Nicolson had fifteen secular priests, eleven Jesuits, four Benedictines, one Augustinian Canon, and five Irish Franciscans working in the Highlands and Islands under his jurisdiction.

In some parts of Scotland, particularly in the southern Lowlands, the Calvinist bigotry of the Covenanters still survived. The Kirk Sessions still maintained powers over faith and morals which exceeded those of the Inquisition at any period of its history. There was one important exception, however: ecclesiastical censure was no longer followed automatically by civil action. Neither had the Church Courts power over life and death. If they enforced fines, they could not enforce payment. The sanction was public ignominy, and that depended on public opinion. Unbelief and contempt for religion, and mockery of the Kirk and its censures, in the spirit of Robert Burns, was the inevitable result later on.

The Kirk still believed that it had the right to interfere in the private life not only of all its own members, but also of persons who adhered to other Christian denominations. The crimes and vices of layfolk were treated rigorously and, in a sense, the persecution of both Episcopalians and Papists was in keeping with the spirit of the age. Here the Kirk had the support of the State, because both these minorities could be regarded as dangerous rebels plotting to overthrow the government—and up to a point this was true enough. On the other hand, the covenanting fervour had never taken strong hold north of Aberdeen, where the greater number of non-Catholic lairds and their people showed little enthusiasm for Presbyterian polity. The Lord's Supper does not appear to have been administered in Aberdeen itself by Presbyterian ministers until 1704, fourteen years after the abolition of prelacy.

During the first quarter of the eighteenth century morals tended to grow more lax and the faith luke-warm and cold. In the North-East the majority of the people remained loyal to the Episcopalian clergy, who refused to take the oath of allegiance, yet in many cases retained possession of their manses, living on their stipends. * Such was the background against which Bishop Nicolson lived in retirement at Preshome, with Bishop Gordon as his coadjutor after 1706.

Bishop Nicolson's associations with Jacobite plots, 1707-8.

It must not be supposed that the now aged Bishop of Peristachium *in partibus* devoted himself exclusively to prayer and pastoral work at Preshome. He was quite ready to be used by political agents to promote their schemes to restore the Stuart dynasty. From the point of view of the Government he was a rebel,

* Cf. H. G. Graham, *The Social Life of Scotland in the 18th Century* (1909), p. 272.

because he appears to have had no scruples about giving practical help to the secret agents of a foreign power which was at war with Britain.

Among the spies employed by Louis XIV was Colonel Nathaniel Hooke, an adventurer and soldier of fortune, who at one time was an Anglican chaplain in Monmouth's forces and was pardoned by James VII after the rebellion of 1685.   By way of gratitude he joined both the King's religion and the French army in Ireland. In 1706 Hooke was sent to Scotland to find out how far the Jacobite nobles were prepared to give their support, if French troops were landed, and he reported that an invasion at the moment would be too risky.   Soon after the Treaty of Union became law in the spring of 1707, he sailed again for Scotland.   Louis and his Ministers believed that the time had come to strike a blow, but they wanted detailed information of the probable strength of Jacobite assistance.

Hooke did well to land at Cruden Bay on the coast of Buchan, because the inhabitants, taken as a whole, were " agin' the government", and notorious smugglers.   He was given shelter by the Earl and Countess of Erroll at Slains Castle, perched on the edge of the red granite cliffs, from which escape would have been easy by boat. He travelled around the counties of Aberdeen and Banff, staying with most of the leading Jacobite lairds, and also with Bishop Nicolson more than once. On his second visit to Preshome he fell ill, and he remained in the Enzie district until his health was recovered.   Then he returned to Slains Castle, where he met one of his most active fellow-plotters, a secular priest named James Carnegie, usually referred to in letters as ' Mr Hall'.   This elusive character is known to have had at least eleven aliases. *

Hooke got back to France without being arrested as a spy.   He convinced Louis XIV that the majority of the Jacobite nobility and landed gentry, strongly opposed to the Act of Union, were eager to overthrow the Government and the result was that a French squadron sailed from Dunkirk in March 1708, bound for the east coast of Scotland.   It had no success, however.   Contrary winds drove the ships out of the Moray Firth on to the North Sea and after a very stormy passage James VIII and his French supporters landed at Dunkirk.   Such was the end of this attempt to replace the Stuarts on the throne of Britain.

* Carnegie, born in 1669, was a kinsman of the Earl of Southesk. As a youth he was reconciled with the Catholic Church and became a student at the Scots College, Rome, where he was ordained priest in 1696. The following year he began work on the Scottish Mission, where he remained on and off until 1729. During much of this time he was constantly employed as a secret Jacobite agent. After an adventurous career he retired to France, and acted as Procurator of the Mission until 1734. Bishop Gordon and some of his clergy had such a high opinion of this somewhat unconventional priest, that they hoped that he would be nominated as coadjutor after the death of Bishop Wallace (See p. 129). Having returned to Scotland, he died at Edinburgh in 1735 after a brief illness.

The only result was that Queen Anne adopted drastic measures to cower the rebels, among whom were numerous leading Catholics. The Scots Law of Treason was adjusted to the English code and many Scottish Jacobites were imprisoned. Although Bishop Nicolson sent Bishop Gordon to Edinburgh, to confer with influential persons about their release, nothing was gained by this long winter journey from Banffshire. Gordon nearly lost his life in a snowdrift.

On the other hand it was arranged to send Mr Carnegie (*alias* Hall, etc., etc.) to London, where somehow he managed to ingratiate himself with the Duke of Queensberry, Secretary of State for Scotland, and the Earl of Dartmouth, Secretary of State for England. It was a remarkable achievement, for this cloak-and-dagger priest was certainly guilty of high treason by violating his allegiance to the reigning sovereign and stirring up a foreign invasion. Yet he used his back-stairs influence to such effect that he got orders sent in the Queen's name to all the Lords Justiciaries in Scotland that Papists were not to be persecuted for their religion, provided that they lived peaceably and raised no disturbances. For the next three years they were more or less unmolested.*

Bishop Gordon's first Visitation of the Highlands in 1707, and Bishop Nicolson's Visitation of the Lowlands, 1708.

Shortly after the Act of Union had been passed in the summer of 1707 Bishop Gordon left Banffshire for a Visitation of the Highlands and Islands. He was accompanied by a young deacon from Rome, a Mr Daglish (or Douglas), who spoke Gaeilc. By a circuitous route through Glenlivet and Badenoch they reached Glengarry on June 10. Here they had their last meal of white bread and meat for several weeks, for the Highlanders then existed mainly on barley bread, milk oatmeal and cheese. The journey was continued on foot along rough mountain paths, where their feet were seldom dry. Many Catholics were confirmed in Knoydart. Two days were spent on the Island of Eigg, where the Bishop and two priests heard confessions and said Mass. Among other islands visited were Rum, South Uist, Barra, Vatersay, Benbecula and Canna. Having returned to the mainland, the Bishop raised Mr Daglish to the priesthood at Borrodale in Knoydart on July 25. †

* For a detailed account of the invasion of 1708, see *The Secret History of Colonel Hooke's Negotiations in Scotland, in Favour of the Pretender* (London, 1760), but now completely superseded by the edition of Hooke's letters by W. D. Macray in the Roxburgh Club (1870). There are also handy excerpts and comments by C. S. Terry, *The Chevalier de St George and the Jacobite movements in his favour, 1701-1720* (London, 1921). Far too little has been disclosed of the political and highly secret activities both of Bishop Nicolson and of James Carnegie.

† This was not the first sacerdotal ordination in Scotland since the Reformation. On March 11, 1704, apparently in Strathbogie, Bishop Nicolson raised Peter Fraser to the priesthood in the utmost secrecy. Ordinations to the priesthood were not ventured upon in England until 90 years later.

Before the Visitation was ended, towards the end of August, more than 2,200 persons had been confirmed. The Bishop, utterly exhausted and suffering from fever, was cared for, at Balnacraig on Deeside, by his brother who was a Doctor of Medicine.*

The following year, in spite of the troubled political situation described in the previous section, Bishop Gordon managed to visit the scattered Catholics in Angus, Perthshire, the Lothians, Niths-dale and Galloway. He reported that in the south-west of Scotland many of the Presbyterians were " so superstitious and pharisaical that they thought it a profanation to contract friendship, or to have any connection, with those whom they looked upon as heathens and idolaters . . . As for priests, they looked upon them as so many monsters." †

Relations were now much more amicable between the secular clergy and the Jesuits. On May 26, 1709, Bishop Gordon informed Fr. Michaelangelo Tamburini, General of the Society of Jesus, that all the Fathers working on the Scottish Mission were submissive and obedient to his authority. He could hardly find words in which to express his admiration for their piety and zeal. Four Jesuits were working in the Highlands, and seven in the Lowlands, but some were in great financial straits, because they were unable to obtain money from France owing to war-time conditions. ‡

A Seminary opened on Loch Morar, 1714.

The Peace of Utrecht, signed on April 11, 1713, between Great Britain with her allies and France, secured the Protestant succession for England and Scotland. There appeared to be no chance of another Jacobite rising, so Bishop Nicolson and his Coadjutor decided that it would be safe to open a small seminary, which would prepare boys for the colleges abroad and enable others to be ordained at home. Nothing of the kind had been founded in the British Isles since the Reformation.

An island in Loch Morar, on the west coast of Inverness-shire, was chosen as a suitably remote spot for the seminary. Mr George Innes, who had studied at the Scots College, Paris, and was a brother of Lewis and Thomas Innes, was appointed first head-master. There were seven boys at the start. The following year Bishop Gordon, who had been learning Gaelic to enable him to preach and hear confessions in that language, made a second Visitation of the Highlands and Islands, during which he confirmed over 12,000 persons, of whom about half were converts.

The Jacobite Rising of 1715–16.

Queen Anne died on August 1, 1714, and was succeeded by

---

* A Report of the Visitation, sent to Propaganda, commended the apostolic labours of Bishop Gordon. (Cf. Bellesheim, op.cit. vol. iv, p. 181).

† Forbes-Leith, op.cit. vol. ii, p. 243.

‡ ibid, vol. ii, pp. 258-61.

The Seminary at Scalan, Glenlivet (1717-1807).

Tombae, Glenlivet, Banffshire. The present church was built in 1829, but there was a regular succession of priests here from 1687.

George, Elector of Hanover and Duke of Brunswick-Luneberg, who became King George I of Great Britain and Ireland. The immediate result was that the Jacobites started to plot again for the restoration of the Stuart dynasty, presuming that few people in Britain wanted to be ruled by a German prince, even if he happened to be a Protestant.

Although Bishop Gordon was just as much of a convinced Jacobite as Bishop Nicolson, he does not appear to have approved of the rebellion, which started with the Earl of Mar raising the royal standard at Braemar on September 6, 1715. James VIII sailed from Saint-Malo and, disguised as a sailor, landed at Peterhead on December 22. His sojourn in Scotland lasted less than two months. On February 4, 1716, he boarded the French ship Marie-Thérèse off Montrose, and a week later came ashore at Waldam between Calais and Gravelies. Such was the end of 'The Fifteen'.

The only result was another outburst of Protestant fanaticism, combined with a terror of further invasion by France. Many of the Catholic nobility and landed gentry in Scotland had been involved in this latest act of treason against the Hanoverian government. They were imprisoned, deprived of their titles, and had their estates confiscated.

In a report which Bishop Gordon managed to get through to Rome, dated November 19, 1716, he informed Propaganda that Scottish Catholics were in danger of annihilation and it almost looked as if their religion was on the verge of disappearing from the country.

Bishop Gordon opens a seminary at Scalan in Glenlivet, 1717.

The little seminary on Loch Morar had been closed as the result of 'The Fifteen', but two of its students who got out of Scotland were at the Scots College in Rome. In 1716 Bishop Gordon decided to open a seminary in the Braes of Glenlivet, which formed part of the Duke of Gordon's lands in Banffshire, and where most of the people were Catholics. Surrounded by mountains on all sides, and far from any road, the Braes were difficult of access. At the far end was a small roughly-built heather-thatched cottage, or 'but-and-a-ben', hidden by juniper bushes, close to a burn of brown peaty water. Used as a hide-out since 1715 by Mr John Gordon, the missionary in Glenlivet, it was known as Scalan. *

By 1717 a few boys had been brought to Scalan and Mr George Innes, the first Superior of the seminary on Loch Morar, was put in charge of them. He was soon succeeded by Mr John Tyrie and in 1720 Mr Alexander Grant (brother of the future Bishop James Grant) looked after this humble seminary. †

* The name is said to have been given it from the sticks fixed in the ground and interwoven with twigs forming the small huts.

† Hugh Macdonald (consecrated as first Vicar-Apostolic of the Highland District in 1731), came from Morar as one of the first students.

I

For the next eighty-three years many priests for the Scottish Mission were educated at Scalan in conditions utterly different from those they would have enjoyed at any of the Scots Colleges abroad. Writing in 1762, Bishop John Geddes explained that "the climate here is cold and you have commonly much snow in the winter, but in the summer the place is not at all disagreeable".* The masters and boys were cut off from all contacts with the outside world as completely as the fourth century hermits in the Egyptian Desert. It was a system of education which had disadvantages as well as advantages. †

Death of Bishop Nicolson, 1718.

Although Bishop Nicolson had taken no active part in the Jacobite rising of 1715, after its failure he was arrested and imprisoned at Fochabers. On his release he returned to Preshome, where he died on October 12, 1718, aged seventy-six. His body was laid to rest in St Ninian's Cemetery. ‡

* Cf. W. J. Anderson, 'Scalan' in *Innes Review*, Autumn, 1963, p. 94.
† For further details of life at Scalan, see pp. 118-9, 194-7.
‡ His grave is in a corner of the walled enclosure, and his name is recorded on the base of a granite cross, erected about fifty years ago, with those of about thirty missionary priests who were buried here.

CHAPTER FOUR

SECOND VICAR-APOSTOLIC
1718-1731

Bishop Gordon's efforts to obtain a coadjutor, 1718–1731

ON THE DEATH of Bishop Nicolson the whole of Scotland came under the jurisdiction of Bishop Gordon, then aged fifty-four. His health was poor and he begged Propaganda to give him a coadjutor. He also wrote to James VIII, whose headquarters had been at Urbino in the Papal States since he left Avignon in the summer of 1717, requesting him to use his influence at Rome in favour of Mr John Wallace. Cardinal Sacrapanti was informed that the King was personally acquainted with this "very pious priest, equally humble and learned."

Had word of these negotiations between Bishop Gordon in Scotland and the ' Old Pretender ' in Italy reached George I and his ministers, it might have been awkward. In February 1719 James left Urbino for Spain, planning to lead another invasion of Scotland, a quixotic affair which ended with the surrender of a small band of Spanish troops at Glenshiel, at the head of Loch Duich, on June 10 that same year. The King went back to Italy, and on September 1 his marriage took place at Montefiascone with Maria Clementina, grand-daughter of John Sobieski, King of Poland. The Pope allowed the royal couple to live in the Piazza dei Apostoli at Rome, where Papal cuirassiers mounted guard daily outside the Palace, just as at the Vatican and the Quirinal. Clement XI also presented James with the Savelli Palace at Albano as a summer residence. *

Wanting to show the world that he was still Defender of the Faith, James VIII went on nominating bishops, both Catholic and Episcopalian. By pulling strings at Propaganda he managed to persuade the Pope and the Cardinals that John Wallace would make an ideal coadjutor for Bishop Gordon, and on April 8, 1720, this convert Episcopalian, in his middle sixties, was appointed coadjutor to Bishop Gordon, as titular Bishop of Cyrra on the

---

* This display of papal protection and support of the Stuart royal family did not make things any easier for Catholics in Britain. Sir Horace Mann, from 1737 to his death in 1786, was continuously in Italy, chiefly in Florence. He knew everybody of importance, and had an accurate and sound knowledge of everything that was going on. He took care that the Jacobite gossip reached London, and he was far from being the only Hanoverian agent in Italy.

upper Euphrates. From the King's point of view what mattered most were the social status and political opinions of the candidate, not his qualifications for active mission work. Mr Wallace had proved himself a loyal Jacobite for more than thirty years. He was also a friend of several of the Scottish nobility who were plotting and praying for the restoration of the Stuarts.*

For nearly nine years Mr Wallace had been living in Edinburgh under the protection of the widowed Duchess of Gordon—herself a militant Jacobite—when the news reached him of his nomination to the episcopate. With a special dispensation from Rome, Bishop Gordon was able to consecrate him with the assistance only of priests, and on October 1, 1720, the function took place at Edinburgh in the utmost secrecy, possibly in the house where he lived on Moultries Hill behind what is now the Register House.

Bishop Wallace is a somewhat enigmatic figure. His intensely devotional spiritual letters to Bishop Gordon are, to say the least, eccentric. Before his consecration he had spent only one year in mission work and afterwards, when he was accused of neglecting his duties as a coadjutor, he always pleaded ill health. It may have been true. He had reached the age of sixty-six when he became a bishop. On the other hand, he made many converts, including Mr Dickson, Provost of Forfar, whose son entered the Scots College, Paris, but died there when still an acolyte.†

State of the Scottish Mission in 1722-4.

The joint report of the Scottish Mission, sent to Propaganda by

---

* Born about 1654, John Wallace was the son of Patrick Wallace, Provost of Arbroath. Brought up as an Episcopalian he may have been ordained to the ministry, but was reconciled with the Roman Church in 1686, probably due to the influence of the Earl of Perth, whose tutor he became in 1681. Wallace followed his noble patron into exile, and for some years lived with the court at Saint-Germain-en-Laye. He visited Rome with the Earl in 1695. Then he entered the Scots College, Paris, as a 'gentleman-boarder'. Bishop Gordon met this middle-aged convert in 1706, and with great difficulty persuaded him to return to Scotland. On April 14, 1708, Bishop Nicolson raised him to the priesthood at Preshome. Next we hear of him living at Arbroath, where he ministered to the few scattered Catholics in Angus. He was arrested and ordered to appear before the Justiciary Court at Perth for having apostasised to "the Popish religion, also for trafficking and perverting others." He managed to escape imprisonment, and retired to Edinburgh.

† Six months before Bishop Wallace's consecration, all informed Europe was talking about a Scotsman who had recently conformed to the Roman Church, clearly a necessity for him in his financial career, and whose downfall was more sudden than his rise to world-wide fame. This was John Law (1671-1729), the notorious financier, who by 1719 had acquired the entire control of French trade in the East Indies, China and the South Seas. He founded the disastrous so-called Mississippi Scheme, having already founded a private Bank. He and his family were generous benefactors to the Scots College, Paris, but he ended his days in poverty at Venice, where he died after receiving the last Sacraments. Some at least of his benefactions seem to have survived the financial debacle which ruined so many.

Bishop Gordon and Bishop Wallace in October 1723, reads like the fulfilment of the signs of the end of the world as foretold in the twenty-fourth chapter of St Matthew's Gospel —"the abomination of desolation set up in the holy place." *

Throughout Scotland violent enmity against Papists was being stirred up and a new Oath of Allegiance had been approved by Parliament in 1723. This had to be taken by all persons without exception, under pain of confiscation of property, banishment and imprisonment. The Oath was phrased in such a way that no Catholic could take it without virtually renouncing his religion. As the result of intervention by some of the foreign ambassadors, however, the Oath was modified the following year.

Bishops Gordon and Wallace informed Propaganda that the seminary at Scalan and a few Catholic schools in the Highlands were still carrying on, in spite of attacks by some of the more bigoted ministers. Bishop Wallace, together with eleven layfolk, was arrested one Sunday morning while hearing confessions before Mass in the dowager Duchess of Gordon's house in Edinburgh. After a brief confinement in prison he was released on bail. He ignored a summons to appear, and was declared fugitive. Nevertheless he was bold enough to remain in Scotland, and Bishop Gordon left him in charge of the Southern Lowlands, while he devoted himself mainly to the Highlands.

In the summer of 1723 Bishop Gordon made another visitation, more strenuous than any of the previous ones. More than 2,090 persons were confirmed and others reconciled with the Church, during his three months' journeys. Although the Bishop was exhausted when he returned to Preshome, he continued to lead a life of great austerity and self-mortification. From time to time he went to the Braes of Glenlivet, where he met the professors and students at Scalan, in constant fear that the seminary would be raided by English soldiers.

It was also in 1723 that George I made a grant of £1000 for the promotion of Protestantism in the Highlands and Islands. The itinerant preachers, catechists, and teachers, who with the support of the S.P.C.K. were striving to stamp out Popery, received another generous benefaction from the Royal Bounty Committee formed in 1724. Further assistance was given them by the Commissioners of the Forfeited Estates, when they began operations. It was not lack of money that prevented Papists being converted to Presbyterianism, except in a few cases.

It is difficult to form an accurate idea of the number of Catholics in Scotland during the seventeen-twenties. We have the figures recorded by the Vicars-Apostolic on the one hand, and those supplied by the General Assemblies of the Established Kirk on the other. In 1722, when the ministers were trying to make the Assembly send more preachers and catechists to the Highlands and

---

* Cf. Bellesheim, op.cit. Vol. IV, Appendix X, pp.377-80.

Islands, they may have been exaggerating when they reported 4,000 persons given over to idolatry and superstition in Barra, South Uist, Benbecula, Canna, Eigg, Rum and other islands, as well as in Knoydart, Morar, Moidart, and Ardnamurchan on the mainland.* There were other fairly numerous groups of Catholics in Glengarry, Glenmoriston, Glenurquhart and Strathglass, all lying west of Inverness. On the Duke of Gordon's extensive lands in Banffshire the preachers hardly dared to carry on their evangelistic work. Catholics had increased in certain parts of Aberdeenshire too. On the other hand they were decreasing steadily in the southern Low-lands, except in and around Edinburgh, and the Northern Highlands beyond Inverness remained almost 100 per cent. Presbyterian.

Bishop Gordon generally stayed at Scalan during the summer months, and in 1722 he drew up a few short Rules for the students. † They begin with the intimation that as "the design of the house is to educate a few youths in piety and learning, and to fit them to instruct others, it seems necessary to keep off all such company as may give them the wrong impressions or disturb them in their business, and to put them upon such methods as are most proper for attaining at what they aim at."

The "scholars" were bidden to "converse as little as possible with strangers"—not that there can have been very many in this remote spot—and to "shun the company of women entirely." Only with the master's permission were servants or workmen allowed to eat, play or discourse with the students, who were for-bidden access to the kitchen. They were to be "well taught to pray always seriously, and from the heart to seek God's blessing upon everything they do". Not only had they to "make some pious lecture every morning and afternoon", but they also had to "meditate in an easy and solid manner as soon as they can be made capable", and for half-an-hour twice daily. The "scholars" had to go to Confession every fortnight, and "communicate once a month at least". Mass was normally celebrated only on Sundays and holidays before breakfast, but Bishop Gordon recommended that it should be said "several days a week"; also that they should recite "some part of the Church Office both in the forenoon and afternoon" on Sundays and holidays, "which 'tis necessary the master should say with them and direct them". Their studies were "to be proportioned to what their health can bear, and let them seek leave, when they want it, to go out a little even out of time of recreation to refresh their spirits by walking." Instruction in the "French and Irish or Highland languages" was ordered; also

---

* Cf. MS Report to the Assembly of 1722, quoted by Donald Maclean in *The Counter Reformation in Scotland* (1931), p. 205.

† Cf. W. J. Anderson, 'Bishop Gordon's Rules for Scalan', in *Innes Review*, Autumn, 1963, pp. 106-9; 'The College for the Lowland District of Scotland at Scalan and Aquhorties, Registers and Documents', ed. by W. J. Anderson, in *Innes Review* (Autumn, 1965), pp. 89-212.

"Geography, Chronology, History and Critick" besides "some little of the Greek, and likewise of Rhetorick, when they know the Latin pretty well." The more advanced students in philosophy and divinity also learned Hebrew, if they had "a genius for tongues."

Attention must be paid by the masters to the health of the boys and youths, making sure that they got eight hours of rest and sleep daily. A quarter of an hour was enough when they arose at five in summer and six in winter "for putting on their clothes (which should be done quickly and modestly), for combing their heads and washing their hands". It was not possible for "young folk who study much to keep their health without a great deal of exercise, walking and diversion," and the regulation of all this had to be left to the master's prudence, "according to the proper times and seasons, and to every one's age, state of health, and genius." Besides daily recreations, the scholars were permitted one whole afternoon weekly.

Such was the manner of life led at Scalan and, taken all round, the conditions were probably no more austere than what most of the boys and youths would have experienced in their own homes. There were three classes of students: "Boarders; those for trial; and Members". The first group paid six pounds sterling per annum for board. They had to bring with them two or three pair of blankets, and "be in tolerable good clothes, with three shirts at least, three pairs of stockings, and new shoes".*

Reprisals between Papists and Protestants in Banffshire, 1720-25.

From the point of view of the S.P.C.K., Banffshire was a spiritual ' black country', a veritable Sodom and Gomorrha; a sink of iniquity where idolatry and superstition had to be rooted out. Almost an embodiment of the Whore of Babylon, or the Beast with seven heads and ten horns, was Alexander, second Duke of Gordon, who succeeded his father in 1716. He lived at Gordon Castle in princely style. Sinister stories were told of his luxury, vice, splendour and, above all, his tyranny over Protestants. It was rumoured that the Duke corresponded with other leading Papists at home and abroad—even the Pope! His eldest son had been named Cosmo, in honour of Cosmo de Medici, the Grand Duke of Tuscany. Handsome in appearance, kindly in disposition, liberal to his numerous tenants and generous to the poor, the Duke was regarded as the most powerful opponent of Protestantism in Scotland during the reign of George I.† The preachers, catechists and teachers appointed by the S.P.C.K., though assisted by many royal and other benefactions, were making little headway in Banff-shire, where another Gordon, the Popish Bishop, himself a kinsman of the Duke, had his residence.

---

* These rules for classes of students were made later.

† He had married an Anglican, the Lady Henrietta Mordaunt, 2nd daughter of Charles, Earl of Peterborough and Monmouth.

*Shenval, on the borders of Aberdeenshire and Banffshire.
A succession of priests from 1728 to 1793 served a hidden
chapel in what was known as the 'Siberia of Scotland'.*

*Tomnagylach, Glen Rinnes, Banffshire. Mass was
celebrated here from 1731 to 1773 for the benefit of the
then numerous Catholics.*

120

A memorial addressed to the Government in 1720 stated that " to such a height have the Papists and Jacobites arrived in the Duke of Gordon's country that Protestant friends of the Government are in hazard of their lives. Thomas Miller in Fochabers, who lately renounced Popery, has had his house set upon by a mob of Papists the 21st of May last, and he with his wife and family beat, and some of them dragged by the feet to the door, and his goods abused, and part thereto taken away, and this rabble was hounded out by one Thomas Clapperton, a violent Papist." *

Other instances of the persecution of Protestants by the Duke of Gordon's tenants were reported in 1720. Harry Forrest of Fochabers was so "rabbled" that he and his family had to leave the district. Even worse, in April that same year two elders of the parish of Gartly, near Huntly, "were set upon by three gentlemen of the Duke's ground, and beat in an inhuman manner, one of them to the effusion of blood and danger of life."†

Two years later the General Assembly at Edinburgh was informed that the Papists in Fochabers had stripped two Protestant boys naked in the open street, and ordered the "common officer" to whip them, which he did.‡ Whether this occasion to use the 'tawse' on these two Banffshire 'loons' was because of their religion, or for some more obvious breach of the peace, was not stated : the crime lay in the fact that the police had dared to strip and belabour Presbyterian bairns. Next it was reported that Walter Scobie, a school teacher maintained by the S.P.C.K., had been beaten and bruised by a Romish rabble.

In September 1725 an itinerant preacher named Walter Morrison, formerly a teacher in the Enzie district, had the effrontery to call at Gordon Castle. He informed the Duke that he intended to hold a Protestant service in St Ninian's Chapel the following Sunday. § As might have been expected, the Duke refused to consider such a request, pointing out that the chapel was the burial place of his family and Catholic tenants.

Next day Morrison arrived with some men. They broke a window, put in a boy and he unfastened the door. A prayer-meeting took place, at the close of which Morrison said he would do the same on the coming Sabbath. On Monday the Episcopalian Earl of Findlater, Sheriff of Banffshire, dined at Gordon Castle and was asked by the Duke to check further violations of private property, which he promised to do. Another service did take place at St Ninian's, but as the window had been repaired and the door barricaded, Morrison and his congregation had no choice but to worship in the open air. There is a story that a party of Papists

---

* Cf. Maclean. op.cit. p. 211, quoting MS 68, National Library, Edinburgh.

† ibid, p. 211.

‡ *Records* of the General Assembly, 1722.

§ It had been rebuilt by the 1st Duke of Gordon in 1687 on the site of an old chapel, and Mass was still celebrated there occasionally.

from Fochabers, with faces blackened to prevent recognition, attacked and wounded some of the Protestants, driving them away, although it was against the Duke's orders. *

A lurid account of how the Popish mob had set upon the Protestant evangelists was sent to the Royal Bounty Committee, in which it was stated that: "with great clamour, rage and fury . . . uttering many execrable oaths, and cursing the foresaid preacher and his congregation and reproaching our Holy Religion, calling it domn'd religion, and swearing that it shall never get footing there, and after they had violently dispersed the people who came to hear the word, they did pursue the preachers through the several roads by which they were obliged to flee to save their lives . . . Protestants were discouraged and were frightened into apostasy and people accordingly were leaving their farms."

Never since the Reformation had Catholics in Scotland dared to defy Protestants so openly. The above stories show the power wielded in Banffshire by the second Duke of Gordon. At the General Assembly of 1723, the Royal Commissioner drew attention to these disturbances, mentioning " the restless endeavours of Popish emissaries in perverting many to the errors of the Church of Rome and withdrawing them from their duty and allegiance to His Majesty". Most of the ministers present had no doubt that the 'woman on the scarlet beast', 'the great mother of harlots', was riding around the North-East, 'drunk with the blood of the saints'. Her followers were rebels at heart, "promoting the interests of a Popish pretender", whose divine right to the thrones of England, Scotland and Ireland was recognised by the Pope.

Something had to be done to check this papal aggression, so on November 30, 1723, an Order in Council was issued from Whitehall, bidding the Lords Justiciary and all local Justices, magistrates and other officials in Scotland to enforce the penal laws more rigorously.

This would soon be made easier, because George I was considering building strategic roads in the Highlands, to enable English troops to move across the mountains and to penetrate into the heart of certain Papist enclaves with greater rapidity than hitherto. The work, however, was not started until 1726. Meanwhile the Jacobites went on plotting behind the scenes.

Apparently in that same year an inner circle of Jacobites persuaded Mr James Carnegie (alias Hall), who has been mentioned previously in connection with Bishop Nicolson, to go to King James in Rome with certain information which it was not safe to put down in writing, even in cypher. He made the long journey without being molested, but the Scottish Jesuits seem to have heard of it, and accused the papal nuncio in Paris of favouring Jansenism, hinting that many of the secular priests in Scotland

* G. Hutcheson, *Days of Yore, or Buckie and District in the Past* (Banff, 1887).

were already tainted with this heresy.   Carnegie did not remain
long in Rome.   Having done his secret business with the King,
he slipped back to France, where friends advised him to present
a memorial to Cardinal Fleury, the Prime Minister, concerning the
persecution of Catholics in Scotland.   More back-stairs plotting
went on.   Carnegie had a secret meeting with the Cardinal at
Fontainbleau, where the court was in residence, but Fleury was
non-committal.   The astute statesman gave Carnegie a letter
addressed to the French ambassador in London, and there the
ambassador explained to the Scottish priest that the right moment
had not yet come to show the Cardinal's diplomatically worded
proposals for persons of influence. Realising that nothing more
could be done to promote the cause of Catholicism in Scotland by
hole-and-corner plotting and scheming, this priest-politician made
his way north incognito, and reported the result of his negotiations
to the Jacobite leaders, who had sent him to Rome.

It is not easy to understand the mentality of James Carnegie,
who appears to have been convinced that he best fulfilled his
vocation as a priest by devoting himself mainly to dangerous
espionage activities, and that in the long run these were promoting
the greater glory of God. Nevertheless the abbé Macpherson —
himself a secret agent—wrote in after years that Carnegie's
"eminent good qualifications were so conspicuous and so greatly
valued by Bishop Gordon and his clergy, that he had their
unanimous suffrages to be Coadjutor in place of Bishop Wallace.
But his humility, which was not the least of his virtues, withstood
all their entreaties." *

Bishop Gordon asks Propaganda to appoint a Gaelic-speaking bishop for the Highlands and Islands, 1726

The British Government were not left in ignorance of what the
Jacobite nobility were doing to restore the Stuart dynasty, so it is
not surprising that in 1726 bodies of light troops were sent to scour
the glens for the purpose of arresting priests in the Highlands. Mr
Shaw was the only one captured, and he was imprisoned at
Inverness.

On August 13 that same year Bishop Gordon and Bishop
Wallace wrote a joint letter to Propaganda, recommending that a
Gaelic-speaking vicar-apostolic should be nominated for the Highlands and Islands. They explained that in the Highland districts
the recent persecution had been violent; almost the worst which
had occurred for one hundred and sixty years. What alarmed the
Calvinists was that the number of Catholics had increased three-
fold, notwithstanding all the efforts to crush them. †

The two bishops added that " King James of England " (a proof
of their Jacobite loyalty) had " in a very strong letter " written to

---

* *Scotichronicon*, p. 533.
† Cf. Bellesheim, op.cit., vol. iv, appendix xi, pp. 381-3.

the Cardinal Prefect of Propaganda, insisting on the need of a vicar-apostolic for the Gaelic-speaking parts of Scotland. Not content with this, the King had petitioned Benedict XIII to nominate Mr Alexander James Grant for this office. *

Mr Grant was " a man of great knowledge, piety and zeal, but naturally diffident and timid, which exposed him to many inconveniences. Still Bishop Gordon judged him the most proper person to be made Bishop in the Highlands, and induced him to accept that office." † He left the Braes of Glenlivet and spent some time in Paris on his way to Rome. We are told that " being very awkward, and of mean appearance, it was thought proper not to introduce him to the great personages of that City." Then he was ordered to return to Scotland, and told that his Bulls of Consecration would follow. He ran out of money on arriving at Genoa, was laid low with both ague and depression. The Bishop-elect wrote to Paris explaining his plight, but got no answer. The abbé Macpherson related that " his imagination was diseased." Meanwhile the Bulls of Consecration had reached Scotland. Letter after letter was dispatched to Rome, and from Rome, but nothing more was heard of Mr Grant. Whether he retired into a monastery, or died unknown, has never been discovered.

Benedict XIII divides Scotland into two Vicariates, 1727.

King George I died on June 11, 1727, and on July 23 (or 27) Pope Benedict XIII ratified the division of Scotland into two Vicariates, the Highland and Lowland Districts. A delay of more than four years took place before any appointment was made. Bishops Gordon and Wallace renewed their previous petition, and proposed Mr Hugh Macdonald as a substitute for the vanished Mr Alexander Grant, begging for a speedy decision because of the rapid increase of Presbyterian ministers, teachers and catechists in the Highlands and Islands.

In the spring of 1728 Bishop Gordon wrote to Cardinal Sacrapanti, requesting him to ask the Pope to inform the Emperor of Austria and other Catholic sovereigns of the sufferings of the priests and layfolk on the Scottish Mission. He hoped it would be possible for them to plead with the British Government, so that relief could be guaranteed at the ensuing Congress where deputies of most of the Powers in Europe were expected.

In spite of his poor health, Bishop Gordon made another Visitation of the Highlands and Islands that summer. The weather was bad, with constant rain and winds. More than once the Bishop was exposed to great danger when crossing raging seas in an open

---

* Grant, a native of the Enzie District, after a distinguished career at the Scots College, Rome, had spent seven years on the Mission. He learned to speak Gaelic after he had been put in charge of the seminary at Scalan.
† Scotichronicon, p. 561.

boat, or when penetrating mountain glens on foot. He confirmed over a thousand persons, many of whom were converts.

Death of the second Duke of Gordon, 1728.

In the autumn of 1728 the Duke of Gordon decided to go to London in the hope of trying to induce the Government to issue orders that persecution of his Catholic tenants must cease. The strain of riding more than five hundred miles in both directions hastened his death, which occurred on November 28. His body was taken from Gordon Castle to St Ninian's Chapel, where it lay in state, the coffin surrounded by tapers. His eight-year-old son, Cosmo, Marquis of Huntly, who became the third Duke, served the Requiem Mass. This appears to have been the last time that the Chapel was used for Catholic worship. The burial took place in the south choir-aisle of Elgin Cathedral, where many Gordon ancestors had been laid to rest.

As was the usual custom in the case of a mixed marriage until the Encyclical *Magnae nobis* of Benedict XIV (1741), which declared the Church's repugnance to such unions, and insisted that the children of either sex must be brought up as Catholics, a pact had been made by the Duke and Duchess that their sons would be educated in their father's religion, and their daughters in their mother's. What happened after the funeral was that the chapel at Gordon Castle was closed, and the chaplain, Mr Robert Gordon, who had held the post for ten years, was dismissed.* Protestant tutors were engaged for the four boys, and on Sundays they were taken to Protestant worship. The Episcopalian Dowager Duchess, however, remained on friendly terms with Bishop Gordon, and did not evict or molest Catholic families on the young Duke's estates.†

There were rumours that Bishop Gordon was trying to kidnap the two elder sons, and send them abroad to be brought up as Papists. This led to his arrest, but the Duchess used her influence and he was soon released. In 1729 Propaganda wrote to the Nuncio at Paris, requesting him to consult Mr James Carnegie, as to the chances of getting the Duke and his brothers away from their mother, so that they could be brought up in their father's religion. It appears that 'Mr Hall', having discussed the matter with Cardinal Fleury and Louis XV, decided although abducting the boys would certainly promote the greater glory of God, it would be too dangerous, and possibly harm the Jacobite cause. ‡

---

* He retired to Edinburgh, where he became Procurator of the Mission, which office he retained until 1740.

† Her youngest son, Andrew, born in 1717, visited Rome in 1755. So deeply impressed was he by Benedict XIV, that he was reconciled with the Church, and had his children brought up Catholics. One of the 2nd Duke's grandsons, Lord George Gordon (1751-95) became notorious as the instigator of the 'No Popery' riots in 1780. (See pp. 181-2)

‡ Cf. Forbes-Leith, op.cit., vol. ii, p. 315.

The Protestant missionaries who intensified their efforts to convert Papists in the Highlands and Islands had more than enough justification for regarding them as rebels as well as idolaters. It distressed Bishop Gordon that owing to his age and infirmities he was unable to make another Visitation of his Gaelic-speaking flock. He appealed to Propaganda again and again to nominate a bishop, and recommended Mr Hugh Macdonald as "a member of a most illustrious clan, and a man of great experience of the country". Although "rather young, he was more remarkable for his zeal and piety than for his birth." * On September 17, 1730, James VIII wrote to the newly elected Pope, Clement XII, highly commending this priest as a Vicar-Apostolic for the northern part of his Kingdom.

In the summer of that year Bishop Gordon managed to make a Visitation of the Lowlands, even as far south as Galloway. After his return to Banffshire he composed the first Pastoral Letter by a Catholic Bishop in Scotland. Dated October 29, 1731, it was addressed "to all the Churchmen [priests] and honourable Catholic gentlemen in the Highlands of Scotland". Previous to the issue of this Pastoral, word had come from Rome that Hugh Macdonald had been nominated first Vicar-Apostolic of a Highland District.

* ibid, p. 318.

CHAPTER FIVE

LOWLAND & HIGHLAND VICARIATES
1731-1768

Bishop Hugh Macdonald and the Highland Vicariate, 1731-8.
Hugh Macdonald was the son of the Laird of Morar, born apparently in 1699. As stated already, he was one of the first students at the school on the island in Loch Morar in 1711.[*] His studies were completed at Scalan, where he was ordained priest by Bishop Gordon in 1725. Then he returned to Morar as a missionary, but later on spent a year at the Scots College, Paris, at the time when the Jansenist controversy was nearing a crisis. He remained in France until word reached him that he had been nominated bishop. Leaving Paris while crowds of convulsionaries were still surging around the tomb of the Jansenist deacon in the churchyard of St. Médard, he returned to Scotland. His consecration as titular Bishop of Diana in Numidia took place in Edinburgh on St Luke's Day, October 18, 1731, and was performed by Bishop Gordon, assisted by the now very frail Bishop Wallace.[†]

One of Bishop Macdonald's first acts was to reopen the seminary on Loch Morar, and by June 1732 there were three or four students. In a report to Propaganda, dated March 18, 1732, he explained how necessary was an educational establishment of this sort, and wrote: "Whilst I ponder over a remedy for so great an evil, this seems to me the most efficacious—that a seminary be started in this Highland District for the training of youths for the ecclesiastical state. It will thus happen that the youths who will in future be sent to the colleges abroad will be better prepared, whilst others, being ordained in this country, will make up for the small number of those who come back as priests from the colleges. How comes it, indeed, that of the Highland youths who, after the most careful selection, have been sent abroad, so large a proportion give up the ecclesiastical state, and, returning to the vanities of the world, belie the hopes which had been placed in them?" [‡]

The Bishop, with his experience of life in Paris, evidently felt temptations of great cities on the continent; and that it would be

[*] See p. 105 note †.
[†] See p. 116.
[‡] Cf. 'Glenlivatensis' in *St Peter's College Magazine*, vol. xix (1950), pp. 133-9; also 'The Highland Seminaries, I'; also Odo Blundell, O.S.B., *The Catholic Highlands of Scotland* (1909), *The Western Highlands* (1917).

better for them to be trained amid their own mountain fastnesses, out of touch with the world. Another advantage: these youths would not forget their native Gaelic, which usually happened after four to six years overseas.

It was made clear enough to Cardinal Domenico Rivera, who had been appointed Protector of the Scottish Mission, that the Catholic Highlanders were so poor that there was no hope of establishing a proper seminary unless Propaganda was prepared to give financial help.

For the next few years Bishop Hugh kept up a ceaseless begging campaign on behalf of his seminary. The small island in the deepest lake in any part of Europe, except a submarine valley on the south coast of Scandinavia, became almost too well-known to the officials of Propaganda, and to Mr William Stuart, the Roman Agent. The island (Eilean Ban) lies half a mile from the shore, and was large enough for a good garden, so there was no need for the boys to leave their natural enclosure—not that the five to six miles distant hamlet of Arisaig could have offered much in the way of what the Bishop referred to as " the vanities of the world."

Three years after Hugh Macdonald had become the first Vicar-Apostolic of the Highland District, there took place the death-bed submission to the Catholic Church of Rob Roy MacGregor (1671-1734). The greater part of his life had been spent in cattle-lifting, and exacting money for affording protection against thieves. He was notorious as a freebooter throughout Scotland. It is not surprising that Mr Alexander Drummond, the Jansenist chaplain at Drummond Castle, Perthshire, is said to have " frequently groaned, crossed himself, and exacted a heavy remuneration before he absolved his penitent for the many mortal and venial sins of his long life. *

When Rob Roy lay dying in his home among the mountains, he asked for a priest to give him the last Sacraments. We are told that he "did not pretend, when pressed closely on the subject, to justify all the tenets of Catholicism, and acknowledged that extreme unction always appeared to him as a great waste of oil." The priest is said "to have found the dying hero a little slow to understand the universal nature of Christian forgiveness. "I forgive my enemies', said Rob, but (catching the eye of Robin Og), 'look you to them".†

* Cf. Hamilton Howlett, *Highland Constable* (1950), p. 280. Alexander Drummond, a former student of the Scots College, Paris, was regarded as the most rigid Jansenist priest in Scotland.

† Rob Roy was buried in the kirkyard at Balquhidder in 1734, where his supposed grave is still pointed out. His son, Robin Og, was reconciled with the Church before he was executed in 1754, and his body was laid to rest beside those of his parents.

Bishop Gordon continues his apostolic labours in the Lowland District.

Relieved of the care of the Highlands and Islands, Bishop Gordon was able to concentrate on the scattered Catholics in the Lowlands. It is reported that he was " so much revered for his prudence and piety that every Catholic, whether he was of the clergy or laity, wished him to be present at the settling of matters of any importance; and his zeal and charity could not refuse them.*

In April 1732 Bishops Gordon and Wallace wrote a joint letter to Propaganda. They said that "there is not one of the missionaries but does more work than three could do with any degree of convenience. Of this, however, they do not complain; their zeal for the glory of God, and the salvation of souls makes such fatigue easy for them. But to be in real want of the most pressing necessaries of life is too much for human nature to bear. How often since I had charge of this Mission, with a heart pierced with the deepest grief, have I known these apostolic men, after travelling the whole day through snow and rain from one village to another, assisting the sick, instructing converts, and comforting the distressed, retire at night to their miserable habitations, where they had not fire nor meat to relieve oppressed nature. Many have the heroic charity to lose their lives under these miseries rather than abandon their charge; but this cannot be expected of all. Hence, if their Eminences wish to preserve religion in that country, they must make some permanent addition to the usual allowance granted to the Missions of Scotland from their first establishment." When there were only ten missionaries, two thousand five hundred crowns yearly were assigned to them; now there are about thirty, and the income is the same." †

For the past three or four years Bishop Wallace had been living in retirement in Edinburgh, cared for by the Dowager Duchess of Gordon. She died on July 16, 1732, and his own death took place there on July 11, 1733, in his eightieth year. Bishop Gordon wrote: "His value is known to few but God. I cannot express what esteem I have of him." It is recorded that Bishop Wallace's " charity to the indigent was so great, and his contempt for all worldly riches so high, that though he had a genteel patrimony from his own family, and was extremely parsimonious and sparing on himself, there were not enough effects belonging to him found after his death to bear the charges of his funeral." ‡

Considering the troubled state of the country, it is surprising that Bishop Gordon ventured to publish instructions in 1733 on

* Forbes-Leith, op.cit., Vol. II, p. 324.
† ibid, p. 325.
‡ Some account of the state of religion in Scotland from the year 1710 to the year 1729, by the Rev. John Thompson'. Cf. Forbes-Leith, op.cit. Vol. II, p 326.

J

how to gain the Indulgences of the Jubilee Year "by making visits to the ordinary places of meeting, or any other remarkable old places of devotion in the divers parts of the kingdom."

It was also in 1733 that a book was published in London (with a Testimonial from the Presbytery of Edinburgh), which did much harm to Catholics in Scotland. It was entitled *The Memoirs of John Gordon of Glencat, in the County of Aberdeen.* The author stated that he had spent " thirteen years in the Scots College at Paris, amongst the Scottish clergy"; explaining that his purpose was to lay bare " the absurdities and delusions of Popery"; also to give " the history of Baianism, Jansenism, and the Constitution *Unigenitus,* confuting the Infallibility of the Romish Church". An appendix contained " some short but full answers to any questions that can be proposed by a Papist". Glencat's story seems to be more or less factually true, apart from minor details, but it is fairly obvious that he was temperamentally unfitted to become a priest on the Scottish Mission, though his strange career as a penitent rendered it very great service. He never got further than the diaconate.*

Another Scottish Catholic about this time who led an unhappy life, but from different reasons to those of Gordon of Glencat, was George Douglas, second Earl of Dumbarton (1697-c1750). From his youth he wanted to be a monk or friar, and as there were no religious communities in Scotland, he wandered around the Continent, moving from one monastery to another, always short of money, and constantly borrowing from friends. He even appealed to the Pope and to James VIII. The latter advised him to find a good spiritual director, and stick to his counsel. But this was just what Dumbarton could not do. He continued to be a rolling stone until he found comparative peace at last with the Jesuits at the Scots College, Douai, where he died about 1750.

The first schism in the established Church of Scotland, which took place in 1733, did not affect Catholics. Under the leadership of the Rev. Ebenezer Erskine, a group of ministers and layfolk

* He was a nephew of Mr Robert Gordon, who had been chaplain at Gordon Castle from 1718 to 1728. Having been educated at Scalan, he was sent to the Scots College, Paris, where he spent 13 years. The value of his often scurrilous memoirs is that he does manage to recreate the atmosphere of Paris at the time of the Jansenist controversy. Having given up his religion, Glencat became involved in the career of an adventuress who called herself the Countess of Gordon, also Countess Dalco, Madame Kempster, and other titles. He returned to Scotland with this lady, then he moved to London, where about 1742 he was reconciled with the Church by Bishop Challoner. He took up business as a wine-merchant and acted as London agent for the Scottish Vicars-Apostolic and the Scots College, Paris. His status was irregular owing to the existence of a Mrs Gordon, who did not die until 1765. He helped several priests who had abandoned their status; also former clerical students who were in London, concealing their Catholicism. Among them was James Gibb (1682-1754), who became an architect, best known for his London church of St. Martin's-in-the-Fields. Glencat died on November 1, 1770.

formed themselves into what was called 'The Associate Presbytery'. Bishop Gordon and his clergy were in contact with some of the Nonjuring Episcopalians, for most of them were staunch Jacobites, though broken up into three factions because of differences over details of ritual and ceremonial. *

Mr Alexander Smith appointed coadjutor for the Lowland District, 1735.

After the death of Bishop Wallace in 1733 it was expected that he would be succeeded as coadjutor by Colin Campbell, one of the Campbells of Lochnell, and a brother to Sir Duncan. He had been reconciled with the Church at Aberdeen in 1716, as a young man. Bishop Gordon had a high opinion of this convert and sent him to the Scots College, Paris, where he was ordained priest in 1722. On his return to Scotland he accompanied the Bishop on his Visitations of the Highlands and Islands, his great asset being native Gaelic speech. Campbell got the wrong side of his Bishop, and started behind the scenes negotiations in high places to secure his nomination as successor to Bishop Wallace. But he was passed over in favour of Mr Alexander Smith, whose consecration as titular Bishop of Misinopolis in Turkey took place in Edinburgh on November 13, 1735. †

Bishop Smith took up his residence in Aberdeen, where he remained until 1741, when he moved to Edinburgh.

The Jansenist Controversy

The 'auld alliance' between Scotland and France had often done more good than harm in the past, and such was the case during the second half of the seventeenth century when the professors and students of the Scots College, Paris, were inevitably affected by Gallican and Jansenist opinions, as were all Catholics in France to a greater or lesser degree, except when they were directly opposed to these tendencies.

---

* Thomas Innes, who became Vice-Principal of the Scots College, Paris, in 1727, was a close friend of Dr. Gilbert Wauchope, an Edinburgh Catholic who lived in London, and who acted as agent between the Dutch Jansenists and a group of non-jurors, some of whom regarded their nonconformist sect as the 'Orthodox British Church' and were hopeful of bringing about union between themselves and the Russian Orthodox Church. (Cf. C. B. Moss, The Old Catholic Movement, its Origins and History, 2nd ed. 1964); and B. Skechley, A.A., 'The English Non-Jurors and the Orthodox Church, in Unitas, Winter number 1960, pp. 232-8).

† Alexander Smith was born at Fochabers in 1684. He entered the Scots College, Paris, at the age of 14, and returned to Scotland as a deacon in 1709. His ordination to the priesthood took place at Preshome on Easter Eve, 1712. Having worked on the Mission for six years, he became Procurator at the Scots College, Paris, retaining this office for ten years, when Mr Carnegie (alias Hall) took his place. By 1730 he was back in Scotland, working in Angus. His health broke, so he was glad of a retreat in his old college, where news reached him that Propaganda had nominated him coadjutor to Bishop Gordon.

Gallicanism, so it should be explained, is a collective name for the body of doctrine which asserted the more or less complete freedom of the Catholic Church from the ecclesiastical authority of the Papacy. This opinion can be traced back to about three hundred years after the death of Charlemagne in 814. Gallicanism was being taught at the University of Paris in a primitive form during the Great Schism (1378-1417). What were known as the Four Gallican Articles, which were affirmed by the Assembly of the French clergy in 1682, were the result of a dispute between Louis XIV and Innocent XI over the appointment of bishops and the revenues of vacant sees. They were condemned by Alexander VIII in 1690, and by Louis XIV three years later, but they continued to be taught in most French seminaries, and were made a test for admission to academic degrees and public offices. Gallicanism is merely another word for Erastianism, the theory that the Church should be subordinate to the State.*

Jansenism, in the strict sense, consisted of five propositions taken from the writings of Cornelius Jansen (1585-1638), Bishop of Ypres, which were first condemned by Innocent X in 1635. Jansen maintained (1) that without a special grace from God, the performance of His commandments is impossible to men, and (2) that the operation of grace is irresistible; and hence that man is the victim of either a natural or supernatural determination, limited only by not being violently coercive. The theological teaching was outwardly expressed by a general harshness and moral rigorism.

The Jansenist movement gained many adherents among the more devout French Catholics, who realised that the Church badly needed reforming. The moral laxity of the court, also that of the private lives of many of the bishops and clergy, was enough to make any serious-minded person a Jansenist. The heresy was an almost inevitable reaction from the Humanism of the Counter-Reformation, which tried to make the practice of religion as easy as possible. Jansenism, on the other hand, was a dour, dreich presentation of Christianity. Its asceticism was nothing if not rigorous. There were few pleasures which were not regarded as sinful. Priests often abstained from celebrating Mass for long periods as a penance. Among layfolk the habit of voluntary abstention from the sacraments came to be regarded as a mark of sanctity. No Jansenist was so holy as Monsieur de Paris, the deacon who was said to have passed two years without even making his Easter Duties.

In 1713 Clement XI condemned all the substantive tenets of Jansenism in the bull *Unigenitus*, which reaffirmed several previous papal denunciations of the heretical opinions. The more rigid Jansenists refused to accept the bull, and were persecuted. Some

* Under the Stuarts the doctrine of the divine right of Kings was upheld, not only by Catholics, but also by non-juring Anglicans, and was, indeed, the religious basis of Gallicanism.

took refuge in the Netherlands, where Jansenism was at first tolerated, and then encouraged by successive Vicars-Apostolic. In 1723
the Dutch Jansenists repudiated papal authority and nominated
for themselves a schismatic Archbishop of Utrecht. Such was the
origin of the present-day Old Catholic Church in Holland. *

Most of the professors and students at the Scots College, Paris,
were swept up into the Gallican and Jansenist movements, and
none more so than Thomas Innes (1661-1744). † He acquired
his first-hand knowledge of Jansenism with the Cistercian nuns
of Port-Royal; and had also acted as assistant to the *curé* of the
parish there, whose austerities were much talked about. This is
how Thomas Innes obtained his admiration for Jansenist piety,
but what must be remembered is that he was a historian before all
else, interested in facts rather than ideas. In 1733, for the sake
of peace, he left the Scots College, and stayed with Lord Edward
Drummond, who was an ardent Jansenist. ‡ He is justly
renowned for his contributions to Scottish historical scholarship.
His death took place after a long period of illness at the Scots
College, on January 28, 1744, aged eighty-two. §

On the other hand, it must not be supposed that the Scots College at Paris represented the religion of the majority of Catholics in
Scotland during the first quarter of the eighteenth century, even if
the austerity of the lives of many of the missionary priests might
suggest that they were Jansenists at heart. Only a minority of them
had been trained in France. In 1733 a certain number of priests
wanted Bishop Gordon to enforce signing a document accepting the
bull *Unigenitus,* but he would not do so. His opinion was that
on the whole the Jansenist heresies were not prevalent among either

* From this body many small schismatic sects have evolved. After 1870
the Church of Utrecht linked up with the Old Catholics in Germany and
Switzerland. (Cf. C. B. Moss, *The Old Catholic Movement* (2nd ed. 1964);
and P. F. Anson, *Bishops at Large* (1964).

† See p. 85 note *. The second son of James Innes, he was sent to
France at the age of 15, entering the Paris College in 1691. He soon showed
exceptional gifts as a historian, and was appointed Prefect of Studies in
1701. So far as his letters show—there are more than 600 of them in the
Blairs College archives—the Jansenist interest began quite late. Accusations against him started about 1719. In his later letters until his death
in 1744, Innes became quite indiscreet and partisan on theological matters.

‡ Lord Edward firmly believed in the supposed miracles performed at
the grave of the deacon, François de Paris, who died in 1727. He was buried
in the cemetery attached to the Church of Saint-Médard in Paris, where
some very strange things occurred. In 1732 the cemetery had to be closed
by the police on account of the mass-hysteria of the convulsionaries. Hence
the famous epigram affixed to the gateway: *"De parte du Roi défense à
Dieu de faire miracles en ce lieu".* There were other Scottish Jacobites
who believed in the 'miracles' alleged to have been performed by the
Jansenist deacon after his death. (Cf. Ruth Clark, *Strangers and Sojourners
at Port Royal* (Cambridge, 1932), pp. 247-51; and R. A. Knox, *Enthusiasm*
(Oxford, 1950), pp. 375-6).

§ The *Innes Review,* from which so many quotations are made in this
book, derives its name from this missionary priest and historian. It is the
organ of the Scottish Catholic Historical Association.

the clergy or the laity, so action was unnecessary. Eventually he gave way, imposed a formula, and requested his priests to sign it. This was reported to Propaganda on March 29, 1734. *

That same year, Mr Colin Campbell, possibly realising that there was no hope of his being raised to the episcopate, organised a meeting of disgruntled priests at Clashmore in Glenlivet. Among them was Mr John Tyrie, who, with Campbell, concocted a plot against Bishop Gordon. Also present was a Benedictine monk, Dom. Marianus Brockie, who had been Superior at Erfurt from 1719 to 1727, and who worked on the Mission from that year until 1739.† The year following the Clashmore meeting a scandal occurred and Tyrie was banished to Morar. He soon managed to get abroad, and Campbell followed him. Both made their way to Rome so that they could air their grievances against Bishop Gordon to Propaganda, intending to accuse him of encouraging Jansenism.

At that time Jacobitism and Jansenism were closely associated. Loyalty to the 'King over the Water' resulted in not only Catholics but also the English and Scottish Nonjurors taking refuge in France, where they were welcomed by Gallican-minded bishops and priests. ‡ When Thomas Innes was in London supervising the publication of his *Critical Essays* which were published in 1729, his host was Gilbert Wauchope, a doctor of medicine, one of the Catholic Wauchopes of Niddrie Marischal, near Edinburgh. The doctor and his nephew acted as intermediaries between the Dutch Jansenists and the English Nonjurors. § It may be doubted if Bishop Gordon was aware that the then Vice-Principal of the Scots College at Paris was keeping company with Jansenists in London. Either at the Wauchopes', or at the bookseller's, Innes became acquainted with Pierre-Francois Courayer (1691-1776), a Canon Regular of Sainte-Geneviève, Paris. After the French bishops had finally condemned his treatise defending the validity of Anglican ordinations (first published in 1723), excommunicating him at the same time, he sought refuge in England in 1728. Here he spent the rest of his life, dependent on Anglican charity, though he never abandoned communion with Rome for that of Canterbury. ** Then, as today, the Ecumenical Movement sometimes leads to contacts between strange people, and such were some of Thomas Innes's friends, a few also being on friendly relations with the other professors at the Scots College, Paris.

After Charles-Vintmille de Luc succeeded the ever vacillating

* Cf. Bellesheim, op.cit. Vol. IV, p. 202, note 1.

† Another trouble-maker behind the scenes was Dom Wm. MacGregor, a monk of Würzburg, who had been a missionary from about 1724 to 1730.

‡ Cf. Henry Broxap, *The Later Non-Jurors* (Cambridge, 1924).

§ Innes also met the abbés Etemare and Le Gros, who had been sent to England by Archbishop Wuytiers, in the hope of obtaining the support of the Vicars-Apostolic for the now Schismatic Church of Utrecht.

** Cf. E. Préclin, *L'Union des Eglises gallicanes et anglicanes* (Paris, 1928).

Chapel of the Scots College, Paris (1672).

Cardinal de Noailles as Archbishop of Paris in 1729, the civil authorities began to interfere with bishops and priests who were reported to have given the sacraments to persons suspected of Jansenism, often refusing them Christian burial. The Scots College thus became almost the last stronghold of the heresy in Paris.

On January 2, 1736, Abbot Bernard Baillie of Ratisbon wrote a strongly worded letter to Propaganda, obviously based on information from the two monks mentioned above, in which he mentioned "ravenous wolves in sheep's clothing", who under the pretext of restoring pure doctrine and primitive discipline, were causing parties and divisions among Scottish Catholics.* It was clear enough that the Abbot was attacking the Scots College, Paris, as the source of the troubles. This, however, was not the only information which reached Propaganda.

Mr John Tyrie and Mr Colin Campbell had wasted no time after their arrival in Rome from Scotland, though their welcome had not been too cordial. They were bold enough to denounce Bishop Hugh Macdonald for not having signed the formula against Jansenism. † It was not long before the Roman authorities began to suspect these two Scottish priests with a grievance. Their next step was to denounce the Congregation of the Holy Office, i.e. the Inquisition, for encouraging heresy. But Tyrie and Campbell did not know Rome very well, and they were double-crossed in their machinations. Tyrie tried to get at a minor official of Propaganda, who listened to his stories, having known him in the past as a fellow student. He promised the fullest support, but what he actually did was to repeat the gist of the conversations to the other side, in the person of Mr Stuart, the Roman Agent. The latter's opinion of the so-called 'Pilgrims' was summed up in the words: "They are sib Kilpit's swine, for wherever they are they'll aye have their nebb in an ill turn."

Detailed instances of false statements and even of direct substitution of documents by forgeries were discovered eventually by Propaganda. Having gained nothing by their 'pilgrimage' to Rome, Campbell and Tyrie made their way back to Scotland where they got a cold reception from the clergy.

The Visitation of the Scots College, Paris, 1736

Propaganda could not dismiss all these charges made against the bishops and other clergy of the Scottish Mission.   In the autumn of 1736, the Secretary of the Congregation wrote to the Nuncio in Paris, Mgr. Raneiro Dolci, titular Archbishop of Rhodes,

---

* Bernard Baillie was a professor of philosophy at Erfurt from 1698 to 1717, then director of the seminary at the Scots monastery at Ratisbon. He was elected abbot in 1721, and died in 1743. He was also President of the University of Salzburg.

† Later on the Bishop proved that this was a lie.

requesting him to examine into and report on the state of the Scots College.

The status of this College was peculiar; it had been given a royal charter after its foundation in 1602, and papal privileges had been conceded by Paul V and Urban VII in 1617 and 1643, but it was not a so-called 'pontifical college', like the Scots College in Rome. Strictly speaking it was only the Prior of the Carthusian monastery in Paris who had the right to make a visitation, because the College had been put under his immediate jurisdiction after the death of Archbishop Beaton in 1603. Had the Archbishop of Paris been asked to conduct the visitation, the consent of the King would have been necessary. According to Gallican principles even the Pope needed royal approval to interfere. Clement XII was in his eighty-fifth year, growing blind and often bed-ridden. There had been more than enough trouble with Louis XV and the Church in France, involving several papal bulls and briefs against Gallicanism and Jansenism, so it can be understood why the Congregation of Propaganda, which of course had no jurisdiction in a Catholic nation like France, with a state-controlled Church, could not act directly; in fact, the Congregation had no authority to entrust business in Paris to anybody. Even the Nuncio could only deal with the Scots College as a French educational establishment under royal patronage, not as a seminary for training priests for the Scottish Mission. Most of the French bishops, and certainly Louis XV, could have protested that visitation was a violation of Gallican principles, which were still taught openly.

Archbishop Dolci happened to be away from France at that moment, so the Visitation was carried out by a young Italian monsignore, Niccolò Lercari, who belonged to a Genoese family which had produced several distinguished ecclesiastical diplomats. He would have found no difficulty in investigating the private as well as the public lives of everybody connected with the Scots College, from the Principal down to the servants. All he had to do was consult the then Lieutenant-General of the Police—René Hérault. * The Paris police of the *ancien régime* was a highly organised body with its own detectives and spies (known as *mouchards*). At one time it was reckoned that a quarter of the maids and lackeys in the city added to their wages by domestic espionage. We may be certain that Hérault had a detailed dossier on every man and woman in Paris suspected of Jansenism, as well as of crimes and trivial offences. † Had Lercari wanted to evade a visitation, likely to be difficult, he could have asked the

---

* His Predecessor, Marc-René de Voyer de Paulmay, Marquis d'Argenson, had taken a leading part in the suppression of the Abbey of Port-Royal in 1707, followed by the digging up of the corpses of all deceased nuns, and carting them away as heretical.

† It was he himself who pinned the famous epigram on the gate of the graveyard at Saint-Médard forbidding Jansenist miracles by order of the King (See p. 133 note ‡.)

Lieutenant-General of the Police to obtain a *lettre de cachet* from Louis XV. The rest would have been easy: the armed *sergents* and *archers* could have arrested the professors and dismissed the students without the nunciature being implicated in any way.

It did not take long, however, for Lercari to collect more than enough gossip and scandal to work up into a Report. On March 4, 1737, he transmitted to Propaganda an impressive-looking document written in Italian.* On its face-value this Report was nothing if not convincing. It started off by stating that there was no doubt that pure Jansenism was being taught at the College, that the professors had shown no signs of submitting to the Constitution *Unigenitus* (1713), and that five years later they had the temerity to appeal to a future General Council. This in itself was more than enough proof that the College was tainted with Gallicanism as well as Jansenism. Next certain individuals were mentioned by name, including the Procurator, Charles Whytford, and the Prefect of Studies, Thomas Innes. Lercari explained that: "Thomas later resigned that office to his brother George, and there is also there Lewis Innes, their uncle, known as the Abbé, and formerly almoner to James II. These three Inneses, all alike Jansenists, joined Whytford on the appeal, and they have always resided in the College. There is no doubt that Whytford has recalled his appeal, but the act has not been published in Paris, where he would be bound to repair the scandal which he has caused. It is not known that George Innes or Alexander Gordon, the present Prefect of Studies, has made an act of acceptation of the bull [*Unigenitus*], so that little regard should be paid to the letter subscribed by them in 1735, and sent in order to justify themselves in the eyes of the Sacred Congregation; and the more so, as they keep up the same correspondence as before with the Jansenists, and are entirely dependent on Thomas and Lewis Innes, the latter being themselves appellants, and retaining absolute power over the community, in which to the opinion of all the Catholics of Paris, Jansenism is taught just as much as it formerly was."

The young Italian diplomat showed no discretion in what he wrote about Thomas Innes, and said: "Not only as Prefect of Studies did he insinuate the very contrary to Catholic doctrines, but being at the same time confessor at St Barbe, he brought thither his students to perform their spiritual exercises, and to receive Jansenist instructions which were at that time being given there; nor is it known that he has since changed his opinions."

The statements about Lewis Innes almost amounted to libel and defamation of character, for Lercari was bold enough to inform Propaganda that "He has perverted the Scots, who are residing at the royal palace at Saint-Germain-en-Laye, and he is at the moment the director of all those families, and regarded by

---

* An extract of the Italian original was given by Bellesheim, op.cit. Vol. IV, appendix XVIII, pp. 408-13.

them all as their apostle. Among his disciples is my Lord Milton, and, to still greater extent, his relation, my Lord Perth*, who is so far committed in favour of Jansenism that he would not even be present at the mission given last year by the Jesuits in the city of Saint-Germain, retiring during that time to Paris, to the Scots College. From this it can be inferred how much harm had been, and is still being done by this Lewis in the College, where he is looked on as an oracle."

Incriminating evidence was piled up, paragraph by paragraph but reading between the lines it is impossible not to wonder how much of it was based on the tales of *agents-provocateurs*. Reference was made to certain students who had been expelled from the College, also to others who had received holy orders outside the Archdiocese of Paris, so that they did not have to sign the formula against Jansenism. It was insinuated that priests who came on from the Scots College, Rome, had stayed in Paris "to be instructed in controversy and morals" before starting missionary work in Scotland, and became "in consequence imbued with the errors of Jansenism." † Lercari insisted that the first measure of an urgently needed reform of the Paris College would be the instant removal of the three Inneses. Although the Italian monsignore had no first-hand knowledge of Scotland, and was merely the acting-secretary of the Paris nunciature, he had the audacity to write: "There are but few missionaries, and of these a large proportion are affected with Jansenism. Among the most notorious are Alexander Drummond, who refused to subscribe to the formulary; Andrew Hacket, and Robert Gordon, authors of a catechism since condemned at Rome; George Gordon of Scalan, who published a letter contesting the authority of the Church; Patrick Leith, known in Edinburgh by the impious lectures he has delivered against the Apostolic decrees; George Duncan, brought up in the seminary at Scalan, and taught by Innes and Paris; and John Gordon, who refused to sign the formulary, and is now publishing in Scotland an account of the pretended miracles of Monsieur Paris." ‡

Niccolo Lercari showed his want of caution even more by going on to accuse the seventy-one-year-old Bishop Gordon of "not being untainted with Jansenism . . . According to report, he has led away many Catholics [in the Lowlands]; he has employed on the Mission disaffected ecclesiastics, without ensuring himself of

---

* The "Lord Perth" mentioned was James, the 3rd titular Duke, who succeeded his father, who died at Paris, in 1720. He was wounded at the Battle of Culloden in 1745, and died unmarried during his passage to France, and was succeeded as 4th titular Duke by his only brother, Lord John Drummond, whose estates were forfeited.

† Lercari felt it worthwhile to mention John Law, "the notorious Scotsman, who possessed such influence in France at the time of the Regency, that he gave the College a large quantity of bank shares or notes". (See p. 116 note †).

‡ The Jansenist deacon, mentioned already, who died in 1727.

their submission to the Constitution. He permits Catholics to read books written by Jansenists, notwithstanding that many of the more fervent Catholics have represented to him the evil that results from such permission; he gives every token of partiality for the suspected clergy; he keeps up a close correspondence with Thomas and Lewis Innes; he has constantly sent youths to the College at Paris, although he cannot have been in ignorance of the errors taught there; he has examined and approved of the before-mentioned catechism, which has already been condemned in Rome; he has opposed, more than anyone else, the subscription of the formula sent from Rome—and finally, he has chosen for his coadjutor, Mr Alexander Smith, a man much suspected in these parts, and fearing to find his choice opposed, he has obtained his appointment, and consecrated him, without any of the Catholics knowing anything about it." *

So the accusations and insinuations continued, line after line, always in the same tone. The ordinary reader would have formed the impression that the Catholic Mission in Scotland was riddled with heresy, and that hardly a priest was not suspect. Lercari warned Propaganda that if Bishop Smith were to succeed Bishop Gordon as Vicar-Apostolic of the Lowland District "the Mission would greatly suffer". He had no hesitation in stating that it was already "in a very bad state". Almost the only cleric for whom he had a good word was Bishop Hugh Macdonald, of whom he wrote: "He has been spoken of to me with the highest praise, as well with regard to doctrine, as to his true zeal for religion, so that the most entire reliance can be placed in his orthodoxy." This is surprising, because the first Vicar-Apostolic of the Highland District had been one of the first pupils at the suspect college at Scalan. His subsequent studies had been conducted at Paris, where he was under the influence of the Innes brothers.   The long Report ended with the affirmation that nothing had been achieved by the creation of two vicariates for Scotland in 1731, and that "all the more fervent missionaries" were hoping that they would soon be re-united under one Vicar-Apostolic, as had been the case from 1694 to 1727.

What is noticeable about the whole Report is that no documentary evidence was produced for any of the accusations made. They appear to have been based merely on the verbal statements of persons consulted.   So far as they deal with the Paris College, it is fairly safe to conclude that most of the information was supplied by the Police, whose duties ranged from the inspection of brothels, gaming-houses, hospitals and prisons, to the perusal of theological books for signs of heresy. A specially close watch

---

* Considering that the briefs, nominating this priest to the office of Bishop, had been drawn up by Propaganda and sent off from Rome on September 19, 1735, Lercari's statements must have surprised the cardinals when they read the Report.

was kept over all aliens, and even the mistresses maintained by English or Scots *milords* were duly noted down in the dossiers. The junior member of the corps diplomatique, had he bribed the police, may have found the visitation of the Scots College much easier than other jobs which fell to him in the absence of the Nuncio.

The Report failed to convince Cardinal Riviera and the officials of Propaganda that things were as bad as Lercari made them out to be. They discovered that the source of most of his Scottish information was Colin Campbell, whose statements, as they were probably aware already, could not be taken as conclusive. It was well known in Rome that this priest had a grudge against Bishop Gordon, and that his judgment was biased. Campbell had used his considerable knowledge (though his learning was not very great), and he was hampered by having no Italian and no fluency in Latin, to defame Mr Robert Strachan, the priest who had reconciled him with the Church. Having been trained at the Scots College, Paris, Campbell had little difficulty in understanding the reputation of the Ineses. John Tyrie was less guilty, being merely Campbell's understudy—indispensable to him because he spoke Italian as a student at the Scots College, Rome, from 1711 to 1719. It was Tyrie who put into tolerable but not very correct Italian Campbell's long and mainly calumnious reports.*

The results of Lercari's Report on the Scots College, Paris.

So far as the *'Collège des Ecossais'* was concerned, the immediate effect of Mgr. Lercari's Report was that it ceased to be a seminary for training priests for the Mission. For the next twenty-six years the professors merely devoted themselves to the education of the sons of Jacobite noblemen and landed-gentry. They took the line that the students had never been compelled, only encouraged, to adopt the ecclesiastical state. More than ever before this high-class educational establishment in the Rue des Fosses Saint-Victor, which was under royal patronage, served as the *rendezvous* for the 'Scots Colony' in Paris. It became a hot-bed of Jacobite plotting for the restoration of the Stuart dynasty;

---

* On his return to Scotland, Tyrie was sent to Tombae in Glenlivet, where he remained until 1745, when he became a chaplain to the Glenlivet and Strathavon contingent of Gordon of Glenbucket's regiment. He followed Prince Charles into England, and remained with him until after the Battle of Culloden, where he was wounded. His house was burned by the English soldiers and everything destroyed. His latter years were spent in the lonely Cabrach of Banffshire, where he died at Shenval in 1755.

Campbell, who left Rome with Tyrie in 1738, was sent by Bishop Hugh Macdonald to work in the Highlands. He joined the Jacobite forces as chaplain in 1745, and died of wounds received at the Battle of Culloden. Bishop Smith wrote: "would that he could have washed out by his blood the calamities which he was the first to inflict on this most peaceful mission."

The facts recorded about Campbell and Tyrie have been taken from the collection made by Canon Clapperton about a century ago, now in the Scottish Catholic Archives. He had read all the relevant letters and documents, and discussed them with Bishop Kyle, who had already done so.

a combination of an academy and club, conducted by comfortably off clergymen.

On July 21, 1738, Clement XII, then aged eighty-six, issued a brief, worded almost identical with his apostolic letter of two years before, ordering that the Scottish missionaries, secular and regular, should subscribe to a formulary accepting the bull *Unigenitus* of 1713. This document also made reference to the Catechism, composed in 1702 by the Oratorian priest Pouget, at the request of Charles Colbert de Croissey, Bishop of Montpellier, but condemned by the Holy See in 1712 and 1721 for alleged Jansenist tendencies. How far it was ever used in Scotland is uncertain.*

Primarily the formula was directed against two humbler works— elementary catechisms for layfolk and children composed by Andrew Hackett and James Carnegie, copies of which are now very rare. Their fault was that they were mainly translations of small French books, adapted from the Montpellier Catechism, the French originals being condemned as well as the Scottish versions. †

If a verdict is required, it can only be said that the unpolished material on this delicate matter is abundant, very difficult to interpret and tedious to read, but there was little or no *theological* Jansenism in Scotland at any time. Bishop Gordon can be acquitted without a stain on his character. The Scots College, Paris, however, cannot be dismissed as innocent, because Thomas Innes, and to some extent but in varying degrees his devoted pupils were sympathisers with many Jansenists. ‡ It would also be true enough to say that Jansenist influences penetrated into many places in Scotland, as they did into most countries of Europe. §   No good purpose is served by equating hostility to the Society of Jesus with Jansenism. It is correct enough to say that all Jansenists were anti-Jesuit, this was part of their platform. But in the long run it is doubtful if the Jansenist troubles in Scotland would have occurred had it not been for that small group of rebellious priests, who in 1733 held a secret meeting in Glenlivet under the leadership of Colin Campbell and John Tyrie. They were at the root of all the scandals

---

* A sumptuously-bound copy of this large book intended for priests, a kind of Manual of Christian Doctine, which came from the Scots College, Paris, is preserved at Blairs College.

† They were printed, almost certainly in Edinburgh, though no place is stated, between 1724 and 1733.   When they were condemned in 1738, Bishops Gordon and Macdonald were directed to warn the laity against reading heretical or suspected books, and to suppress them by every possible means.

‡ If there were any Jansenists in Scotland during the first quarter of the 18th century, they would be found at Drummond Castle, Perthshire, where Mr Alexander Drummond (mentioned on p. 128) was chaplain until his death in 1742.

§ One of the last strongholds of the heresy was Tuscany, mainly because of the anti-papal policy of the Grand Duke Leopold. It lingered on in France until after Napoleon's Concordat of 1801; and even after this survived as the secret conviction of a limited number of French Catholics, especially in religious communities.

that followed, so determined were they to undermine the authority of Bishop Gordon, whose declining years were much disturbed by the long drawn-out controversy.

Bishop Gordon's last eight years as Vicar-Apostolic of the Lowland District, 1738-46.

Bishop Gordon, now an old man in constant ill-health, continued to make visitations of his wide-spread Lowland Vicariate. During the summer of 1738 he arranged to replace the original huts at Scalan which formed the college by a small but decent built house. He had already bequeathed all his property for the support of the students. In 1741 they had much to suffer owing to the failure of the crops in Glenlivet and Strathavon, when many people died of starvation.

A most depressing picture of the Scottish Mission was painted in the Report sent to Propaganda on February 5, 1743. The Bishop wrote: "Alas for our misery! The conversion of heretics does not advance, nor do such examples of virtue and holy life shine forth among Catholics as was the case in past times, in those bygone years when concord, unity and peace flourished. We have often, with great sorrow, complained of the disturbing factions and seditious combinations formed by certain of the missionaries; and would that we could at length hope that an end might be put to them, so that we might be able to breathe freely for a time, and peacefully rejoice in the work of our sacred office. But they do not cease with their seditious and turbulent language to disturb the mission, and greatly to obstruct the progress of the faith. For while, on the one hand, they harass by their malicious arts the best and most useful of our missionaries, on the other they deceive themselves and impose upon some of the younger clergy by their calumnies, seducing such of their penitents as are weak or ill-disposed to underhand suspicions and whispered insinuations, and turning them against the others." *

A contemporary reader of this Report might well have formed the opinion that, so far as dissentions were concerned, the Episcopalians, the Papists, and the nonconformist Presbyterians were all on much the same level.

Freemasonry was gaining adherents all over Europe at this time. The Grand Lodge of England had been founded in 1717, and that of Scotland in 1736. Two years later, three months before Clement XII made his second demand on the Scottish missionaries to subscribe to the formula against Jansenism, he condemned the anti-Christian spirit of the secret society of Freemasons in the bull ' In eminenti '. At that time the Pope inflicted the penalty of excommunication on all its members. A fair number of broad-minded Catholics were Freemasons, and remained so in

---

* Cf. Bellesheim, op.cit. Vol. IV, appendix XV, pp. 395-9.

defiance of the papal bull.   Among them was the Scotsman, Sir
Alexander Ramsay, who became Grand Chancellor of the French
Masons in 1734.* After his death in 1743 Vespers of the Dead
was solemnly chanted in the parish church at Saint-Germain-en-
Laye. Among the mourners was Charles Ratcliffe, Earl of
Derwentwater, in his official capacity as Grand Master of the
Freemasons of France.

By 1745 Bishop Gordon had reached his eightieth year.   As
he recalled a half-century of mission work, he may well have
wondered what was the fate in store for Catholics in Scotland.
He could remember the Revolution of 1688, and the fall of the
Stuart dynasty. He had witnessed the Union of the Parliaments
of England and Scotland in 1707, and the failure of the Jacobite
risings in 1708 and 1715. In August 1745 came the news that
Prince Charles Edward had landed in Moidart and unfurled his
standard at Glenfinnan; in September, reports of his victory at
Prestonpans.

The Bishop was staying at Thornhill, not far from Drummond
Castle, south-west of Crieff in Perthshire, where he was being cared
for by Mrs Mary Drummond.   In January 1746 the Jacobite
troops repulsed General Hawley at Falkirk, and the Prince, moving
northwards, must have passed near Thornhill. The Bishop, however, was spared news of the final defeat at Culloden on April 16,
for his death took place on March 1. He was buried at Inner-
peffray, where there is a small collegiate church, with the tombs
of several members of the Drummond family. †   Before his body
was moved from Thornhill, an advance party of Hanoverian
soldiers attacked Drummond Castle, already partly demolished
to prevent its occupation.

The Jacobite Rising of 1745 and its effect on the
Catholic Mission in Scotland.

The doctrine that a monarch in the hereditary line of succession has a divine and indefeasible right to his kingship and
authority, and that for a subject to rebel against him is the worst
of political crimes, caused almost as much suffering to Catholics
in Scotland as the persecution they had endured for their religious
beliefs during nearly two hundred years. For a considerable
period before 1745 there had been very little violent molestation
of Papists in Scotland, although the penal laws were always
hanging over their heads and they were excluded from all civil
and military employments. Taken as a whole, they were able to
live in comparative peace.   In some of the more remote parts

---

* Ramsay had maintained that Masonry dates from the close association
of the Order with the Knights of St. John of Jerusalem, and was convinced
that the old Lodges of Scotland had preserved the secrets of true Masonry
which had been lost by the Grand Lodge of England.

† John, Lord Drummond, had endowed it with four chaplains in 1506.

of the Kingdom public worship was carried on openly. Most Catholics hoped and prayed that sooner or later the Stuart family would be restored to the throne of Britain, because they believed that this would release them and give them again the privileges of free-born citizens. But they were realistic enough to see that the moment had not arrived. For the Jacobites to attempt another rising with the aid of foreign forces would merely make things worse.   Nobody understood this better than the two Vicars-Apostolic and most of their clergy, no matter how loyal they might be to the 'King over the Water'.*

Bishop Hugh Macdonald was returning to the Highlands from Edinburgh after a meeting of the Bishops and their Procurator in July 1745. On arriving in Lorne, he met Macdonald of Kinloch Moidart, who told him that Prince Charles Edward, with no more than a handful of French troops, had already arrived off the west coast. The Bishop went on north to Moidart, where the French frigate *Dourtelle* was anchored near Borrodale on Loch-nam-Uamh. He was rowed out to the ship and introduced to the Prince, who was disguised as a priest. He informed him candidly that the country had not been expecting the invasion until the following year—that any attempt at the moment would endanger his own person and probably ruin his best friends. Although he begged him to return to France in the same ship, until there was a more favourable opportunity, 'The Young Pretender' paid no attention either to his warnings or to those given by Macdonald of Boisdale. The latter sailed back to Uist and appears to have prevented the islanders as wll as those on Barra, from rallying to the Jacobite cause.

Having landed, and moved east to Glenfinnan at the head of Loch Shiel, the Prince presided over the hoisting of the royal standard before a gathering of the clans that was a motley crowd of little more than 2,000 men. The Bishop then appointed several of his priests as chaplains to the forces. †   They wore Highland dress, with sword and pistol, and were given the rank of Captain.

After the final defeat of the Jacobite forces at Culloden on April 16, 1746, Bishop Hugh Macdonald, his brother and Lord Lovat went into hiding on Loch Morar. Some English sailors who had landed at Arisaig discovered them there and set fire to the college buildings, "merrily adorning themselves with the spoils," as is recorded.   The Bishop was taken prisoner and after brutal treatment was put aboard the ship.   Eventually he managed to escape and got across to France, where he found a refuge at the Scots College, Paris.   Although he wanted to go to Rome, he

* Cf. Forbes-Leith, op.cit. Vol. II, p. 332, where the opinions of Bishop Geddes are quoted.

† Among them were Alan Macdonald (nominated confessor to the Prince), Aeneas MacGillie, James Leslie, John Tyrie, Colin Campbell, William Grant, John Gordon. Gallus Leith, O.S.B. (later Abbot of Ratisbon), and William Grant, O.S.B.

K

was advised to remain in France, so that he might be nearer his flock and able to return to Scotland more easily when things quietened down. An Irish Franciscan offered to take him to Spain, to beg funds for the Highland Vicariate, but he felt it more prudent to remain in France. The French Government took compassion on this destitute prelate and granted him a pension, which he enjoyed until his death in 1778.

Following the Battle of Culloden, orders were issued that all Papist chapels or places where Mass was being celebrated must be demolished, and all priests arrested. A chapel in the Enzie District was one of the first to suffer. The vestments were taken to Fochabers and burned in the main street. What happened in Glenlivet is best told in the words of Bishop John Geddes: "I think it was on the morning of the 16th of May [1746] that the detachment of the troops surrounded Scalan and orders were immediately given for setting the house on fire nor was it long before these orders were executed. Mr Duthie with a sorrowful heart from one of the neighbouring hills was looking down on the affecting scene. * He saw his habitation surrounded with armed men whom he knew to be then full of barbarous fury; in a short time the smoky flames began to ascend; he would soon perceive the roof fall in and after a little while there was nothing left but ruins. This was to him and to others a dismal sight but the worst was that it seemed to be only the beginning of evils; they knew not what was to follow nor where nor when these barbarities were to end; the entire extirpation of the Catholics out of Scotland was loudly threatened and was justly to have been feared without the interposition of Divine providence in their favour. When the soldiers had completed their shocking work and done all the harm they could get done at Scalan they departed thence to carry terror and mischief to other places, and then Mr Duthie ventured down to take a nearer view of the ruins they had left, making at the same time the reflection which such circumstances would not fail to suggest." †

Next came the burning of the priest's quarters at the Bochel in Glenlivet, the chapel in Strathavon and another in Strathbogie. At Mortlach and elsewhere, vestments and furnishings went up in flames.

Many priests were arrested and imprisoned. There was wild

---

* This priest, a former student of the Scots College, Paris, had been placed in charge of Scalan in 1742, replacing Mr Alexander Gordon, who had been superior since 1736. Mr Duthie had already sent away all the students, and had hidden the vestments, sacred vessels, and other movables before the soldiers arrived at Scalan.

† Cf. W. J. Anderson, 'Scalan', in *Innes Review* (Autumn, 1963).

‡ Among the Jesuits were Frs. Charles Farquharson and his brother John; and Fr. Alexander Cameron of Lochnell. The secular priests included Mr Alan Macdonald, Mr Alexander Forrester, Mr James Grant (the future Bishop), Mr Alexander Godsman, and Mr George Duncan. Fr. Alexander Gordon, S.J. died in prison at Inverness in 1746.

plundering throughout the Highlands by the Duke of Cumberland's troops, based mainly at Inverness, Fort Augustus and Fort William. Their barbarity extended even to women and children, who were tortured and sometimes killed. The "hellish crews of red-coats" (as a contemporary Presbyterian writer called them) "who came as vermin from Flanders and England, as if the floodgates of hell had been opened, bellowing forth their horrid curses and blasphemous oaths and robbing, stealing and ruining all where they came, sheltering all their villainies with this nick-name, 'ye are rebels, though never so innocent'." *

By this time ' Bonnie Prince Charlie ', after five months of wandering around the Highlands and enduring much hardship, had sailed from Loch-nan-Uamh in a French vessel. He was disillusioned. On this same shore he had landed full of hopes thirteen months before. He did not remain long in France, for he was banished by Louis XV in 1748 after the Peace of Aix-la-Chapelle, when the war between Britain and France ended.

So terrified were countless loyal Englishmen and women of "the danger which his Majesty and all his Protestant subjects are exposed to, from the restless Plots and Machinations of the very worst set of People under heaven that profess the Christian Name, the Papists of the British Dominions," that in 1747 an anonymous writer published a pamphlet in London, addressed to the Duke of Newcastle. † Its object was to make the general public realise the " Dangers arising from Popery and Disaffection occasioned by the seizing of certain Papers in a Popish Chapel in the North-West Highlands of Scotland." ‡ They were printed in extenso, and helped to fan the flame against the 'Scarlet Woman' and 'The Beast' as nothing had done for some time.

The writer went on to explain: "Many of these People are most cruel and barbarous Thieves and Murderers, as well as Traitors. *The Pretender to His Majesty's Crown* may be truly said to have a Standing Army, ever ready for his Service. And amongst these, McDonalds more especially, will be found a great body of relentless Foes to the Protestant Name. Here the *Roman Vicar Apostolical*, and his subordinate Tools the *Missionaries*, exercise their Functions

---

* Quoted from the *Active Testimony* (1749) by Donald Maclean, *The Counter Reformation in Scotland, 1560-1930* (1931), p. 225, note 2.

† The 1st Duke (1693-1768) had been rewarded for his services against the Jacobites after 1715. He became Secretary of State under Walpole in 1724, and Prime Minister in 1756.

‡ These documents consisted of what were described as (1) "Bishop Gordon's Mandate to the Popish Clergy and Laity in the Highlands, 29th October, 1731;" (2) "Instructions for Mr John Tyrie . . . in a meeting held at the Isle of Morar, *in Montanis*, April 1735"; "List of the Popish Missionaries in the Lowlands and Highlands of Scotland, as they stood *Anno* 1740"; (4) "Articles of Agreement, dated 1st May, 1742, betwixt Bishop McDonald and his brother John McDonald, for the latter to board and maintain five Boys, and a Master to teach them"; and (5) a letter addressed "à Monsieur L'Abbé Stuart, Agent du Clergé d'Ecosse à Rome." (written in cypher).

almost as freely as if tolerated by Law, in spite of the unwearied Opposition they meet with from the legal and loyal Protestant Clergy and Schoolmasters . . ." *

Anybody having read these papers, so it was pointed out, would realise that "the *Pretender*, whom the Bishop here calls their *Sovereign*, actually directs the Affair of this Mission as a *Sovereign*, as far as his Holiness will permit any secular Sovereign to do so." There was no shadow of doubt "that every Papist in these Kingdoms" was "alike invariably, though not alike explicitly, our determined implacable Foes". Something had to be done, and that speedily, "for clearing the country of such poisonous weeds" in the shape of the five boys being educated in the Popish Seminary hidden away in "the barren Highlands," by establishing more Protestant schools, where "true Religion, Loyalty and Industry" were taught. Horror was added to horror, and in conclusion the Duke was reminded that "The Papists of the British Dominions have, in very truth, no just *Claim to Protection, while they refuse that Fidelity and Allegiance to* OUR ROYAL HEAD, *which are the implied conditions of it. That though they live amongst us, they cannot be properly said to be* of us, *since their Religion, Education, Maxims, Inclinations, Affections and Allegiances, all are* foreign; and they have nothing that *truly denotes them* BRITONS, *but their Names and Language!"* †

During the summer of 1747 Mr Duthie managed to rebuild part of the Scalan quarters, but it was not until the summer of 1749 that he was able to assemble a few students, and the Rules drawn up by Bishop Gordon in 1722 could be enforced again. It is recorded that "much prudence and caution was necessary", because until 1756 there were nearly always two parties of soldiers stationed in Glenlivet, with express orders to arrest priests wherever they could find them, and with the promise of a reward for every arrest made. Even as late as 1752 the seminary was visited one night, and a strict search was made, but Mr Duthie had been forewarned of the danger by a friendly sergeant or his wife, and got away before the ' red-coats ' arrived.

On December 13, 1747, Bishop Smith addressed a very long Report to Propaganda, stating that, in spite of great dangers, he had managed to visit most of the priests in the north, as well as those districts where Catholics were left without Mass or the sacraments because the clergy had been driven away or imprisoned. Several had died and there were no priests to replace them. He described the many chapels and houses which had been burned down by the Hanoverian soldiers. Worse than the material

---

* Letter to the Most Noble Thomas, Duke of Newcastle, p. 7.
† ibid, p. 24. Some of the sixteen cyphers given in the letter to the abbé Stuart are worth mentioning: Hamburgh—Rome; Amsterdam—Paris; Mr Cant—The Pope; The Change—Propaganda; Physician—Bishop; Birly—Jesuit; Mr Arthur—The King, i.e., the Pretender.

desolation, however, was the harm done by a handful of rebellious priests, of whom some still persisted in their errors. He begged to be given a coadjutor, adding: "It is needful that the proper remedies should be applied without delay to the evils under which clergy and people have been, and still are, suffering; for our little bark, albeit much tossed about by the waves, is by the singular goodness of God not yet overturned. If, however, it be abandoned by the Holy See, needs must that it perish."*

Having discovered that several Catholic youths had been smuggled out of Scotland to be educated abroad, the Government ordered that all priests stationed in Glenlivet, Strathdon and Donside, and anywhere else where Papists were numerous, must be arrested. These measures were directed against Bishop Smith in particular. After lying in hiding for some months, he escaped to England. For nearly a year the Lowland District was without a resident bishop. †

When this news reached Rome, the Agent, Mr Peter Grant, reported it to Propaganda and the Cardinals asked the Catholic sovereigns of Europe to order their ambassadors in London to intercede on behalf of the persecuted Scottish Catholics. Bishop Challoner, Vicar-Apostolic of the London District, managed to induce the Duke and Duchess of Norfolk to approach the Duke of Argyll, and make him realise that he ought to support the Austrian, Bavarian and Sardinian ambassadors in their negotiations with George II and his ministers. At the same time Henry Benedict, Duke of York, the younger son of James VIII, who had been ordained priest and made a cardinal in 1748, secured a fairly generous subsidy from Propaganda for the relief of the clergy in Scotland.

It was not until the summer of 1751 that Bishop Smith ventured to return to Scotland. On his arrival in Edinburgh he heard that several Catholic prisoners at Carlisle had been condemned to death, and that there was no priest there to minister to them. ‡ And this priest actually managed to get into the gaol with the Blessed Sacrament hidden on his person, heard the confession of the prisoners, and gave them Holy Communion. Then he hurried back across the Border without being molested.

Some time in 1750 the 'Young Chevalier' paid a secret visit to London, where he was reconciled with the Church of England in St Mary-le-Strand. Nine years later he published a statement in which he explained how he had made " a solemn abjuration of the Romish religion, and did embrace that of the Church of England as by Law established in the 39 Articles", in which he

---

* Cf.Bellesheim, op.cit. Vol. IV, p. 196, and appendix XVI, pp. 399-405, where the Report is given verbatim.

† Mr Alexander Gordon was nominated Pro-Vicar for the south, and Mr John Godsman for the north.

‡ Duncan had been ordained at Scalan in 1732 instead of at Paris, to avoid signing the formulary against Jansenism.

hoped to "live and die".* This event, once it became known, and the immoral life being led by 'Bonnie Prince Charlie', more than anything else dashed the last Jacobite hopes. It eliminated many of the Prince's leading supporters, not on moral grounds, but because they were firmly convinced that the Catholic lady, Clementina Walkinshaw, with whom he was living openly, was a Hanoverian spy.

In 1749 Bishop Hugh Macdonald returned to Scotland from France by way of London. He decided that it would be safer for him to remain outside the Highland Vicariate, and for the next three years he lay hidden in the Cabrach District of Banffshire. He was now an old man and much broken down by all he had been forced to endure, mainly because of his Jacobite principles.

Commissioners for Annexed Estates were appointed in 1752 to administer lands forfeited by the Jacobites and that same year, Bishop Hugh felt it safe to return to his Vicariate. Rumours were soon flying that he had been commissioned to recruit men in the Highlands for the French army and, considering his close associations with the 'rebels' in 1745, this was quite probable. He changed his name and hid himself in the Lowlands until the storm blew over.

It is hard to believe that Catholic support of the 'Forty-Five' was not a wildly imprudent and disastrous gamble. This is not because of the failure of the rising itself and the aftermath of the Battle of Culloden. If this Jacobite rebellion had succeeded, the best that could have been hoped for was the re-establishment of an anti-papal Episcopalianism. 'Bonnie Prince Charlie' had never been a pious Catholic like his father and grandfather, and he was very far from being the charming and romantic figure of popular legends. He seems to have been devoid of religious convictions, considering his " solemn abjuration of the Romish religion " for political reasons, four years after his defeat at Culloden, and his acceptance of it again later on, when it was to his material advantage. In temperament the ' Young Chevalier ' was as unstable as his great-uncle, Charles II.

What admits of no doubt is that the failure of the ' Forty-Five ' held back the progress of the Catholic Mission in Scotland for more than a quarter-of-a-century. It also led to wholesale destruction of many of the castles and country houses which had sheltered mission priests for nearly two hundred years. No real advance was made until after the Vicars-Apostolic, clergy and laity accepted the *de facto* government in 1780.

James Grant nominated coadjutor to Bishop Smith, 1755

In a Report dated November 1, 1753, Bishops Smith and Macdonald entreated Propaganda for coadjutors without further

* Cf. Sir Charles Petrie, *The Jacobite Movement (1959)*, p. 417.

delay. The former was aged seventy-one and the latter although only fifty-four, had been very ill and near death. Both realised they were unable to attend episcopal duties. Discipline of the Mission had grown lax during the troubled years after the 'Forty-Five', when so many priests were on the run, in danger of their lives. So the two Vicars-Apostolic asked if the Regulations which had recently been drawn up for the English Mission, approved by Benedict XIV on May 30, 1753, might be extended to Scotland. The Superior of the Jesuits had already promised to obey them if they became law in the Scottish Vicariates. To make the situation more difficult Abbot Bernard Stuart of Ratisbon had informed Bishops Gordon and Macdonald that all the missionary funds in Germany had been lost, and he could not train any more priests for Scotland without a guarantee of financial support from Rome.*

At home there was not a penny to spare. Some of the priests were complaining bitterly about the unfair way in which the last grant from Propaganda had been distributed. †

More than a year elapsed before word came from Rome that Mr James Grant had been nominated as coadjutor to Bishop Smith, with the style of titular Bishop of Sinita in Numidia. Born at the farm of Wester Bogs in the Enzie district of Banffshire in 1706, he had been educated at Scalan and the Scots College, Rome. After his ordination in 1734 he continued his studies in Paris, first at the Oratorian College of Notre-Dame-des-Vertus, which, unknown to him at the time, was strongly tainted with Jansenism. Having discovered this, Mr Grant transferred himself to the seminary of Saint-Nicholas-du-Chardonnet until he returned to Scotland the following year. He worked in the Braes of Lochaber, on South Uist and on Barra. In 1746 he was nearly arrested at Castlebay, Barra, by the crew of an English ship, but managed to escape to a nearby island where he eventually was captured, taken to the mainland and imprisoned first at Mingary Castle and later in the common gaol at Inverness. Having been liberated he retired to his brother's farm in Banffshire to regain his health. Then he was put in charge of Catholics in the coastal parish of Rathven, where he remained until he was informed of his election to the episcopate. After his secret consecration by Bishop Smith as titular Bishop of Sinita (an ancient port in Algeria) in Edinburgh on All Souls Day, November 2, 1755, Bishop Grant usually resided at Preshome until 1761, when he moved to Aberdeen.

As to Bishop Macdonald, he was arrested again a few weeks after Bishop Grant's consecration, and only released from prison on giving bail for a large sum of money. He was ordered to remain

---

* Abbot Stuart had to resign his office in December 1753 for other reasons than finance and ill health, and died in Italy two years later. He was succeeded by Dom Gallus Leith, who had been a Jacobite chaplain in the 'Forty-Five'. (See p. 145 note *.)

† Cf. Bellesheim, op.cit., Vol. IV, p. 198; also appendix XVII, pp. 405-8.

at Duns in Berwickshire until called for. His trial took place in Edinburgh early in 1756, when he was accused of being by habit and repute a Popish priest. Yet it could be proved only that he was a bishop, and his advocates pleaded that the laws against priests did not apply to prelates. This legal quibbling occasioned a long delay and consultation with lawyers in London. Finally a sentence of banishment was given against him. It is not clear how he managed to stay on in Scotland, but having changed his name, first to Mackenzie, and then to Scott, he slipped away to the North-East. For about four years he lodged with Mr Thomas Brockie at Shenval in the Cabrach. In the summer months the Bishop ventured to make secret visitations of parts of the Highland Vicariate. After the death of Mr Brockie in 1759, he generally spent the winter months with Gordon of Dorlethen at Auchintoul, beside the Deveron, near Marnoch. The Highland Vicariate was in sore need of priests. Again and again Bishop Macdonald begged the Roman Agent without success to send him some Irish Franciscans.

During the seventeen-fifties the two Vicars-Apostolic must often have been driven nearly desperate, what with the lack of missionaries, and never enough money to maintain them. Bishop Grant had no choice but to remain at Preshome, and could give little help to the aged and infirm Bishop Smith. The Scots College, Paris, which, as has been stated already, had ceased to train youths for the priesthood, required a new prefect of studies. Only two priest were left there: Mr Gordon, the Principal, and Mr Ruddock, the Procurator. Eventually Mr William Duthie, who was still in charge of the college of Scalan, was sent to Paris. In 1758 Bishop Macdonald managed to visit France again. After his return he wrote to Cardinal Spinelli that he was "now an old man, much broken down by the fatigues of his office and hardships of these disturbed times." He renewed his appeal for a coadjutor, but had to wait another three years before it was granted.

The religious condition of the Highlands during the 1750s

Taken all round the cause of Protestantism had gained little from the brutal efforts made by the Duke of Cumberland and his red-coats to quell the rebellious Highlanders, the majority of whom were Papists. In 1755 Dr Alexander Webster had compiled a census in which he estimated that the total of Romanists in Scotland was 16,303. *   It is not easy to see how these figures were

* He arranged them in the following groups:—
Presbytery of Edinburgh, 185; Presbytery of Dumfries, 35; Presbytery of Kirkcudbright, 261; Presbytery of Lanark and Renfrew, 5; Presbytery of Stirling and Clackmannan, 10; Fife, 8; Kincardineshire, 17; Perthshire, 194; Aberdeenshire, 2,200; Banffshire, 3,150; Elginshire, 90; Inverness-shire, including Outer Isles, 5,664; Ross-shire, 20; Argyllshire, including Kilmonivaig and small Isles, 4,329; (MS 89, National Library, Edinburgh (quoted by Maclean, op.cit. pp 230-1); see also figures in *Scottish Population Statistics*, ed. by James Gray Kyd (Edinburgh, Scottish History Society, 3rd Series, Vol. XLIII, 1952).

correct, but they give a general idea of the Catholic population of Scotland at the middle of the eighteenth century.   In spite of constant persecution, there had been a fairly steady increase since the Revolution of 1688-9.   For instance the number of Catholics in the Highlands and Islands had been doubled in about fifty years—an increase from 5,417 to 10,187 in the same area. In the Lowlands the numbers had risen only from 527 to 766.

In 1760 the General Assembly appointed two ministers to investigate the religious state of the Gaelic-speaking parts of Scotland.   They submitted a report the following year, when Mr John Walker, the parish minister of Moffat, was chosen by the Trustees of the Annexed Estates (set up in 1752 to visit the Highlands and Islands so that a better idea could be obtained of their spiritual and moral condition. The first of his reports did not appear until 1765.   It conveyed the impression that in most districts "the Popish Religion " was visibly increasing, due to "the assiduity of the Roman priests ", whose "Foreign Education ", and "politik Religion " gave them a dangerous influence "over the minds of the people".   In Glenmoriston and certain other parts of Inverness-shire Protestantism "was decaying and Popery increasing".   Mr Walker continued: "As Popery prevails, every attempt towards the moral and civil improvement of the inhabitants will meet with obstruction, and even the progress of the arts of industry will be prevented . . . The baleful influence of the Popish religion, wherever it is generally professed, is visible even in the face of the country.   There not only the morals and the manners of the people, but the very soil is more rude and uncultivate . . ."

This Lowland minister attributed the growth of Romanism in the Highlands to "the relaxation in the execution of the penal laws against the priests and people of that communion, and the vast extent of the parishes.   The execution of the penal laws is what no good men would wish to see, if the hurtful consequences they are meant to obviate can be prevented by other methods; and it seems more worthy of the constitution of this Kingdom, and of the Church of Scotland, to obtain the end proposed to them by more generous and humane ones, if by such the means can be obtained."

Dr Hyndman, who was the first minister sent to the Highlands, reckoned that there were 11,120 Papists among the total population of 110,307.*   Four secular priests and two Jesuits were ministering to widely scattered flocks. They had to contend all the time with the increasing efforts being made by the teachers and catechists maintained by the S.P.C.K. and Royal Bounty Committee. Some of those employed by the former organisation were fully trained for their work. It is related that they had to be "men of piety, loyalty, prudence, gravity, competent knowledge

---

* Bishop Hugh Macdonald's estimate of his flock in 1762 was "as near as he could judge, 12,000", so there was not much difference between the Protestant and Catholic reckonings.

of literature, and other Christian and other necessary qualifications suited to their respective stations." They were commissioned to make " the full light of the Gospel shine everywhere, and its teaching communicated to all who sit in darkness"— as Papists were presumed to be. Convinced that " Popery, the foe of liberty, which enslaves and mind and corrupts the heart", was making " daily and too successful attacks " on the innocent Highland folk, these lay-preachers and catechists, who were all well paid for their evangelistic labours, went on striving " to diffuse the principles of a religion which alone make loyal subjects, useful citizens, and good men ". Some of them were handicapped because they could not speak the barbarous language of these ignorant and uncouth men, women and children. They regarded the Bishop of Diana *in partibus* and his priests in much the same way as St Paul and his disciples looked on Demetrius and other workmen who made silver shrines of the Goddess Diana.* Popery must be driven out of the Highlands and Islands, but not with an uproar.

The more enlightened ministers, who were keeping themselves informed about current affairs, could afford to be benevolent towards Papists, for they had reason to believe that Romanism as a system would die a natural death, sooner or later. Throughout western Europe hostility towards the Jesuits was rapidly developing into open antagonism against papal domination. " It was a complex movement, in which Bourbon absolutism and other governmental autocracy, the effects of Jansenist hostility to the Society of Jesus, the influence of the free-thinking and free-living 'Philosophies' and 'Encyclopaedists', and the underground ferment of the coming Revolution all had their part." † Both the S.P.C.K. and the Royal Bounty Committee may have felt that God was working in a mysterious way to bring about the final downfall of Babylon the great, with whom the kings of the earth have committed fornication." ‡ On the other hand it was fortunate that in 1761 another schism had taken place in the Church of Scotland, when the so-called 'Relief Kirk' was established.§

Mr John Macdonald consecrated as coadjutor to Bishop Hugh Macdonald, 1761

Benedict XIV had been succeeded as Pope by Clement XIII on July 6, 1758. George II had died on October 25, 1760, and his grandson, George III, was now King of England, Scotland and Ireland. The following year Henry, Cardinal of York, the younger brother of ' Bonnie Prince Charlie ', was nominated Bishop of Frascati, and about the same time Propaganda finally gave Bishop

---

* Cf. Act, XIX, 24-41.
† Donald Attwater, *A Dictionary of the Popes* (1939), p. 286.
‡ *Rev.* XVIII, 2-3.
§ It had been preceded by the sect known as the Glassites in 1730, with a sub-schism called Sandemanians, sometimes referred to as the 'Kail Kirk' because of its agapes of vegetable broths.

Hugh Macdonald a coadjutor in the person of his nephew, Mr John Macdonald.

Son of Donald Macdonald of Ardnamurchan and Catherine Macdonald of Morar, Bishop Hugh's sister, the new Bishop was born in 1727. He was sent to the Scots College, Rome, in 1743, and after his ordination in 1752, worked in Lochaber for two years. Then he was sent to South Uist, where he received the news of his appointment. Crossing the Minch, he made his way to Banffshire, and after a retreat at Scalan, he was consecrated at Preshome by his aged uncle, assisted by Bishops Smith and Grant, on September 27, 1761, with the title of Bishop of Tiberiopolis in Phrygia (Asia Minor). *

Indulgences granted for the Jubilee Year, 1762.

In 1762, the year after Bishop John Macdonald's consecration at Preshome, Britain declared war against Spain, and the suppression of the Society of Jesus was being urged in France by many influential people. It was also a Jubilee Year at Rome, so Bishop Smith decided to write a pastoral letter to the clergy of the Lowland Vicariate, explaining how some Plenary Indulgences could be obtained by the faithful. This was the first attempt made in the post-Reformation Scottish Mission to encourage more frequent reception of the sacraments of Confession and Holy Communion.† This pastoral letter also directed layfolk how to administer Baptism when no priest was available, and warned priests to make sure that people were really dead before they were buried hastily.

Bishop Smith's Report on the Lowland Vicariate, 1763.

In 1763, Bishop Smith, now in his eighty-first year, sent a detailed Report of the Lowland Vicariate to Propaganda. ‡ The total number of Catholics was given as 6,279. § They were served by eighteen priests, of whom eleven were seculars, and seven regulars, i.e. six Jesuits, and one Benedictine. It was reckoned that about 1,000 Catholics had been either banished, killed, or fled from Scotland after the 'Forty-Five'. **

Based at Edinburgh, and covering an area of about twenty miles around the city, were Mr Alexander Gordon, and two Jesuits—Fr. Joseph Duguid, and Fr. Patrick Gordon (usually

---

* He returned to the Outer Isles after his consecration, and in 1764, was in charge of Barra and South Uist, with Mr Alexander Forrester helping him. (See p. 159.)

† For the conditions of gaining these Indulgences, the priests were referred to the Appendix of Bishop Challoner's edition of the Roman Ritual.

‡ Cf. Forbes-Leith, op.cit., Vol. II, pp. 358-9.

§ In 1754 the estimated population of Scotland was 2,372,634.

** Many served in the French army at an earlier period. There had been roughly 6,000 Scots Catholics in the British forces during the war between Britain and France in 1756, some who had been sent to America, and never returned.

known as John Johnstone). There were two secret chapels. Mr
Gordon had 180, and the Jesuits 130 communicants. Fr. George
Maxwell, S.J., whose headquarters were at Terregles House, three
miles north-west of Dumfries, ministered to a district of about
fifteen miles, with 253 communicants. Further west in Galloway
Fr. John Fraser, S.J., acted as chaplain to another Maxwell household at Munches, near Dalbeattie, where 132 persons had made
their Easter Duties. Mr Charles Cruikshank, who in his earlier
years had troubled the Vicars-Apostolic by supporting Colin
Campbell and John Tyrie, was chaplain at Traquair House,
Peeblesshire, with only 17 regular communicants.

So effectively had the old religion been stamped out, that no
more than 59 practising Catholics had been found in the peninsula
of Fife and the County of Angus. They were under the care of
Mr Robert Grant, who acted as chaplain to Bower of Methie.
Mr George Gordon, a former student of the Scots College, Paris,
was chaplain to the dowager fifth Duchess of Perth, a daughter
of the Earl of Traquair, who lived at Stobhall, the ancestral home
of the Drummonds, eight miles north of Perth. The communicants,
within an area of roughly ten miles, mustered 157. Mr Alexander
Godsman, aged sixty-five, a cousin of the saintly Mr John
Godsman, of whom more will be said, served an immense district
around Drummond Castle, near Crieff (including Glasgow), but
only 84 of his widely scattered flock had made their Easter Duties.

Aberdeen had two hidden chapels in 1763, one under the care
of Mr George Gordon (known as 'Scalinensis' for the sake of
distinction, and the other of Fr. William McLeod, S.J. The
former reported 125, and the latter 135 communicants within an
area of eighteen miles of the city. Fr. Alexander Duguid, S.J.,
whose two brothers George and Joseph were also Jesuits, usually
resided with the Frasers of Strichen, and served roughly 140
Catholics in the Buchan District of Aberdeenshire, covering an
area of about thirty miles.

Glenlivet had the largest Catholic population in the Lowland
District. Mr William Guthrie, a former student of the Scots
College, Rome, reckoned that he had 1,100 communicants in his
mission, the extent of which was only ten miles. Bishop Smith
described him as a priest "full of zeal and rare prudence".* Mr
John Geddes (the future Bishop), said to be a "worthy, learned,
and pious missionary", combined the charge of the College at
Scalan with ministering to Catholics in the Braes of Glenlivet.

Mr George Hay, then aged thirty-five—another future Bishop
—looked after the eastern part of the Enzie District of Banffshire.†
His Easter communions at Preshome came to 900. The sixty-four-
year-old Mr John Godsman was in charge of the mission in the

---

* This latter quality was needed when dealing with people whose chief
means of livelihood was the illicit distilling of whisky.
† See p. 185 note *.

St Ninian's, Tynet (1755).

St Gregory's, Preshome (1788).
See p. 203

157

parish of Bellie, with his chapel at Tynet, with 708 practising Catholics. *

In Upper Banffshire, both Strathaven and Strathisla (with its centre at Keith) lacked missionaries in 1763. The former district could muster 800 and the latter 159 communicants. Mr William Reid, once a student of the Scots College, Rome, now aged fifty, and in feeble health, had charge of the Mortlach mission, a flock of 430 within an area of eight miles. † The wild and isolated districts of Auchindoun, Glenrinness, and the Cabrach were served by Dom. John Baptist Menzies, O.S.B., a monk of Ratisbon, who worked on the Mission from 1756 until his death at Auchintoul, near Aberchirder, Banffshire, in 1799. His communicants in 1762, some of whom came from as far off as eighteen miles, were 250.

Mr William Duthie, a convert from Episcopalianism, had been in charge of the mission at Huntly, Aberdeenshire, since 1761 (after his sixteen years at Scalan and three years in Paris) and had 350 practising Catholics within an area of ten miles. From time to time he visited the Garioch District. The Catholic population was greatly reduced in numbers, and hardly needed a resident priest. The estimated 170 communicants on Deeside were ministered to by Fr. William Grant, S.J., whose mission covered about eighteen miles. ‡

Bishop Hugh Macdonald's Report on the Highland Vicariate, 1764.

It was on April 4, 1763, that Cardinal Spinelli asked the two Vicars-Apostolic to forward a census of their missions. Bishop Smith managed to compile his report without much difficulty and forwarded it to Propaganda. § It was much more difficult for the sixty-four-year-old Bishop Hugh Macdonald to draw up a census owing to the widely scattered nature of the Highland District. **

---

* It was in 1755 that Mr Godsman enlarged a newly-built sheep-cote between Auchenhalrig and the farm at Tulloch as a semi-permanent chapel. He had been living here for about twenty years, disguised as a farmer, saying Mass in barns, usually at night, so as to avoid arrest. This long, low building, with its white harled walls, did not assume its present shape until about 1787, when it was lengthened considerably to provide space for an increased congregation. St. Ninian's, Tynet, was restored and refurnished in 1961, under the direction of Ian G. Lindsay, R.S.A. It is the oldest post-Reformation Catholic place of worship in Scotland still used for public services.

† It was not until 1817 that the Earl of Fife started to lay out the streets of Dufftown, situated within the parish of Mortlach.

‡ These details do not always agree with those given by Canon Clapperton in his Memoirs of the Scottish Missionary Priests, which contain many obvious blunders. (Cf. Roderick Macdonald, 'The Highland District in 1764', in *Innes Review*, Autumn 1964, pp. 140-1).

§ See pp. 155-7.

** The total number of Catholics in the Highland District was estimated at 13,166, i.e. more than double those in the Lowland District (6,279).

After Cardinal Spinelli's death, Cardinal Albani withheld payment of a legacy from him until he received full details of the state of the Scottish Mission. Not until May 7, 1764, was Bishop Hugh able to forward what is called a "Description of the Highland Vicariate" and it was addressed from "Preshome at the mouth of the river (Spey)".*

The titular Bishop of Diana began by explaining to Cardinal Albani the immense area under his jurisdiction, that the missions were far apart and each needed at least one priest. He stressed that travelling between the mission stations was for the most part extremely difficult, because they were divided by rough mountains, lochs and arms of the sea. Some stations were very remote, like Barra in the Outer Hebrides, with five smaller islands adjacent to it. Sixty miles from the mainland, they lay exposed to the Atlantic Ocean and were inaccessible throughout the whole winter, because of the tempestuous nature of the seas. These islands were looked after by Bishop John Macdonald of Tibetropolis (consecrated in 1761), who was young and strong. 1,200 Catholics depended on his ministrations. Although there were very few Protestants on Barra and the smaller islands, they included some of the gentry.

North of Barra was the island of South Uist, beyond which was Benbecula. The former was about twenty-four miles long and five miles broad, the latter eight miles in diameter. It was reckoned that Mr Alexander Forrester, a former student at the Scots College, Rome, had 2,503 Catholics under his charge. He was in poor health, living in poverty and squalor, and utterly cut off from other priests. The Bishop described him as "a very old man, indeed truly worthy, simple and good, but broken by age and labour, for he has suffered both prison and exile for the Faith." † These two stations obviously required more than one missionary but the only assistance available was from Bishop John Macdonald, who had to do the work of a missionary in addition to his other duties, because of the scarcity of priests.

Nearer the mainland lay the two small islands of Canna and Eigg, the former separated by thirty miles of open waters, the latter by fifteen. There were 250 Catholics on Canna, and 350 on Eigg, with 24 on the mainly Presbyterian adjacent islands of Muck and Rum. At one time these four islands had a missionary of their own, but now all they got was a visit perhaps two or three times a year from the nearest priest on the mainland. He told Cardinal Albani that Canna and Eigg each demanded a priest, because of

* Cf. Roderick Macdonald, 'The Highland District in 1764', in *Innes Review* (Autumn, 1964), pp. 140-50; F. Forbes and W. J. Anderson, 'Clergy Lists of the Highland District, 1732-1828', in *Innes Review* (Autumn 1966), pp. 129-84. This long article (with map) gives much fuller details than those found in Gordon's *Scotichronieon* (pp. 627-36).
† ibid, p. 147.

"the terrible seas which make it nearly always dangerous to travel from one to the other ".

Mr William Harrison (*alias* Henderson or Hatmaker), a former student of the Roman College, then in his sixty-first year, had charge of a very large district on the mainland coast, including Moidart, Arisaig and South Morar. * When occasion permitted, he also ministered to the Catholics on Canna and Eigg.   The Bishop related that "the maritime area of Moidart is a very mountainous country, so much so that even a horse is of no use for travelling.   The whole region is Catholic, and no-one of any sect ever set foot in it until last year, when by the authority of the Government a minister was sent with his servants to take up residence and try to lead the faithful people into the errors of heresy.   (This is done now in all the Catholic parts of the Vicariate).   This region is twenty-two miles long, and at its widest is six miles wide.   It contains 817 souls, besides another 77 scattered among the neighbouring Protestant regions, and whose needs are supplied by the missionary of Moidart." †

Separated from Moidart by the Sound of Arisaig and Loch Ailort, as well as by high and rugged mountains, was the district of Arisaig, twelve miles long and four miles wide. The population of 739 was entirely Catholic. Adjoining this district was South Morar, not very broad, but fifteen miles long.   The Bishop explained: "It is extremely rough country, so that in some parts it is difficult to travel even on foot.   But it is all Catholic, and contains 318 souls.   Now, if the places themselves were considered, and the number of souls in them, it must be admitted that each of these three last mentioned regions would require a missionary to itself.   In fact, to do the work properly, any missionary in any one of these stations would have enough to do and more; but alas, through all these areas there is no-one to serve the faithful people except Mr William Harrison, who has to attend as best he can to the islands of Canna and Eigg also.   He has been hitherto indefatigable, a man of burning zeal for the salvation of souls, in whose service he has endured, and continues to endure, incredible hardships.   Having so many areas to cover, he scarcely ever spends two consecutive nights in one place, but must go travelling through these rugged mountains, although he is already worn out with toil and advancing age; for he came to the mission from our college in Rome in 1737." ‡

Then there was North Morar, separated from South Morar by the large loch of the same name, with 409 Catholics.   North of this district lay the region of Knoydart, twenty-four miles long and six wide, also entirely Catholic.   Mr Alexander Macdonald, who

* In 1734 Harrison had been associated with Colin Campbell and John Tyrie in their efforts to defame the two Vicars-Apostolic.
† ibid, p. 148
‡ ibid p. 148.

*The Church of Our Lady and St Bean, Marydale,
Inverness-shire (1866). There was a succession of
priests in Strathglass from the latter part of the 17th
century.*

began work on the mission in 1747 after being a student at the Roman College, ministered to 400 souls in North Morar and 1,000 in Knoydart. The Bishop stated that he was young, never spared himself, and did what he could for the flock entrusted to his care. His labours were not made easier by the distances between the places he had to visit and the rough mountains between them.

Glengarry was the most important mission in the Highland Vicariate. It extended over seventy-two square miles, mostly to the west of Loch Oich in Inverness-shire, and the country was so rough and broken that it was useful only for the summer grazing of sheep. Mr Aeneas McGillis, was the priest there. Then aged forty, he had charge of 1,400 Catholics. * The priest, like Mr Harrison, had been associated with Campbell and Tyrie during his training at the Roman College, where he was ordained in 1740. Described by the Bishop as "a very prudent man, and full of the Apostolic Spirit", he was not only in charge of Glengarry but ministered also to 1,270 Catholics in Braelochaber and the Braes of Badenoch. This was a very large region, twenty-two miles long, seven miles broad and full of lofty mountains. It should have had at least two missionaries and the Bishop was certain that the hardships Mr McGillis had to endure made it humanly impossible for him to look after the three regions much longer. In 1762 the Bishop had taken up his abode in Glengarry, and was doing what he could for the people round about him, but at the age of sixty-five and very infirm, he could not move around much.

Fr. Norman McLeod, S.J. (alias McHardy), " a labourer full of zeal and unsparing of himself", had charge of the Strathglass mission, a populous district ten miles long and six miles wide, to the south-west of Inverness. The Laird was a Protestant but among his tenants were 1,321 Catholics " according to the most careful count." Another missioner was obviously needed for so many people.

Included in the Highland Vicariate, because all the Catholics were Gaelic-speaking, was the mission of Glencairn, north of upper Deeside in Aberdeenshire. Fr. Charles Farquharson, S.J., looked after 612 Catholics in this mountainous region. He was " a man of long-standing repute, simple and upright, but unfortunately grown old and broken by innumerable labours, imprisonment and exile endured for the Faith."† Fr. Kenneth McKenzie, S.J., ministered to about 900 souls in and around Braemar. Much younger than Fr. Farquharson, he was better able to carry on his apostolate in a large area.

In order to understand what these missionary priests had to

* The Bishop wrote: "On the border is a Government fort and a village nearby in which there are many Protestants, but the rest of the region is all Catholic". This referred to Fort Augustus, erected after the rebellion of 1715, and enlarged by General Wade in 1730.
† ibid, p. 149.

endure two hundred years ago, it must be remembered that conditions in the Highlands and Islands were utterly different from what they are today. There were no towns, railways, telephones (far less air-services), no state institutions for carrying letters and parcels, and very few shops. There were no roads fit for coaches —more often than not merely rough tracks, over which it was too dangerous to ride on horse-back. Sea voyages were usually undertaken in small open boats.

If a priest fell ill, it might take weeks before any of his fellow missioners got word of it and even longer in the case of a priest stationed on one of the Outer Hebrides. There was seldom the chance to go to confession, or seek counsel and advice from another priest. The missioners in the Highland District only rarely met their Vicar-Apostolic and very often they had to depend on their own judgment in emergencies. Such were the men whom Propaganda again and again grudged supporting. The cardinals and monsignori in Rome either lacked the imagination to picture their surroundings or perhaps felt that Scotland did not count for much in the now world-wide mission field.

Further efforts to maintain a seminary in the Highland Vicariate, 1765–74

Heroic efforts were still being made to educate a few youths for the priesthood in the Highland Vicariate. In 1765 Bishop Hugh Macdonald informed the Roman Agent, Mr Peter Grant, that vigilant watch was being kept over his movements by "a number of idle ministers, who, having no Presbyterians in their parishes, have no other occupation than acting as spies upon their Catholic neighbours." * The Bishop had sent some of his "prentices" (as he called the students for security reasons) to board in private houses around Fochabers, so that they could attend local schools and receive private tuition from Mr John Godsman at Auchinhalrig.†

The following year Bishop John Macdonald informed the Roman Agent that he hoped to re-open a seminary somewhere in the West Highlands, and said: "I expect now to settle somewhere here [Glenfinnan]; it is thought that I shall have a few young people with me to prepare for the trade, and I hope for your help." In July 1678 Bishop Hugh wrote that he had received "Francis Macdonald, who has been at school for two years now under the care of Mr Godsman, but as the keeping of the boys at Fochabers has become very charitable to me, and they are not so well taught as I would wish, I have begun a new shop in the West under the direction of Mr Tib and Mr Allen, one of the

* Cf. 'Glenlivatensis', 'The Highland Seminaries, II', in *St. Peter's College Magazine*, Vol. IX (1951), p. 20.
† See pp. 156-8.

young travellers lately come to us, is to be constantly with the apprentices to teach them." *

Writing again in August 1769, Bishop Hugh said that "Mr Allen is still at shop"; adding that "little Alexander Macdonald" was on his way to the Scots College at Douai, although "too young and too little advanced in his studies for that place, having been here little more than half a year. This is an inconvenience we have been long under for not starting our shop sooner, but I hope shall be removed in time."

The future prospects of the 'shop' in Glenfinnan were not quite so hopeful, because on October 21 that same year Bishop Hugh informed Bishop Grant that "to provide students [for the foreign colleges] at the West shop does not answer expectations. Mr Tiber settled down last year in such a troublesome place that his house is full of people every night, and by his last accounts to me, he says he cannot keep apprentices for less than £20 a year. This gives great uneasiness to me, and I am sometimes thinking to bring the subjects back to Fochabers, where I can keep them much cheaper. It will continue this season."†

Financial straits of the Jesuit missionaries owing to the cessation of support from abroad by 1767

Both in the Lowland and Highland Vicariates the Jesuit missionaries were finding it hard to make both ends meet, having lost many wealthy friends and benefactors whose Scottish estates had been sequestrated after the 'Forty-Five'. By 1767 their position had become acute with the suppression of the Society of Jesus in Portugal, Spain and France, together with the dispersal of its members in Brazil, the East Indies and the Two Sicilies. The General, Fr. Lorenzo Ricci, was watching the slow death-agony of this once world-wide and almost omnipotent religious institute. Within a few years he himself would be imprisoned in the Castle Sant'Angelo at Rome, and treated as a criminal until his death in 1775. No longer could he give any financial help to the handful of Jesuit missionaries in Scotland.

On July 27, 1767, a meeting of the Vicars-Apostolic took place at Preshome, where a letter from Fr. Patrick Gordon was read and discussed. He explained that he could now maintain only five out of the ten Jesuits who were working on the Mission. So the Bishops resolved to donate £20, and agreed that if more Jesuits came to Scotland they would be supported from the funds intended only for the secular clergy. It was also agreed that on the death

---

* ibid p. 21. "Mr Tib" was John Macdonald, titular Bishop of Tiberi-opolis. It must be admitted that Bishop Hugh's attempts to keep the seminary secret were easy of detection, had his letters been read by government spies.
† ibid, p. 21.

of any of the Jesuits, their places would be filled by secular priests. These measures were reported to Propaganda.

The death of Bishop Smith (1767) and the appointment of Mr George Hay as coadjutor to Bishop Grant (1768)

For several years the venerable Bishop Smith had travelled on horseback from Edinburgh to Glenlivet—a distance of nearly 200 miles—so that he could drink goat's milk at Scalan.* He had great faith in this cure, also in the bracing air of Upper Banffshire.

He died at Edinburgh on August 21, 1767, aged eighty-three. Bishop Grant, then sixty-three, found himself in sole charge of the Lowland District. One of his first actions was to send Mr George Hay from Preshome to look after the Catholics in and around Edinburgh, where he also acted as Procurator of the Vicariate, in place of Mr Cruickshanks who retired to the Cabrach.

In a reply to the letter to Propaganda, notifying the death of Bishop Smith, Cardinal Castelli asked Bishop Grant to propose two or three of his priests for nomination as coadjutor. He also mentioned that he had procured the services of two Irish priests for the Scottish Mission.† On October 5, 1768, Propaganda dispatched briefs from Rome (without a *congé d'élire* from King Charles III), nominating Mr George Hay as coadjutor to Bishop Grant, with the style of titular Bishop of Daulis in Greece. The documents arrived in Edinburgh in January 1769, at the same time that the ambassadors of the Bourbonist Naples, Spain and France were presenting themselves one after the other before Clement XIII, demanding the complete suppression of the Society of Jesus throughout the world.‡ George Hay was born at Edinburgh on August 24, 1729.§ By the eighteenth century the Hays were staunch Jacobites and devout Episcopalians. George's mother, Mary Morrison, taught him to say his prayers, night and morning. Having been educated in Edinburgh, he began the study of medicine at the age of sixteen as a surgeon's apprentice. It is not surprising that he joined other medical students who ministered to wounded Jacobite soldiers after the Battle of Prestonpans in 1745. He then spent four months as an infirmarian with the Jacobite forces and after being taken prisoner he was detained in Edinburgh Castle for about three months. Then he was moved to London, where he was imprisoned for a year. During the year George was visited by a Catholic publisher, named Meighan, and for the first time heard Catholic doctrines defended. When he was

---

* A new house had been built there in 1767.

† A Mr Mackenna was sent to the Highlands, and a Fr. Dominic Braggan, O.P., found his way to Glenlivet, where he assisted Mr Guthrie.

‡ A consistory was called for February 3 to examine the matter and on the eve of that day the Pope had a stroke and died.

§ His father was a solicitor, and descended from Dugald Hay of Linplum, whose second son, George, was an ardent disciple of John Knox.

released in June 1747 and allowed to return to Edinburgh, he withdrew for political reasons to Kirktown House, where he stayed with his relative, Sir Walter Montgomery. Here he came across a copy of John Gother's *A Papist Misrepresented, or a two-fold Character of Popery* (first published at London in 1665). He read it carefully and about a year later, on his return to Edinburgh, he was received into the Catholic Church by Fr. John Seton, S.J., on December 21, 1748.

Meanwhile George continued his medical studies, although the penal laws made it impossible for him to graduate at the University or obtain his diploma at the Royal College of Surgeons. All he could do was to open a shop and sell drugs. Then came the opportunity to leave Scotland as surgeon on a ship bound from Leith to the Mediterranean. Finding himself in London, he called on Bishop Challoner, who told him that he showed signs of a vocation to the priesthood. The Vicar-Apostolic of the London District also wrote to Bishop Smith in Edinburgh and arranged for the young convert to enter the Scots College, Rome. *

George's engagement with the Leith merchants ended when he landed at Marseilles. Going on to Rome, he entered the Scots College on September 10, 1751, and he remained there eight years, without returning to Scotland until after his ordination to the priesthood on April 1, 1759. His journey back to Edinburgh took over four months and then he continued north to Preshome, to act as curate to Bishop Grant. They led an austere comfortless life, even sharing a room to save a fire and a candle at night. One of Mr Hay's first acts was to restore the nearby Chapel of the Craigs, which had been gutted by English soldiers in 1746, and soon after it was re-opened a false alarm was given one Sunday morning. When Mr Hay was about to start Mass, somebody rushed in with the news that a soldier had been seen approaching the chapel. However, the bright red waistcoat of a worthy inhabitant of Fochabers had been mistaken for military uniform. Confidence was restored, and the service proceeded.†

Mr Hay remained in the Enzie District for eight years and his medical knowledge made him the friend of Protestants as well as of Papists, for he rode around the country on his pony, visiting anybody who was sick or infirm. From time to time Bishop Grant sent him to Edinburgh on business connected with the Vicariate. His preaching too attracted Protestants as well as Papists. Catholics were fairly numerous at New Byth, a hamlet about twenty-five miles east of Preshome, and once after he had preached a sermon there, a Presbyterian was heard to say: " If he preached here always, we would never go anywhere else."‡

* Cf. Edwin H. Burton, *The Life and Times of Bishop Challoner* (1909), Vol. II, p. 151.
 † *Scotichronicon*, p. 48.
 ‡ ibid, p. 56.

Shortly after moving to Edinburgh, in 1767, Mr Hay obtained Bishop Grant's permission to take on a house in Blackfriars Wynd, off High Street, to serve both as a chapel and a residence for the priest. He explained that the partition wall between the dining-room and the kitchen could be "put up and taken down at pleasure", and this would accommodate "a good number of persons on occasions". Realising that the gentry might object to being mixed up with the riff-raff, he added that "people of the better sort" could be seated in another room, and "would hear perfectly well". This hidden Papist 'house-church', reminiscent of early Christian places of worship, continued to be used for nearly twenty years.*

* ibid, p. 58.

CHAPTER SIX

LOWLAND & HIGHLAND VICARIATES
1769-1811

Bishop Hay's secret consecration, 1769

ALTHOUGH IT WAS nearly a quarter of a century since the Jacobite forces were defeated at Culloden, both Episcopalians and Papists were still suspect in the eyes of the British government, for the more romantic-minded Jacobites had not entirely lost hope of the restoration of the Stuart dynasty. In the summer of 1769 Bishop Robert Forbes of Ross and Caithness arranged to meet Bishop Robert Gordon, an English Nonjuring prelate of Scots descent, who normally lived in London. They had a hole-and-corner rendezvous near Moffat, in Annandale, and there they discussed the possibility of arranging for Charles III to marry a pious Protestant lady, in the hope that she would bear him a son. His Catholic mistress, Clementina Walkinshaw, had only given him a daughter, Charlotte, born in 1753. She retired to a convent in Paris in 1760, and was known as Countess Alberstrof.

George Hay, though still a Jacobite at heart, took a more realistic view of the political situation than these two Nonjuring bishops and others who shared their yearnings for the return from Italy of the now middle-aged and far from 'bonnie' Prince Charlie. This, however, did not prevent his consecration being carried out almost with the secrecy of the confessional, and in the same clandestine manner as Bishop Nicolson's in 1695.* Edinburgh would have been far too dangerous. Because the bishop-elect was so well-known and popular on the Banffshire coast, Preshome would have been even more risky. The safest place seemed to be the Braes of Glenlivet. So it came about that on the morning of Trinity Sunday, May 19th, 1769, Bishop Grant, assisted by Bishop Hugh Macdonald, consecrated George Hay as titular Bishop of Daulis in Greece. They were crowded together in a small upper room of the college of Scalan, which had been rebuilt two years before, and for motives of prudence the certificate that he had taken the prescribed oath and made the usual profession of faith

---

* 'The Young Pretender' returned to communion with Rome in 1759 after nine years of more or less nominal communion with Canterbury.

was not forwarded to Rome. * Bishop Hay returned to Edinburgh, and Bishop Grant took charge of the Enzie District, for the saintly Mr John Godsman had died on April 1st, that same year, aged seventy-one.† There was no priest who could be spared to take his place.

English Catholics asked to assist the Scottish Mission, 1769.

The destitution of most of the missionary priests was the first business to which Bishop Hay gave his attention. Many were homeless, living from hand to mouth and roaming around the countryside. They were little better off than vagrants but, unlike the blue-gowned 'Gaberlunzie men', they had no royal licence to beg from door to door. There was a great scarcity of vestments, altar linen and liturgical books.

The dowager Lady Traquair promised the help of Mr William Constable of Everingham, a member of the Yorkshire family which had helped to keep the faith alive since the Reformation, and acting on her suggestion the Bishop drew up a memorial describing the state of the Scottish Mission. It was forwarded to Bishop Challoner, Vicar-Apostolic of the London District since 1758.

The response was immediate. Collections were made in two of the London chapels and the English bishops granted permission to Lady Traquair and Mr Constable to beg for money. The latter sent Bishop Hay £100 as his own contribution. On July 5th, 1769, Bishop Challoner informed Bishop Hay that he had shown the memorial to "a person of great honour and virtue," who promised a donation of £1,000 for the relief of priests in Scotland. All he asked in return were their prayers "for R.J. deceased".†

Removal of the Scots College from Madrid to Valladolid, 1770.

Early in 1770 Bishop Hay asked Mr John Geddes to go to Spain and find out whether anything could be done about reopening the Scots College at Madrid. It had been closed after the Jesuits were expelled by Charles III in 1767, because of a rumour that the Society was plotting to dethrone him. All the Fathers had been deported. The majority had settled in the Papal States, the only place in Europe where they could be fairly sure of safety, and that would not be for long. The Spanish ambassador in

---

* It was not until Bishop Hay happened to be at Paris in 1772 that he wrote out in his own hand, and entrusted the paper to Principal Gordon of the Scots College for transmission to Propaganda, confirming that he had taken the oath and made the profession of faith.

† See p. 166.

‡ It is probable that the benefactor was the young Lord Petre, whose father, Robert James, 8th Baron Petre, of Ingatestone Hall, Essex, had died in 1742.   (Cf. Burton, op.cit., Vol. II, p. 152).

London, on the recommendation of Bishop Challoner and Bishop Talbot, his coadjutor, made arrangements for Mr Geddes's journey.

The Madrid College had been of very little use to the Mission since it was opened in 1627,* for apparently not more than three secular priests were sent to Scotland in a hundred and forty years. Mr Geddes, having acquired an unwanted Jesuit property at Valladolid, arranged for the College to be re-opened there and he was appointed its first rector, an office he held until 1780.†

Fifteen boys left Scotland for Spain in 1770. To avoid suspicion they were divided into two groups, one group sailing from Aberdeen, the other from Leith. On their arrival in London the lads were looked after by a Mr Coghlan, a Catholic bookseller, who had visited George Hay when he was a prisoner in 1746, and discussed the Catholic religion with him.

The new College was not ready for occupation when they reached Valladolid, so they lodged at the English College.‡ King Charles of Spain and the Two Sicilies granted a royal charter, which stated that the purpose of the College was, "according to the intention of the Founder, the education of Scottish priests, who are to return to their own Country, to preach the Holy Faith, take care of the Catholics already in that Kingdom, and labour for the conversion of heretics."§

The Scots College at Douai reopened under secular priests, 1772.

Louis XV had totally suppressed the Society of Jesus throughout France in April 1764 and this involved closing the Scots College at Douai.** The French Government, however, recognised that the Vicars-Apostolic had a legal claim on the property, which had been sequestrated. After long-drawn-out negotiations, permission was granted for the College to be re-opened.

The government reserved the right to nominate a secular priest as its rector, on the recommendation of the Scottish Bishops, and their choice fell on Mr Robert Grant, brother of the Abbate Grant, the Roman Agent. Bishop Hay decided that he had better visit Douai in person, with the hope of raising funds in France, and to settle other business. On his way through London he called on Bishop Challoner, whom he had not met since he was a young layman, working as a ship's surgeon. This was probably

---

* Cf. W. J. Anderson, 'The Rule of the Scots College, Madrid, 1647', in *Innes Review* (Autumn, 1964), pp. 189-91.

† See p. 186.

‡ Founded by Cardinal Allen in 1589.

§ *Scotichronicon*, p. 75.

** The Fathers retired first to Dinant, at that time within the Austrian Empire, taking with them all the richest ornaments of the chapel, including the relic of St Margaret, and leaving behind them many debts. (See p. 300)

the occasion when the two Bishops made a pact that whosoever should outlive the other would celebrate Mass three times a week for the repose of the soul of the deceased. *

From Douai, Bishop Hay went on to Paris, accompanied by Mr Grant, but without obtaining any financial help from the College. The Papal Nuncio showed no interest. The Bishop of Arras was the only member of the hierarchy who offered to assist. We are told that "On the whole it was evident that unless they would stoop to court intrigue, and solicit or purchase the influence of some of the King's mistresses, their errand was hopeless. To this Dr Hay would not consent, and so the whole scheme fell to the ground. It affords an instructive example of the utter hollowness to which matters had come, both in the French Church and State, inviting, as they too surely did, the terrible scourge of a Revolution, unsurpassed in horror in the annals of the world.†

The disillusioned Bishop returned to Scotland by way of Douai, and reached Edinburgh after a voyage from Dunkirk towards the end of March 1772. Ten pounds worth of books which he had bought at Paris were seized and destroyed when unshipped at an English port.

Suppression of the Society of Jesus by Clement XIV, 1773

On August 16, 1773, Clement XIV suppressed the Society of Jesus throughout the world.‡

The Scots College at Rome shared the same fate as those at Madrid and Douai, because it had also been staffed by Jesuits. Next had to be solved the problem of what could be done with the ten members of the Society working on the Scottish Mission. Their formal submission to the authority of the Vicars-Apostolic took place on October 6th, 1773. Bishop Hay wrote to Bishop Grant describing this incident, and said: "They were most ready and willing to comply, and accordingly writ over the Form of the Submission both at once, and then delivered it into my hand, upon which I rose and embraced them with the tenderest affection which they mutually returned, and hoped we should always find them most submissive and obedient; and I assured them they should never have reason to complain or regret the change of their

* Cf. 'Memoirs of Bishop Hay', prefixed to Bishop Strain's edition of his works (Edinburgh, 1871).

† *Scotichronicon*, p. 99.

‡ A passage in the brief *'Dominus ac Redemptor'* conveys the Papal attitude: "Guided, we trust, by the Divine Spirit, impelled by the duty of restoring harmony in the Church, convinced that the Society of Jesus can no longer fulfil the purposes for which it was founded, and moved by other reasons of prudence and governmental policy which we keep to ourselves, we abolish and annul the Society of Jesus, with its offices, houses and institutions." It is doubtful if the Pope believed all the charges against the Jesuits made by most governments in Europe. He took the line of least resistance.

Superiors on our part . . . This being finished, we drank tea together, and were very frank." *

Other Jesuits, not present at this meeting, made their submission later, either personally or in writing.

All the funds of the Scottish Jesuit Mission were tied up in France, or had already been confiscated by the Government. The Superior, Fr. Patrick Gordon, seems to have been convinced that the Society would soon be restored, and consequently held up the business of the Vicars-Apostolic getting hold of them for nearly seven years.

Persecution of Catholics on South Uist, 1770-2

Since 1768 the Laird of Boisdale, Alasdair Mor Macdonald, had been persecuting his tenants on the island of South Uist. Encouraged by this lapsed Catholic laird, who had already ordered his people to eat flesh meat in Lent, the Presbyterian schoolmaster began to attack their religion, then started to corrupt their morals in more ways than one. All this was a cause of much anxiety to Bishop Hugh Macdonald.

At Whitsuntide, 1770, Boisdale told roughly three hundred families that unless they renounced Popery and became Presbyterians, they would be evicted from their homes. It astonished him when they replied that they were prepared to give up their crofts, even to beg bread from door to door, rather than abjure their faith. The laird did not want to be deprived of their services, so he compromised by telling the parents that they could remain Catholics, provided their children were brought up as Presbyterians. They flatly refused to consider such terms.

Macdonald of Glenaladale, in Moidart, and certain other Catholic lairds on the mainland proposed a remedy. Land on the island of St John at the mouth of the river St Lawrence had already been bought by Glenaladale, who had sold his Scottish estates. He offered to take the people of South Uist to Canada, and to act as their leader.

Bishop Hay was informed of this scheme. It roused him to write and have printed what was entitled *'A Memorial for the suffering Catholicks in a violent persecution for Religion at present carried on in one of the Western Isles of Scotland'*. Having recorded the story of the persecution, he continued: "Now as the only way to provide for these heroic sufferers is to get them to

---

* *Scotichronicon*, pp. 118-9.

† The 10 Fathers were as follows: Patrick Gordon (*alias* John Johnstone), Superior of the Mission; William McLeod (Aberdeen), William Grant and Alexander Duguid (Aberdeenshire), Joseph Duguid (Edinburgh), John Fraser and Sir Alexander Strachan (Galloway), and three more in the Highlands. Besides these there were other Scottish Jesuits on the continent, formerly on the staffs of the Colleges at Madrid, Rome and Douai.

St John's Island, where the above mentioned gentleman will provide them with land on the most advantageous terms, although it is not in his power to carry them over; and as it is impossible to raise such a sum of money in their own country as would be required for their passage, provisions and the other necessities for a new colony, the only resource they have under God, is to recommend themselves to the charity of all well-disposed Catholics, hoping the above plain narrative of their case will not fail to excite pity and compassion." *

Bishop Challoner received a copy of this *Memorial*, and lost no time in enlisting the practical sympathy of English Catholics. Collections were made in the chapels of the foreign embassies in London, with the result that quite a large sum of money was forwarded to Scotland.

Early in 1772 Glenaladale visited South Uist in company with Bishop John Macdonald to arrange for the removal of the people to Canada. Their extreme poverty made it impossible for them to contribute anything toward the expenses, and this led to a further delay. Later on, that same year, a ship sailed with two hundred and ten persons on board. A hundred came from South Uist, the rest from the mainland. The emigrants were accompanied by a priest, Mr James Macdonald.

Letters took a long time to cross the Atlantic. When the first news came from St John's Island it was clear enough that most of those exiles were in great misery and destitution. The island was covered with virgin forest and had never been cultivated. Within less than a year some of the people began to regret having left Scotland. Nevertheless in 1776 Bishop Hay was able to inform Mr Geddes at Valladolid that the Uist people were doing extremely well on St John's Island, far better than if they had remained at home. As for Boisdale, realising that he had done himself no good by evicting so many of his tenants, he began to give almost unlimited toleration to those whom he favoured. He even allowed priests to celebrate Mass in his house at Kilbride on South Uist. Yet he was never reconciled with the Church and died a nominal Presbyterian.

State of the Highland Vicariate during the 1770s

The depopulation of the Highlands and Islands went on steadily, and it was not only Catholics who emigrated to North America. Between 1740 and 1775 more and more crofts in Glengarry, Glenmoriston, Glen Urquhart, and Strathglass (all in Inverness-shire) were abandoned. Families from the counties of

---

* Cf. Odo Blundell, O.S.B., *The Catholic Highlands of Scotland: The Western Highlands and Islands* (1917), p. 37.

† It has been stated that roughly 20,000 emigrated between 1763 and 1773; and that another 30,000 followed between 1773 and 1775.

Argyll, Perth, Ross and Sutherland crossed the Atlantic, never to return. The great exodus, however, was from the islands—North and South Uist, Skye, Lewis, Arran, Jura, Gigha and Islay.

The chief reason for the rapid decline in the population of the Highlands and Islands was so that good farm-land in the glens and the straths might be turned into sheepwalks, because sheep-farming offered a short way out of the difficulties which faced most of the landlords. The evicted families were driven to the more or less barren sea coasts, where they were expected to support themselves by fishing, unskilled labour or begging. *

When war broke out in 1775 between Britain and her American colonies it became dangerous to face a voyage across the Atlantic. Already Highland families were drifting south in search of employment. Most of them settled in and around Glasgow, which had risen by leaps and bounds since the start of the tobacco trade in 1718. But this trade collapsed in 1776 owing to the American War of Independence. The opening of iron works near Glasgow helped to increase the Catholic population by migration from the Highlands and Islands. Although there was still no permanent chapel in Glasgow, mass was celebrated occasionally in private houses. The first cotton mill was not opened until 1779. When more followed, there was a further increase of Catholic Highlanders, looking for jobs in the Clyde Valley.

Meantime Bishop Hugh Macdonald had died on March 12, 1773, and was buried in Kilfinnan in Glengarry, having ruled over the Highland Vicariate for forty-two years. His nephew, Bishop John, did everything humanly possible to recruit candidates for the priesthood and to train them. The subject was mentioned in the Bishop's Annual Letter to Propaganda in 1774, where it was stated: "Tiberiop [Bishop John] is in such difficulties that he cannot take up his residence in any one district. He is often at a loss to know what districts to attend to first. Even if he could comply with all the requests, he could not afford them much permanent help. It was with much regret and with great injury to religion that he was forced to close the little seminary which he had started a few years previously. He could, however, not possibly spare anyone to attend to it." †

Nevertheless, Bishop John made a fresh start in 1775, and ordered "a cargo of books" to be sent to him, which included

---

.* What the material conditions of the Highland Vicariate were like in 1773 can be found in James Boswell's *Journal of a Tour to the Hebrides*, published in 1785. It was during the first year that this lapsed Catholic travelled around the Highlands and Islands with Dr Samuel Johnson. By this time the eldest son of Lord Auchinleck, a Scottish judge, had developed such a fear of Papists, that he even had scruples of engaging a Catholic Bohemian as his servant. (Cf. *Boswell in Search of a Wife*, ed. by Frank Brady and Frederick A. Pottle (1957), p. 351).

† Cf. Blundell, op.cit. p. 109.

Samalamen Lodge, near Glenuig, Inverness-shire, was a seminary from 1770 to 1803.

Mortlach, in the parish of Cairnie, Aberdeenshire, was a meeting-place for the Vicars-Apostolic during the 18th century.

four copies of Ovid's *De Fastis*, five copies of Cicero's *Select Epistles*, besides several Latin grammars.*

The problem was to find a suitable place. A farm near Fort Augustus was considered, but eventually it was decided to re-open Buorblach, i.e. the so-called 'West Scalan'. Priests were needed badly, because trained Presbyterian evangelists were still active in the Highlands, doing their best to convert Papists from idolatry and superstition, and turn them into loyal subjects of George III.

Bishop Hay was asked by Bishop John to send "Jamie Cattenach from East Scalan as a model of regularity and discipline" to other students. In February 1777 came a request for books, and in May reference to the "incredible sum" which had been spent on 'West Scalan' that year. There were no funds upon which Bishop John could draw—nothing corresponding to those of the S.P.C.K. and the Royal Bounty, which educated and maintained the Presbyterian propagandists. "Tiberiop" was always in financial difficulties, due, so it seems, to his open-hearted generosity to everybody who appealed for help. It was not without reason that Bishop Hay invariably referred to him as "Good Bishop John ".

In a letter to Bishop Hay on January 9th, 1779, Bishop John said he was proposing to buy "a lot at the lower end of Loch Morar, including five farms, viz. the two Mallaigs, Glasnachardoch, Buorblach, and Beoraid ". His death took place on May 9th that same year, and he was buried at Kilchoan beside Loch Nevis in Knoydart.

Bishop Hay was in London when the news reached him, and he wrote to Mr John Geddes: "Alas! my Dear Friend, I am now all alone; our worthy and most valuable friend, Mr Tiberiop, is no more . . . You will more than easily imagine that I can describe the situation we all must be in, on that melancholy event. May Almighty God, in His infinite mercy, look upon with pity, and direct us what to do."

His next step was to ask the senior priests of the Highland Vicariate to collect the votes of their brethren for a successor to the late Bishop. Their choice fell on Mr Alexander Macdonald, who had been working on the Isle of Barra since he was raised to the priesthood in Rome in 1765.† There was a long delay, however, before Propaganda confirmed this nomination. It was not until Passion Sunday, March 12th, 1780, that Mr Alexander Macdonald was consecrated as titular Bishop of Polemo in Asia Minor. The ceremony took place at Scalan. Special permission had been obtained from Rome for Bishop Hay to carry out the consecration, assisted only by two priests.

---

* *Scotichronicon*, p. 176.
† He was a native of South Uist, son of the Laird of Bornish, and was born in 1736.

First efforts to obtain Catholic emancipation, 1777.

There was an urgent need for more recruits in the Army, after the outbreak of the American War of Independence in 1775, and largely because of this the British Government realised that the penal laws must be relaxed, not only in England but in Scotland. Two years later a confidential agent, Sir John Dalrymple, was sent to the Highlands to find out what Catholics were in favour of the war, whether they would join the forces if invited, and what changes in their religious and legal statutes they would demand for their services. Sir John discussed the matter with Bishop Hay in Edinburgh, and on February 18, 1778, the latter submitted a written reply. He said: Were the whole Penal Laws against them to be repealed, and them restored to all the rights and privileges of their fellow subjects, this would doubtless attach them wholly to His Majesty's person and government for ever . . . But as a total repeal is not to be thought of, in the present state of affairs, and perhaps not even to be wished for, in my humble opinion, the removal of three impedimenta would suffice to effectuate what you propose, and would be necessary for that purpose." *

The three impedimenta were: (1) the repeal of the laws against all hearers and sayers of Mass; (2) the repeal of the statutes which allow the Protestant seller of an estate to take it back from the Catholic purchaser without returning the price, and of those statutes which enable the Protestant heir to take the estate from the Catholic proprietor; and (3) the abolition of that part of the attestation oath which concerns religion, so that recruits should be required to swear fidelity to the King and obedience to the laws of war.

Having consulted many influential people in Scotland, the Agent returned to London. There he showed Bishop Hay's reply to the Prime Minister, Lord North, and other members of the Cabinet who were in the secret of his mission. The situation was desperate, because in March 1788 diplomatic relations between Britain and France had been broken off, after it was discovered that Louis XVI was helping the American colonies in their efforts to gain independence.

Much correspondence followed between Bishop Hay and Bishop Challoner and the latter's coadjutor, Bishop Talbot. It appears that Bishop Challoner, now aged eighty-seven, was afraid that any relaxation of the penal laws was dangerous. A fair number of English Catholics shared this point of view. It was not until Sir John had got in touch with a young lawyer, William Sheldon, that he managed to make any headway with the proposals. Eventually Bishop Challoner modified his opinions and drew up a document, which was signed by himself and the other English

* ibid p. 145.

M

Vicars-Apostolic, as well as Bishop Hay, asking for free toleration without reference to particular grievances.

So it was that the Catholic Relief Bill (England) was carried through both Houses of Parliament without a single division, and received the Royal Assent on June 3rd, 1778.

The partial relief granted to English Catholics did not extend to Scotland. Presbyterians, taken as a whole, were determined to oppose the emancipation of Papists with every means in their power and they lost no time in organising resistance. Almost the only outstanding personality who adopted a liberal attitude was Dr William Robertson (1721-93), the famous historian and Principal of Edinburgh University. Although he managed to convince the greater number of the members of the General Assembly that a repeal of the penal laws was required, not only by political expediency but by the humane spirit of the Gospels, he did not reckon with the majority of his countrymen. After Parliament met again in the autumn of 1778, a bill was introduced abolishing the penal statutes of Scots Law. The effect was instantaneous. The whole nation rose up against it almost to one man. "The Established Church, the Secession Church, the Relief Church, joined in the cry. Synods, presbyteries, kirk-sessions, passed resolutions against the obnoxious bill. Town councils, guilds, corporations, clubs, societies joined hand in hand to keep the Papists down. The remotest districts of the north caught the infection, and joined in the clamour. The Incorporation of Cordiners in Potterow, the Seven United Trades of Montrose, the Porters in Edinburgh, the Berean Chapel, Carubber's Close, the Society of St Crispin, the Society of Journeymen Staymakers, the Coal-hewers in and about Carntyne, the Friendly Society of Gardeners, butchers, sailors, flaxdressers, weavers, masons, all vied with each other in expressing their abhorrence of the proposed repeal. Seventy-nine ecclesiastical courts, two counties, forty-one burghs, twenty-four towns, eighty-four parishes, fifty-five corporations, and twenty-one private societies, recorded their hostility to the measure, as fraught with ruin to the interests of the Protestant religion." *

From the Butt of Lewis to Berwick-on-Tweed, from the Shetland Islands to the Solway Firth, men and women were smitten with almost maniacal anti-Popish mass-hysteria. The smouldering embers of the old Covenanters' fires burst into flame—war to the death, and "To Hell with the Pope!" Broadsheets and pamphlets were printed and sold.†

* John Cunningham, *The Church History of Scotland* (Edinburgh, 1882), Vol. II, p. 386. All these addresses, declarations, and resolutions were collected and published in an octavo volume of 356 pages, entitled *Scotland's Opposition to the Popish Bill.*

† In Edinburgh one of them was entitled *The Brave and Spirited Resolution of the Ministers, Members and Congregation of the Gaelic Church, against the intended Popish Bill, with Popery Dissected, and the price of each Sin, Pardon, Purgatory Opened.* Even more hair-raising, and better

The Synod of Glasgow and Ayr, realising the gravity of the situation, ordered that the second Tuesday of December 1778 was to be observed as a strict and solemn Fast. Protestants were bidden to gird up their loins and unsheath their swords against "that cruel superstition which has so often been drunk with the blood of the Saints — that unjust superstition which the more it advances, the more powerfully it operates in pulling up the foundations of the Protestant state." Scots men and women were warned of "the astonishing progress of this detestable, cruel and unjust superstition—so much the more alarming, as it appears not only in remote and uncultivated corners, but in the most populous and improved parts of the land." *

Meanwhile the Glasgow ministers in particular were fanning the flame of anti-Popish hatred in sermons and speeches. One of the most militant was the Rev. Daniel McArthur, who was almost out of his wits for terror of the ascendancy of Popes, Papists and anti-Christ. His fast-day sermon, entitled *The Church of Rome, the Mother of Abominations,* preached in the Black Friars Kirk, was printed in pamphlet form. Dr. William Porteous delivered a sarcastic but more subtle discourse in the Wynd Kirk on the perils of Popery.

There were no more than about twenty Catholics resident in Glasgow in 1778, most of them poor Highlanders who met in a small back room off the High Street, on Sunday mornings, if a priest came to celebrate Mass, and it is therefore difficult to understand why Presbyterians were so alarmed at the largely imaginary growth of Romanism. Even before the prescribed fast-day, a mob attacked a handful of people making their way on a Sunday morning to worship, casting mud and stones at them. At least one house in which a Papist lived was burnt. No less than eighty-five societies were soon formed in Glasgow alone, with a total membership of over 12,000, each determined to suppress idolatry and to oppose the giving of any relief to Romanists.†
Since the total population of Glasgow did not then amount to more than 38,000, this zeal for promoting what was believed to be Bible

---

value for the money was *Sawney's Defence against the Beast Whore Pope and Devil.* It contained an engraving showing "the Beast" with seven heads and ten horns, upon which rode "the Scarlet Whore of Babylon" with the cup of her sorceries in her right hand. Sawney himself was shown in full Highland costume, holding a shield and a standard, and brandishing a claymore. Other figures in the group were the Pope "Man of Sin", wearing a triple tiara, a rosary and keys stuck into his girdle, offering absolution to George III for his breach of the oath. Over the seven-headed Beast flew a fearsome black Devil, with a coronet destined for the Lord Advocate.

* Cf. *Glasgow, Past and Present* (Glasgow, 1856), Vol. III, p. 499.

† They were in close touch with Lord George Gordon in London, and sent him a gold snuff box in token of appreciation for his courageous efforts to crush Popery.

Christianity is remarkable. In emulation of the Old Testament prophets, some of the worthy citizens smashed the windows of the upper-room chapel and took care that it was purged of all superstitious symbols — if there were any! It was not until 1782 that the much persecuted Catholics felt it safe to rent a small back-room at the foot of the Saltmarket, and meet there for Mass when a priest came to minister to them.

While all this was going on, Bishop Grant was living in Aberdeen, too old and infirm to do anything to assist his persecuted flock. He died in the chapel-house off Justice Street on December 3rd, 1778, aged seventy-three, and in the forty-fifth year of his episcopate. His burial took place in the pre-Reformation grave-yard of *Santa Maria ad Nives*, commonly known as the 'Snow Kirk', the name perpetuated in the present Snow Cemetery. After his death Bishop John Macdonald wrote to Bishop Hay: " Bishop Grant was one of the few who in their whole life escaped all censure, because censure could find no access to one who entered on the stage of the world with the maturity of old age, and whose conduct from the beginning was regulated to the most solid maxims of prudence and religion."

In more recent times Bishop Kyle called him "the greatest bishop in Scotland, because he wrote short letters and wasted no words."

By the close of the year 1778 pent-up Protestant emotions in Edinburgh could not be held back. After Hogmanay the city resounded with the cry of "Knock down, kill, burn all Papists!" Nothing quite like this had happened since the winter of 1688-9, when news reached Scotland that James VII had fled to France and that William of Orange had come over from Holland to restore the Protestant religion.* After ninety years the smouldering embers of Presbyterianism burst into flame with new fury. The magistrates kept aloof and took no active measures to check rioting.†

A violent attack was made on the newly opened chapel-house in Chalmers' Close, regarded by the Protestant mob as a spiritual brothel kept by the Whore of Babylon. That same day, February 2nd, when Catholics in more peaceful parts of the world were carrying out the ceremonies of Candlemas, another gang filled with Covenanting zeal set fire to the recently opened chapel-house in Blackfriars Wynd, having forced an entry. One of the priests, however, managed to escape with some of the vestments, a chalice etc. Damage was also done to the houses of Catholic layfolk. Eventually the Riot Act was read but without much effect. Thanks to the magistrates, there were no similar scenes at Aberdeen, but

---

* *Scotichronicon*, p. 156.
† Cf. *The Scots Magazine*, Vol. XL (1778) and Vol. XLI (1779), which contain contemporary accounts of riots in Edinburgh and Glasgow.

elsewhere attempts were made to destroy property owned by Papists.

Bishop Hay arrived back from London, and when he noticed a crowd in the street near his house, he asked an old woman what was the reason. She replied: " O sir, we are burning the Popish chapel, and we only wish we had the Bishop to throw into the fire."* He beat a hasty retreat and found refuge in the Castle for a few days.

On February 12th, 1779, it was announced that the government had finally decided to give no relief to Papists in Scotland and when the General Assembly met in May, most of the ministers rejoiced at this great victory for Protestantism. Bishop Hay had lost most of his library, and the two Edinburgh chapels had been desecrated. Seeking compensation he returned to London but first he addressed a letter to the Lord Provost of Edinburgh, making claims for damages done by the mob. No answer was ever received.

Further efforts to obtain relief for Scottish Catholics

The Bishop, having reached London, wrote and had printed a *Memorial*, in which he described what Catholics had endured during the recent riots. He managed to get it circulated among members of the Government and a petition based on this *Memorial* was presented to George III by Lord Linton. The cause of the persecuted Scottish Catholics found a warm partisan in John Wilkes. This always outspoken politician had supported the American colonists in their war with England, and he never ceased trying to obtain freedom for everybody. Edmund Burke, the famous historian, also took up the cause with characteristic eloquence and tenacity, and wrote ironical replies to more than one of the ministers who sent him copies of sermons and other documents filled with scriptural arguments against giving relief to Romanists. Principal Robertson tried hard at the General Assembly that same year to make the ministers adopt a more reasonable and humane attitude towards Papists, but without success.

The only result was the passing of a Government motion that the repeal of the penal laws in Scotland was both dangerous and inexpedient, but deploring the militant opposition on the part of the mobs. Bishop Hay's negotiations in London led to nothing, except that he did receive compensation for damages done to property. This enabled him to repair and reopen the chapel in Blackfriars Wynd in August 1780.†

In the meantime Lord George Gordon, grandson of the militant Catholic second Duke of Gordon, continued to stir up a fear of Popery in England. " Very earnest and rather mad, with his long

---

* Cf. *Scotichronicon*, p. 160.
† It became known as 'The Highland Chapel'.

red hair and solemn face, he harangued the poor of London almost as an equal. * For five days in June, 1780, rioting went on. Newgate prison was burned down and three Catholic chapels were desecrated. Much damage was done to private houses and business properties belonging to Papists. Rioting also took place in some other parts of England. †

Changes in ecclesiastical discipline, 1780.

In January 1780, six months before the Gordon riots in England, Bishop Hay decided to make several changes in ecclesiastical discipline in the Lowland Vicariate.   Considering the troubled state of the times, it is rather surprising that he should have ordered his priests to observe February 1 (Candlemas Day) as an occasion for " public prayers " (Mass), with a sermon and the distribution of blessed candles.

What is more significant of a change of Catholic mentality in Scotland was the directive that a special prayer must be recited before Mass on all Sundays and Holy Days of Obligation "commending to the mercy of God our Sovereign, the King, the Queen and all the Royal Family", by whom were meant George III and Charlotte Sophia of Mecklenburg-Strelitz — not Charles III and Louisa of Stolberg-Gedern.‡ Since 1774 the former 'Bonnie Prince Charlie ' had been leading a sordid existence in the Palazzo Guadagni at Florence.   He had gained nothing by his " solemn abjuration of the Roman religion" in 1750.§ It is doubtful if he was ever a practising Catholic after he was formally reconciled with the Holy See some years later.**

There was a certain priest in the Lowland Vicariate who had

---

* David Mathew, *Catholicism in England* (1936), p. 142.

† Eventually Lord George lost all support and declared himself a Jew. He was arrested for libel, and died in prison on the feast of All Saints, 1783.

‡ It was not until August 24, 1788, eight months after the death of Charles III, which ended almost all hopes of the restoration of the Stuart dynasty, that the Synod of the Scottish Episcopal Church resolved that on and after May 25 the following year King George III and his family should be prayed for in public services. This order greatly distressed the few remaining loyal Jacobites, who regarded Henry, Cardinal Bishop of Frascati, the younger son of James VIII, as their *de jure* sovereign.

§ See p. 149.

** In 1780 his wife, who had been carrying on a liaison with the poet Vittorio Alfieri for about five years, deserted him and retired to a convent in Rome. Known as the Countess of Albany, she was soon installed in the Palazzo della Cancellaria, where she lived more or less openly with her lover.   Charles III, left alone in Florence, summoned his natural daughter, Lady Charlotte Stuart, to keep him company.   She was legitimated, and given the rank of Duchess, but on the understanding that this in no way affected the right of her Cardinal-uncle to the throne of Britain.   She was already the mother of three children whose father is supposed to have been Archbishop Ferdinand de Rohan, first of Bordeaux, then of Cambrai.

been a constant source of worry to Bishop Hay for sixteen years.
This was Mr Alexander Geddes, a brilliant but eccentric
character. *

Since 1769 he had been assistant missionary in the western
part of the Enzie District, where his somewhat unconventional
ecumenical activities made him popular with Presbyterians. It
was reported that "he could ridicule the infallibility of the Pope,
and laugh at images and relics, at rosaries, scapulars, obits and
dirges, as much as could the most inveterate Protestant in his
neighbourhood."†

Not content with this he boldly criticised Bishop Hay's
administration of the Mission funds, which led to an episcopal
reprimand. After this Mr Geddes found reasons for taking a long
holiday in London. Anti-clerical society where criticising die-
hard bishops was the correct thing just suited him. He met Dr
Samuel Johnson, Lord Petre and many other distinguished people,
Catholic and non-Catholic, who treated him with great respect.
The literary world of London proved so congenial that after his
return to Scotland Mr Geddes informed Bishop Hay that he wished
to resign his post at Auchenhalrig (now known as Tynet) and
remove himself to the more intellectually emancipated environment
of the Metropolis.

His resignation was accepted, but he lingered on in the North-
East, hob-nobbing with the nobility and landed gentry.   One
Sunday when visiting Cullen House, he proposed "by way of a
frolic" that his host, Lord Findlater, and his guests should be
driven over to Banff so that they could listen to a popular preacher
at the parish kirk. It is not absolutely certain, however, if Mr
Geddes accompanied the party, but gossip was spread that he had
been seen worshipping in a Presbyterian kirk.

Bishop Hay happened to be staying in the Enzie District that
weekend, and after hearing what may have been a garbled version
of the story, he summoned Mr Geddes for an interview, which
seems to have been reasonably friendly.   Geddes, however, wrote
a satirical account of it and this came to the ears of the Bishop,
who wrote on May 9, 1780: "I am sorry to find that the offence

---

* Born near Preshome in 1737, he showed signs of abnormal precocity
even before he became a student at Scalan at the age of 14. His career
at the Scots College, Paris, between 1758 and 1764 was exceptionally
brilliant. The professor of the newly-founded chair of Hebrew at the
Sorbonne wanted him to remain on and teach that language. After his
ordination Geddes returned to Scotland, where he worked first at Dundee,
and then at Traquair House as private chaplain, occupied with biblical
and philosophical studies. Then after nine months in Paris, he was back
again in Scotland in 1769, this time as curate to Mr John Godsman in
the Enzie District. Soon he became such a popular preacher that the
chapel had to be enlarged. Mr Geddes speculated in house property and
lost money over it. In his leisure moments he translated selected Satires
of Horace and had them printed.

† Cf. James Mason Good, *Memoirs of Dr Geddes* (1803), p. 36.

taken at your conduct is daily increasing. Your debts are a matter of great clamour, and I fear will turn out much to your dishonour. I also understand that you are become a hunter, contrary to the Sacred Canons of the Church, and to the no small scandal of the Catholics in that country, and the late unhappy step you took that Sunday when I was in the Enzie, has found its way to this place [Aberdeen], and met me in different places in Buchan, to the great offence and scandal of all our people. Even those of your best friends are grieved to the heart about it, and the more so, as it appears that one of the principal channels by which it came to this place was from yourself, in a ludicrous letter you wrote on the subject." *

Geddes replied at once, but without satisfying the Bishop, who told him that he must leave the Enzie District within a month or be suspended from exercising his priesthood. It was not until the autumn, however, that he departed, first to Traquair House and finally to London, armed with letters dimissorial from his Vicar-Apostolic. By this time Marischal College, Aberdeen, had conferred on him the degree of Doctor of Letters, apparently in recognition of his translation of the selected Satires of Horace.†

Shortly before this scandal in the North-East, Bishop Hay set to work on a Pastoral Letter, copies of which reached his clergy towards the end of February, 1780. The titles of its four sections almost suggest that they were inspired by the particular priest who indulged in hunting, ran into debt, preached heresy, and consorted injudiciously with Protestants, for they were: (1) On the Sanctity annexed to the Priesthood; (2) On the Sanctity required for the Pastoral Charge; (3) On the Sanctity that belongs to the Character of the Apostle; and (4) on the Sanctity which the Church requires of her Ministers. Rules were given for clerical behaviour, amusements which priests must avoid, and virtues they must strive after. In later years the Abbé Macpherson summed up this Pastoral Letter: "Because it demanded too much, it did no good."‡

---

* ibid, p. **187.**

† The subsequent 22 years of this volatile but erudite priest's career are outside the scope of this book. Lord Petre made him an allowance, enabling him to make and get published parts of a translation of the Bible which were condemned by three of the English Vicars Apostolic. Eventually Dr Geddes was suspended from all ecclesiastical functions, and died in 1802, Bishop Douglass (Vicar-Apostolic of the London District) refused permission for a requiem Mass, because the French priest who had given conditional absolution to the dying man could not confirm his repentance, so the funeral had to be carried out with Anglican rites. Robert, 10th Lord Petre, the son of Dr Geddes's former benefactor, paid for a marble tombstone in Paddington Cemetery, with the inscription (taken from the deceased's writings): "Christian is my name, and Catholic my surname; I grant that you are Christian as well as I, And embrace you as my fellow disciple in Jesus. And if you are not a disciple of Jesus, still I would embrace you as my fellow man ". (Cf. Bernard Ward. *The Dawn of the Catholic Revival in England, 1781- 1803* (1909), Vol. II, p. 247).

‡ *Scotichronicon*, p. **179**, footnote.

Having urged his clergy not to follow in the footsteps of poor Mr Geddes, but to aim at heroic sanctity, Bishop Hay sought and obtained permission from Rome for a reduction in the number of holidays of obligation, which were now limited to ten. Vigils annexed to the festivals were dispensed as days of fasting, but fasting was enforced on the Wednesdays and Fridays in Advent. As the feast of SS. Peter and Paul (June 29) sometimes fell in the barley harvest, the Bishops were authorised in such cases to allow manual labour in the fields, provided that the workers assisted at Mass. *

There were five students at Scalan, supported partly by friends, partly on funds left by Cardinal Spinelli. The Superior was Mr James Paterson.

What must be remembered is that Bishop Hay's rigid directives to the clergy of the Lowland District, with the insistence on their refraining from all worldly amusements, were issued within a year of the 'No Popery' demonstrations in Scotland and shortly before the Gordon Riots in England. They dressed as laymen and kept out of sight so far as possible. Most of them had to travel long distances, usually on foot, to keep in contact with their widely scattered flocks, some of whom thought themselves lucky if they

---

* In a Report of the Lowland District sent to Propaganda in 1780, the following details were included.

Town or District	Catholics	Communicants	Missioners
Dumfries	308	256	John Pepper,
			ex S.J.
Munches	168	114	John Fraser
Edinburgh	800	No returns	Robert Menzies
			John Thomson
Drummond Castle			James Cameron
(including Glasgow)	118	82	Alex Innes
		No returns	(from Paris)
Stobhall	130		William Hay
			(from Rome)
Strathavon	500	—	Vacant
Glenlivet	810	—	Jas. Macgillivray
			ex S.J.
Shenval	127	—	Paul Macpherson
Huntly	325	220	Charles Maxwell
			ex S.J.
Mortlach	371	No returns	William Guthrie
Strathisla	220	—	Alex Menzies
			O.S.B.
Bellie (Tynet)	750	—	George Mathison
Rathven (Preshome)	1150	—	John Reid
			(from Rome)
Aberdeen	470	230	Andrew Oliver
Buchan	130	No returns	Alex. Duguid
Deeside	240	—	William Grant
			ex S.J.
Traquair	—	—	C. Cruickshank

got to Mass even twice a year.   The so-called 'chapels' were usually large rooms or lofts above private houses. *

Consecration of Mr John Geddes as coadjutor to the Lowland District, 1780.

Since the death of Bishop Grant at Aberdeen on December 3rd, 1778, Bishop Hay had been in sole charge of the Lowland District.   In September the following year Propaganda notified Mr John Geddes, then Rector of the Scots College at Valladolid, that he had been chosen as Bishop Hay's coadjutor.   His consecration as titular Bishop of Morocco was postponed until St Andrew's Day (November 30th), 1780.   The function took place in the chapel of the Salesian nuns at Madrid. The consecrating prelate was Francesco Antonio Lorenzana, Archbishop of Toledo, assisted by the Bishops of Urgel and Almeria.   Having returned to Valladolid, Bishop Geddes started for Scotland on February 23rd, 1781. He ordained three deacons at the Scots College at Douai, sailed from Ostend to Margate, and finally reached the Enzie District of Banffshire by way of London, Edinburgh and Perth. By the end of November he had settled in Edinburgh, Bishop Hay having decided to make his home at Aberdeen. Judging from the autobiographical notes left by Bishop Geddes, he led a very active life between 1782 and 1786, making long and frequent journeys around the Vicariate.†

At a meeting of the Vicars-Apostolic in June 1781, it was decided that Bishop Hay should go to Rome.   Under the government of Propaganda, what are known as 'ad limina' visits by bishops 'in partibus infidelium' were by no means encouraged, unless they were specially invited or summoned to do so.   It was not merely a question of expense, or indeed danger of attracting attention from a suspicious or hostile government; there was also a possibility that a Vicar-Apostolic might try to appeal to the Pope against Propaganda.‡ George Hay certainly showed enterprise and originality.   He asked and obtained permission, taking care that his journey was kept secret, even from the Scots Colleges at Paris and Rome.   His own clergy were not informed of his ultimate destination. He travelled incognito, under the *alias* of ' Signor Scotti '.

A coach took him from Edinburgh to London in four days.

* A semi-permanent chapel had been opened at Aberdeen in 1774, on the site of St Peter's, Justice Street, erected in 1803.   It was enlarged in 1782.

† Cf. W. J. Anderson, 'Autobiographical Notes of Bishop John Geddes', in *Innes Review* (Spring, 1967), pp. 36-57. For details of the earlier career of John Geddes, see p. 170.

‡ Normally English Vicars-Apostolic never visited Rome either. It is, to us, strange to reflect that the greatest of them, Richard Challoner (1691-1781), never in all his life, so far as is known, set foot in Rome, though a bishop for forty years.

Having driven on to Margate, he boarded a vessel bound for Ostend and, after a fifteen hours voyage, transferred to canal barges by which he reached Ghent, thence by coach to Brussels. Finding that the Nuncio was taking a cure at the fashionable watering place of Spa, 'Signor Scotti' moved on there. The Nuncio received him most cordially, and arranged a select dinner party. Among the guests was the mother of Princess Louisa Maximilienne of Stolberg-Gedern, the runaway wife of Charles III, now known as the Duchess of Albany. * So on via Aix-la-Chapelle and Cologne the titular Bishop of Daulis reached Würzburg and Ratisbon. In both places he was entertained by the Scottish Benedictines. Having passed through the Tyrol, the Republic of Venice and the Papal States, the Bishop eventually arrived at Rome. It appears that the choice of this devious route was to preserve his incognito, and he had good reasons to give Paris a wide berth.

So far as doing business, it was an unfortunate moment. Most of the Roman officials were *'in villegiatura'*, enjoying their summer holidays. The Bishop, having informed the Scottish Agent, the Abbate Grant, of his arrival, the latter sent a coach to convey him to the villa at Marino, where the students gave the Vicar-Apostolic of the Lowland District a warm welcome.†

The Abbate belonged to that type of priest whom Cardinal Manning called a "diner-out", and whom Bishop Hay neither understood nor approved of. He had reached the age of seventy-three at the time of the Bishop's visit to Rome, and the latter, entirely on his own authority, without the approval of Cardinal Albani, the Protector of the Mission, appointed Mr John Thomson as assistant Agent.‡

* See p. 182 note **.

† Peter Grant (1708-84) was born in Glenlivet and educated at Scalan and the Scots College, Rome, where he was ordained priest in 1735. He returned to Scotland, but two years later was appointed Roman Agent after the murder of Mr William Stuart. Grant—described as " a man of fine parts, and of good taste in Classical knowledge; and strict honour, integrity, and sweet temper; very obliging and agreeable in conversation", soon made a niche for himself in Roman Society. He became a *cicerone* to the English and Scots gentry on the ,Grand Tour', and who wanted a papal audience. As a personal friend of Clement XIV, he expected to be made a cardinal sooner or later, but the sudden death of this Pope in 1774—there were stories that he was poisoned—put an end to those dreams.

‡ This autocratic action on the part of the Vicar-Apostolic of the Lowland District, decided the Abbate to revisit Scotland. After a gay time in Paris, with many dinner parties, he went on to England by way of the Scots College at Douai. Then followed a round of mostly Protestant country house visits in England and Scotland. By the time that the Abbate got back to Rome he was exhausted. He died on September 1, 1784, and was buried in the chapel of the Scots College. A memorial was erected to him, chiefly at the expense of the Earl of Bute and Mr James Stuart Mackenzie. Cf. William J. Anderson, 'Abbé Peter Grant, Roman Agent for the Scottish Catholic Mission, 1738-1783, in *St Peter's College Magazine*, June 1957, pp. 4-8).

One day the Cardinal Duke of York sent a coach so that the Bishop and the Abbate could dine with him at Frascati, where episcopal hospitality was on a lavish scale. Sixty horses were kept in the stables at La Rocca and many coaches for the benefit of guests. But in spite of this outward magnificence the Cardinal Duke set an example to some of his colleagues in the Sacred College by the rectitude in which he carried out his pastoral duties. His generosity to the poor was proverbial.* He promised to help in every way in promoting the objects of Bishop Hay's visit to Rome.

On moving to the Scots College after his rest at Marino, the Bishop received a call from Cardinal Leonardo Antonelli, who placed a coach and horses at his disposal for ceremonial visits. This must have embarrassed him, after the humble manner of his life in Scotland.† There was plenty of business to be done once the cardinals and officials returned to Rome after their summer vacations. First on the list were amendments to the *Statuta* drawn up by Bishop Nicolson in 1706.‡ There were also problems to be solved connected with the Scots College at Paris. Mention has already been made of the fact that it had ceased to accept clerical students. It had not sent a single priest to the Mission between 1739 and 1764. A new Ritual for the missionaries was also needed and a large annual grant of money. Bishop Hay managed to arrange for these two matters. Propaganda finally approved certain amendments in the Statutes, and they were printed at Rome immediately.§ After long discussions the cardinals refused to permit the appointment of a Scottish secular priest as Rector of the Scots College, Rome. It continued to be directed by Italian superiors until it was closed in 1798, after Napoleon's army captured Rome.

Having ordained several students in the college chapel and been received in private audience by Pius VI, Bishop Hay left Rome after Easter 1782. He broke the homeward journey at Paris and there some of the questions he asked at the Scots College were not appreciated by the staff, who reminded him that he had no

* Cardinal de Bernis, the French ambassador at Rome from 1769 to 1791, maintained a standard of living that must have shocked Bishop Hay. When he paid a simple call he contented himself with no more than ten coaches, but on any state visits his magnificent vehicles were accompanied by 22 footmen, 8 runners, 8 pages, 10 beadles, 8 grooms, a mounted Equerry and Master of the Household, 4 gentlemen ushers, 8 valets, and the requisite number of coachmen and postillions (Cf. Sir Marcus Cheke, *The Cardinal de Bernis* (1958), p. 231).

† Until this visit to Rome he was unfamiliar with episcopal ceremonial, and when celebrating Mass had always given the Blessing as a priest does. (Cf. *Scotichronicon*, p. 213).

‡ See p. 105.

§ The *Epitome Ritualis Romani in usum Missionum Scotiae* appeared without name or place or printer, but with the date 1783. Actually it was printed in London.

jurisdiction over this establishment. He landed at Margate by way of Douai and Ostend towards the middle of June. All the liturgical books, relics, rosaries, medals, etc. which he had brought from Italy were seized as contraband, and it cost the Bishop a fine of six guineas to recover his property. He reached Edinburgh during the second week of July, having been absent from Scotland a whole year. At a meeting of the Vicars-Apostolic at Scalan, in August, Bishop Geddes was appointed Procurator of the Mission, with residence in Edinburgh.

Bishop Alexander Macdonald and the Highland Vicariate, 1780–91

Bishop Alexander Macdonald's reports to Propaganda after his consecration as titular Bishop of Polemo on March 12, 1780, usually mentioned the increasing depopulation of the Highland Vicariate as the result of turning so many of the glens into sheep-runs. The Presbyterian ministers were also losing almost as many of their flocks as the result of widespread emigration. From Skye alone some 4,000 persons emigrated between 1772 and 1791. Otherwise life went on fairly quietly. The 'No Popery' riots in 1778-9 hardly affected the more remote parts of the Vicariate.

In October 1790 a sloop sailed from Greenock round the Mull of Kintyre and up the west coast to Moidart with a cargo which included furniture and domestic utensils for the farmhouse college. The Bishop on account of his failing health had already begged Propaganda to give him a coadjutor. He died at Samalaman on September 9, 1791, shortly after his return from the annual meeting of the Vicars-Apostolic, which that year took place at Gibston, near Huntly.

Bishop Hay's life at Aberdeen, 1782-88.

Bishop Hay was aged fifty-three when he went to reside permanently in the little chapel-house at Aberdeen. There he led a life of spartan simplicity, spending most of his time writing books* but occasionally practising his knowledge of medicine and issuing prescriptions to poor people. He wrote frequently to Bishop Geddes in Edinburgh, taking care not to refer to places or persons by their correct names. So Scalan was called 'Patmos', and a Visitation a 'walking tour'. He was inclined to be hypochondriac and often mentioned his own health. His only diversion appears to have been to take tea at Miss Rankine's Boarding School for young ladies, where his 'pleasant conversation' was much appreciated. It is recorded that "he would then call for a little music, and, asking some of the older pupils for their new song, would himself sing it, at sight, with perfect ease and

---

* These included the second part of The Sincere Christian, later on renamed The Devout Christian.

accuracy.   All the young ladies were expected to present
themselves on Sunday at the altar rails for their catechism".

Apparently Miss Rankine felt that it was not quite genteel
for her pupils to mix with the lower orders, so the Bishop agreed
to receive them in his own room on Sunday afternoons, " where
they always found him in a purple cassock, and a purple velvet
cap on his head, where he talked to them kindly and cheerfully." *
Miss Rankine's establishment was highly superior.   The Bishop
recommended it to a Miss Balfour from Orkney, saying that there
was " a very decent good table and tea twice a day".   The
advantage of boarding there was that a girl was sure to meet
" some of the most respectable persons at Aberdeen."

On his 'walking tours' around the Vicariate, the Bishop is
recalled as " a tall figure, striding along and wrapped in a Highland
plaid, with a Highland boy behind carrying a knapsack".   He
regarded the Braes of Glenlivet as a health resort, and was firmly
convinced that his habitual rheumatism was greatly benefited by
bathing in the cold brown peaty water of the Crombie burn.   Later
on, when he grew more frail, he felt justified in mounting on a big
grey horse. But whether he was walking or riding, his servant
Cummings, who served him for twelve years, carried the Mass
vestments and medical requisites without which his master never
travelled. All were packed into a large leather valise. If it rained,
he bade Cummings take shelter under his plaid. Before setting out
on a 'walking' or 'riding tour' he calculated how much money
he could save by rigid economy.   When he was approaching a
Catholic house, notice was sent on ahead.   An altar was fitted
up in a barn or byre, with a blanket for a reredos, and there the
Bishop heard confessions, gave advice to all who asked for it, and
often alms as well, not to mention some homely remedy for their
ailments.

On December 14, 1784, in the upper-room Episcopalian chapel
in Longacre, Aberdeen, Bishop Hay's neighbour, Bishop John
Skinner, assisted by Bishops Robert Kilgour and Arthur Petrie
(vested in black gowns and white bands) laid hands on Mr Samuel
Seabury (1729-96) as first Bishop for the Protestant Episcopal
Church in the United States of America.†

It is not known what Bishop Hay's reactions were when he
was told about that but he must have been distressed that the
Established Church of Scotland was being affected more and more
by liberalism in doctrine. The broader-minded ministers were
termed 'Deists', because they held that Christianity was more a
code of ethics than a divine revelation. There were also the
scholarly, leisured and beneficent 'Moderates', men of wide and
mellow culture. Bishop Hay and his priests owed a lot to them

* *Scotichronicon*, p 272.
† A concordat was drawn up "between the Catholic remainder of the
ancient Church of Scotland and the now rising Church in Connecticut".

indirectly, because they believed in toleration and disapproved of the persecution of Papists. They were sure that with the spread of education and culture Roman Catholicism would die a natural death; persecution merely kept it alive among the ignorant. They dismissed Popery as a moribund superstition.

The spiritual descendants of the old Covenanters were only to be found in the southern parts of the Lowland Vicariate. They included the Cameronians (now known as the Reformed Presbyterians), the Associate Synod (generally referred to as the Seceders), who were split into the mutually excommunicate Burghers and Anti-Burghers. Far more heterodox, however, were the followers of Mrs Elspeth Buchan, who regarded herself as a sort of reincarnation of the Third Person of the Trinity, who had been called by God to lead the chosen people into what they hoped would be their Israel—actually the largely Catholic Nithsdale in Dumfriesshire. *

Bishop Geddes' life in Edinburgh during the 1780s

The titular Bishop of Morocco led a very different sort of life from that of the titular Bishop of Daulis in Aberdeen. The latter, in fact, was often worried by what he regarded as the worldliness of his coadjutor. In after years the Abbé Macpherson wrote of Bishop Geddes: "His learning was great, his piety, affability, humility, and that natural disposition of obliging everyone, as far as it lay in his power, were all qualities so engaging that it appeared impossible for anyone who had an opportunity of being for any time in his company not to respect and love him."

What must be remembered is that, unlike Bishop Hay, Bishop Geddes had spent nearly eleven years as the rector of a college in a Catholic country. Quite at home in the society of Spanish grandees, cardinals, archbishops, bishops and monsignori, he had acquired a *savoir faire* which enabled him to carry on a very real apostolate in Edinburgh. Many of the leading citizens coveted his friendship. Within a short time prejudice against priests broke down and a much greater tolerance towards Papists in general was achieved. Bishop Geddes became a *persona grata* in the somewhat exotic society-world of the 'Modern Athens'. It was the golden age of Edinburgh and he was always a welcome guest at any social function.

The Bishop was often invited to the famous supper parties given by the erudite but eccentric lawyer, Lord Monboddo, at his town-house at 13 St John Street. Sir Walter Scott recorded in after years that "the best society, whether in respect of rank or literary distinction, was always to be found there". The guests sat down at a candle-lit and flower-strewn table, and had the choicest wines poured into their glasses from rose-garlanded decanters of Grecian

* After the death of their foundress in 1791, the Buchanites were driven further west. The remnant found a home in North America.

pattern. The hostess was Mondoddo's daughter, Eliza Burnett, whose beauty was the talk of the town.

It was at Monboddo's that in December 1786 Bishop Geddes met Robert Burns for the first time. The Kilmarnock edition of his poems had been published five months previously and he was being lionised by the *intelligenza*. On January 17, 1787 — four days after the Grand Lodge of Scotland had toasted Burns as 'Caledonia's Bard'—the Bishop wrote to Mr John Thomson, the Roman Agent: "One Burns, an Ayrshire ploughman, has lately appeared as a very good poet. One edition of his Works has been sold rapidly, and another by Subscription is in the Press." *
On March 26 he informed the same correspondent: "There is an excellent poet started up in Ayrshire, where he has been a ploughman; he has made many excellent poems in old Scotch, which are now in the press for the third time. I shall send them to you. His name is Burns. He is only twenty-eight years old; he is in town just now, and I supped with him once at Lord Monboddo's, where I conversed a good deal with him, and think him a man of uncommon genius; and he has, as yet, time, if he lives to cultivate it." †

The first letter from Burns in which Bishop Geddes is mentioned is dated November 4, 1787.‡ Writing to Mrs Dunlop, he said: "I have outraged that gloomy, fiery Presbyterianism enough already, although I don't spit in her lugubrious face by telling her that the first [i.e. the finest or best] Cleric I ever saw was a Roman Catholic — a Popish Bishop, Geddes." §

It was on December 4, that same year, that Burns first met the Edinburgh 'blue-stocking' Mrs Agnes MacLehose, who was then a grass-widow. They started to address each other as 'Clarinda' and 'Sylvester' in almost daily letters. She wrote to him on January 10, 1788: "When you see Bishop Geddes, ask him if he remembers a lady at Mrs Kemp's on a Sunday night who listened to every word he uttered with the gaze of attention. I saw he observed me, and returned that glance of cordial warmth which assured me he was pleased with my delicate flattery. I wished that night he had been my father, that I might shelter me in his bosom." **

It says a lot for the Bishop's tolerance that their friendship deepened. In 1789, the year when Burns began duty as an Excise officer, he borrowed Geddes' copy of the Edinburgh edition of his

---

* *Scotichronicon*, p. 161. The Edinburgh *Poems* were published on April 21, 1787.
   † ibid, p. 161.
   ‡ The Edinburgh edition of the Poems printed among the list of subscribers all the Scots colleges and monasteries abroad, excepting Rome. which at that date still had an Italian rector.
   § Cf. James Darragh, 'The Geddes Burns', in *St Peter's College Magazine*, December 1948, p. 127.
   ** ibid, p. 127.

poems and returned it with additional verses transcribed. They are thirteen in number, written on the flyleaves at the front and back of the volume. Accompanying the book was a long letter, dated February 3, 1789, and written from Ellisland, near Dumfries, where Burns had settled in June 1788. It starts with the salutation " Venerable Father "—most unusual at that period when the appellation of 'Father' was reserved for the regular clergy.*

There was another side to the character of Bishop Geddes which may well have helped him to become such a close friend of Burns. His boyhood had been spent among farmers and crofters. He knew all about country life. And when the shortage of priest made it necessary for him to serve outlying districts, he usually made journeys from Edinburgh on foot.† This worried Bishop Hay, who begged him to give up walking if he found it too fatiguing, but he explained: "When I get out hence, after conversing with God, I foresee, as well as I can, what I have to do in Glasgow and by the way; and concert all my measures."

He enjoyed visiting the old castles or churches he passed, and took a keen interest in archaeology. One day he wrote humorously: "Bishop Hay recommended me to go north on horseback; but was not in the end displeased at my having gone on foot, especially as by this means my horses eat none of his grass; and he readily approved of my walking through Banffshire and Aberdeenshire as he could not well spare his Scalan horses."†

The 'Highland Chapel' in Edinburgh during the 1780s.

In 1783, a year after his return from Rome, Bishop Hay rented a tenement house on the east side of Blackfriars Wynd, off the High Street in Edinburgh. The top flat was furnished as a chapel and reached by a common turret-stair. It became known as the 'Highland Chapel'. For about eight years the priest in charge was Mr Robert Menzies.‡ The Rev. W. J. Anderson reminds us that "in the second half of the eighteenth century there were many Gaelic speakers in Edinburgh; necessarily all spoke some Scots for communication with their employers but undoubtedly they spoke only Gaelic among themselves. They were of all classes. Highland chieftains and lairds visited Edinburgh, some had houses and with them they brought their ladies, and both laird and lady had servants, often numerous. Highland costume

---

* After passing through many hands, the 'Geddes-Burns' found its way into the Henry E. Huntington Library at San Marino, California, in 1918.

† The first real roads in Scotland, as compared with mere tracks for pack-horses, were not built until General Wade started making a few in the Highlands after 1726. Later on local Turnpike Trusts began to construct modern roads in the Lowlands. Before this, people travelled only when they were forced to do so, and then on horse-back. The first regular stage-coach service between Edinburgh and Glasgow was started in 1749. It took 12 hours to cover the 44 miles journey.

‡ *Scotichronicon*, p. 299.

was worn and was fashionable. The Act of Parliament of 1746 proscribing 'clothes called Highland clothes' (always excepting military use) was repealed in 1782 . . .

"[Mr Menzies'] flock in Blackfriars Wynd included at least some of the City Guard . . . Also included were sedan-chairmen who knew Edinburgh society and might, for a consideration, reveal to what address they might have taken a lady. Then there were the Edinburgh 'caddies'. All of these were quite predominantly Highland and Gaelic-speakers. Readers of the complete edition of the letters of Robert Burns will meet Highland servant-girls, some unfortunately of easy virtue and quite illiterate."

Both Catholic and Protestant Gaelic-speakers had to be provided with books needed for worship and instruction. The latter were fairly well catered for by the Rev. Joseph Robertson MacGregor, minister of the Presbyterian Highland Chapel, and later on by the Duncan MacCraig, who served the second chapel (St Oran's), and published a new version of the Shorter Catechism in Gaelic. In 1781 Mr Menzies issued a Gaelic Abridgement of Christian Doctrine by "A Lover of Truth", and entitled *Ainghearradh na Teagisg Chriosduidh*. It was printed in London by the Catholic firm of James Peter Coghlan. In 1785 followed a Scots Gaelic version of the Imitation of Christ, with the title of *Leanmhuin Chriosd ann Ceithear Leabhraicheanm* which was printed in Edinburgh.

Mr Menzies died in October 1791, as the result, so it was said, of "pecuniary embarrassments", leaving nothing of value but his watch. He had carried on a zealous apostolate in Edinburgh, teaching both reading and writing, as well as conducting Sunday Schools, where the Catechism was taught. "The value of [his] unostentatious services began to be felt when death had put a period to them. Many of the poor Highlanders were lost, for want of a priest who could speak the Gaelic tongue. It was next to impossible to secure such a one for the Lowland District."[*]

Bishop Hay at Scalan, 1788-91.

It was in the early summer of 1788 that Bishop Hay transferred his quarters from Aberdeen to Scalan, where he remained for the next three years. The reason given was that Mr Dawson, who was in charge of the College, had been obliged to retire because of his health. The Bishop's first job as Rector was to complete the house which had been begun in 1767. Then he set about cutting down the expenses of the establishment by rigid economies, paying what he called "a handsome board" for himself. Writing to Bishop Geddes on August 10, 1788, he said: " Who knows but Scalan may yet turn out to be of good service in place of Scots

* *Scotichronicon*, p. 329.

shop in Rome . . . our present subjects are all promising."*

Scalan played such an important part in the revival of Catholicism in Scotland between 1717 and 1799 that it may be as well to give further particulars of the place. The so-called "Seminary" was situated at the far end of a wide amphitheatre, surrounded by heather-covered hills. A stranger today, motoring from Dufftown or Speyside to Tomintoul, might not notice the narrow entrance to the Braes of Glenlivet—a gorge through which flows the Crombie burn, a tributary of the Livet Water, over-shadowed by a rounded hill, known as the Bochel. The buildings of Scalan, reached by a rough cart-track from the road that ends at Chapeltown, are invisible until one is quite close to them.

They remain in much the same condition as when Bishop Hay lived there, except that the original thatched roofs have been replaced by slates. The arrangement of the interior of what is not much more than an ordinary farm house has been modified by subsequent partitions. The Bishop occupied a room on the ground floor, next to what was the library, and a diningroom-study at the other end. Upstairs were the students' dormitories, and a tiny chapel where the Blessed Sacrament was reserved. This chapel, immediately above the Bishop's room, was reached also by a stone staircase outside the house. The buildings of what once formed a courtyard are now in ruins. On its north side was another chapel, fitted up when the indoor oratory became too small for the congregation.

The life at Scalan was austere. It is recorded that "the bell rang at six in the morning; and the boys, who wore the Highland dress of black and blue tartan, with home-made shoes [brogues], performed their morning ablutions in the Crombie. They had meat for dinner only twice or thrice a week, vegetables, oatcakes, and sowans [sifting of oat husks, boiled in water] supplying its place on other days. Their breakfast and supper consisted of oatmeal porridge . The Bishop invariably dined with the boys. In the house he generally wore a long coat, or reading gown, of blue and red tartan, spun by the thrifty housekeeper, Annie Gerard ".

She is said to have been even more economical than the Bishop, unwilling to spend one extra penny. Sometimes he had to reprimand her for starving the boys as well as his guests. The Bishop's faithful servant, John Cummings, used to relate how his master always rose very early, long before anyone else was awake, and engaged in solitary prayer in the tiny oratory with its altar-piece of the *Ecce Homo*, which a Lady Chalmers had pre-sented to the original chapel in Blackfriars Wynd, Edinburgh. He lectured to the students on mental philosophy, metaphysics,

* Cf. 'The College for the Lowland District of Scotland at Scalan and Aquhorties; Registers and Documents', ed. by W. J. Anderson, in *Innes Review* (Autumn, 1965), pp. 89-212.

St Peter's, Aberdeen (1774-1803).

natural theology and logic, in addition to the classics.*

The whole life at Scalan must have been a mixture of plain living and high thinking. The household usually consisted of two masters, half-a-dozen boys and a few servants.   There was plenty of peat-fuel for heating, an ample supply of water, local-grown oatmeal (the staple diet), milk from cows, and eggs from hens, so this isolated community was more or less self-dependent * What must be remembered is that Scalan was never a 'seminary' in the modern meaning of the word. It was something almost unique in Catholic educational establishments during the eighteenth century.

News from the outside world took a long time to reach the Braes of Glenlivet, but eventually the masters and students heard that the man whom some of them still regarded as King Charles III had died in Rome on January 30, 1788. Fearful of offending the British Government, Pius VI had refused to let him be buried with royal honours in Rome, so the funeral took place in the cathedral at Frascati, where the Cardinal—now King Henry IX—did as he pleased in the details of ceremonial.   By this time, how-ever, few Jacobites were left who believed that the Stuart dynasty would ever be restored.

What worried Bishop Hay far more was the report of a revolu-tion in France, with the fall of the Bastille on July 14, 1789.   Ever since his visit to Paris seven years before, he had been hoping to acquire direct control of the Scots College, so that it could resume its work of training priests for the Mission.   To him, the College and all its possessions, including its valuable archives, were directly his responsibility.   Although Mr Alexander Gordon, the Principal since 1778, fully realised the hopes and needs of the missionary priests in his native country, he did not see eye to eye with Bishop Hay.   Printed pamphlets appeared, deplorable in their language on both sides.   Word reached Scalan that Louis XVI and the royal family were in prison; that French bishops and priests were seeking refuge in England. It was fairly obvious that the Scots Colleges at Douai and Paris would soon be closed.

Catholic life in the Lowland Vicariate at the time of the outbreak of the French Revolution

Less than a decade had passed since the ' No Popery ' riots of 1778-9 and although no official relief had as yet been granted to Papists in Scotland, both priests and layfolk were enjoying much greater freedom than at any previous period. Banns of marriage, however, still had to be published in the parish kirk and only ministers of the Established Church could perform regular

---

* Among his text books were Thomas Reid's *Essays on Intellectual Powers of Man* (Edinburgh, 1785), and *Essays on the Active Powers of the Human Mind* (Edinburgh, 1788).

† The many illicit stills in Glenlivet could provide whisky if needed.

marriages. The fees payable were a serious matter to poor people. Sometimes priests had to find the money for Catholics to be married by ministers.*

The education of children too remained a serious problem. It was still forbidden to send them out of the country to be educated, though this law was not enforced with great rigour. There were no Catholic schools in the Lowland Vicariate for poor children. It was not until 1790 that Bishop Geddes managed to obtain a definite assurance that Catholic boys and girls, sent to Protestant Charity Schools like the one opened in Glenlivet at an earlier date, would not be forced to learn the Shorter Catechism. They were to be taught only to read and write, with a little arithmetic.

It is difficult to discover how many of the estimated 17,000 Catholics in Scotland about 1780 could read and write. In 1762-3 statistics divided the total into 12,900 Highland and 6,230 Lowland. Twenty years later the proportion had not changed much. Since the majority of the Lowland Catholics were illiterate, there could have been little demand for spiritual reading matter in English or Lallans. There would have been only a very small market for Catholic editions of either the whole Bible or the New Testament and only a minority could have afforded to buy them.† In 1796 Bishop Hay arranged for the publication in Edinburgh of the Douay Bible (1609) in five volumes, priced at 3s a volume, but only a dozen copies were sold in Glasgow, which is not surprising.‡

The Rev. W. J. Anderson reminds us that: "A bishop who embarks in Bible-publishing has at once a vested interest in the sale of Bibles but, while not forgetting that, we must try to be as objective as possible. If I had to express an opinion it would be that Bishop Hay's attitude was one of cautious encouragement, though *cautious* is too weak a word, for in this matter Hay was nervous and timid; and for that he had very good reason . . . Now of the three types of Christian envisaged by Hay — Sincere, Devout and Pious — we need only study the Pious Christian. Nowhere, so far as I know, is there any hint that it might be a duty for a Christian to own or even read a Bible as a complete book. Naturally Hay assumes knowledge of those parts of Scripture read at Mass, and he himself provides for the Pious Christians a generous selection of Scripture texts and short passages on which to

---

* The position of Catholics in Scotland differed widely from that in England. Dues for baptisms had to be paid to the Session Clerks or Beadles of the parish.

† In 1796 Bishop Hay imported a copy of an edition of the whole Bible published at Dublin, printed on cheap paper. It cost him £1 11s 6d. This was a lot of money at that date.

‡ Cf. W. J. Anderson, 'Father Gallus Robertson's Edition of the New Testament, 1792', in *Innes Review* (Spring, 1966), pp. 48-59.

meditate. Sometimes he gives references only and that assumes access to a Bible.

Prior to 1796 Scottish Catholics who could read, and were rich enough to buy copies of the Bible, appear to have used the Authorised Version, and there was no ban on doing so. So afraid was Bishop Hay when it came to printing a Bible himself, that he kept his name out of it entirely. Probably what gave him the courage to launch out as a publisher was that during his visit to Rome in 1781 he heard about the 'Biblical Movement' there. Antonio Martini, the newly consecrated Archbishop of Florence, had published his Italian version of the Scriptures, with a warm commendation from Pius VI. It was a large-scale scholarly work, yet it became a ' best-seller '.

After Bishop Hay's return to Scotland Bishop John Geddes and Fr. Gallus Robertson (a Benedictine monk of Ratisbon, working in Edinburgh) began the translation of the New Testament which appeared in 1792. Previous to this Bishop Hay was so scared by the number of changes made by them that the final printed version was the unrevised Challoner edition of the Douay-Rheims New Testament (1749). The 'Robertson' New Testament, when it went out of print, was superseded by the 'Bishop Hay ' one. *

Apart from the Catechisms produced by James Carnegie and Andrew Hacket, and later by Bishop Alexander Smith (1750), there were no simple books of instruction for layfolk during the eighteenth century. The situation was very different in England, where edition after edition of books of instruction appeared. Scottish missionary priests were afraid to compose catechisms, lest they should be accused of Jansenist heresies, for Fr. Anderson points out: "Somehow in Scotland we have long memories and never let things die down." *

The laws of fasting and abstinence remained unchanged. Bishop Hay refused to consider their mitigation, through fear that people might be encouraged to dispense themselves still further. After all, the Presbyterians had fast days before their infrequent communion Sundays. It would never do for Catholics to set them a bad example by laxity in self-discipline.

Funerals were still carried out more or less secretly, and with no external solemnity. On the other hand, once the religious function (if any) had been performed and the coffin laid in the grave, no limit was imposed on the secular aspects of mourning.

---

* 3,000 copies were printed, of which 1,350 copies were taken by the two English vicars-apostolic, Douglass and Gibson. So the Hay Bible was really produced for the English market, partly because Edinburgh printers were then undercutting those in London. Only a small number of copies were sold to Scottish Catholics. The first edition of the Old Testament in four volumes also consisted of 3,000 copies.

† ibid, p. 54.

Usually Catholic prayers were said in the house before starting to the cemetery. *

Public worship (usually referred to as 'Prayers') seldom consisted of anything more than a low Mass, preceded by a sermon. So far as externals went, there was not much to choose between Catholic and Episcopalian worship in Scotland. There was always the danger that the magistrates or civil authorities would appear at "Public Prayers", so a priest was probably often tempted to rush through Mass as quickly as possible. There were no statues even in the semi-permanent chapels. Only the bare essentials of Catholic worship were to be found.† If a Presbyterian managed to slip into any Papist 'meeting-house' during divine service, he might well have been excused if he formed the impression that the Mass was merely a meaningless mummery, carried out in a dead language, with lots of bowing and scraping by the priest.

Presbyterian worship had always included the singing of metrical versions of the psalms, but there was no music at all in Catholic services. Bishop Hay refused to allow such a dangerous novelty, when attempts were made by priests to liven up the Mass by hymn-singing. Bishop Geddes was not alone in trying to persuade him to adopt a more tolerant point of view, but to no purpose.

Fr. Gallus Robertson, mentioned already, the chaplain to the Maxwells of Munches in Galloway, received a severe rebuke from Bishop Hay when he asked permission to make a few changes in the traditional ritual and ceremonial—"I must and do insist on you observing the common practice of making the sermon before Mass, and on your giving up the singing. If this occasions any trouble to yourself, you have only yourself to blame for it, from the rash step you have taken, and you must extricate yourself the best way you can . . . In these unhappy times . . . Innovations, Changes and an itch for pretended Reformations seem to have in some degree pervaded all ranks of people."‡

* At the funeral of Mr George Gordon, the priest at Scalan in 1737, care was taken to order the following drinks for the refreshment of the mourners:—an anker of whisky (equal to 10 gallons); 2 dozen bottles of claret; 3 dozen bottles of port wine; 1 dozen bottles of white wine; and a fair supply of shortbread and biscuits. This was nothing extraordinary, and what would have been expected at any decent funeral in the 18th century—Papist or Protestant.

† The same austerity existed in the typical Episcopalian 'meeting house' at this period, for it hardly differed from the average Presbyterian kirk in its plan and furnishings, even if the doctrines preached from its two or three-decker pulpit tended to be more Catholic than Calvinist. The communion table never displayed either a cross or candlesticks. Both the bishops and priests conducted services in black gowns.

‡ Scotichronicon, p. 405. The sermon came first, and was followed by long vernacular prayers, with ' Acts of Faith, Hope, Charity ' etc.—much longer than the 'Bidding Prayers' given in the official text of the Rite of Low Mass approved by the Scottish Hierarchy in 1965.

This " short, stout, merry little monk " (as he is recalled) ignored the liturgical directives of his Vicar-Apostolic, quite possibly maintaining that he was bound by the Ratisbon Benedictine 'Use', not "the common practice" of the Scottish Mission. Indeed he was a forerunner of the modern Liturgical Movement because he introduced lectors, i.e. "Psalm-readers", in the chapel on Sundays, and even formed "a set of elders, so called, to form his Council, respecting the poor". Mr John Pepper, the chaplain at Terregles, wrote in 1798 : "He used, but whether he continues I don't know, to have singing and ranting Psalms of his own translation, which I must confess I think most improper in a Roman Catholic chapel in this part of the world. It is now a common saying in this country that Mr Robertson's prayers are not the same as at Terregles and Kirkconnell." *

Bishop Hay was not impressed by the reports sent to him of liturgical experiments made in the chapel at Tynet and Edinburgh, in spite of the fact that they resulted in much larger congregations. Before introducing hymn-singing at Tynet, Mr Matheson took the precaution of securing the approval of the local Presbyterian ministers.† When the Bishop heard that a *Te Deum* had been chanted in the chapels at Aberdeen and Edinburgh in thanksgiving for the recovery to health of George III in April 1789, he was horrified; denouncing it as "an Innovation in the service of God, and in the public discipline of the Church". Mr John Thomson, the Roman Agent, agreed with him, and wrote that it was "a mere whim of the Scottish Catholics to wish for music in their chapels; a thing which ought to be the last to be thought of."‡

But the people, having started corporate participation in worship, were not going to be stopped by the Bishop of Daulis *in partibus*. At Christmas, 1789, Mr Robert Menzies allowed the congregation at the Highland Chapel in Edinburgh to sing the *Adeste Fideles*. This seventeenth or eighteenth century hymn of French or German origin is said to have "speedily become a *furore* in the town; apprentice lads whistled it in every street; the very blackbirds in the squares joined in the chorus, it was said."

The lively tune which the boys whistled seems to be of English origin, and exists in a MS of 1746 at Clongowes College, Ireland, and in MSS of a later date in non-Catholic institutions in England. The description 'Portuguese Hymn' sometimes attached to the *Adeste Fideles* comes only from its use, in the late 18th century, in the Portuguese Embassy Chapel, London.

* ibid, 406.

† (He was told by them that it was strange that Papists had so long neglected enriching their services with music, especially in view of the fact that since 1753 Sir Archibald Grant of Monymusk had been leading a movement in the North-East to improve the music in both town and country parishes of the Established Church.

‡ ibid, p. 290.

Even a fire which damaged the chapel at Stobhall in 1789 helped to convince Bishop Hay even more that it was his duty to "put a stop to the Singing-Scheme". He entreated Bishop Geddes to enforce the joint resolution of the Vicars-Apostolic against disedifying liturgical innovations.

Until this time there had been no glamour or romance about Catholic worship in Scotland to attract Protestants, for this was the last thing that anybody wanted to do. First Communion was often postponed for years because of fear of irreverence and lack of true understanding of the august nature of the Sacrament. The laity were discouraged from making their Confessions or receiving Holy Communion more frequently than at the times of the so-called "Indulgences", i.e. the greater festivals. The preparation for Communion was almost as long drawn-out as that of the Episcopalians and Presbyterians for their even less frequent administrations of the Lord's Supper. Thanksgiving for Holy Communion would be prolonged for several days.

Devotional life centred round the weekly Sunday "Prayers", a simple low Mass; the observance of many abstinence and fasting days; the reading of a few well-known spiritual books, and more rarely the Bible, for there was only Challoner's translation, and copies of it were few and far between.* This austere type of Catholicism was the result of both the Penal Laws and a Calvinist environment. It is doubtful if French Jansenism played any part in creating it.

Bishop Geddes took a very different line from Bishop Hay, and tried from time to time to make him see differently. He could not understand what dangers were inherent in reverent singing in Catholic chapels. He reminded Bishop Hay that Sunday afternoons were times of peculiar risk to young persons, for which reason they ought to be attracted by a little music to attend "Christian Doctrine", and so be kept off the streets. He even went so far as to write: "This would likewise be a preparation at a distance, for our having a High Mass sung on some Festivals, to the great edification of the faithful, and when we shall see it expedient. Your predecessor was very desirous of seeing this; and what he said to me on that subject was one of the reasons I had for making Church Music to be taught at Valladolid, which I wish were done in all our Houses abroad. I beg you will consider all this, and I hope you will give a favourable answer to our petition."†

* The original version of Challoner's *Garden of the Soul* (1740) was much used by layfolk in Scotland. They read the 'Meditations during Mass', not only when they could not attend 'Public Prayers' for lack of a priest, but also while low Mass was being celebrated. In Bishop Hay's time copies were imported from England and sold in the Lowland Vicariate. The Meditations were adapted in some of his own devotional writings.

† ibid, p. 294.

Bishop Hay, however, remained obdurate. He considered the possible effect of hearty singing on the Sabbath morning — for instance in Blackfriars Wynd — and he had not forgotten what an Edinburgh mob could do. It was too dangerous to draw attention to Catholic worship, which ought to be kept as secret as possible. So far as he was concerned, Scottish Catholics were still in the same state as the early Christians at Rome who had to meet in the catacombs. He flatly refused to permit any sort of music in the chapels of the Lowland Vicariate. It was not until after his death in 1811 that a few liturgical changes were made. The Sunday morning services continued to consist of a sermon and long prayers in the vulgar tongue, followed by a more or less silent Low Mass celebrated in Latin.

What must be remembered is that, unlike London, Edinburgh never had any foreign embassy chapels. In London, every Sunday throughout the greater part of the seventeenth and eighteenth centuries, these provided Sung Masses and Vespers (with Benediction), which attracted Protestants by the music and ornate ceremonial. Catholic life in London centred round the chapels maintained by Spanish, Portuguese and Bavarian envoys, with whom the Vicar-Apostolic's relations were sometimes difficult.

It was with considerable reluctance that in 1788 Bishop Hay gave permission to Mr John Reid, the priest in charge of the eastern part of the Enzie District, to erect a new place of worship at Preshome which would look like a church and thus be liable to desecration by Protestants. This chapel, planned to hold seven hundred persons, was opened on Whit Sunday, 1790, and this is how it has been described: "As built it was a wide rectangular church with harled walls and freestone dressings. With flanking staircase pavilions, well disposed round-headed openings, and a pedimented gable inscribed 'DEO 1788' and adorned with urn finials, its west end is a charming product of eighteenth century taste in which Italian Baroque has been skilfully naturalised to a Banffshire setting . . . Mr John Reid was himself a product of the Scots College, Rome, and there is little doubt that he is largely his own architect for the work."*

The Earl of Findlater, whose Catholic wife sometimes came over from Cullen House to worship at Preshome, presented a copy of Caracci's painting of St Gregory the Great as the altar-piece.† Lady Findlater provided two holy water stoups of Portsoy marble,

* George Hay, *The Architecture of Scottish Post-Reformation Churches.*
† This instance of the dedication of the church resulting from the presentation of a picture seems to have become the normal sequence of events later on. In the case of the chapel at Dufftown, Banffshire (1824), the original altar-piece—an Italian 'Scourging at the Pillar'—promised by Lord Fife, did not materialise. Eventually an 'Assumption' after the manner of Poussin was acquired, so the chapel was dedicated to Our Lady of the Assumption. The same thing happened at Keith in 1831 (See p. 252).

and Bishop Geddes donated a handsome tabernacle. The opening of this chapel at Pentecost 1792 can be regarded as the dawn of a 'Second Spring' for Catholicism in Scotland. It more or less coincided with crowds, bearing the red bonnet of liberty, marching to the Tuilleries, and the first battle of the French Revolutionary War.

Bishop Geddes's visit to France, 1791

At the meeting of the Vicars-Apostolic held at Gibston near Huntly in August 1791 it was decided that Bishop Geddes should be sent to France, so that he could enquire into the affairs of the Scots College, Paris. His status would be that of Deputy and Procurator for the Mission. Powers were granted to him by Bishop Hay and Bishop Macdonald, and five priests who acted as administrators of the Mission's temporal affairs. Twenty-four influential Catholic laymen added their signatures to the document presented to him before he left Edinburgh for London by coach on October 16.

His mission was a delicate one, because Mr Gordon, the Principal of the Paris College, argued that it had always been and ought to remain an independent establishment. None of the Vicars-Apostolic had ever known much about the College, except Bishop Gordon who had been a student there. Neither Bishop Hay nor Bishop Macdonald seems ever to have studied or even to have seen its Statutes, and they therefore had no powers as Visitors. There had always been a definite *esprit-de-corps* among the Paris-trained missionaries. To all intents and purposes, they regarded the Principal of the College as their Religious Superior, even after they returned to Scotland. As has been stated already, the College had always been a hot-bed of political Jacobitism.*

Bishop Geddes reached Paris on December 23,† having landed at Calais and gone on to Douai. He was informed that he could not lodge at the Scots College, "because the house was in some confusion, a theft having been committed by a servant in the English Seminary", so he had to be content with other accommodation. When he did call on Mr Gordon he "found him more friendly than expected", and he was allowed to examine the archives—even to translate part of a Chinese Grammar. Courtesy calls was made on the British Ambassador, the Papal Inter-Nuncio, Mgr. Salomon and other important people. He noted in his journal (Section 51): "From my first arrival in Paris I had been endeavouring to get some account of the Bishop of Rodez, but until now I have only learned that he was in town, but none could tell me at

* See pp. 131-2.
† While staying at the Scots College, Douai, his arm "was electrified by Mr Poynter of the English College (the future Vicar-Apostolic of the London District) for a rheumatic weakness in it."

what place. At last, he having heard of me at Lord Gower's, sent the abbé Cook to Mgr. Salomon who conducted me to the Bishop. This prelate is a son of the family of Castlehill, by name Seignelay-Cuthbert, or Colbert, and was sent to the college of Paris when he was only eleven years of age at the desire of his uncle who had a rich benefice in France. Here he remained as a pensioner for three and a half; he afterwards studied in French seminaries, embraced the ecclesiastical state, was Grand Vicar of Toulouse, and distinguished himself among the clergy of France, and was made Bishop of Rodez in 1781. He had been a member of the first National Assembly, but refusing to take the Constitutional Oath, he had been obliged to leave his diocese, and was now living in a retired manner with only one servant. He made me very welcome to him . . ."*

On January 4, 1792, Bishop Geddes attended a meeting of the National Assembly, where, to his surprise, one of the ushers ('huissiers') walking up and down to keep order was a Mr Rose from Edinburgh.

Nothing was gained by this trip to France, even if the Bishop did discover "remarkable things" in the Statutes of the Scots College (shown him by the Prior of the Carthusians). He arrived back in Edinburgh four months later and there he compiled an account of the unsuccessful negotiations between himself and Principal Gordon, which he dictated to the abbé Macpherson and authenticated by his own signature on July 16, 1794.

There was a meeting of the Vicars-Apostolic at Scalan in August 1792, after which they sent their usual annual Report to Propaganda. Bishop Geddes returned there the following year but his health steadily grew worse. When he was moved to Aberdeen on October 22, 1793, the journey took five days.†

After the massacres in Paris early in September 1792, when the prisons were broken open and about a hundred priests were among over 1,200 persons slain, the affairs of the Scots College settled themselves. Principal Gordon fled to London, where he was befriended by the eighth Earl of Buchan. He continued to regard himself as the lawful guardian of the College and its properties,

---

* It seems that the Bishop was a grandson of John Cuthbert, 8th Laird of Castlehill, near Inverness, who married Jean Hay of Dalgetty, only daughter of William Hay, episcopalian Bishop of Moray, who died in 1707. Apparently she set out to provide for one (or two) of her grand-sons on the death of their father, George Cuthbert, and called in the aid of French Catholic relatives, among whom was an abbé Alexander Colbert. There is a story that the abbé came to Scotland about 1780, and bought back the sequestrated Castlehill estate, which passed to his brother. George, who was Provost Marshall in Jamaica. But the whole story is confused and contradictory, and there are different versions of it.

† He remained in Aberdeen until his death on February 11, 1799.

*The Seminary at Aquhorties, near Inverurie,
Aberdeenshire (1797-1811).*

*The College on the island of Lismore, Argyllshire
(1803-1829).*

and his agents in Paris managed to prevent the settlement of any claims made by the Vicars-Apostolic.*

By the winter of 1792 French refugees were arriving in Scotland from England, some finding work in the mills at New Lanark, others tried to earn their living by teaching.

Mr John Chisholm consecrated as fourth Vicar-Apostolic of the Highland District, 1792.

During Bishop Geddes's absence in France, Bishop Hay was informed by Propaganda that Mr John Chisholm had been nominated Vicar-Apostolic of the Highland District, in succession to Bishop Alexander Macdonald, who had died on September 12, 1791.† Mr Chisholm, with the title of Bishop of Oris in Mesopotamia, was consecrated in Edinburgh by Bishop Hay on February 12, 1792, with no external solemnity.

The seminary at Samalaman needed his immediate attention. Studies were being neglected — the eight boys spent more time working on the farm than at their studies — and the establishment was heavily in debt. Conditions appear to have been squalid, for the new Bishop wrote to the Roman Agent that "East Scalan" was "a palace in comparison with West Scalan"‡ In 1794 he mentioned the constant effort of "keeping up and repairing the old huts and thatch that cannot stand against the storms on this coast." The isolation of Samalaman added to the difficulties. Provisions had to be brought thirty or forty miles. The following year there were eight boys, all of them very poor and unable to provide their own clothes. Expenses mounted daily and matters went from bad to worse. On January 30, 1798, Bishop Chisholm wrote to Bishop Hay that it was impossible to keep Samalaman open any longer.

Having inspected properties on the islands of Eigg and Mull, in 1803, Bishop Chisholm bought a farm on the island of Lismore from Campbell of Dunstaffnage and it cost the Highland Vicariate about £5,000, a stiff sum in those days. Very little has been recorded about this seminary on the island of Loch Linnhe, where

---

* Had it not been for the quarrel between Gordon and Bishop Hay, Mr Pitt, then First Lord of the Treasury and Chancellor of the Exchequer. would have bought the surviving archives of the College, but it could not be decided who was their legal owner. Certain documents remained in Gordon's hands until his death in 1818, after which they found their way to Edinburgh and then to Blairs College. Most of the archives which were deposited with the Paris Carthusians were lost or destroyed.

† John Chisholm was born in Strathglass in 1752, and was educated at the Scots College, Douai, until the Jesuits were expelled from France. He resumed his studies there after the College was put under the direction of secular priests. He returned to Scotland following his ordination in 1777, and his first mission was in his native Strathglass.

‡ Cf. 'Glenlivitensis', 'The Highland Seminaries, III', in *St Peter's Magazine*, Vol. XX (1952), p. 119.

a small cathedral had been built in 1236, when it became the seat
of the diocese of Argyll with a chapter of secular canons. The
seminary, which carried on for twenty-six years, never evolved
into what Bishop Chisholm hoped it would be—"a renowned
Academy, where every branch of education would be taught in
style." * Life on this fertile island, nine-and-a-half miles long,
cannot have been easy. Everything needed for the Seminary had
to be brought from Glasgow or Greenock by sea—even the cargoes
of coal and bricks—and it was a long journey round the Mull of
Kintyre for Skipper McLaughlin's little vessel.

Nevertheless, many priests were educated on Lismore, and in
after years they all worked in the Highland District. The island
remained the residence of its Vicars-Apostolic until the students
were moved to Blairs in 1829.†

Glasgow's first resident priest and permanent chapel, 1792.

Until about 1780, Glasgow did not require a resident priest
because there were seldom more than half-a-dozen Catholic
families living in and around the city. Once or twice a year the
chaplain at Drummond Castle, Perthshire (about fifty miles
distant), rode over to say Mass.‡ Bishop Hay used to visit Glasgow
from time to time, when he was living in Edinburgh, and after 1781
Bishop Geddes occasionally made the forty-four miles walk in
each direction to celebrate Mass, mainly for the benefit of the
Misses Fletcher of Dunans, two convert ladies from Argyllshire.
Four years later Mr Alexander Geddes on a very short visit
ministered to them, but at first he refused to let any outsiders assist
at his Mass, for fear of trouble.

The Catholic population of Glasgow had begun to increase
after the first cotton mill was opened in 1779. The cotton-weavers,
who formed a trade union in 1782, included Gaelic-speaking
Highlanders who had been evicted from their homes, when their
crofts were turned into sheepwalks. Then there were also Irish
families coming over to Scotland seeking employment.

A young priest, Mr Alexander Macdonall (1760-1840), was
sent by Bishop Alexander Macdonald in 1792 to look after the

---

* In 1814 Sir Walter Scott, when making a tour of the lighthouses for
the Commissioners, wrote: "We coasted the low, long and fertile island of
Lismore where a Catholic bishop, Chisholm, has established a seminary
of young men intended for priests, and has a better thing, a valuable lime
work. Reports speak well of the lime, but indifferently of the progress
of the students." (ibid, p. 31).

† The two Bishops Chisholm and other priests were buried on the island
of Lismore.

‡ In 1969 the estimated Catholic population of the Glasgow Archdiocese, which comprises only the City and the County of Dunbarton
(a quite small area), was 325,830. The 98 parishes were served by 690
priests (secular and regular).

Highland Catholics in Glasgow.* Not only did he secure jobs for them, but he acted as their devoted pastor. Through the influence of the Monteiths (the chief owners of the cotton mills) and several leading citizens, Mr Macdonell soon found permanent quarters for a chapel—a disused tennis court in Town's Court off Mitchell Street, of which the Duke of Hamilton was the landlord. Some of the manufacturers provided three hundred seats, and became security for the rent. All were Protestants, but "they were alive to the advantage of having sober and industrious men in their employment; and, above all, the poor Catholics had God to trust in".

Mr Macdonell celebrated his first Mass in Glasgow's first permanent Catholic chapel on October 21, 1792, four months after Britain declared war against France. The fear of a French invasion was making Protestants more tolerant towards Papists.

As might have been expected, Bishop Hay was nervous of what could happen as the result of opening this chapel, and he wrote to Bishop Geddes a fortnight later: "I am much afraid that Mr Macdonell had a little touch of the common turn too prevalent among us; yet considering the difficulties he must be exposed to, in setting up house in such a place, and in such circumstances, I am very willing that he get the town quota for a little."

On December 8 he wrote again more optimistically, and said: "Mr Macdonell is of a forward and intrepid disposition; but I have often seen that when Providence has a mind to being about any event, he qualifies the instruments he makes use of for that purpose; and very often, a certain degree of boldness produces much better effects than too much timidity. I trust in God that that will be the case with our friend there."†

The Catholic Relief Act (Scotland) 1793.

Freedom of worship for Scottish Episcopalians was granted in 1792. The following year, on April 22, the Lord Advocate, Henry Dundas (created Viscount Melville in 1802), obtained permission to introduce a relief bill for Scottish Roman Catholics.‡ It passed the House of Lords on May 24, and received the royal assent on June 3.

A month later, on July 11, the titular Bishops of Daulis and Morocco presented themselves to the Sheriff-Substitute of Midlothian, so that they could take the Oath, Abjuration and

---

* Born at Inchlaggan in Glengarry in 1760, he was educated at Buorblach on Loch Morar; and afterwards at the Scots Colleges at Paris and Valladolid, where he was ordained priest in 1787. His first mission was in the Braes of Lochaber, where he worked for five years.

† *Scotichronicon*, p. 334.

‡ ibid, p. 335. About this time the magistrates of Dundee offered Dom William Pepper, a Benedictine monk of Wurzburg, who had been in charge of the mission since 1782, to petition the Government for the extension of the Catholic Relief Bill to Scotland.

Declaration as prescribed in the recent Act. Two days after this, the Bishop of Daulis sent out copies of a pastoral letter in which he expressed his sense of gratitude towards the Government, set forth the duty of loyalty to the State, and maintained that Catholics were bound to pray for their earthly ruler. In conclusion he begged them to use their recovered liberty "with prudence and moderation, so as, by their quiet and peaceable demeanour, to convince the world that they were not unworthy of the favour lately bestowed on them . . . To gratitude they were bound to join a sincere repentance for their own sins and the sins of their forefathers, which had provoked the Divine anger against them." *

It was not charity towards a persecuted minority in Scotland that caused the Relief Act to be rushed through both houses of parliament and given royal assent. Catholics had to thank the French Revolution for their partial emancipation. The massacres of September 1792 had been followed by the execution of Louis XVI in January, and war against Britain and Holland was declared on February 1. Then began the reign of terror, the beheading of Queen Marie Antoinette, and the worship of the goddess of reason, enforced in November 1793. The government was alarmed by the activities of societies known as 'Friends of the People', which had been formed in England and Scotland. It was known that risings were being planned to take place in Edinburgh, Dublin and London in support of the revolutionaries in France.†

What Scottish Catholics actually gained by the Relief Act was the peaceful possession and free disposition of their property. On the other hand they were still excluded from almost every public office, including that of teacher or professor of any subject. They still had to have their banns of marriage published in the parish kirk, to be married (if a regular, as distinct from a valid marriage was essential) by the parish minister, and to pay dues for baptism to the parish official. If a Protestant consented to be married by a priest, he or she was liable to fines and kirk censures. But the revised form of abjuration to which Catholics were now obliged to subscribe granted them freedom from all pains and penalties imposed by former Acts (especially those passed in the first Parliament of William III in 1689). Although for political reasons it had become necessary to tolerate the existence of a Papist minority in Scotland, it was not considered safe to grant them anything in the nature of full emancipation.

Bishop Hay had now left Scalan and taken up his residence in Edinburgh. On December 26, 1793, he received a call from a papal envoy, Mgr. Charles Erskine, who had been sent by Pius

* ibid, p. 348.
† In 1792 Thomas Paine, who had published *The Rights of Man,* had fled to France to escape prosecution. His *Age of Reason* appeared the following year.

VI to confer with the British Government mainly about the numerous French bishops, priests and layfolk who had sought refuge in England by this time.* Being a British subject he was entitled to enter England without permission or passport. The police and customs officers, who had been advised of the arrival of this distinguished papal diplomat, showed him the utmost courtesy on the journey from Margate to London.† After a round of visits to his Protstant kinsfolk in Fife, Mgr. Erskine on his return journey southward spent ten days in Edinburgh without even seeing Bishop Hay or returning his calls, though he promised to do so. It is recorded that "the Bishop felt this keenly, as he had hoped to press the interests of the Scots College on his old fellow student at a personal interview."‡ After his return to London, however, the Papal Envoy found time to answer the two letters received from the Bishop while he was in Scotland, and said: "Edinburgh is a charming town; every view of it and from it is picturesque; and that mixture of old and modern engages not only the eye, but the imagination. As for its society, I must say it is the pleasantest I have ever met with; and I shall never forget the civilities I have received there."

There was no reference in this letter to the Scottish Mission but its affairs were outside the immediate business for which Mgr. Erskine had been sent to Britain by the Pope. This probably explains why, as an astute diplomat, he associated almost entirely with Protestants.§

In the meantime quite a number of Catholics in Scotland, sharing the opinions of Robert Burns, were glorying in the French Revolution. One of the extreme Catholic republicans was William

---

* Son of Colin Erskine of Cambo, Fife, by Lady Anne Erskine, daughter of the 3rd Earl of Kellie, Charles was born at Rome in 1739. He was brought up by the Cardinal Duke of York, Cf. Ian Docherty, 'Cardinal Erskine and the Cardinal Duke of York', in *Innes Review* (Autumn, 1965), pp. 217-8). In 1770, having taken the degree of Doctor of Law, he was made Pro-Auditor and Promoter of the Faith (otherwise 'Devil's Advocate'), also a domestic prelate, canon of St Peter's, and dean of the college of consistorial advocates. In 1783 Mgr. Erskine received minor orders from the Cardinal of York and was then ordained subdeacon, but he was never raised to the priesthood, even after he became a Cardinal in 1801.

† As for the postillions, divining from this special treatment the quality of the traveller, they took care, on each change of the post horses, to announce with emphasis to the postillions who succeeded them, the *Ambassador of the Pope!* This was done all the whole way to London, and Erskine could not perceive that the news was received in any sinister manner, but rather with an increased desire to serve him." (W. Maziere Brady, *Anglo-Roman Papers* (1890), p. 129).

‡ *Scotichronicon*, p. 366. Erskine had entered the Scots College, Rome, in 1748, but left after five years because he would not take the Mission Oath, and subsequently studied Law.

§ Some of his relatives wanted him to seek a dispensation from the Pope and get married, so that he could beget heirs, for there was no direct line of succession to the earldom of Kellie.

Maxwell of Kirkconnel but even Bishop Geddes had not been unduly perturbed by what he saw during his visit to Paris in 1792.* As to the heterodox Dr Alexander Geddes, now living in London, he was quite convinced that Britons ought to support the fight for freedom in France.

In 1794 Robert Watt, a one-time government spy and agent-provocateur, was arrested in Edinburgh and charged with high treason for planning an armed insurrection in connection with the Friends of the People.† He was convicted and hanged. At the same time, but separately, an Edinburgh Catholic, the goldsmith David Downie, who was a treasurer of the society, also stood in the dock. He, however, was respited and finally transported, probably to Botany Bay.‡

Although Downie had openly described Bishop Hay as "turned recruiting-sergeant for King George", the Bishop visited him in prison. So did Mr Alexander Cameron, later rector of the Scots College at Valladolid.§ In September 1794 Bishop Hay issued to his clergy a Latin pastoral which was nothing if not patriotic in its sentiments. Brimful of gratitude for the end of two hundred and thirty-three years of the Penal Laws, it included a generous recognition of the fair deal which the Government had been giving to the Catholic Mission in Scotland.

With the death of Mr John Thomson in November 1792, another priest had to be found to take on the duties of Roman Agent which he had fulfilled for ten years. The Vicars Apostolic chose Mr Paul Macpherson, who left Edinburgh in August the following year.** Considering the troubled state of Europe, it is surprising that the journey to Rome took him no more than two months. He was faced with many difficult problems, the chief of which was the state of the Scots College, which was still under the charge of Italian secular priests.

Mr Alexander Macdonell helps to organise a Catholic regiment, 1794.

One result of the Relief Act of 1793 was that Scottish Catholics could now serve in the British Army without having to give up their religion. The Government badly wanted recruits and a good

---

* See p. 205.

† See p. 210.

‡ Cf. William J. Anderson, 'Davie Downie and the Friends of the People', in *Innes Review* (Autumn 1965), pp. 165-79.

§ The latter wrote to Bishop Geddes in Aberdeen, asking if it would be in order for him to hear Downie's confession before the trial; if he refused to disclose the whole story of the attempted rising, could he be admitted to the sacraments (ibid. p. 171). Downie was a person of standing in the Edinburgh Catholic congregation.

** Born in 1736, his father being a crofter in Glenlivet, he was educated at Scalan, Rome, and Valladolid. After his ordination in 1779 he worked successively in the Cabrach District, at Aberdeen, Stobhall, and Edinburgh.

number of Catholics of high social standing wanted to be officers. At the same time there were more than enough unemployed High-landers drifting around the Lowlands in search of jobs to swell the ranks. It struck some of the Highland lairds that it would benefit their men if a wholly Catholic regiment, staffed only by Catholic officers, could be raised. Mr Alexander Macdonell, still in charge of the Glasgow mission, was really responsible for forming this regiment. *

On February 26, 1794, a meeting took place at Fort Augustus. Marmaduke Maxwell of Terregles presided and among others present were Bishop Chisholm, the chief of Glengarry and Mr Macdonell. There it was decided that a regiment should be formed—called the Glengarry Fencibles—to consist of ten com-panies of fifty-seven men each, with the usual complement of officers and non-commissioned officers. A picturesque uniform was devised, consisting of a close-fitting scarlet jacket, with a kilt and plaid of the Macdonald tartan (dark green, blue and red). The officers would have broad-bladed, basket hilted claymores and skean-dhus (dirks), in addition to their long Highland pistols.

Bishop Hay was alarmed when he heard what had taken place but by that time it was too late to oppose the formation of this Catholic regiment and he felt he must tolerate the project. But "wishing to know the matter to the bottom", he made further enquiries and ended by writing to Bishop Geddes: "The facts are but too true, and the effects of the remedy, if adopted, lie in the hands of Providence. I am much edified with Glengarry. He is an amiable young gentleman, and I hope will one day be an honour and support to his Country and to his Religion."†

The Protestant Duchess of Gordon was also opposed to the formation of the Glengarry Fencibles, because her son, the Marquess of Huntly, was trying to raise a similar regiment. As most of his tenants in Aberdeenshire and Banffshire were Catholics, it was to be expected that they would prefer to enlist an all-Catholic body. At first George III declined the offer of a Scottish Catholic regiment, but when Henry Dundas, now Secretary of War, intervened, permission was granted for setting up the Glen-garry Fencibles. The Colonel was Alexander Macdonell of Glengarry, the Lieutenant-Colonel, Charles Maclean, and twenty-one out of the twenty-eight officers were either Macdonalds or Macdonells. Mr Macdonell was appointed chaplain, although this was still illegal, and so he became the first Catholic chaplain in the British Army since the Reformation.‡

The subsequent career of this Highland priest, although outside

---

* See p. 208.
† *Scotichronicon*, p. 367.
‡ The regiment was immediately sent to the Isle of Guernsey, where it remained until 1798, when it was moved to Ireland, in case there should be a French invasion. The Fencibles were disbanded at Glasgow in 1807.

the scope of this book, must be recorded briefly. After the Glengarry Fencibles were disbanded in 1802, he spent most of his time negotiating with the government for the emigration of his people to Canada. He followed them in 1804, and was put in charge of St Raphael's Mission in Glengarry County, "the Cradle of the Church in Ontario". This remained his base for twenty-five years, while he travelled immense distances, sometimes on horse-back, sometimes on foot or in Indian birch canoes, administering the Sacraments and keeping in touch with his flock. For ten years he had no priests to assist him. In 1812 he re-organised the Glengarry Fencibles, and became their chaplain once again. During the two years' war against the United States (1812-14) he was present at several engagements.

Upper Canada was removed from the jurisdiction of the Bishop of Quebec in 1817, and Mr Macdonell was appointed first Vicar-Apostolic. His consecration as titular Bishop of Roina took place at Quebec on December 20, 1820. * Six years later Bishop Macdonell became the first prelate to rule over the newly erected Diocese of Kingston, and first Bishop in Upper Canada. So greatly was he respected that in 1831 he was made a member of the Legislative Council and accorded the title 'Honourable'. This one-time missionary in the Braes of Lochaber never ceased working to obtain government grants for church and school purposes. He made five voyages to Europe and raised immense sums of money for promoting religion and education. He died at Dumfries during a visit to Scotland, and in 1861 his body was brought back to Canada and re-interred in Kingston Cathedral.† He is remembered as a great missionary, prelate and patriot — the Apostle of Ontario.‡

The part played by Mgr. Charles Erskine in Scottish Catholic affairs between 1793 and 1802, while he was acting as papal envoy to Britain, is often forgotten. During those nine years he managed to establish excellent relations with the Court of George III and with the British Government. This subdeacon-monsignore, with his tact, charm of manner and savoir-faire, made the perfect liaison officer at dinner-parties and other social functions. There were never any Protestant demonstrations against him.§

Catholic Life in Scotland between 1793 and 1811.

One effect of the French Revolution was the sudden increase of Catholic clergy in Britain. At one time there were over five thousand French priests in England, besides nineteen bishops. They helped to break down prejudice against Catholics and, on the

---

* King George IV presented him with an episcopal ring.

† See p. 257.

‡ Cf. D. R. Macdonald, 'Macdonell, Alexander' in *Catholic Encyclopedia* (1910). Vol. IX, pp. 489-90.

§ It was largely due to his negotiations that the Government decided to give financial help to the Scottish Vicars-Apostolic and clergy.

whole, were treated with both compassion and respect. Many of those who had sought refuge in Britain returned to France after the Concordat of 1802, but others remained, refusing to accept Napoleon as the *de facto* ruler of their country.

Our knowledge of the clerics who found their way to Scotland is deficient, owing to the small amount of official data which has been discovered so far, but there were many more French *emigré* priests living in the Lowland District between 1789 and 1814 than is generally realised.* The majority supported themselves by teaching, became friendly with the ministers of the Established Church and moved freely in the upper classes of society. A few offered their services as domestic chaplains or assisted the priests in the Vicariate by saying Mass for them. More use could have been made of them if they had only learned to speak English.

Bishop Hay tried to obtain the help of at least one French priest, to whom he was introduced by the Bishop of Saint-Pol-de Léon, during a visit to London. It is recorded that Bishop Hay had a long conversation with this priest "in which he took occasion to lay before him the difficulties of the Mission, both as to food and labour. He heard afterwards that this young Emigrant had been hurt by what the Bishop had said, as if it had seemed to imply a suspicion that these difficulties would discourage him."†

Some time after this incident, one of the French priests who was brave enough to face life on the Scottish Mission asked permission from Bishop Hay to celebrate Mass without a server, because there was not a single Catholic in the place where he was then living. It is related that "in the circumstances, the Bishop gave his permission, on Sundays and Holidays, but afterwards doubting his authority to do so, he made an application to Rome on the subject.‡ We are not told what answer was received. It is probable that the majority of the *emigré* priests often found themselves in the same position, and they may not have troubled to seek a dispensation from the Vicar Apostolic of the Lowland District.

On January 6, 1796, Charles-Philippe, Comte d'Artois, the youngest brother of Louis XVI, took up his residence at Holyrood Palace, after several years of exile from France, most of which he had spent in Germany.§ Here he lived until 1810 at the expense

---

* Cf. James McGloin, 'Some refugee French clerics and laymen in Scotland, 1789-1814', in *Innes Review* (Spring, 1965), pp. 27-55; also J. E. Handley, 'French Influences in Scottish Catholic Education,' ibid, (Vol. I, 1960), p. 22.

† *Scotichronicon*, p. 369.

‡ ibid, p. 370.

§ Louis XIV had been guillotined on January 21, 1793, and Queen Marie Antoinette on October 16 that same year. The Comte d'Artois had to be smuggled to Scotland for fear of being arrested for debts incurred for supplies to his troops.

of the British Government, and in spite of great poverty he tried to keep up the dignity of his court. It appears that at first the Comte and his household attended Mass on Sundays and Holidays in the Blackfriars Wynd Chapel and this must have embarrassed Bishop Hay, for among the ladies was the Comte's current mistress, Madame de Polastron, who for the sake of propriety had quarters in a house near the Palace. *

A court chaplain was obviously necessary, so the Comte applied to one of the French bishops exiled in London, requesting a priest of humble origin, who could not expect to have his meals with royalty. So it was that the abbé Jean-Baptiste de la Til (sometimes spelt Latil) found himself in Edinburgh. A room in Holyrood Palace was fitted as a chapel, where Mass was celebrated, de la Til having been given the rank of Almoner.†

This French Catholic community, centred around Holyrood, had little contact with members of the congregation who worshipped in one of the two chapels in Edinburgh, but occasionally there were visits to or from some of the Scottish nobility. Other people turned up at the Palace, such as emissaries from Louis XVIII, far away in Poland, or secret agents from La Vendée. Most of them wanted money.‡

The life led by the majority of the *emigré* French priests in Scotland was utterly different from that of the make-belief court at Holyrood. Having to earn their living by teaching, they were in daily contact with ordinary people. In their own way they carried on a hidden apostolate by breaking down centuries of prejudice against 'Romanism' and 'Popery'. They were, in fact, what we now call 'Worker-Priests'. Typical of them, for instance, was the abbé Capperon (usually known as Mr Capron), who died at Greenock in 1805, having taught there for many years. This one-time *curé* at Limoges celebrated Mass at Paisley before the first resident priest was appointed. The abbé Lemonnier—a former *vicaire* in the Archdiocese of Rouen — taught in Glasgow from

* His wife, Marie-Thérèse of Savoy, had been left behind at Turin. Later on she moved to Graz, where she died in 1805.

† On December 22, 1802, Bishop Hay informed Bishop Geddes that he was sending a box from Aberdeen to Edinburgh containing "a Thurible, with its Boat and a Remonstrance or Soleil for the Exposition of the Holy Sacrament . . . They are all of silver, and belonged originally to the Chapel of Holyrood House, when the Duke of York dwelt there. Monsr. Latil wished much to have the use of them for his little Congregation . . ." (*Scotichronicon*, p. 433). In 1803 the abbé reconciled on her death-bed the Duchese de Guiche (another of the Comte's mistresses), who was buried with Catholic rites at Holyrood. The following year—again a death-bed repentance—the abbé gave the Last Sacraments to Madame de Polastron. After this the Comte began to practice his religion seriously. (See p. 255.)

‡ Cf. Marjory Weiner, *The French Exiles 1789-1815* (1960) p. 134. In 1799 an arrangement was made with his creditors that enabled the Comte d'Artois to travel around Britain.

about 1798 and was saying Mass in Greenock ten years later. In 1813 the abbé Despréaux, who had been a professor of Latin in the Collège d'Avranches, opened a French Academy at Greenock, after teaching in Paisley. In 1816 he issued a printed prospectus begging "the Humane and Affluent Inhabitants of Paisley" to contribute towards building a school for Roman Catholics. Many of them, so he pointed out, were "little accustomed, as yet, to the restraints which civilised society imposes".* It appears that this Norman priest quarrelled with Bishop Cameron, who assumed charge of the Lowland District after Bishop Hay's breakdown in health in 1804. On August 5, 1809, the former wrote to Mr Andrew Scott (placed in charge of the Glasgow Mission in 1805): "I fear Despreaux goes to Paisley, and I am sorry for it. His faculties for saying Mass will depend on his behaviour."†

The canonical status of these *emigré* clergy was often somewhat irregular. Not all of them bothered to obtain faculties from the Vicar Apostolic of the Lowland District. They regarded themselves as under the jurisdiction of their own bishops, some of whom were exiled in London or elsewheree in England.‡

Working in the Dumfries area, and acting as chaplain at Terregles as late as 1810, was the abbé Cabart Danneville, formerly Vicar-General of the Diocese of Bayeux. He too was a source of worry to Bishop Cameron by his grievances, real or imaginary. Then there was "Mr Bricon, French Clergyman", who got as far north as Aberdeen, where he advertised both private tuition and public classes. In 1797, the abbé d'Ancel (later a Bishop), well versed in history, mathematics and astronomy, became a teacher at the Banff Academy, but he returned to France some time after the Concordat.§ The abbé Daraux had a school in Dundee until about 1814. The abbé Quentin was teaching in the Perth Academy in 1797, and in 1805 the abbé César, a Doctor of the University of Paris, was doing the same "with much propriety of accent and pronunciation".** It is probable that M. Lagrandierre, one-time Vicar-General of the Diocese of Lisieux, was the first priest to celebrate Mass at St Andrews since the sixteenth century. He was conducting classes in French and

---

* McGloin, op.cit., p. 35.   Mr William Rattray, the first resident missioner at Paisley, had been appointed in 1808.   He opened what was called a "large and commodious chapel" the following year.
† ibid, p. 35, note 22.
‡ Among other French priests who maintained themselves by teaching in or around Glasgow during the first decade of the last century were the abbés Perchley, Halley, Nicolas, and Dufour.   All belonged to dioceses in Normandy.
§ In 1803, while the present St Peter's Church in Aberdeen was being built, he assisted the Rev. Charles Gordon, and said Mass in the Concert Hall on Sunday mornings.
** ibid, p. 45.   It was not until 1830 that Perth got its first resident Scottish priest.   The nearest chapel was at Stobhall, about 7 miles distant.

Drawing there in 1794, but he returned to France in 1802. *

The abbé l'Evesque, one-time *vicaire* of Manneville in the Diocese of Bayeaux, lived in Edinburgh from 1791 till 1813, teaching French and celebrating Mass for priests who needed help in their missions. He offered advice on architecture to Bishop Cameron after the latter had bought land in 1812, on which to build a new chapel.

Never since the Reformation had there been so many more or less redundant priests in Scotland. For a time there must have been a superfluity of clergy in the Lowland District. " But, one fact clearly emerges—Scotland sustained a little Norman Conquest of her own, and she was the richer for the experience."†

In spite of his age and infirmities, Bishop Hay remained active, and in the autumn of 1794 he began to negotiate for the purchase of the Oxhill estate in the Enzie, so that the students could be moved there from Scalan. By this time it was clear enough that there was no immediate hope of re-opening the Scots Colleges at Douai and Paris, and it looked as if many youths would have to complete their education for the priesthood in Scotland. But the price demanded by the Duke of Gordon was too high, and in the end Bishop Hay felt he must look for other quarters. Finally in August 1796 he decided to negotiate with Leslie of Balquhain for a ninety-nine years' lease of the farm of Aquhorties, about four miles west of Inverurie, Aberdeenshire. An agreement was completed, but it was not until the summer of 1799 that the house (with accommodation for thirty students) was ready for the reception of the students. Bishop Hay took up his residence at Aquhorties in June, and towards the end of July the boys left Scalan, which had been a seminary for eighty-two years.‡

Thanks to the efforts of Mr John Farquharson, who had succeeded Mr Macdonell as priest in charge of the Glasgow mission

---

* Other French priests who remained in Scotland for shorter or longer periods were the abbé Dausque (Boulogne Diocese), who was teaching in Edinburgh between 1798 and 1802; Gaultier (St Malo Diocese), who acted as Bishop Cameron's confessor for several years; Gossier (Rouen Archdiocese), tutor to the 7th Earl of Fingall's children in 1813; Le Hardy (St Malo Diocese), who taught at Musselburgh between 1800 and 1801; Paulmier (Lesieux Diocese), teaching in Edinburgh in 1801; Robin (Rouen Archdiocese) and Tiothoin (Doctor of the Sorbonne). The last two taught French, etc., in Edinburgh between 1799 and 1802.

† McGloin, op.cit. p. 55. There was at least one refugee nun in Scotland—Lady Emilia Drummond, daughter of the Duke of Melfort, titular Duke of Perth. She returned to her convent near Rouen some time after 1802.

‡ Mr John Sharp and Mr Alexander Badenoch were put in charge of the students, with Mr John Gordon acting as Procurator. In 1801, Mr Sharp was replaced by Mr William McDonald. During the next 15 years there were several changes in the staff. (cf. W. J. Anderson, 'The Aquhorties Register', in *Innes Review*, Autumn, 1963, pp. 170-89. An alphabetical list of the students is given on pp. 190-5).

in 1794, a new chapel was opened in October 1797. It was located in Boar Head Lane, opposite the Infantry Barracks.* He begged all over Scotland for money — even from "indigent Highlanders and strolling Irish "—but he could not pay off his debts and did not manage to extricate himself until 1799.

Owing to the loss of all foreign funds, the financial position of priests in Scotland had become worse. They numbered fifty in 1798, and forty-five of them were dependent on a common fund. The following year a small grant was made by the British Government for the support of the Mission. The business had to be kept secret, lest militant Protestants should discover that the State was helping to propagate Popery. Each Vicar-Apostolic was to be paid £100 annually, a Coadjutor £50, and a sum was given to augment the stipends of priests to bring them up to £20 a year. The negotiations were made with Lord Castlereagh (1769-1822), Keeper of the Privy Seal, who became Chief Secretary of State for Ireland in 1796. Two of the Catholic intermediaries were Mgr. Erskine and Sir John Cox Hippersley, both of them diplomats and lawyers. Neither the priests nor the laity knew where the money came from. The grant continued until 1804.†

As a temporary measure in war-time, partly to compensate for the loss of foreign colleges, it was welcome enough, but there were risks attached. No Government grant in payment to bishops and clergy could be accepted without suggesting the right of the State to control, at least by a veto, all appointments. The possible dangers of any such suggestion do not need to be enumerated. Royal and political appointments to bishoprics led to some of the worst evils in pre-Reformation days, and in other countries until more recent times.

Napoleon Bonaparte had invaded Italy in 1796, and the following year demanded that Pius VI should disband his army, surrender Avignon to the French, and a large part of the Papal States in Italy. On February 10, 1798, General Berthier captured Rome and declared a Republic. The Pope fled to Siena, and later to the Carthusian monastery at Galuzzo near Florence. A fortnight later French troops occupied the Scots College, but Mr Paul Macpherson managed to get away with twenty-two students — English, Irish and Scots. They were given permission to travel through France.

On their arrival in London the refugees were treated like heroes.

---

* Mr Farquharson said Mass occasionally as far away as Ayr and Inveraray, where there were a few Catholics. He made the long journeys on foot, because he could not afford to hire horses. The Mission Fund allowed him no more than £18 a year.

† When Castlereagh's *Correspondence and Dispatches* were published between 1847 and 1853, and the facts became known after half-a-century, the grant was violently criticised by Catholics even more than by Protestants.

Macpherson was presented to the Prince of Wales and to the Duke of York. He was interviewed by the Speaker of the House of Commons and by leading ministers. He had managed to bring with him from Rome some of the College archives and had also secured part of the archives from the Scots College, Paris. Later on he secured the Stuart papers which were handed over to the royal collection at Windsor Castle.

Negotiations had been going on for several years to obtain another coadjutor for Bishop Hay but owing to the troubled state of Europe, and Rome in particular, it was not until 1797 that Mr Alexander Cameron was chosen by Propoganda.* His consecration as titular Bishop of Maximianopolis (which may have been in either Palestine or Pamphylia) took place in Madrid on October 28, 1798, but he remained in Spain for the next four years, undertaking all the episcopal duties of the aged and infirm Bishop of Valladolid; also settling differences between the Rector and students of the Irish College at Salamanca. It was not until 1802 that Bishop Cameron arrived in Scotland, when he took up his residence in Edinburgh. There, so we are told, "his shining talents and polished manners brought him into acquaintance of the higher circles, and gained him their esteem, while his easy and amiable deportment endeared him to the lower orders."†

Bishop Geddes had died at the chapel-house in Aberdeen on February 11, 1799, after a long illness. He had never fully recovered from the fatigues of a walking-tour in 1790, when he travelled on foot from Glasgow to the shores of the Pentland Firth and crossed over to the Orkney Islands to stay at Kirkwall. After the magistrates had entertained him with great civility, he visited his old friends, the Traill family, on the Island of Sanday. The return journey on the mainland was also made on foot. After 1793 he usually spent the summer months at Scalan, but latterly he remained in Aberdeen, devoting himself to literary work.‡ He was buried in the Snow Churchyard in Old Aberdeen.

Pius VI died in exile at Valence in the south of France on August 29, 1799.§ A few weeks later the French troops evacuated

* Born at Auchindryne, near Braemar, in 1747, he was educated at Scalan and the Scots College, Rome. After his ordination in 1772 he returned to Scotland and was put in charge of the Strathavon mission. In 1780 he was appointed rector of the Scots College, Valladolid, as successor to Mr John Geddes, a post he held for 17 years.

† *Scotichronicon*, p. 459.

‡ His books include *The Life of St Margaret of Scotland, A Treatise against Duelling, Some Useful Information concerning the History of Religion in Scotland,* and *A Method for a Scotch Clergyman to direct him from Youth until the Last.* The first two only were published. He left MSS of interest to students of Scottish Catholic history, notably on the Colleges, especially Paris and Madrid.

§ Mgr. Erskine organised and paid for the pontifical Requiem Mass for Pius VI, held in St Patrick's, Soho, London, on November 16. He was not the only Scottish prelate in the sanctuary, for among the seven

Rome, and the next Pope, Pius VII, was able to return there the following year. The Concordat of 1801 between Napoleon, now first Consul, and the Holy See made it possible for Mr Paul Macpherson to go back to Rome, with the hope of regaining possession of the College property for the Scottish Mission.   He informed the Bishops: " Our college and its vineyard are in a deplorable state. The chapel has been used as a stable, the college itself occupied by squatters, and the vineyards taken over by some rascally farmers, headed by the *custode*, Giuseppe Longhi, a very prince of unjust stewards." *   Mr Macpherson put everything right by slow stages. A decree was obtained that all future rectors of the College should be chosen from the Scottish secular clergy, and he himself was the first of them.

French prisoners of war raised problems both for the Vicars-Apostolic and their priests, for at one time there were between 12,000 and 15,000 of them in various parts of Scotland. Those who were given parole increased the Catholic population considerably, and made abundant social contacts within a fairly wide area round their places of confinement. Some were strongly anti-clerical, and were welcomed by the local Freemason's Lodges. Not a few of these unwanted aliens became notorious as skilful forgers of banknotes. They were a mixed crowd, including Poles and Spaniards as well as French, and even Americans captured from privateers. Presbyterian efforts to make the prisoners read the Bible do not appear to have been very successful. Little has been recorded about the ministrations of Scottish Catholic priests to these unfortunate men.

The Scottish Vicars-Apostolic, unlike the English ones, were spared the embarrassment of having to deal with three French bishops who refused to recognise the Concordat made between Pius VII and Napoleon (now First Consul) in 1801.†   One of them was Mgr. Seignelay de Cuthbert, the Scots-born Bishop of Rodez.‡ It must have infuriated him that his small diocese had been united with that of Cahors, as the result of a drastic reduction in the number of sees, and nomination of new bishops by the State. So he remained in England.   There he made it awkward for the Vicars-Apostolic by granting faculties to French priests, who, like himself, preferred to remain in exile.   John Gibson Lockhart relates that at the time of the Revolution, when the Bishop escaped from France to England by way of Germany, his

---

bishops was Mgr. Colbert de Seignelay, Bishop of Dodez, who gave one of the five prescribed Absolutions.   Never since the Reformation had such a spectacular Catholic function taken place in Britain.

* David McRoberts, op.cit. p. 9.

† This led to the formation of the schismatic sect known as '*La Petite Eglise*. The bishops and most of their priests were reconciled with the Holy See, except the Bishop of Blois, who ruled over this body until his death in 1829. The *Petite Eglise* lingered on in parts of France until the close of the century. (Cf. P. F. Anson, *Bishops at Large* (1964), pp. 91, 299-300).

only luggage was a huge wig-block, without which he never travelled, and which he honoured with the title of 'Monsieur le Chevalier de Rodez.' This now elderly 'bishop at large' paid at least one visit to his native country and stayed with Protestant friends at Bothwell Castle, Lanarkshire. * Apparently without the authority of Bishop Chisholm, Vicar-Apostolic of the Highland District, the deposed Bishop of Rodez extended his travels to the Western Isles, with the vague idea of leading colonies of emigrants to Canada. It was a task for which he was quite unsuited.†

Pius VII recalled Mgr. Erskine to Rome in 1802. There he was created a cardinal two years later and made Protector of the Scottish Mission in succession to Cardinal Albani. He took a keen interest in the affairs of the Scots College, of which Mr Paul Macpherson was now the Rector. The Scottish Vicars-Apostolic wrote to thank him for all he had done on their behalf since his arrival in England as papal envoy in October 1793.

Meanwhile the abbé de Latil had not been confining himself to ministering to the exiled Comte d'Artois at Holyrood Palace. In the summer of 1803 he offered Bishop Cameron the well-paid post of Chaplain to the Spanish Embassy in London, where he would be in charge of the small but stately chapel, described as "a fair specimen of Italian architecture", which had recently been opened in Manchester Square.‡ Bishop Hay was extremely annoyed when he heard of this proposal, and expressed his feelings in a very long letter to his coadjutor, dated September 13, 1803. Pointing out that there were political reasons behind it,§ he said: "Of all the afflictions that I have met with, since I had my present Charge, the proposal contained in the abbé Latil's letter to you, is the most poignant. Those were only personal, but this extends to the interests of Religion and pierces all my rational faculties to the quick . . . I cannot with safety to my own soul approve and much less consent to you having anything to do with it. *The Abbé and Bishop of Arras, you say, foresee great advantages to our Mission by your acceptance of the offer;* that may be, but it would be too great a price to endanger the anger of God to gain the whole world . . ."**

* The episcopal wig-block got lost on the journey. " Rather than appear in any way dishevelled as to *coiffure,* he chose to come down to dinner in his own venerable grey hair, which being very much admired by the ladies, the Bishop never again resumed his wig." (Cf. Marion Lochhead, *John Gibson Lockhart* (1954) p. 177.

† He died in London in 1813, about five months after pontificating at St Aloysius, Somers Town, which had been built by the French *emigré* priest, the abbé Carron, with the help of the abbé Nerinck.

‡ The Bishop had been rector of the Scots College, Valladolid, for eighteen years, and spoke Spanish fluently.

§ France and Spain were allied against Britain. Their combined fleets were defeated at the Battle of Trafalgar on October 21, 1805.

** *Scotichronicon,* p. 438.

When Bishop Cameron heard that if he accepted this offer he would have to reside permanently in London, he declined it with thanks. Bishop Hay wrote to Propaganda explaining that for health reasons the time had come for him to hand over the business of the Lowland Vicariate to his coadjutor. He had been living with the students at Aquhorties since 1799, and for several years he had been unable te celebrate Mass in public. On August 15 — not long before Pius VII set out from Rome for Paris, to crown Napoleon as Emperor of the French—the Bishop reported to Propaganda, in reply to a list of questions sent him, that Catholics were now permitted the free exercise of their religion; that there were twenty-eight missionaries in the Lowland Vicariate, all of them seculars, and all but three engaged in active work. Each priest received £10 annually from a common fund, which was not nearly enough for his maintenance. Mixed marriages were fairly numerous, but were usually conducted by a priest. The chief difficulty, as in the past, was a lack of missionaries and money to maintain them. *

On October 25, he had a stroke, but recovered sufficiently to make several more journeys from Aquhorties to Edinburgh, and back again.† It was not until June 1805 that documents arrived from Propaganda, dispensing him from the recitation of the Breviary, and at the same time placing the Vicariate under the sole charge of Bishop Cameron.

Three months after this Bishop Cameron travelled to the Island of Lismore, and there on September 15 he consecrated Mr Aeneas Chisholm as coadjutor to his brother, Bishop John, who was the fourth Vicar-Apostolic of the Highland District. The consecrand was given the title of Bishop of Diocaesarea in Palestine.‡

After Pius VII had been arrested by French troops in July 1808 and imprisoned at Savona on the coast of Liguria, Cardinal Erskine feared the worst. He urged Mr Macpherson to sell the Scots College at Rome while there was the chance to do so, and clear off to Scotland with the profits. Europe was in a state of turmoil. Charles IV of Spain and his son had abdicated in favour of Napoleon, and the Peninsula War had started. But Macpherson did not take the Cardinal's advice. As a result he was imprisoned

---

* Cf. Bellesheim, op.cit. Vol. IV, p. 269.

† After 1807 it was possible to travel between Aberdeen and Port-Elphinstone, near Inverurie, by a " swift gigboat " on the Canal, drawn by two horses.

‡ Aeneas Chisholm was born in Strathglass, and was educated at the Scots College, Valladolid. Ordained priest there in 1783, four years later he was appointed Prefect of Studies at the re-opened Scots College at Douai. After his return to Scotland in 1790 he spent the next fifteen years mainly working in his native Strathglass, where he built a new chapel, " of a very superior description", so it was reported.

on August 10, 1808, with other clergy of British nationality, but he was soon released and managed to stay on in Rome, looking after the affairs of the College and its villa at Marino. Finally deported in 1811, he found his way back to Scotland and was put in charge of the Huntly mission by Bishop Cameron.*

Death of Bishop Hay, 1811

Bishop Hay died at Aquhorties on October 15, 1811, in his eighty-fourth year. Mr James Sharp, the Procurator of the College, was nothing if not thrifty. He ordered a coffin to be made by Mr Webster of Inverurie "in a plain but decent style" and got Miss Hamilton of Aberdeen to make "the grave clothes". The deceased prelate was not buried in his purple cassock, still less with his ring or pectoral cross, which still exist. There was no pontifical Requiem Mass, because Bishop Cameron, who was then single-handed in Edinburgh, did not feel justified in leaving the congregation without a priest. Even so, the more than 150 miles journey by coach in each direction would have cost a lot of money. Leslie of Fetternear gave permission for his former episcopal tenant to be buried in the family burial-place, i.e. ground around a ruined chapel on the north bank of the Don. No priests attended the obsequies, except Mr Charles and Mr John Gordon. Among "a number of very respectable gentlemen" present were Sir Archibald Grant of Monymusk, Gordon of Manar, Menzies of Pitfodels and local ministers. The Earl of Kintore expressed regrets for his enforced absence. On October 22 Mr Sharp wrote to Bishop Cameron, starting off " Much Honoured Sir,", which at that time was the correct mode of address for bishops: "I was duly favoured with your apology for not attending Bishop Hay's funeral, and I take the first leisure moment to acquaint you with the manner in which matters were conducted on that occasion . . . Our boys all dressed in mourning accompanied the hearse and made a very decent appearance. I got a waiter from Aberdeen who laid down dinner and served up things in a fashionable style; he was assisted by Mr Menzies' servant. I offered the head of the table to Mr Leslie which he very properly declined in favour of Mr Menzies, who acquitted himself very handsomely in the capacity of chairman. Mr Bannerman took the other end of the table; all appeared easy and happy on the occasion. Mr Menzies gave a number of appropriate toasts, which were drunk with much good humour. All the company dispersed about six o'clock . . . The expenses attending the funeral will be considerable and swallow up a good portion of that money which was destined for other

* Cardinal Erskine, having lost all his property in Italy, was ordered by Napoleon to leave Rome to retire to Paris. He died there on March 20, 1811, and was buried in the Church of Ste. Geneviève, which was transformed into the Panthéon in 1830.

purposes; but these charge must be frayed whatever the consequence. I hope you will have no objection to my distributing
Bishop Hay's old clothes among the servants and the poor. I believe his whole wardrobe though exposed would scarcely fetch
twenty shillings." *

No inscription was ever erected over Bishop Hay's grave, and
eventually the exact spot was forgotten.† Yet this was in keeping
with the character of the man, who had always tried to lead a
hidden life, and who had a horror of any sort of display.‡ His
writings are his lasting memorial. They express a type of solid
piety, breeding a spirit of fortitude and patience, which is quite
alien to that of our own age. The present generation would find
his books dull and ponderous, nevertheless they evoke the atmosphere of the time of persecution, when it cost something to be a
Catholic in Scotland.§

* Cf. W. J. Anderson, 'St Ninian's, Fetternear, and the burial of Bishop
Hay', in *Innes Review* (Autumn, 1963), pp. 196-204. James Gordon, one of
the boys who followed the hearse, wrote to his mother that all he got for
the funeral was "a pair of black stockings and a crape." The servants and
the housekeeper got "stuff of cotton" for their mournings.

† In 1849 James Leslie of Fetternear built a new chapel in the grave-
yard.   Ten years later St John's was erected at the other end of the
policies (See p. 305 note *.). Previous to this, Catholics in the district had
attended Mass either in the domestic chapel of Fetternear House, or, after
1852, in the new church opened at Inverurie.   The Fetternear estates were
broken up after the house was burned down in 1919.   St Ninian's Chapel,
long since abandoned, was demolished in 1962.

‡ His second successor, Bishop Paterson, had a very different sort of
obsequies in 1831 (See pp. 256-8).

§ An edition of his Works in 5 volumes, edited by Bishop Rigg, was
published by the authority of Bishop Strain at Edinburgh in 1871.   There
are various MSS by Bishop Hay in the Scottish Catholic archives, many
of them written in his own shorthand.

P

CHAPTER SEVEN

LOWLAND & HIGHLAND VICARIATES
1811-1827

Paul Macpherson chosen as secret-agent by the British Government, 1812.

The death of Bishop Hay marked the end of a chapter in the history of the Catholic Mission in Scotland. During the next sixteen years many changes took place, leading to the division of the country into three Vicariates. By the spring of 1812 the Vicars-Apostolic of England, Scotland and Ireland found themselves unable to communicate with Propaganda. Pius VII was still a prisoner in France, separated from his Curia and the rest of the Church, which to all intents and purposes lacked a Pope from 1809 to 1814.

One day Mr Paul Macpherson received a letter from Bishop Poynter, Vicar-Apostolic of the London District, and another from Sir John Cox Hippersley, requesting him to go to London so that certain business could be discussed. This, it was explained, was so confidential that it could not be committed to paper. * On his arrival in London from Huntly, Mr Macpherson met Sir John, who revealed the secret—nothing less than that the British Government intended to release Pius VII from his prison at Savona. Macpherson, he suggested, should find his way to Savona, effect a meeting with the Pope and warn him to be ready to escape when the moment came. Then the Scots priest was to inform the British Minister in Sardinia of what he had done and discovered. Sir John also told Macpherson that, although he was not authorised by the Government to pay expenses, they would be paid out of his own pocket. The secret-agent set off from London and, on landing at Morlaix in Brittany, heard that the Pope had been moved from Savona to Fontainbleau, near Paris.† So he moved on to Rome, where he inferred that the Scots College was not going to be sold. In the absence of the Pope and most of the Curia, Mgr. Quarantotti was acting as head of Propaganda, and Macpherson soon gained his support.

In 1813 a Bill for the full emancipation of Catholics had been

* Cf. Bernard Ward, *The Eve of Catholic Emancipation*, Vol. II, p. 72, note 1.
† Pius VII had to be given the last Sacraments when crossing the Alps, but he recovered. On Napoleon's return from his Russian campaign, negotiations for a new concordat were begun.

introduced into Parliament, although it was bitterly opposed by
Dr Milner, Vicar-Apostolic of the Midland District from 1803 to
1825. On occasion he used strong and almost abusive language
against Macpherson. Quarantotti, however, issued a favourable
report on the Bill and this was dispatched to London. Meanwhile
Pius VII, liberated by Napoleon, was back in Rome. Macpherson
by this time was mixed up with this affair. Bishop Milner hurried
to Rome in an effort to stop Catholic Emancipation and Bishops
Poynter and Bramston hurried after him, determined to frustrate
his efforts. Napoleon abdicated in April 1814 and was exiled on
the island of Elba. Cardinal Consalvi arrived in London on his
way to the Congress of Vienna and celebrated Mass in St Patrick's
Chapel, Soho.

When Napoleon escaped from Elba in March 1815, and
resumed power in France, all ideas of Catholic Emancipation were
ended for the moment. Mr Macpherson, unlike the three English
bishops, remained on in Rome after Pius VII fled to Genoa but he
fully expected that all the British clergy would soon be deported.
He wrote to Bishop Cameron: "In that case I shall make my way
back to you again, in the unalterable resolution of never more
putting my foot out of Scotland. That I be obliged to leave Rome
is more than likely. I therefore wish that you would look out for
a small snug charge for me; but it must not be on the East coast
nor a chaplaincy, as the former is against my health, the latter
equally against my inclination. Though I be obliged to put up in
such a dwelling as I was born in, I will be master of my own house.
I am getting on in years, and, as to my health, *non sum qualis eram*
[I am not as I used to be] and must live in my own way."*

The Battle of Waterloo, fought on June 18, 1815, decided not
only the fate of Europe but also that of Mr Macpherson. Shortly
after this he resigned his diplomatic duties and started work on
the re-opening of the Scots College.

Catholic affairs in Scotland, 1811-27

Mr Walter Scott published his poem, *The Lay of the Last
Minstrel,* in 1805, about the very time when Bishop Cameron took
up residence in the 'Modern Athens', and people who regarded
themselves as cultured were now showing an interest in ruined
cathedrals and monasteries, as well as in the more romantic aspects
of medieval Catholicism. More poems followed in quick succession but it was not until 1814 that Scott's first novel, *Waverley,*
appeared. His knowledge of the externals of 'monkery' and
popery became much more informed in the later novels. Although
at the best it was incredibly inaccurate, and largely came from
Fosbroke's *British Monachism,* nevertheless "no English novelist
before Scott had written about Catholics seriously, or had intro-

* McRoberts, op.cit. pp. 13-4.

St Mary's, Broughton Street, Edinburgh (1814).

duced high-minded respectable priests into their books. Scott revived curiosity about Catholicism and, as Newman seems to have realised, paved the way for the acceptance of the Oxford Movement by interesting his readers in the Catholic past."* Scott had little use for Roman Catholicism as a religious system. He regarded it as a superstition "likely to sink into the dust, with all its absurd ritual and solemnities".† Yet his influence in creating greater sympathy for the more picturesque aspects of medieval religion among his compatriots cannot be ignored.

This is apparent even in some of the Catholic chapels which were erected. When St Peter's, Aberdeen, was opened on August 19, 1804, High Mass was celebrated—a function at that date almost unknown in Scotland. It was designed in the ' Gothick ' style of the Regency period, clearly inspired by English models of the Strawberry Hill school.

But it took time for Gothic to become the vogue. The chapels at Paisley and Dumfries, which were erected in 1808 and 1813, were in the Grecian style of architecture. Many more chapels were opened between the one at Greenock in 1816 and the so-called "Saxon" one at Eskadale, Inverness-shire, in 1826. Most of them have little architectural interest.

The need for a decent Catholic place of worship in Edinburgh became apparent in 1812, when Bishop Gordon acquired land in Broughton Street for this purpose. With the notable exception of St George's Episcopal Chapel, built in York Place in 1794, all the churches which had arisen in the city within the past century had been designed in one or other of the Classic styles. Bishop Cameron was sufficiently alive to the latest fashions to risk ' Gothick' for his new chapel. He instructed James Gillespie Graham (1777-1855) to make plans for a place of worship which would be utterly different from any of the newly built Presbyterian kirks in Edinburgh, incidentally giving him the first job there. The conception decided on was a rectangular auditorium with a shallow apse, masked by an English Perpendicular Gothic facade, conveying the impression of a nave with flanking aisles. A contemporary journalist described St Mary's Chapel as an example of " the finest Gothick, with pinnacles according to the antique, which produces a fine effect to those who admire the style adopted."‡ It was opened in the year when *Waverley* was published.

Bishop Cameron, now aged sixty-eight, realised that he needed

---

* Una Pope-Hennessy, *Sir Walter Scott* (The English Novelists series, 1948), p. 62.

† John Gibson Lockhart, *Memoirs of the Life of Sir Walter Scott* (Edinburgh, 1837-8), Vol. V., p. 35.

‡ The altar-piece was a painting of the Deposition from the Cross, attributed to Vandyke. When George IV visited Edinburgh in 1822 he is said to have offered £4,000 for this picture.

a coadjutor, because the Catholic population of the Lowland Vicariate had increased rapidly, mainly due to Irish immigration. Propaganda having confirmed the choice of Mr Alexander Paterson, his consecration as titular Bishop of Cybistra (a Turkish port on the Black Sea) was performed on August 15, 1816, by the titular Bishop of Maximianopolis in the Grecian-style chapel at Paisley, of which the new prelate had been in charge since 1812. *

It was also in 1816, the year when Scott's novel *The Antiquary* was published, that Gillespie Graham's English Perpendicular Gothic chapel, dedicated to St Andrew, was opened in Glasgow. Mr Andrew Scott was appointed to this mission in 1805 and by that time the Easter communicants numbered 450, but within a few years he discovered that the total Catholic population of Glasgow and its suburbs was well over 3,000, most of them poor Irish, working in the cotton mills. The Calton Chapel, which had been used since 1797, had long since become too small to accommodate the crowds. In defiance of criticism, Mr Scott resolved to build a new chapel large enough to hold between two and three thousand worshippers. He was warned by both Catholics and Protestants that such an undertaking was sheer folly. Presbyterians looked on with horror and alarm at the rising walls of the Popish Mass House, facing the Clyde. Under the cover of darkness the more bigoted spiritual sons of the Covenanters attempted to pull down what had been built the previous day. Then, to add to Mr Scott's troubles, the disbanding of the troops after the Battle of Waterloo and the fall of Napoleon led to great destitution, unemployment and even riots. When at last the chapel was completed it was proclaimed to be the most magnificent and most spacious Papist place of worship in the whole of Britain. More than this, Mr Scott had created visible proof that Catholics in Glasgow could be regarded no longer as a small body of despised aliens.

Gillespie Graham's Glasgow facade was more elaborate than the one he had designed for St Mary's Chapel, Edinburgh. The spacious interior, with its arcades and groined plaster ceilings, was provided with galleries supported by massive fluted columns.†
The astonishing thing is that this wonderful evocation of early nineteenth-century romanticism should have been erected by the son of a Banffshire farmer to enable thousands of poor Irish and

---

* Born at Pathhead in the Enzie District in 1766, he was educated at Scalan and the Scots College, Douai, where he remained on as Sub-Principal after his ordination until it was closed at the French Revolution. Then he was put in charge of the Glenlivet mission, where he worked with great zeal until he was sent to Paisley.

† The galleries were removed in 1892 when the interior was refurnished by Peter Paul Pugin to give it a more cathedral-like character. Since then more changes have been made, so that the architect would hardly recognise the place were he able to inspect it today.

St Andrew's, Glasgow (1816).

231

Highland families to fulfil their religious obligations. A big bare hall would have been more practical and less expensive. *

Immigration of Highlanders to Canada, 1817

The immigration of Highlanders, both Catholic and Protestant, to Canada had started in 1772 and it reached its peak in 1817. By far the greater number settled in Nova Scotia. During roughly sixty years approximately 35,000 Gaelic-speaking Highlanders made new homes for themselves in the forests of this colony, which had been separated from New Brunswick in 1784, with the name 'Nova Scotia'. The first two ships arrived at Pictou on Northumberland Sound in 1791. The previous year Mr Angus MacEachern, a student of the Scots College, Valladolid, ordained in 1787, left his mission in the Hebrides and sailed for Prince Edward Isle. He met every ship arriving from Scotland, to advise Catholics where to settle, either in the county of Antigonish or on the island of Cape Breton.†

Another Scots priest, Mr James MacDonald, arrived in Nova Scotia the same year but his health broke down and Mr MacEachern was left alone to minister to the Catholic Highlanders until 1802, when he was joined by Mr Alexander MacDonald, son of Archibald, fourth of Clianiaig, Cadet of Keppoch, also a former student at Valladolid. Other priests joined them at intervals. In 1821 Mr MacEachern was consecrated titular Bishop of Rosa, and given charge of the Apostolic-Vicariate of Cape Breton.‡

One of the most outstanding priests who left Scotland for Canada was Mr William Fraser, a great builder of churches in Cape Breton and Antigonish. In 1825 he was consecrated titular Bishop of Tanes. He became the second Vicar-Apostolic of Nova Scotia and first Bishop of Halifax in 1842. Two years later he was transferred to the newly created Diocese of Arichat on Cape Breton Island, owing to difficulties with his Irish coadjutor, Bishop William Walsh. He died at Antigonish in 1851.** It is worth

* The total cost of St Andrew's, which seated 2,200 persons, was reckoned to be about £15,000—a vast sum in those days.

† The parish of Arisaig in Antigonish county traces its history back to 1792.

‡ In 1829 he was nominated first Bishop of Charlottetown on Prince Edward Is'and. Nova Scotia, hitherto part of the Diocese of Quebec, got its first Vicar-Apostolic in 1817, in the person of Mr Edmund Burke. The Apostolic-Vicariate of Nova Scotia became the Diocese of Halifax in 1842, and was raised to archiepiscopal rank 10 years later.

§ Born in Glencannich in 1779, he studied at Samalaman and at Valladolid, where he was ordained in 1804. For some years he was Principal of the seminary on the island of Lismore.

** For a detailed account of the Highland priests who worked in Eastern Canada, see Angus Anthony Johnston, 'A Scottish Bishop in New Scotland', in Innes Review Vol VI (1955), pp. 107-24; also Macmillan, History of the Catholic Church in Prince Edward Island (Quebec, 1905); and Macleod, History of the Devotion to the Blessed Virgin in North America (Cincinnati, 1860).

mentioning that the Scottish Catholics who migrated to Canada were followed by priests, yet the Catholic Irish who migrated to Scotland during the same period do not appear to have brought a single priest with them. They were often left as sheep without shepherds, except for the ministrations of the far from sufficient Scots priests; hence the wholesale lapses from their religion, especially in Galloway.

Increasing Irish 'Invasion' of Scotland

Writing in 1820, the statistician James Cleland estimated for the previous year the number of Irish Catholics in Glasgow as 8,245 out of a total number of 15,208 Irish in a population of 140,000.* The future Bishop Murdoch, however, when being cross-examined at the trial of the Rev. Andrew Scott v. William McGavin in 1821, stated that the "nominal Roman Catholics" in Glasgow mustered between 14,000 and 18,000.† It was not until 1841 that the classification into ' Irish born ' was made in the census returns, so everything previous to this is an estimate based on general remarks. What is certain, however, is that the nominal Catholics from Ireland were increasing so rapidly, above all in the southern part of the Western Vicariate, that the few priests could not cope with these immigrants.

The Irish bishops gave no sign that they were interested in the spiritual welfare of the ever increasing number of Irish families who abandoned their homes to seek their fortunes in a foreign country, where there was little or no provision for the practice of their religion.

The education of the children of these immigrants was a problem which had to be solved by the Scottish Vicars-Apostolic and their priests. By 1819 a Catholic Schools Society had been established in Glasgow, with the support of a number of the leading employers of Irish labour. The Chairman, Mr Kirkman Finlay, M.P., a Glasgow merchant, stated that " the manufacturers of this country could never have gone on without the emigration from Ireland, or the assistance of the Irish weavers; and, having them, could they retain them in ignorance and debased state, or help them to attain to the character of a population who were able to read and write?"‡

The Society had a board made up of fifteen Catholics and fifteen Protestants. It was stated at the time that schools were being opened "for the purpose of instructing the children of poor Roman Catholics", and that " the rules allow no religion to be

---

* Cf. James E. Handley, *The Irish in Scotland* (Cork, 2nd ed. 1945) p. 108.

† The number of Catholic baptisms at Glasgow had increased from 20 in 1795 to 610 in 1819. They reached a total of 1,542 in 1883. The figures tell us nothing about the parents, e.g. mixed marriages.

‡ Handlay, op.cit. p. 280.

taught, but the Protestant version (of the Bible) is read without note or comment, or explanation by the teachers." *

Three such schools had been opened in Glasgow, located in Bridgeton, Anderston and Gorbals, all districts in which the Irish were most numerous.

Mr Scctt felt that the need for Catholic schools was so urgent that the end justified the means. It is recorded that "rather than see his little ones abandoned to hopeless ignorance, he consented to their being taught to read a Bible not their own. Many now came forward readily from without, with Funds, and Books, and kind and liberal Speeches about opening unto all the blessings of Education; suitable teachers, members of the Congregation, were subsequently appointed."†

One day a cart-load of Protestant Bibles was dumped at the chapel-house in Clyde Street. They were gratefully acknowledged by Mr Scott.‡ So it was that Popery began to be regarded mainly as the religion of the undesirable, but unfortunately necessary aliens of the lower orders of society who provided cheap labour.

To raise money for these schools, sacred concerts (called oratorios) with full orchestras, were performed from time to time. Bigotry still smouldered below the surface, and it was one of these sacred concerts held in St Andrew's chapel in 1818, when the band of the 40th Regiment was an extra attraction and 2,100 tickets were sold at 5s each, that roused a Mr William McGavin to attack 'The Man of Sin' who had again dared to raise his majestic head in Scotland.§ It took the form of a newspaper article in which he criticised its favourable report of the oratorio held for the benefit of the Catholic schools. His sense of timing was excellent, because Scottish Protestants were growing alarmed by the rumours of Catholic emancipation. A heated correspondence was kept up in the *Glasgow Chronicle* for six weeks. The basis of McGavin's attack was that Mr Scott had extorted money to build his new chapel by a sort of poll-tax from the starving Irish.

Matters reached a crisis in 1821, when Mr Scott sued him for libel. The jury court of Edinburgh awarded Mr Scott £100 against

---

* *Great Britain Parliament House of Commons. Answers Made by Schoolmasters in Scotland to Queries Circulated in 1838* (1841), p. 541.

† *Scotichronicon,* p. 467.

‡ Catholic schools were opened at Blantyre and Paisley in 1816, later on at Leith and Edinburgh. By 1825 there were schools in the Glasgow districts of Anderston, Bridgeton, Calton, and Cowcaddens, with 1,400 Catholic pupils, whose ages ranged from 6 to 20.

§ McGavin, born at Auchinleck, Ayrshire, in 1773, had first earned his living as a printer and bookseller, later as partner to a cotton manufacturer. Then he became an Anti-Burgher preacher. He started to attack Popery in weekly pamphlets entitled *The Protestant* in 1818-1822, which went, in collected volumes, through many editions; helping to pay for his defeat in a libel action brought against him. He also republished Knox's *History of the Reformation,* which was widely read. He died in 1832.

St Mary's, Eskadale, (described as "a magnificent Saxon pile, holding 800 grown-up persons without the assistance of galleries") was built at the expense of Lord Lovat and opened in 1826. It replaced two earlier chapels in lower Strathglass, where there had been resident missionaries from about 1687.

McGavin, and a shilling against each of his printers. Two months before the trial the petition for Catholic emancipation, known as the Civil Sword Petition, was rejected on second reading by the House of Lords.

Life in the Highland Vicariate, 1814-27

Quite apart from all this controversy, life in the Highland Vicariate went on quietly. The chief problem to be faced was the poverty of most of the priests, as well as the depopulation of many missions.

Bishop John Chisholm had died on July 8, 1814, and his nephew, Bishop Aeneas on July 31, 1818. It was not until February 26, 1820, that Bishop Paterson consecrated Mr Ranald MacDonald in Edinburgh as his successor, with the title of Bishop of Aeryndela in Palestine. * It was said that "although he lived secluded from the world, he never lost the polish of a gentleman, and had more of the air of refined society than many of those who have, all their lives, moved in its highest circles . . . He combined a simplicity and elegance of manners with a quiet vein of humour peculiar to himself . . . which rendered his society delightful. He rejoiced in the happiness of others, and his own seemed to consist in defusing cheerfulness, and endeavouring to promote innocent enjoyment."†

Five years after he assumed charge of the Highland Vicariate many of his scattered flock were faced with ruin and starvation by the remission of import tax on alkali. Families driven down from their crofts to the sea shore could no longer earn a meagre living by gathering and burning kelp. The Sutherland Clearances between 1811 and 1820 reduced the population of the Vicariate by roughly 15,000. Between 1801 and 1806 more than 13,000 persons left the Highlands and Islands.

Both Bishop Aeneas Chisholm and Bishop Ranald Macdonald resided at the seminary on Lismore. The former had added to the farm and enlarged the buildings, so that they provided accommodation for about a dozen students. In 1820 Bishop Macdonald wrote that he was " refurbishing his old and rusty Latin" to take a class of boys. He had "seven veterans", whom he wanted to send to one of the colleges abroad, and "four recruits", of whom he "could say nothing good or bad as yet". In July 1824 he wrote to Bishop Paterson: "I must tell you *inter nos* that this poor Establishment had been left with such a load of debt, that it will keep me in misery for the remainder of my life, so that in place of increasing the number of boys here, as I did at first before my embarrassments, I must now reduce the number . . . When shall I

* Born in 1756, he studied at the Scots College, Douai, and after his ordination in 1782, he worked in Glengairn, Glengarry, and later South Uist.
† ibid, pp. 464-5.

expect to see you in this Land of Cakes? Bad as times are, I would cheerfully bestow a glass of Toddy on you in Lismore yet."*

Three years later he was waiting impatiently for the students to move from Aquhorties to Blairs College, asking when it would be possible to send the boys there, and close Lismore.†

The buildings of both Samalaman and Lismore are still standing, though forgotten. Their chief work was to have provided priests for Canada, and to have kept the Faith alive in the Gaelic-speaking parts of Scotland, always in conditions of dire poverty. As for the priests of the Highland Vicariate during the first quarter of the nineteenth century, although no longer faced with persecution, they led lives of heroism for the most part, content to do their duty where their Bishops placed them, and never expecting any earthly rewards for their labours.

Reopening of the Scots College, Rome, 1820.

The education of priests for the Mission had been a constant source of worry to the Vicars-Apostolic, ever since the Scots Colleges overseas were closed at the time of the French Revolution. Valladolid had been re-opened in 1816, but it was not until four years later that the Roman College was re-established. Most of the property of the Douai and Paris Colleges had been lost. Two obstacles blocked the way of re-opening the Scots College at Rome—the lack of money and the apparent indifference of the Vicars-Apostolic.   Since 1815 Mr Paul Macpherson had been playing off one Bishop against the other with all his customary diplomacy, informing them from time to time that Propaganda would be annoyed if, now that the buildings had been made habitable again, they did not send students to occupy them.   And endless correspondence was kept up between him and Bishops Cameron and Aeneas Chisholm. It was not until 1820 that his efforts were rewarded, when two students from Aquhorties, Alexander Grant and William Stewart, and three from Lismore, Donald Macdonald, Christopher Macrae and Alexander Chisholm, were dispatched to Rome, and life in the College was resumed again. Macpherson carried on as Rector until May 1, 1827, on which date Mr Angus Macdonald succeeded him. Then he returned to his native Glenlivet, where by strict economy he managed to build a chapel, presbytery and school, which were opened in 1829.‡

* Cf. Alexander S. MacWilliam, 'The Highland Seminary at Lismore', in *Innes Review*, Vol. VIII (1957), p. 35.

† According to the Aquhorties Report (*Innes Review*, 1963) Aeneas Mackenzie, Archibald Chisholm, James Macrae, Alexander Macdonald, and Allan Macdonald came from Lismore in August and September 1828.

‡ Leo XII presented him with a chalice in recognition of his services to the papacy, above all for risking his personal liberty, if not his life, to communicate with Pius VII when he was a prisoner at Savona in 1812.

In 1821 Bishop Cameron sent his coadjutor, Bishop Paterson, to Paris, where after endless negotiations he succeeded in recovering all that part of the Scots Colleges' property in France which had not been sold at the time of the Revolution. This provided twenty-two burses which still enable Scots students to be educated in French diocesan seminaries.*

Bishop Cameron's correspondence with 'His Supreme Highness Gregor I, Sovereign Prince of the Independent State of Poyais'.

The Rev. J. F. S. Gordon related that "Bishop Cameron was wont to regard the years he passed in Spain as the happiest of his life. He often expressed an intention of returning thither, and ending his days in the Scotch College, but appears to have abandoned that idea some time before his death.†

We are also told that "he acquired so correct a pronunciation [of Spanish] that the Natives themselves could not, from his speech, discover him to be a foreigner . . . His superior abilities, and engaging manners, soon made him a favourite at Valladolid, so much so, that his acquaintance was courted by the leading characters of the place."

Among these distinguished people was Sir Gregor Macgregor, who had married a Spanish-American lady, generally referred to in his letters as Josefa. After a roving career Sir Gregor turned up in London with his family, having conferred on himself the titles of 'His Serene Highness Gregor I, Sovereign Prince of the Independent State of Poyais, Grand Master of the Order of the Knights of the Green Cross, Cacique, of the Poyer Nation'. It appears that he had already taken part in the Spanish revolution of 1820.

Macgregor had also made the acquaintance in Spain of Mr William Reid, now procurator of the Scottish Mission. The Macgregor family moved to Edinburgh, and on January 19th, 1823, 'His Serene Highness' requested that special seats should be reserved for him at St Mary's Chapel, suggesting that he intended to appear in state the following Sunday. Some time after this he returned to London, and on August 13th wrote a long letter to Bishop Cameron from the 'embassy' of the 'Independent State of Poyais' at 51 Baker Street, Portman Square. 'The Cacique of the Power Nation' informed the titular Bishop of Maximianopolis: "I am obliged to dispatch the ship *Albion* which sails from this port

---

* The handsome chapel remains in much the same state as when it was built in 1665 and enshrines many memorials to Jacobite nobles who died in France. The Duke of Perth erected the memorial to James VII, with a long Latin epitaph. The College has had various inhabitants, but at the present time it houses a community of Dominican sisters who manage a hostel for forty-five French girl students preparing for the 'licence' at the Sorbonne.

† Cf. *Scotichronicon*, p. 459.

for St Joseph's on the 20th instant. It is intended that my family should pass the winter in Italy and that in the interim I go to Poyais. My *chaplain* has long ago been created Baron Pranaw, a Knight of the Green Cross, and Bishop of Fiolana . . . My Chargé d'Affaires at the Court of Madrid was ordered to remain there when the Cortes *fled* to Seville; he is now accredited to the Regency. Have I done right? I have made fresh overtures to the Regency, the Spanish Ambassador at Paris, and the French Minister at this Court. It appears to me that it would much facilitate my negotiations with the Court of Madrid were I to procure a Roman estate and *title*. This might cover a hundred faults and *whitewash* the revolutionary principles that I acquired from a certain noble relation of my own. I understand that such things are to be bought at Rome — that is that the title goes with the estate. Your Lordship will much oblige me by pointing out how this might be brought about *without delay*. I would go as far as £5,000 to obtain a title with a very few acres. Could I not employ some agent at Rome for me? I fear the Bishop of Fiolana would not stir to be made Archbishop of Crieff. Perhaps your Lordship could point out to me some confidential Agent I might employ in this affair at Rome."*

No doubt the 'Cacique' intended to hand over the £5,000 in the bank-notes he had engraved by Lizars of Edinburgh. He also wanted Bishop Cameron to send out a priest, or priests, as missionaries to Poyais. The 'Independent State' was merely one of the Islas de la Bahia, now called Roatan, off the north coast of Honduras, little more than a pestilential swamp. The colony, as might have been expected, proved a disastrous failure. Some of the survivors who sailed to the Caribbean in the ship *Albion* managed to settle down in British Honduras. 'His Supreme Gregor I' and his Knights of the Green Cross were soon forgotten. Bishop Cameron may have regretted that "his shining talents and polished manners" had "brought him into the acquaintance of the Higher circles, and gained him their esteem" in the case of Sir Gregor Macgregor.† It was a good thing that he did not try to obtain for him an expensive Roman title and an estate, or to find him a confidential agent with the Curia.

Creation of three Vicariates for Scotland, 1827.

Having reached the age of seventy-eight in 1825, Bishop Cameron had an attack of apoplexy, which nearly proved fatal. He resigned in favour of his coadjutor, Bishop Paterson. During the following year the latter went to Rome to try to convince Propaganda that another Vicariate was needed for the Mission.

* W. J. Anderson, 'Sir Gregor Macgregor, Cacique of Poyais', *Innes Review* (Spring, 1966), pp. 60-3.
† *Scotichronicon*, p. 459.

This was due mainly to the great increase in the number of Irish Catholics in and around Glasgow.

The negotiations took a long time, for Leo XII and his Curia were kept busy arranging Concordats with many nations, also organising a spy system to combat the revolutionary Carbonari, a secret society which aimed to rid Italy of foreign rulers by anarchical means. The affairs of the Scottish Mission were of minor importance when compared with increasing the papal armed forces, or confining the Jews in ghetto quarters.

It was not until February 3rd and 13th, 1827, that the Rescripts were signed by Leo XII. The Mission was re-arranged into three Vicariates—Eastern, Western, and Northern. Bishop Paterson was given the Eastern, Bishop Macdonald the Western, with Mr Andrew Scott of the Glasgow mission nominated as his coadjutor with right of succession. Mr James Kyle had been at Aquhorties from 1799 to 1826 as student, professor and rector of studies, but in anticipation of his consecration he was sent to Glasgow to assist the future Bishop Scott. After some delay he was appointed Vicar-Apostolic of the Northern District.

Bishop Cameron died on February 7th, 1828, and was buried in the vaults beneath St Mary's Chapel, Edinburgh. This was the first time since the Reformation that a Catholic funeral for a prelate was publicly performed in Scotland.

CHAPTER EIGHT

EASTERN, WESTERN, & NORTHERN VICARIATES, 1827-1852

Events of 1828

ON SEPTEMBER 21st, 1828, Mr Scott was consecrated titular Bishop of Eretria in western Asia Minor at St Andrew's Chapel, Glasgow. The ceremony was performed by Bishop Paterson, assisted by Bishop Ranald Macdonald and Bishop Penswick, Vicar-Apostolic of the English Northern District. On the 28th of the same month, Mr Kyle was raised to the episcopate as titular Bishop of Germanicia on the borders of Kurdistan. Bishop Penswick was the consecrator, assisted by Bishop Scott, and the function took place in St Peter's Chapel, Aberdeen. *

It was also in 1828 that James Menzies of Pitfodels, a wealthy Catholic laird, who had been Convener of the County of Aberdeen from 1810 to 1823, made over his estate of Blairs, on the south side of the River Dee, six miles from Aberdeen, to the Vicars-Apostolic. The students were moved to Blairs from Aquhorties in the autumn of 1829. Mr John Sharp, then in charge of the Preshome mission, was appointed first president, and he retained the post for eighteen years.

Menzies had intended by this benefaction to place himself in a position by which he could continue helping the Scottish Mission. He retained a suite of rooms in the mansion for his own use, meaning to keep an eye on the professors and make sure that the boys were trained in good manners as well as in morals. But he was too optimistic: Mr John McPherson, who was on the staff in those early days, and who founded the Scottish *Ordo and Directory,* remarked in a letter: "The motto here is, 'Dinna anger the laird'. Sometimes, however, the laird *was* angered, because the Vicars-Apostolic failed to carry out his wishes, above all when they made appointments of which he did not approve. The Bishops, President and staff were relieved when Menzies finally decided that he could stand the life at Blairs no longer and returned to Edinburgh.

---

* Born at Edinburgh in 1798, James Kyle, was the son of an architect of the same name, and Mary Strachan of Banff. Having been educated at the College at Aquhorties he was ordained priest there in 1812. He remained on as Director of Studies for 17 years until 1826 when he was appointed curate at the Glasgow chapel in 1826, where he worked until his consecration.

241

St Mary's, Kirkconnell, New Abbey, Kirkcudbright (1815). The furnishings of this chapel are typical of those built before Catholic Emancipation (1829).

Bishop Kyle worked at Glasgow as Bishop Scott's curate for five months, and then took up his residence at Preshome. He felt it would be unwise to live at Aberdeen because of the great influence wielded there by 'Priest Gordon' at St Peter's Chapel. Preshome remained the Bishop's home until his death forty years later. He enlarged and rebuilt the chapel-house and farm steadings; he also supervised the erection of some of the new chapels in the Northern Vicariate, having inherited a wide knowledge of architecture from his father.

It is recorded that: "Dr Kyle (in 1828) had just then completed his fortieth year. In the full vigour of manhood, possessed of a strong constitution and active habits, and his mind amply stored with knowledge, he was well equipped for the great task before him . . . The fact that he was at Preshome in the centre of [a large Catholic] population doubtless determined him in the choice of his residence. But the quiet, sedentary character of the man, careless of all show, and desirous only to do his work, would doubtless lead to a like decision. Pretence of any kind was to him most offensive. He was content to make slow, if he made sure, progress. He was emphatically a builder-up of his Church. He made no advance except where it was warranted, and he was alike sagacious in counsel, and energetic and persistent in action." *

Catholic Emancipation, 1829

Between 1820 and 1828 the movement towards Catholic Emancipation went on gaining momentum throughout Britain and Ireland, largely through the efforts of Daniel O'Connell (1775-1847). In Scotland there was little or no desire to give further relief to the Papist minority beyond what had been granted in 1793, because of the rapidly increasing number of Irish, who were regarded as a danger to the social and moral welfare of the industrial Lowlands, where most of them settled. Among these incomers were pedlars who passed forged notes, and others who engaged in whisky smuggling. There was also the scandal of the Saturday night saturnalia. Wherever the Irish congregated, these same sinners flocked to Mass on Saturday mornings. Far worse, however, were the activities of the so-called 'Resurrectionists', who earned their living by selling corpses to medical students. Some of these dead bodies were brought over from Ireland.

As early as 1823 a Catholic Association had been formed in Glasgow, encouraged by Daniel O'Connell, with the object of working for complete emancipation. That same year the Irish in Paisley entertained John Lawless, the editor of *The Irishman*, as their guest of honour at supper. 'Catholic Emancipation' was toasted, and the editor of the *Glasgow Free Press* spoke in favour

---

* *Scotichronicon*, p. 644. See also James K. Robertson. 'The Bishop looks at his Diocese', in *Innes Review*, Vol III (1952), pp. 22-32

of it. Even the more widely-read *Scotsman* ventured to print articles in the same strain. In 1828 O'Connell was elected M.P. for Co. Clare, which gave him the long awaited opportunity to press for Catholic emancipation. No sooner had news reached Scotland that the now recognised leader of the Irish was about to introduce a Catholic Relief Bill in Parliament; than petitions against this motion were drawn up by Presbyterians throughout the country. In Glasgow, even schoolboys were urged to sign these documents. There were anti-Catholic riots in several towns.

By the winter of 1828 it was common knowledge throughout Britain that William Burke and William Hare—two Irish Catholics living in Edinburgh—had murdered perhaps as many as thirty people and sold their corpses to the anatomists. Burke was hanged on Hare's evidence on January 18th, 1829, after the fifteenth confirmed murder had been discovered.

Among the crowd of between 20,000 and 25,000 persons who gathered under the shadow of the High Kirk of St Giles, long before dawn on that wet winter morning, was Sir Walter Scott, who secured a seat in a window so that he could get a good view of the hanging. Two priests from St Mary's, Broughton Street, Mr William Reid and Mr Robert Stuart—had already visited Burke in prison the previous night. They accompanied him to the scaffold, and remained by his side until the end. It was reported that " in the face of vast crowds, roaring and shouting, the two priests and the criminal knelt down and prayed. While the hangman was adjusting his rope, one of the priests said to Burke, 'Now say your Creed, and when you come to the words 'Lord Jesus Christ', give the signal and die with his blessed name on your mouth."*

More than 30,000 men and women enjoyed the thrill of gloating over Burke's corpse after it had been removed to the anatomical class-room of the College, where it was exposed on a black marble slab. In spite of the horrible murders committed by these two Irish Papists, about 8,000 persons signed a petition in favour of Catholic emancipation at a crowded meeting in the Assembly Hall, Edinburgh, two months later. The *Scotsman* had already voiced what may have been the general feeling of the country in an article published on December 27, 1828, when it said: " The Irish are, perhaps, more easily softened by kindness than any other people; and it is by good offices, not by blows of persecution, that they are to be reformed. In their present lamentable state we see nothing but the genuine results of a long course of misgovernment."

This horrible affair naturally added to prejudice against the Irish, but no one seems to have attributed it to their religion. Scottish industrialists had long realised that they could not do without cheap Irish labour, so it would pay them to make life

* William Rougead, *Burke and Hare* — *Notable British Trials series.* (Edinburgh, 1921), pp. 274-5.

easier for these immigrants by enabling them to practise their religion without fear of persecution.

What was styled the ' Act for the Relief of His Majesty's Roman Catholic Subjects' passed the Commons and the Lords; and on April 13th, 1829—three months after the execution of William Burke—received the royal assent. It gave Catholics throughout Britain and Ireland the same rights and privileges as their non-Catholic fellow citizens, with the following exceptions: (1) No Roman Catholic priest might sit in the House of Commons (but then as now no parish minister could do so); (2) no Roman Catholic could hold certain high offices in the kingdom, which were specified in detail; (3) a Roman Catholic could be a member of a lay corporation, but he could not vote as such, on the appointment of any officials, in the Established Churches, universities, colleges or schools; (4) he could not attend an English or Scottish university; (5) Roman Catholic bishops could not assume titles to sees; (6) neither could a Papist wear the insignia of his office; (7) priests were forbidden to wear their distinctive costume out of doors; (8) admission to a religious order was a misdemeanour, and punishable by fine or imprisonment in Scotland. This statute, however, did not apply to religious communities of women.*

So far as Catholics in Scotland were concerned, after 1829 they still had to contribute towards the annuity tax for the stipends of ministers of the Established Church. Neither were they exempted from contributing to the support of parish schools, imposed as far back as 1696. If they wished to contract a *regular* marriage, they still had to have their banns proclaimed in the kirk of the parish in which each party resided, having notified the session clerks. This involved fees after proclamation, when the parties were given their certificates. It also remained illegal for a priest to hold a permanent appointment as chaplain to a prison, workhouse or hospital.

The Missions and the Clergy in 1830.

It is possible to form an idea of the state of the Catholic Mission in Scotland the year after Emancipation from the modest publication entitled *The Directory to the Church Service*, which was published by John Johnstone, High Street, Edinburgh.

(a) The Eastern District

It is surprising to find how few places of worship there were under the jurisdiction of Bishop Paterson, who with Mr Alexander Badenoch, James Gillis, John MacPherson and James McKay, served the two chapels in Edinburgh, the one in the Old and the

---

* These sections of the 1829 Act were repealed in whole or in part at subsequent dates. The last 'Catholic Relief Act' passed in 1926 was supposed to remove all penal restrictions left, but there are still a few disabilities on Roman Catholic subjects of the United Kingdom, none of them serious.

St Andrew's, Dundee (1836).

other in the New Town. Three Masses were celebrated in each chapel on Sundays and Vespers was sung following a discourse. The Catholic population of Edinburgh and Leith was estimated at about 1,400. Two schools catered for Catholic children exclusively, with two more which did not exclude Protestant bairns. The Edinburgh clergy also served congregations in process of formation at Dunfermline, Campsie, Falkirk, Haddington and Kirkliston.

Traquair House, Dumfries, New Abbey, Dalbeattie and Crieff had chapels with resident priests. Mr John Geddes, reported as being " the first Catholic clergyman who has resided in Perth since the Reformation," had a flock that consisted of "several hundred destitute Catholics, almost exclusively Irish". Mr Geddes had neither a chapel nor a house, and was obliged " to celebrate divine service in a place that is frequently converted into uses quite unbecoming the sanctity and dignity of our Religion, and into which no Catholic can enter, but with feelings of the most poignant grief, that the Living God is without a Temple where he can be adored in spirit and in truth, and that the sacredness of religion should be blasphemed and held up to ridicule in that very place where its most holy rites are performed."

Mainly for the benefit of about 2,000 Irish in Dundee, Mr Constantine Lee carried out " divine service at eleven a.m., and at half-past two in the afternoon," with the help of a newly erected organ. So far Mr Lee had only a Sunday school.

At St Mary's College, Blairs, in Kincardineshire, the Rev. John Sharp was president and the Rev. James Sharp Procurator, with the Rev. Alexander and William Gordon acting as Professors. It was stated in *The Directory* that " no pains or expense have been spared for the proper accommodation and domestic comfort of the students, and the play grounds are delightful "—a far cry from the primitive conditions at Scalan, Samalamen or Lismore. Only a limited number of boys could be supported owing to the heavy debt contracted in erecting necessary buildings, but " young gentlemen not intended for the ecclesiastical state are received for their education." For them the inclusive terms were £30 per annum. Students intended for the priesthood paid board during the first year. After that, if they were found fit subjects, they were maintained and educated gratis; if not, they either retired or paid for their board. No entrance money was required, but every student had to " bring with him two suits of dark coloured clothes—one of the suits to have a surcoat coat". For the benefit of the small congregation attached to the College, Mass was celebrated on Sunday, " preceded by an exhortation, and followed by Christian doctrine."

Such was the state of Catholicism in the parts of Scotland under the jurisdiction of the titular Bishop of Cybistra in 1830.

(b) *The Western District*

The titular Bishop of Acryndela (Ranald Macdonald), and the titular Bishop of Eretria (Andrew Scott), who acted as his co-adjutor, were responsible for the spiritual welfare of many widely scattered Catholics in the Western Vicariate. Bishop Macdonald lived more or less in retreat on the Isle of Lismore, six miles north-west of Oban. Bishop Scott made his headquarters in Glasgow, where he was assisted by Mr John Murdoch, Mr William Stuart and Mr Charles Grant.

" Divine service " was celebrated in the two Glasgow chapels every Sunday morning at 9 and 11.30. The second Masses were enlivened by music and followed by a discourse. At St Andrew's Chapel a catechetical lecture was given on Sunday afternoons. The Gorbals chapel on the south side of the Clyde served as a school on weekdays, and on Sunday evenings. There were four other Catholic schools in Glasgow and its suburbs, with about 1,300 children on their rolls. Most of them were still supported " by subscriptions given chiefly by benevolent Protestant gentlemen of the city." The cost of the eleven Sunday schools for religious instruction in and around Glasgow was defrayed by Bishop Scott and the parents of the children attending them. It was estimated that roughly 3,000 children made use of these Sunday schools.

Staffing them was a problem. A few teachers were specially trained, but the majority were engaged with no previous experience, and the greater number came from Ireland. The rest were the products of the so-called ' Lancastrian System', "whereby a child became a 'monitor', and assisted the teacher by imparting to younger children what he, or she, had been taught." * Several 'private adventure' schools were started about this time, which were open to all and sundry. Their standards varied as did the teachers. The fees charged were 4d a week. It was not until 1848 that the Catholic "young ladies" of Glasgow were provided with a board-ing school, when Mr Peter Forbes, the priest in charge of the newly opened St Mary's, Abercromby Street, helped a Mrs Macdonald to launch " a select establishment " at 25 Monteith Row, where £25 per annum was the inclusive fee.

In 1830 no attempt had been made to estimate the exact number of Catholics in Glasgow and its suburbs, but during the previous years no less than 1,188 children had been baptised. This in itself indicated a rapid increase in thirty years, because in 1800 a small room was sufficient to hold those attending Mass on Sundays.

One of the Glasgow priests visited Hamilton every month, where he celebrated Mass for between three and four hundred

* Cathures, 'Glasgow City Catholic Schools a Century Ago', in *St Peter's College Magazine,* Vol XIX (1949), pp. 63-72.

people. Another station was in process of being formed at Airdrie, but the poor Irish had to be satisfied with "divine service" only every six weeks. Many more priests were needed in Glasgow, and it must have been difficult for Bishop Scott and his three curates to visit their flocks, for lack of public transport.

Mr John Bremner, who came from Garmouth on the Moray Firth, had succeeded Bishop Paterson in 1816 in charge of the Paisley mission. His district extended many miles around the burgh, and included the villages of Neilston, Crofthead, Gateside, West Arthurlie, Barrhead, Nitshill, Elderslie, Linwood, Johnstone, Beith, Lochwinnoch, Kilbarchan, Bridge of Weir, Crossly and Houstoun. There were Catholic families in all of them, but no chapels. In Mr Bremner's scattered district were three Catholic schools, which were supported mainly by charitable contributions. He admitted that he found it difficult to keep in touch with the children, because at an early age they went to work in the cotton mills, weavers' shops and bleach-fields.

Mr William Thomson—described as "the Reverend Incumbent" of the chapel at Ayr, "a beautiful specimen of Gothic architecture" —held "public service" every Sunday at 11 a.m. This zealous priest from the Enzie District of Banffshire also officiated at Girvan every six or eight weeks. He likewise served Irvine and Kilmarnock every fourth Sunday alternately. His efforts to open a school had been a failure. His flock consisted mostly of poor Irish families, and there were no funds available to maintain a schoolmaster. Mr Thomson reckoned that he baptised at least two hundred babies every year, a proof that the Ayr, Girvan and Kilmarnock congregations were increasing rapidly.

The mission of Wigtownshire, started in 1825, covered an area of nearly 1,000 square miles, in which the estimated total of Catholics was 3,000, practically all of Irish origin. Mr Sinnott "performed divine service" at Stranraer every Sunday and holyday; and he also served Newton Stewart and Gatehouse-of-Fleet occasionally, as well as Whithorn less frequently. He had no permanent chapel anywhere, and conducted his services in hired rooms. This devoted missioner stated in the *Directory* that his flock then numbered "about a twentieth part of the whole population. They are supported by manual labour . . . All of them are poor, many of them miserable. Their dispersion co-operates with their poverty, in rendering the observances of religion difficult to them. They are to be found in every parish, sometimes existing in detached families, or solitary individuals."

The missions at Campbeltown (1809) and Greenock (1816) were developing. Those in the Highlands and Islands, dating from the seventeenth and eighteenth centuries, were a world apart from the mainly Irish missions in the south. Gaelic was the language spoken. * They were under the immediate jurisdiction of Bishop Macdonald, while Bishop Scott was responsible for the mainly Irish missions in the southern part of the Vicariate.

(c) The *Northern District*

The impression given in the 1830 *Directory* is that the Northern District, ruled over by the titular Bishop of Germanicia (James Kyle), was organised more thoroughly than either the Eastern or Western Vicariates. At Preshome Bishop Kyle was assisted by Mr John Maclachlan. The chapel had been provided with " an elegant and powerful organ ", for the edification of the roughly 1,400 persons who formed the congregation. Mr William Cavan, who had charge of the "elegant and commodious chapel" at Tynet, complained that he was "burdened with a considerable debt, beyond the means of the congregation to liquidate". At Portsoy, "the neat and commodious chapel" was served by Mr Alexander Grant. He had a Sunday school, and also officiated at Banff and Foggyloan (Aberchirder) every alternate Sunday. Mr James Sharp, the Procurator at Blairs College, ministered to the Catholic families around Aquhorties. Tomintoul was said to possess "one of the neatest chapels in the North of Scotland".

Mr James Gordon appeared in *The Directory* on behalf of the not yet completed "elegant Gothic" chapel at Tombae in Glenlivet. He also wanted donations to start a Catholic school and to build "an addition to his mansion-house", in which he would "gladly accommodate two or three respectable Catholics as boarders." " To persons of retired and religious habits," he pointed out, " the situation will be most eligible, as the climate is salubrious, and the scenery altogether beautiful and picturesque . . . The post arrives thrice a week, and carriers from Aberdeen once every week."

At Chapeltown, in the Braes of Glenlivet, the Catholic population amounted to between 600 and 700. Interesting information about the missions at Elgin, Inverness, Strathglass, Keith and Dornie in Kintail was given in this source of reference, where there were also details of Catholic life at Ballogie (by Kincardine O'Neill), Huntly, Ardoch (Gairnside) and Braemar, each place with a resident priest.

The Rev. Charles Gordon, assisted by the Rev. Charles Fraser, had charge of Aberdeen. On Sundays there were two Masses in St Peter's Chapel. The second of these was accompanied by music, with a discourse after the Gospel instead of before the service, as was still the custom in most Scottish missions. 'Priest Gordon' took care that his people were well instructed in their faith, for every Sunday at 2.30 p.m. ' Christian Doctrine ' was followed by a catechetical lecture. At 6 p.m. " a discourse on

* Arisaig, Badenoch, Isle of Barra, Fort William, Glengarry, Isle of Eigg, Knoydart, Lochaber, North Morar, Moidart and South Uist.

St Joachim's, Wick, Caithness (1837).

St Thomas', Keith (1831).

some of the controverted points of Religion " preceded evening prayers. It was stated in the *Directory* that the pastors of this chapel, " trusting to the never failing hand of Providence and to the charitable contributions of their flock," had already projected a new and larger school.

The spate of chapel-building that went on in the Northern Vicariate after Catholic Emancipation had no counterpart in either the Eastern or the Western District. The first chapels to be erected were Portsoy, Tombae and Chapeltown (Braes of Glenlivet)—all three in 1829. Keith followed in 1831, and Huntly in 1834. St Mary's, Inverness, and St Joachim's, Wick, were completed in 1837 and St Michael's, Tomintoul, the following year. St Andrew's, Braemar, was opened in 1839, and Elgin in 1843.* All these chapels, with the exception of Keith, Huntly, Wick and Tomintoul, consist of hall-like interiors, lit by pointed and sometimes sash-framed windows, with a Gothic facade, adorned with crockets and pinnacles. In most cases the style adopted was English Perpendicular Gothic. The names of their architects are usually unknown.

The 1831 chapel at Keith was given a Greek cross plan and an impressive Italianate facade, said to have been inspired by St Mary of the Angels at Rome. The Huntly chapel (1834) has a curious octagonal plan, with a pedimented porch, terminating in a Spanish Baroque tower.† Bishop Kyle was the architect, and he also designed the ' Gothick' chapel at Dufftown which had been built in 1825, four years before Catholic Emancipation.

Mr Walter Lovi was the architect responsible for the chapels at Keith (1834) and Wick (1837). He was one of the most energetic priests in the Northern Vicariate. Every summer he left his flock at Keith to spend six weeks at Wick during the herring fishing season, so that he could minister to the crowds of Catholics who flocked there, not only from the Highlands and Islands but also from Ireland. It was for their benefit that he erected the large rectangular-shaped chapel, and gave it a dignified stone facade in the Classic style, adorned with a pediment and pilasters. It was used for only a few weeks during the summer, and was closed for the rest of the year. Massive iron gates protected the chapel from the assaults of drunkards and juvenile marauders. Mr Lovi had visions of designing chapels in many other places, and never ceased begging money for his projects, even in Ireland.

---

* Elgin was eventually dedicated to St Sylvester, to commemorate Thomas Stewart, the murdered Benedictine brother of Sir William Drummond-Steuart (See p. 279). Its cost was largely met by his benefactions. At his death his papers came back to Scotland and are now preserved in the David Laing collections in Edinburgh University, though they might be expected to be at Elgin.

† Huntly was the first post-Reformation Catholic chapel in Scotland to be given a bell.

During the eighteen-thirties most of the clergy of the Northern Vicariate had started to use the two volumes of *Sacred Music for Small Choirs*, compiled by Mr George Gordon, the priest in charge of the Dufftown mission. They contained ten Masses and upwards of 150 hymns and anthems in Latin and English, besides psalm and litany chants. The price of each of these large volumes was one guinea. Mr Gordon "took the plainchant tunes and lines of polyphonic melody which he had been familiarized with in his college days, and harmonised them in a fashion congenial to the rumbling basses and high sopranoed voices of our ancestors. And they were sung, and sung as we could not sing them, to orchestral accompaniments, the very thought of which moves us to sibilations of horrified wonder." *

By degrees *Sacred Music for Small Choirs* was adopted, not only elsewhere in Scotland, but also in England, Ireland and even North America.

The Northern Vicariate remained curiously aloof from Catholic life in other parts of Scotland, apart from continuing to provide priests for both the Eastern and Western Districts. Bishop Kyle did not have to worry about many poor Irish families, except in Aberdeen and Inverness, and they never became a problem as they were in the industrial Lowlands. Most of the clergy had to minister to congregations of a conservative outlook and stable habits, who had inherited the traditions of the penal times—staunch in their faith and undemonstrative in their expression of it.

Catholic life in Edinburgh during the 1830s

For thirty-five years after the passing of the Catholic Relief Bill in 1829, the most outstanding personality in the Eastern Vicariate was James Gillis, in the sense that he tried to merge the little Catholic community in the general life of the nation and to make the fullest possible use of the freedom which had been granted to his co-religionists.

He was born at Montreal on April 7, 1802. His father, who belonged to the Enzie District in Banffshire, had emigrated to Canada as a youth, and grown rich. James was the only son of a marriage with an Episcopalian lady, whose maiden name was Langley, and who was not reconciled with the Roman Church until shortly before her death about sixteen years later. He was sent to the Sulpician College in Montreal, where he acquired a fluency in the French language of which he made good use later on. The family returned to Scotland in 1816. The following year he became a student at Aquhorties, where, so it is recorded, he felt that both the rules and the methods of teaching were a poor substitute for those of the Society of Saint-Sulpice, founded by Jean Jacques Olier in 1642, and which spread to Canada in 1657. In

* J. K. Robertson, op.cit. p. 25.

December 1818 the sixteen-year-old Scots-Canadian sailed from Aberdeen to London with four companions, bound for Paris, where they continued their studies at the Sulpician Seminary of Saint-Nicolas du Chardonnet. Five years later Mr Gillis moved to the Seminary at Issy, reserved for the teaching of philosophy, but owing to a breakdown in health he was obliged to return to Scotland in April 1826. Towards the end of the summer he resumed his studies under Mr Scott, the priest in charge of the Glasgow mission, and was ordained priest at Aquhorties by Bishop Paterson on June 9th, 1827.

After this he spent a few months at Blairs College, where he acted as secretary to Menzies of Pitfodels, whom he had first met when he was a student in Paris. The Laird soon realised that this young priest was more a man-of-the-world and better acquainted with the ways of polite society than the rest of the staff. Following the death of Bishop Cameron in February 1828, Bishop Paterson took up his residence in Edinburgh, and appointed Mr Gillis as one of the curates at St Mary's, where he began to make a name for himself as a preacher. It is recorded that " he did not overlook the accessories of style and delivery", also that "he evinced great zeal for the improvement of Youth, and for training them to habits of piety and virtue." *

In the summer of 1829 the Bishop asked Mr Gillis to make a begging tour in France, for St Mary's needed structural repairs. He preached in several Paris churches, and in other cities. Then he retired to the Cistercian Abbey of La Grande Trappe in Normandy, where he made a retreat. A meeting with the saintly abbé Louis-Marie Baudouin, founder of the Enfants de Marie Immaculée and the Ursulines of Jesus, made him feel that he might have a vocation for the religious life. This led him to make a second retreat under Jesuit direction. The Exercises of St Ignatius finally convinced him that it was God's Will that he should remain a secular priest in Scotland and devote himself to trying to put new life into the now emancipated Mission. Like the prophet Ezechiel he visualised the Mission as " a plain covered with bones "—bones which had "withered away" so that it almost looked as if all hope were lost, and that they were dead men. But no: Mr Gillis remembered the words: " I mean to open your graves and revive you, my people; I mean to bring you home to the land of Israel. Will you doubt, then, the Lord's power, when I open your graves and revive you? When I breathe my spirit into you, to give you life again, and did you dwell at peace in your own land? What the Lord promises, the Lord performs; you will know that, he tells you, at last."†

Mr Gillis's trip to France was cut short by the outbreak of a

---

* *Scotichronicon*, p. 481.
† *Ezechiel*, XXXVII, 13, 14.

revolution in July 1830. After Charles X had abdicated in favour of his grandson, the Duc de Bordeaux, it was more prudent to leave Paris and return to Scotland with the money collected. Then came the news that the King's cousin, the Duc d'Orléans, had made a bid for the throne, and that on August 9 he had been acclaimed as King Louis-Philippe. The Holy See recognised the new Orléanist sovereign.

In November that same year, the seventy-three-year-old Charles X, his son the Duc d'Angoulême, his daughter-in-law, the widowed Duchesse de Berry, and her ten-year-old son, the Duc de Bordeaux (now regarded by the Bourbons as King Henri V), having got away from France, arrived in Edinburgh. Holyrood Palace was placed at the disposal of the royal exiles by William IV, who succeeded his brother, George IV, on June 26th. Before long they were joined by the former abbé de Latil, who had been Archbishop of Rheims since 1817 and a cardinal since 1826. In his old age Charles X developed a piety which almost amounted to bigotry, so anxious was he to make amends for his former dissipated life.*

So it was that within eighteen months of the passing of the Roman Catholic Relief Act, a deposed Catholic King and a Prince of the Church were residing in Edinburgh, as guests of the reigning sovereign of Britain. What more was needed to bring the dry bones of the Scottish Mission to life? Nobody was more assiduous in attendance on the royal exiles than Mr Gillis. He visited them at Holyrood, where conditions were far from regal, in fact somewhat squalid. "The place was like a living tomb. Perhaps that was why Charles, the Duc d'Angoulême, and the Duchess took what seemed a morbid pleasure in being there. This palace of catastrophe and Stuart failures exonerated them from everything but a holy resignation."†

Bishop Paterson allowed Mr Gillis to fit up an elegant box-like pew on the Epistle side of the altar in St Mary's, so that the royal family and their suite could attend Mass there on Sundays and holidays of Obligation. Improvements were made in the *décor* of the tiny sanctuary. Mr Gillis was treated as a honorary royal chaplain.‡

In January 1831 Menzies of Pitfodels moved from Blairs

---

* See pp. 215-6 for details of Charles' first major sojourn in Edinburgh as the Comte d'Artois, when the abbé de Latil acted as his private chaplain at Holyrood.

† Vincent Cronin, *Four Women in Pursuit of an Ideal* (1965) p. 41.

‡ Charles X, the Duc d'Angoulême, and the Duc de Bordeaux (Henri V) remained in Edinburgh for two years and a half. Caroline, Duchesse de Berry, left Scotland after January 27, 1831, when Charles signed a decree stating that she would assume the powers of Regent "if and when she landed in France". She managed to do so the following year, when she raised an army in La Vendée, hoping to dethrone Louis Philippe, but she was taken prisoner and eventually deported to Sicily.

College to a large house at 24 York Place, Edinburgh, and invited Bishop Paterson to be his permanent guest. The house backed on to St Mary's Chapel, and at that date was located in one of the most genteel parts of the city. Mr Gillis also became part of the Laird's household, where he enjoyed every comfort. He was still officially one of the curates at St Mary's.

On February 2, Cardinal Mauro Cappellari, a former Camaldolese Benedictine monk, who had been Prefect of Propaganda since 1825, and so in close touch with the Scottish Mission, succeeded Pius VIII as Pope, with the title of Gregory XVI. A civil war broke out in the Papal States, and Austrian troops were rushed to Rome to quell the mob. At one moment it looked as if the Scots College might have to close down again, but by April 3 the Pope managed to restore order in his dominions.

Bishop Paterson enjoyed the hospitality of Menzies of Pitfodels for only nine months. He died suddenly on October 30th, 1831. No sooner had the news reached Edinburgh than Mr Gillis started to arrange for dignified obsequies such as befitted a prelate. On the arrival of the coffin from Dundee it was placed in a room of the clergy-house, fitted up as a *chapelle-ardente* in the correct French manner. As it was little more than two years since the Roman Catholic Relief Act had received royal assent, there was no undertaker in Edinburgh capable of organising the '*pompesfunèbres* (as they called it in France), but Mr Gillis knew how such things were done in the fashionable churches of Paris.

Carpenters got busy in St Mary's Chapel, shifting some of the front rows of the box-pews with their doors, also the communion rails, so as to make a more spacious sanctuary. Having done this, they erected a platform with steps. Other men draped the walls, including the tall Perpendicular Gothic windows, with yards of black cloth. Escutcheons were painted with appropriate devices, and fixed to the quaint 'Gothick' pulpit with its crocketted sounding-board, and on the front of the gallery. The effect aimed at by Mr Gillis was a *mise-en-scène* as awe inspiring as possible— something that would impress both Catholics and Protestants. Admission would be by ticket only, because of the limited accommodation. Gentlemen ushers were appointed to preserve order and were provided with wands.

By eleven o'clock on the morning of November 8th, every seat was filled. Most of the congregation wore black. History was made when His Eminence Jean-Baptiste-Marie-Antoine de Latil, Cardinal-Archbishop of Rheims, supported on either side by the titular Bishops of Germanicia and Eretria, moved up the aisle. Not since David Cardinal Beaton had a Prince of the Church assisted at a High Mass in Scotland, and that was nearly three hundred years before.

What with the myriads of flickering tapers, the sable hangings, the towering white mitres, the black copes, chasuble and dalmatics, and the clouds of incense, the *tout-ensemble* must have been dramatic. It is recorded that Mr Alexander Badenoch "delivered after Mass a short but well-suited discourse . . . and made a most appropriate allusion to the pestilential scourge [Asiatic cholera] which had reached our shores, in order to impress on the minds of his audience the necessity of being always prepared for Death." Then followed the "Funeral Obsequies", with "the usual Prayers and Ceremonies of Aspersion and Incensation", the mixed choir in the gallery having chanted the *Libera*. Finally the coffin was lowered into a grave immediately under where the episcopal throne stood, facing the stage-box-like pew in which were installed the exiled King of France and his family. So ended what had been the most spectacular Catholic function staged in Scotland since the sixteenth century.

There is evidence that Menzies of Pitfodels put forward to Gregory XVI the name of Mr Gillis as the next Vicar-Apostolic of the Eastern District after Bishop Paterson's death. This petition, however, was never sent to Rome, because Bishops Macdonald, Scott and Kyle felt that this young priest lacked experience. The choice fell on Mr Andrew Carruthers. Feeling ran high, and in 1833 it was suggested that Mr Gillis should leave Scotland and return to his native Canada, and be appointed coadjutor to Bishop Alexander Macdonell, of Kingston, Ontario. * The bulls for his consecration were actually ready in Rome, but were cancelled.†

Mr Carruthers was consecrated in St Mary's Chapel, Edinburgh, as titular Bishop of Ceramis in south-west Asia Minor on January 13th, 1832. The ceremony was performed by Bishop Painswick, Vicar-Apostolic of the Northern District of England, assisted by Bishops Scott and Kyle.‡

Bishop Scott's work among the Irish in Glasgow, 1830–6

Nothing could have been more true in the 1830s than that 'East is East, and West is West, and never the twain shall meet', when applied to the growth of Catholicism in the Eastern and Western Vicariates. Much happened after the death of Bishop

---

* See p. 214.

† The Rev. Remigius Gaulin was chosen in place of Mr Gillis, and consecrated on October 20, 1833.

‡ Andrew Carruthers was born at Glenmillan, Kirkcudbrightshire, on February 7th, 1779. Having studied at the Scots College, Douai, for six years, he returned to Scotland, and was ordained priest by Bishop Hay in 1795, after completing his studies at Scalan. Subsequently he served the missions at Drummond Castle, Traquair House and Munches, also acting as domestic chaplain to their owners. In 1814 he moved to Dalbeattie, where, so it is recorded, he devoted much of his time to a serious study of literature, and was on good terms with the landed gentry, both Papist and Protestant. He also laboured on behalf of the numerous Irish agricultural workers, scattered over Galloway (See p. 249). It was from this rural mission field that Mr Carruthers, then aged 63, was called to rule over the Eastern Vicariate.

R

Ranald Macdonald at Fort William on September 20th, 1832, when Bishop Scott became Vicar-Apostolic.

The first signs of trouble with the Irish immigrants had appeared as early as 1828, soon after the formation of the Glasgow Catholic Association. * The Irish felt that their interests were not being given proper attention by the Scottish priests, and accused them of favouritism. Stormy meetings took place in the Gorbals school-chapel, and after Mr Scott had been raised to the episcopate he often told his largely alien flock what he thought of them—in the broadest Banffshire dialect. The pawky humour in his sermons must have been wasted on most of the congregation, for his vernacular was almost a foreign language to them. Unlike Bishop Gillis he was neither interested in ceremonial nor eager to consort with the upper classes. He was fatherly but firm with his young priests, who loved and respected him. Within a year of the death of Bishop Ranald Macdonald, he was given a coadjutor in the person of his curate, Mr John Murdoch, who like himself was a native of the Enzie District of Banffshire.†

It is worth mentioning at this point that during the century and a half preceding Catholic emancipation, the Enzie District gave more priests to the Mission than any other part of Scotland— probably not far short of fifty. Eight bishops were born within an area of about six miles of farming country beside the Moray Firth. They were James Gordon (Glastirum, 1665), James Grant (Wester Bogs, 1708), John Geddes (Corriedoun, 1735), Alexander Paterson (Pathhead, 1736), Alexander Scott (Chapelford, 1772), John Murdoch (Wellheads, 1796), Alexander Smith (Newbigging, 1813) and John Gray (Buckie, 1813). Had it not been for a constant stream of priests from Banffshire, many thousands of Irish who had settled in the industrial Lowlands, rather than starve in their own country, would have been lost to the Faith.

During the cholera epidemic which swept over Europe, reaching Scotland in February 1832, Glasgow was one of the first places to be smitten. Bishop Scott and his curates were kept busy giving the Last Sacraments to the dying and in burying the dead. Hundreds of children were left orphans. It was the future Bishop Murdoch who found homes for them with decent working-class people. After exhausting all his own private means to feed and

---

* See p. 243.

† Born in 1796 at Wellheads, about a quarter of a mile from the farm of Chapelford, which was Bishop Scott's birthplace, John Murdoch studied at the Scots College, Valladolid, from 1816 to 1821, when he was ordained priest. On his return to Scotland he was sent to Glasgow, where he worked for 12 years, devoting himself to his mainly poor Irish flock, visiting them, not only in the foul closes and tenements of the city, but in many outlying towns and villages where as yet there was no chapel. He took a special interest in the Catholic schools and benevolent societies, and also found time to revise and correct a new edition of the works of Bishop Hay.

support the children, he transformed the Calton Chapel into a Catholic orphanage. *

Bishop Murdoch's apostolate in the Western District, 1833–38

Mr Murdoch was consecrated titular Bishop of Castabala (in what is now known as Lesser Armenia) on October 20, 1833. The ceremony was performed by Bishop Kyle, assisted by Bishop Scott.

The orphans showed their gratitude to their benefactor by collecting enough money to provide him with a gold pectoral cross and chain, also a silk cassock.

In these days, when there is so much talk of the progress of the Liturgical Movement in Scotland, it may come as a surprise to learn that in 1835 Mr Hugh Margey published at his ' Catholic Book Warehouse ' in Glasgow a *Complete Vesper Book* in Latin and English. It contained " full directions of all the Parts, and Directions for using it". The prospectus stated that "as the Vespers are now sung regularly on all Sundays in the Catholic Chapels of Edinburgh and Glasgow, this edition is intended for the use of the Catholics of these places; and the book was never before published in Scotland, and this edition is offered to the Public at half the price of the English editions (bound in leather 1s 6d), it is hoped that the Editor (the Rev. Charles Grant, of St Andrew's, Glasgow) will be encouraged and the book readily bought by the Catholics of this kingdom."

Today there are more than 400 parish churches in Scotland and in not one of them are Vespers sung on Sundays, so Mr Grant's book would have no sales were it to be re-issued.†

Bishop Scott's care for the Highland Missions

Bishop Scott was a real Father in God and one of the greatest of the Vicars-Apostolic. He did not confine himself to visitations of the chapels in and around Glasgow, but made long journeys to

---

* With such deplorable housing conditions, it is not surprising that during the first half of last century Glasgow was visited by four epidemics of typhus fever, three of cholera and one of so-called 'relapsing fever'. The city was never free from typhus, for every influx of poor Irish families led to a fresh epidemic in the overcrowded and unsanitary closes where the common lodging houses abounded. Thirty-one per cent of those admitted to the fever hospital in 1832 were Irish-born and by 1841 the percentage had risen to 41. (Cf. James E. Handley, *The Irish in Scotland, 1798-1845*, pp. 249-50.

† Also in 1835 a Roman Missal for the use of the laity was being sold by Denis Kennedy at his shop in Great Clyde Street, Glasgow, bound in morocco for 12s 6d, and a Pocket Missal for Sundays and Holidays at 7s 6d. The catalogues issued by this firm, and by James O'Donnel, at 3 Broughton Street, Edinburgh, prove that Scottish Catholics six years after their emancipation could take their choice of a most comprehensive selection of books at all prices—in fact, more than are on sale at the present time.

St Mun's, Glencoe (1837). In earlier times the priests of Lochaber worked in this Catholic district.

St Anthony's, Sandaig (1850). There has been a regular succession of priests in Knoydart, Inverness-shire, since 1697.

the most remote parts of the Highlands. * He had gone to live in Greenock early in 1834 and in May 1836 he wrote to Mr John Chisholm at Bornish, South Uist: " If I live another ten years, I hope the Highlands will be in a tolerable state for chapels compared with what it was some years ago. To be able to do so was my principal intention in taking up my residence here [Greenock]. The Irish are very jealous, and had I remained in Glasgow, having charge of money matters there, they would have supposed that I was spending their money on Highland chapels, and made that an excuse for not contributing for their own wants which are certainly great. But as I now never touch a farthing of the money collected there, they cannot blame me for spending their money on Highland chapels."

There was certainly a great need for chapels and ' chapel-houses . Many of the priests had no fixed abodes. Some lived as lodgers, even on crofts. As to the places of worship, very often they were thatched buildings without windows and with the bare earth for flooring. In the whole of Argyllshire and in all the Isles there were only two fairly decent chapels—Campbeltown and Ardkenneth (South Uist). Bishop Scott was even prepared to order food supplies and furniture for the Highland missionaries, and some were not always duly grateful.

For instance, the priest at Arisaig complained on July 30th, 1838: " The first tea you sent me was excellent, but the two you sent me last were shocking bad. Should you send the same a second time you will compel me to transfer my custom to some other tea dealer . . . Please send me in the box out per first steamboat 2 lbs. tea, 16 lbs. raw sugar, 3 lbs. salt, 1 stone best pease meal, ½ doz. large earthen plates for creaming milk in, and a black burnt-china tea-pot."†

Two years before this a mason, working on the new chapel at Ballachulish, asked the Bishop to send him " a spotted frock for a linner as there is none to be had here or in Fort William. They go by the name of Gairnsey frocks." He also wanted " a small plastering trowel". On February 13th, 1835, Bishop Scott wrote to an English benefactor: " This ensuing Spring we must begin to build chapels in six different missions in the Highlands, viz.: Glencoe, Badenoch, Glengarry, Knoidart, Morar and Isle of Eigg. In every one of these missions the walls had been built with dry stone, thatched with turf and heath. Part of the walls have fallen down and half of the roofs are blown away. There are now neither doors nor windows, and the roof being open, there is no possibility of getting a candle to burn at the time of Mass but when it is enclosed in a lantern . . . Unfortunately all the proprietors of

---

* Cf. Roderick Macdonald, 'Bishop Scott and the West Highlands', in *Innes Review* (Autumn, 1966), pp. 116-28.

† ibid, p. 118.

these poor missions, except Glencoe and Morar, are great Bigots, who will thwart as much as possible, in place of encouraging the people to do anything for themselves." *

From Greenock the Bishop carried on an endless correspondence with the local lairds or their lawyers about sites for new chapels. By 1837 he managed to erect a reasonably decent one at Bornish in South Uist. Typical of many another, it consists of a long building with the house attached at one end, under the same roof. The negotiations connected with building chapels in Glengarry and Badenoch were even more protracted. Thanks to Sir Charles Gordon, who was a friend of Menzies of Pitfodels, a beautiful little chapel was opened at Drimnin in Morvern, on the Sound of Mull in 1838.† But troubles started over the priests sent there. One after another was found objectionable by Lady Gordon.

The long and exhausting journeys from Greenock to the remote Highlands and Outer Hebrides ended after October 1845, when Bishop Scott felt obliged to surrender full authority over the Western District to Bishop Murdoch. He died on December 4th, 1846, aged seventy-four, and was buried in the vaults beneath St Mary's, Abercromby Street, Glasgow.‡

Travelling by this time was becoming easier. In 1842 the Edinburgh-Glasgow railway was opened, but Glasgow had to wait another six years before it was linked up with Carlisle and Perth by railways. So Bishop Murdoch, for the most part, still had to make distant visitations by coach or by steamer.

When he was at home he preached twice every Sunday, heard Confessions, visited the sick and the dying, and often supplied in missions where the priests were absent for health or other reasons.

There were many difficulties with which he had to contend, not only from the Irish members of his flock but also from more bigoted Presbyterians. As early as January 1836 the *Scottish Guardian* printed an article entitled 'Bible Burning in Glasgow' and this led to unwelcome publicity for Bishop Murdoch, only three years after his consecration. There followed much correspondence between him and the Rev. James Gibson (later Professor of Church History in the Free Church College, Glasgow). But it was not easy to prove that the Bible exhibited by Mr Gibson "was ever tossed into the flames " or that " a Protestant, not a Catholic hand, did the deed, and that a Protestant hand, whether clerical or lay, did the deed for a vile purpose."§

The staffing of schools was another problem. It was not until 1838 that the so-called 'Monitorial' system (begun ten years before) was officially superseded by the 'pupil teacher' system

---

* Ibid, p. 120.
† It is now in ruins.
‡ This large church in the Classic style was opened in 1842.
§ *Scotichronicon*, p. 397.

under which boys and girls of thirteen years and upwards were 'apprenticed' for five years to a head teacher during school hours. Special tuition was given for one hour daily, followed by a course at the 'Normal School at Hammersmith, London, or at the Liverpool school of the same name. Government aid was given to prospective teachers, and the salaries of head teachers were increased in proportion to the numbers of 'apprentices' under their charge. *

The Eastern District, 1832–1843

Bishop Carruthers took little interest in ecclesiastical affairs outside his own Vicariate. He devoted most of his time to the study of Experimental Philosophy and Chemistry, and liked to think that he was an up-to-date scientist. In the scanty archives of Dalbeattie parish can still be seen a notebook with rough sketches of chemical apparatus. It was said that " To a most refined taste he joined an extensive and intimate knowledge, not only of modern Literary Authors, but also of the Ancient Classics. He wrote Latin with great facility and elegance. Though he left France at an early age, and never visited that country in after life, yet he spoke French with fluency, and with a peculiar correctness of diction and purity of pronunciation. His Conversational powers were remarkable, his inexhaustible fund of Anecdote made him a welcome guest to every acquaintance; and when suddenly called upon to speak on any Public occasion, his observations were always singularly apposite and happy . . . In his intercourse with his Clergy, while he wielded with a firm hand the authority which God had committed to him, he was invariably kind, indulgent, and condescending, and by them, in return, he was beloved and revered as a Father."†

When this titular Bishop of Cybiston was a young man he spent six years at the Scots College, Douai, and then in 1792 he made a hasty retreat from France at the time of the Revolution. He had no urge to take a trip to the continent after that and in all his life he never visited Italy. It is improbable, therefore, that he was deeply moved when at the age of sixty-three he received news in January 1834 that the recently appointed Rector of the Scots College in Rome, Mr Angus Macdonald, had died suddenly aged seventy-six.‡ Next came the report that the students, left without a Rector, had been transferred by the orders of Gregory XVI to the College of Propaganda. The buildings of the *Scozzese* were in a bad state of repair, and had been condemned as unfit for habitation. So far as could be seen, it was the end of the long and

---

* Cf. Cathures, op.cit. p. 67.

† *Scotichronicon,* pp. 466-7 (probably written by J. F. S. Gordon).

‡ The result of visits to the major Basilicas to gain the Indulgences granted by the Pope had proved too much for his frame, already exhausted by old age and illness.

chequered history of this establishment which had trained so many priests for the Scottish Mission over a period of more than two hundred years.

Mr Paul Macpherson's reaction to the news was magnificently courageous.   Although now aged seventy-eight and a chronic invalid, with Bishop Kyle's permission he hurried south from the Braes of Glenlivet to Glasgow, and there he discussed the situation with Bishop Scott, who thought he was not far off death.   Apparently without consulting Bishop Paterson, Mr Macpherson, accompanied by a young school-teacher named Dan Gallagher, sailed from Greenock early in October.   After a voyage of nearly three months they landed at Cività Vecchia late in December 1834. *

Within twelve months of his arrival in Rome, Mr Macpherson had the College buildings repaired and had received back the students from Propaganda.   None of the Vicars-Apostolic at home had any personal interest in the Roman College, and when they failed to find another priest, Macpherson himself took on the duties of Rector.   He was now so frail that he could seldom celebrate Mass and he could no longer write legibly.   Dan Gallagher, the first Irishman to enter the Scots College, acted as his secretary.†

Mr Macpherson never returned to his native Banffshire but died at Rome on November 14th, 1846, in his ninety-first year.   All through his years at the Scots College he had taken a keen interest in the welfare of his students and in ecclesiastical affairs outside the College.   We are told that " feeble as he was, he heard Mass every day, and confessed and communicated every week, and oftener when he found it convenient.   Nor was he even known to absent himself from the tribune during the community services, unless prevented by sickness.   To all he was affable; to visitors he never forgot the urbanity of the polished gentleman; and to the students he was not merely kind and fatherly, he was affectionate, and his affection was proved to be real and sincere by the liberal generosity which ever attended it . . . He was no ordinary man, his life proves him to have been endowed with courage and intellectual gifts of a very high order . . . He displayed also a complete detachment from worldly ambitions and honours; in spite of an immense number of influential friends in Church and State, and in

---

* After leaving Scotland their vessel nearly foundered in a squall off the Isle of Man.   Over a fortnight was spent in beating up the coast from Savona to Genoa, a distance of no more than 23 miles; and another week between Genoa and Leghorn.

† After his ordination Gallaher returned to Scotland and became one of the most zealous missionary priests in the Western District.   He founded the missions of St Joseph's, Glasgow (1850), and St Peter's, Partick (1858), where he died in 1884.   As a young schoolmaster at Blantyre he had taught the elements of Latin to David Livingstone, who had already resolved on a foreign missionary career, although he was still working in a cotton mill.

spite of ample opportunities for preferment, he generously sub-
merged his own ambitions and wholeheartedly and selflessly
devoted his long lifetime to the service of God's Church in his
native land. It is with justice that he has been named the Second
Founder of the Scots College, Rome." *

The year before Mr Macpherson rushed off to Rome to save
the Scots College, Mr Gillis with the approval of Bishop Paterson
started to make arrangements for the foundation of a convent in
Edinburgh.† He was already in touch with two ladies who felt they
had vocations to the religious state—Miss Ann Agnes Trail, and
Miss Margaret Clapperton.‡

Almost inevitably, he decided they must be tested in a French
community, so in August 1833 they left Scotland, bound for the
mother-house of the Ursulines of Jesus at Chavagnes-en-Paillers
in La Vendée.§ Six weeks later these two Scottish ladies were
clothed as novices. Miss Trail took the religious name of Soeur
Agnes Xavier, and Miss Clapperton became Soeur Marguérite
Thérèse. It must have felt strange to cast off the then fashionable
wide skirts, worn over many petticoats to create an hour-glass
silhouette, and be given instead a black habit with a violet girdle.
Instead of the large bonnet which was the vogue at the time, their
headdress was a frilled linen cap, under a white veil during the
novitiate but changed to black after profession. Ebony crosses
were suspended round their necks.

Menzies of Pitfodels bought a house and garden for the projected convent in a secluded lane leading from Bruntsfield Links
to the Grange Road, and early in 1834 he acquired the adjacent
Greenhill Cottage, which he enlarged into a residence for himself.
There he had Mr Gillis as his permanent guest. James Gillespie
Graham was commissioned to design a chapel for the convent. A
contemporary writer said that it was in the "Saxon Style", and

---

* McRoberts, op.cit. pp. 18-20. Macpherson was buried in the College
chapel. A mural tablet was unveiled to his memory in St Mary's, Chapeltown, Banffshire, on August 18, 1946, just before the centenary of his
death.

† Before the Reformation the only female religious community in Edinburgh was that of the Dominican nuns, known as St Katherine of Senis
(Sciennes), founded in 1517 and suppressed in 1569.

‡ Miss Trail, born in 1798, was the daughter of the Rev. Dr. David
Trail, minister of Panbride, Angus. She became Catholic during a visit
to Italy in 1826 and was received into the Church by Cardinal Odescalchi.
Mr Gillis first met her when she was staying with the Benedictine nuns
at Hammersmith, London.

Miss Clapperton had known Mr Gillis since childhood. She was a
native of Fochabers and much younger than Miss Trail.

§ This congregation, was founded by the abbé Louis-Marie Baudouin in
1802. The first member, Madame Charlotte de la Rochette (Mère Saint
Benoit), gathered round her a group of ladies who devoted themselves to
teaching and the care of the sick. The Institute spread to Italy, France,
Spain, Holland, Canada, England, Wales, West Africa and South America.
In 1960 it had 1,352 members and 90 convents.

would be " the *chief d'oeuvre"* of the architect. It was not completed until June 1835.

Sister Agnes Xavier and Sister Margaret Teresa had not yet completed their full twelve months' canonical novitiate, when they left Chavagnes-en-Paillers and, after a few weeks in London, arrived at Edinburgh in the early autumn of 1834. As their convent was not ready for occupation, they stayed with a Mrs Stevenson, until they moved into their home on December 26th. Bishop Carruthers celebrated the first Mass in an improvised chapel, after which (so it was reported) " the guests sat down with the bishop and priests to an elegant *déjeuner,* provided by the orders of good old Mr Menzies." * Meanwhile nine French Sisters had arrived from France to make up a community.

The 1835 *Directory* informed its readers that "the twofold object which the ladies of St Margaret's Convent have in view is the education of their own sex, both in the higher classes of society and among the poor; and the relief of the destitute and of the sick".

For the sum of thirty guineas per annum—with extras for French, Italian, Drawing, Music, and Dancing—the young ladies were instructed in English, Grammar, Writing, Arithmetic, Geography, History, Outlines of Astronomy, Natural History, Needlework (plain and ornamental) and the Use of Globes. The "cheerful and well-aired Infirmary" offered "the convenience of a warm bath." The uniform was a buff gingham for summer and "brown stuff" in the winter. White dresses were worn on Sundays. Each young lady on entering the school had to bring with her a knife, a silver fork and spoon, and half a dozen *serviettes*; also two pairs of sheets and half-a-dozen towels. Classes were provided for the daughters of gentlemen not attending the school, who "might wish to perfect themselves in the higher branches of painting, whether in miniature or oil, etc."

Some of the Sisters started to visit the sick poor in their own homes, and a small house off the Canongate was rented. In 1835 Mr Gillis bought Milton House, where the Sisters ran a day-school and dispensary. Bread, potatoes, etc., were distributed three times a week and a small number of orphans were also cared for.

This was how the religious life for women was revived in Scotland after an interval of nearly three hundred years. It was due almost entirely to the zeal of Mr Gillis, who remained the never failing friend and adviser of the mainly French community, in all matters, both material and spiritual. Protestants as well as Catholics were curious to inspect a real live nunnery instead of a ruined monastery. The French Sisters, with their exquisite manners, welcomed callers and were usually able to break down Presbyterian prejudices. Thanks to the late Sir Walter Scott for the most part, people who regarded themselves as cultured now

* *History of St Margaret's Convent* (Edinburgh, 1886), p. 34.

took an interest in the romance and glamour of the Middle Ages. It must have been thrilling to find all this come to life at St Margaret's Convent. *

Yet it is hardly correct to call this a 'revival', because pre-Reformation nunneries in Scotland were few, feeble and unsatisfactory. Five medieval dioceses never had even an attempt at a religious house for women.

After the death of Charles X in 1836, his sixteen-year-old grandson, the Duc de Bordeaux, revisited Scotland and Mr Gillis arranged a magnificent reception for him at St Margaret's Convent. The youth (now regarded by supporters of the Bourbons as King Henri V of France) was led to a throne "with a neat dais of crimson velvet, surmounted by a crown, and the fleur-de-lis, with the initial *H* in gold beneath it." Miss Kyle of Binghill, one of the pupils, played on the piano the tune *'Henri Quatre'* as an *entrée*. The following Sunday, the young King assisted at Mass in St Mary's, Broughton Street, where his special pew was adorned with a crown and fleur-de-lis.†

These royal revels may seem irrelevant to the history of the Catholic Mission in Scotland, nevertheless it was part of the background against which Catholic life in Edinburgh developed during the first decade following emancipation—utterly remote from what was going on in Glasgow at the same time.

On August 22nd, 1837, two months after the accession of Queen Victoria to the throne of Great Britain and Ireland, Bishop Carruthers made history by consecrating the first altar in Scotland since the Reformation. This was in the Chapel of Marmaduke Constable-Maxwell of Terregles. *The Dumfries Times* reported: " We would ask Christians of all creeds, whether it does not furnish matter for much congratulation, that they may now mark the time as having arrived when liberality has so far extended its benign influence on this community that all classes of Her Majesty's subjects are allowed to worship God in the way they may consider most consonant with their consciences? . . . It is also worthy of remark, that some of the sacred vessels used by the Bishop and

---

* The Convent was not the only Catholic school for young ladies in Edinburgh. Miss Fraser (an 'old girl' of the Bar Convent, York) had already opened 'St Mary's Seminary' at 14 Scotland Street, where she offered " a good and fashionable education at a moderate expense". A year or two later a Mr Harkin started a small but select boarding school for " boys of the higher classes " at 7 Hill Street.

† In 1835 a richly illustrated folio volume entitled *Souvenirs des Highlands voyage à suite du Henry V en 1832* had been published jointly at Edinburgh and Paris. The lithographed frontispiece depicts "Henri V en costume de Highlander site de Glen-Croe". The then twelve-year-old Duke assisted at Mass on the Sunday he spent at Fort William, and presented the chapel there with a painting of Our Lady. Cf. R. Macdonald, 'The Picture of the Madonna in St Mary's, Fort William', in *Innes Review* (Autumn, 1966), pp. 193-5.

Clergy on this occasion were the direct gift of James VII of Scotland and II of England."

Shortly before this Terregles function, Bishop Carruthers heard that Propaganda had agreed to his request that Mr Gillis might be chosen as his coadjutor. Owing to some verbal errors in the documents which required correction, twelve months passed before the consecration took place.

The bishop-elect made sure that the rubrics of the *Caeremoniale Episcoporum,* as revised by Benedict XIV in 1752, would be carried out meticulously. The function took place in St Mary's, Broughton Street, on Sunday, July 22nd, 1838, with what was described as " unusual splendour". The consecrating prelate was the dynamic, recently secularised monk of Ampleforth, Bishop Baines, Vicar-Apostolic of the English Western District, who was assisted by Bishops Kyle and Scott. Bishop Carruthers, vested in full pontificals, occupied a temporary shrine in the tiny sanctuary. Bishop Murdoch was the preacher. The consecrand was given the title of Bishop of Limyra, i.e. Myra, the port on the coast of Cilicia, where St Paul transhipped to a vessel bound from Alexandria for Italy. *

This consecration, so far as ritual and ceremonial were concerned, must have been far more splendid than the coronation of Queen Victoria, which had taken place in Westminster Abbey on June 28th. Soon after it was over, Bishop Carruthers moved his headquarters from Edinburgh to Blairs College, where he remained for the next four years, leaving Bishop Gillis in charge of the southern part of the Vicariate. The latter lost no time in returning to his beloved France, where he occupied the pulpits of several churches in Paris, for he was much sought after as a preacher.

Lyons was his next stopping place, for the chief purpose of this journey was to procure funds from the Association for the Propagation of the Faith for the Scottish Mission.† But his request was turned down, on the plea that the Association assisted missionaries only in overseas continents. So the Bishop returned to Paris, where he was more successful with another organisation known as the *Oeuvre du Catholicisme en Europe,* which had recently been established. It had been given the blessing of Mgr. de Quélen, who had succeeded Talleyrand as Archbishop of Paris in 1821. The titular Bishop of Limyra got back to Edinburgh in May 1839.

The following year various improvements were carried out in St Mary's, Broughton Street. The sanctuary was enlarged and an episcopal throne erected, also a new altar, pulpit and organ, said

---

* Acts XXVII, 5-6.
† This organisation had been founded at Lyons in 1822 for assisting the spread of the Gospel by means of prayers and alms for the support of missionaries.

to be "the finest and best in the city" at that date.*

Next came the foundation of the so-called 'Holy Gild of St Joseph', an association for assisting priests in their old age. By also defraying funeral expenses, it restored some dignity, not to say *decency,* to burials.

Always eager to bring the externals of religion in Scotland into line with those in continental countries, especially France, the Bishop introduced the devotion of the *Quarant 'Ore,* or Forty Hours Prayer. The chapel of St Margaret's Convent was chosen for this first prolonged Exposition of the Blessed Sacrament, when it was started on Quinquagesima Sunday 1842.†

In September that year Queen Victoria paid her first visit to Edinburgh while staying with the Duke and Duchess of Buccleuch at Dalkeith Palace, and Bishop Gillis arranged that the children should shower down bouquets on the cortège as she drove along the Canongate. It was reported that " Her Majesty smiled graciously" on the Sisters and the little ones, while " Prince Albert fastened one of the flowers in his button-hole, and the royal pair bowed repeatedly in acknowledgment of the tribute of loyalty offered them."‡

All this sort of thing may sound trivial, but the incident was typical of the Bishop's flair for publicity. If nothing else, he was a born ecclesiastical showman. After all, what was the good of Catholic emancipation if one did not get the fullest possible value out of it? Two years before this he had staged the funeral obsequies of Bishop Alexander Macnell, of Kingston, Canada, who died at Dumfries. After a solemn requiem, carried out with much pomp in St Mary's, the coffin was transported in what was described as "a magnificent Funeral Car" to St Margaret's Convent, where it was deposited in the vault until it could be shipped across the Atlantic.

A trip by Bishop Gillis to the Scots Monastery at Ratisbon in August 1843 had to be cut short, for on arriving at Munich he heard of the death of his friend and benefactor, Menzies of Pitfodels. He hurried back to Scotland, arriving in time to arrange *pompes funèbres* more spectacular than any for which he had been responsible previously. We are told that " Nothing was ever forgotten that could add to the *moral* effect which he strove to

---

* It was not until nearly twenty years later that organs began to be used in Presbyterian kirks, and not without much opposition in some parishes. It appears that the first organ installed was in a new church at Anderston, Glasgow, in 1860. Shortly after this the Old Greyfriars Kirk in Edinburgh was provided with what was called a 'kist o' whistles'.

† A year before this, Bishop Gillis arranged for the band of the 29th Regiment to accompany the singers at a High Mass which was followed by a *Te Deum.* This was on the occasion of the re-opening of the church after refurnishing and decoration, and also to give thanks for the safe birth of the Princess Royal—the first of Queen Victoria's nine children.

‡ *History of St Margaret's Convent,* p. 103.

produce, and certainly the funeral that took place on All Souls' Day was such as left a lasting impression upon all who witnessed it. St Mary's Church was beautifully decorated for the solemn occasion; the windows darkened, the paintings covered with mourning; the gallery and pulpit draped and ornamented with the escutcheons of the deceased; in the centre of the church a splendid catafalque with pillars supporting a canopy of black cloth and ermine surmounted with plumes, etc. From the centre a large burnished crucifix rose up above all the rest, and was the most conspicuous object there." *

The titular Bishop of Limyra presided as chief mourner, vested in a Roman purple *cappa magna*, black stole and white mitre. The elaborate music of Mozart's *Requiem*, accompanied by a small orchestra, added to the length of the function. The pontifical Mass, sung by Bishop Kyle, with Bishop Murdoch as preacher, must have been dramatic. The darkened church was dimly lit by a profusion of torches and large sepulchral urns in which spirits-of-wine burned. It is recorded that " the population of Edinburgh were taken by surprise on viewing the magnificent and unwonted pageantry of the Funeral Cortège, as it set out from the Church and proceeded through the most public streets to the Chapel of St Margaret's Convent, to the Crypt under which, as to their last resting place, the mortal Remains of the deceased were that day consigned."

Here is the order of the procession:

Two mutes on Horseback;
Twelve Baton-men;
The men of the Congregation, all in deep mourning;
The Standard-Bearers and Standard;
The Council of the Holy Gild of St Joseph;
The Members of the Gild;

THE FUNERAL CAR,
drawn by six beautiful horses led by grooms, and bearing the Sarcophagus, containing the body of the deceased, surmounted by the large and burnished crucifix, rising above the plumes, and flanked by three members of the Holy Gild, carrying lamps of most elegant design on handsome shafts;

The Deceased's Private Carriage,
followed by twenty-five poor men who had been clothed at Mr Menzies' expense, bearing torches;

The private carriage of the Right Rev.
Dr. Gillis, with His Lordship as Chief Mourner.
The Bishops and Clergy in mourning carriages,
each drawn by four horses;

* ibid, p. 105

The Trustees of the Deceased;
The Pall Bearers,
And the private friends of the Deceased, all in carriages. *

More than 50,000 persons lined the streets on that November morning to watch the stately free pageant provided by the Papists. The great Disruption had taken place on May 18, 1843, six months before the funeral obsequies of the laird of Pitfodels. At the General Assembly, three hundred and ninety-six members, afterwards increased to four hundred and seventy, withdrew as a body, and constituted themselves as the first Assembly of a new Free Church, with Dr Thomas Chalmers as Moderator. For many years the Scottish Kirk had been tied and bound by parliamentary supremacy, and this break-away appeared to be the only method of getting rid of London rule, which in its own way was more irksome than the control still exercised over the Catholic Mission in Scotland by the Congregation of Propaganda in Rome. The Disruption inspired Bishop Gillis to deliver some controversial lectures in Edinburgh. He believed that ere long there would be a miraculous revival of the 'Old Religion', influenced by this schism in the Established Church.

One of the more pressing worries for Bishop Carruthers and Bishop Gillis was the increase of Irish families in the Eastern Vicariate. By 1840 they abounded in and off the Cowgate, Leith Walk and other parts of Edinburgh. Some were small shopkeepers and tradesmen, but the vast majority were poverty-stricken. Kelso, Jedburgh, Galashiels, Dunfermline and Kirkcaldy also had groups of Irish immigrants. In 1841 it was reckoned that there were 7,100 native-born Irish in the county of Angus, the greater number of them working in the flax and linen mills at Dundee. Three years later the treasurer of the Edinburgh Charity Workhouse stated that there was " nothing so difficult as to deal with than the Irish poor". Their influx into the city, he said, was "dreadful."†

In March 1843, Bishop Gillis, gave evidence before the Charity Commissioners that within the districts of the Canongate, the West Church and the city, about 200 Catholics exclusive of pauper children were in receipt of indoor, permanent outdoor, or temporary relief out of a Catholic congregation in Edinburgh of about 14,000. He was certain that in many cases the Irish poor were refused relief by the public authorities as much because they were Catholics as because they were aliens. Priests were not allowed to instruct Catholics in the Poorhouse, although nine-tenths of them were Irish.‡ Both old and young Catholic inmates of the Poorhouse were forced to attend Protestant worship in the chapel—by the resident governor who was also the chaplain.

* *History of St Margaret's Convent,* pp. 106-7.
† Handley, op.cit. p. 196.
‡ ibid, pp. 109-202.

The Western District, 1839–1849

The spread of 'Romanism' in Scotland, due almost entirely to the steady influx of Irish families and their settlement in the industrial areas of the Lowlands, continued to scare Protestants. By 1841 the Irish-born in the country amounted to 126,000, i.e. roughly 5 per cent. of the total population. *

Three years later a speaker at the Poor Law Inquiry of 1844 drew attention to the " extreme tendency to unhealthy increase among the Irish labourers, having nothing, no artificial wants, no habits of foresight, marry at sixteen or twenty and are grandfathers at thirty-five."†

Nowhere was this more frequent than in the southern part of the Western District. The *Reports of 1842 on the Sanitary Condition of the Labouring Population of Scotland* gave an appalling picture of the state in which most of the Irish families, for whose spiritual welfare Bishop Murdoch was responsible, lived in the towns and villages. Scottish industry, however, could not do without Irish labour, and so these aliens were tolerated as part of the machines in the mills, mines and factories. They were hated by most of their neighbours, because the vast majority were Papists. " Stern Calvinistic spirits in the Church of Scotland viewed with dismay the rise of the symbols of Catholicism in their midst, and rallied their countrymen against them with the hoary and unsuccessful slogan of: 'No Popery!' "‡

The invasion of Scotland by starving and destitute Irish families had become a public menace by December 1845. The failure of the potato harvest over several years resulted in more than a million Irish dying of starvation and diseases which accompany malnutrition. Those who could not afford the cost of the voyage across the Atlantic entered Britain at three main points—Liverpool, the South Wales ports and the Clyde, or slipped in by the little harbours on the Galloway coast. Glasgow was soon overrun with

---

* The 1841 census statistics showing the number of Irish-born persons in the chief towns gives a rough idea of the increase in the number of Catholics:—

	Population	Irish-born
Glasgow (and suburbs)	274,533	44,345
Edinburgh (and suburbs)	166,450	6,187
Aberdeen	64,767	841
Dundee	62,794	5,672
Greenock	36,836	4,307
Kilmarnock	19,956	1,624
Airdrie & New Monkland	20,511	2,074
Perth	19,293	217
Montrose	15,096	103
Dumfries	11,409	417

† Cf. Handley, op.cit. p. 90, note 2.
‡ ibid, p. 294.

St Mary's, Abercromby Street, Glasgow (1842). Since 1816 St Andrew's had been the only Catholic chapel in the city.

273

Irish beggars, many of whom were forcibly deported. Between June 15 and August 17, 1847, roughly 26,335 persons, mostly destitute, had landed at Glasgow from Ireland, the majority " absolutely without means of procuring lodging even of the meanest description. As in Liverpool, they crept into such shelter as they could find. An old disused barn in the Gorbals was occupied by more than fifty people. A cellar at No. 95 Bridegate, measuring ten feet by ten, held eight adults and no fewer than seventeen children." * Not long after this an epidemic of fever broke out. Of the 9,390 cases recorded, 5,316 were Irish.

The following quotation from a contemporary source will give an idea of the life led by Bishop Murdoch and his priests during the 1847 fever epidemic:

"The Infirmary was crowded with patients to excess; the Old Poor House, Great Clyde Street, was changed into a temporary Fever Hospital. Famine and pestilence were raging in Ireland, and the famished and fever-stricken were arriving in this country in hundreds and thousands — for a time at the rate of nearly a thousand per week. They had no homes — no spot on which to lay their aching heads. They sought admittance to the Fever Hospital, and were refused for want of room. Unable to proceed farther, they lay down on the open space just before the door of the Chapel House, which was covered with grass and trees at that time. There they remained until, by death or otherwise, room was made for them in the Hospital.

"At the same time, fever raged in every corner of Glasgow. Three of the clergymen of St Andrew's Church were laid prostrate. None remained to attend the sick but Dr Murdoch, and one faithful companion—the Rev. John Shaw. He went out after breakfast to twenty or thirty sick calls, and returned in the evening about five or six o'clock, weary and fatigued. He took a little hurried refreshment, and away he went again until ten o'clock at night. He then began his regular night - shift amongst the forlorn immigrants in the open air; and there and then he gave them the Last Sacraments, like soldiers on the battle field. He would kneel on the damp ground—or, when very deaf, he would lay himself down beside them on the wet grass, and hear their Confessions with the greatest care, with no covering over him but the canopy of Heaven. This he continued for week after week, when it was well-known his own physical strength was all but hopelessly exhausted."†

Eventually Bishop Murdoch did break down, and the crisis came on the first Sunday in May, 1847, when he was preaching during the second Mass. He had a sudden and complete loss of

* Cecil Woodham-Smith, *The Great Hunger: Ireland 1845-9* (1962), p. 279.
† *Scotichronicon*, p. 501 (probably written by J. F. S. Gordon).

memory. Although after a long rest he was able to fulfil normal episcopal duties, it was more than a year before he dared risk another sermon. He obviously needed a coadjutor, and Propaganda appointed the Rev. Alexander Smith, whose consecration as titular Bishop of Parium (the modern Kamares in Anatolia) took place in St Andrew's, Glasgow, on October 3rd, 1847. * The ceremony was performed by Bishop Murdoch, assisted by Bishops Kyle and Carruthers. *

Bishop Murdoch's coadjutor had already had eleven years' experience of working among the Irish. They formed the bulk of his congregation at Greenock, where the kirk treasurer of the East Parish Kirk openly expressed regret that there was no authority to send them back to their own country and commented: " they are the greatest plague we have".†

As a matter of fact, a fair number of Irish vagrants and beggars apprehended by the police were deported, and a paid official was employed at Greenock to deliver them to the captains of steamers. The situation at Paisley was much the same. At one time in the 'forties there were 629 Irish families on the relief funds, and 208 others had been struck off because they had not resided for the required number of years in Scotland. The Rev. John Bremner, who had been in charge of the mission for thirteen years, stated in 1840: " I would consider, speaking of my own congregation, that the Irish should get fairer play than they do get. I have seen instances where they had been refused relief, and where thèy had a fair right to receive it". On being asked whether they were refused because they were Irishmen, his answer was " No doubt of it."‡

Priests working in other missions in Lanarkshire and Renfrewshire told the same stories of how their mainly Irish flocks were often boycotted by the public authorities when needing relief. The priests had to shoulder all the burdens, because there were as yet no Catholic social workers, and no religious orders of men and women to assist them. Not only in Glasgow, but also in Greenock, Dumbarton, Paisley, Hamilton, Ayr, Kilmarnock and other towns and villages destitute Irish families were crowded together, mostly in bug-infested tenement houses.§

* Alexander Smith, born in the Enzie District on January 24, 1815, was educated at Aquhorties, Blairs, and the Scots College, Rome. Forced to return to Scotland for health reasons he was ordained priest in 1836, at Greenock, where he worked for 6 years. In 1842 he was moved to Paisley and he remained there until his consecration.

† Cf. Handley, op.cit. p. 207.

‡ ibid, p. 207.

§ It was reckoned in the 1840s that 1 in 8 of the total population of Glasgow was attacked by louse-borne typhus. There were several cholera epidemics. Tuberculosis and rickets were rife. Until 1855 Glasgow's water-supply came from the Clyde, fouled by general refuse and drainage. The first Medical Officer of Health was not appointed till 1863. The first Fever Hospital was opened two years later.

In 1846 a Glasgow priest who visited Tourcoing, the manufacturing city in the north of France, happened to call at the convent of the Franciscan Sisters of Our Lady of the Angels, where he told the community of the dearth of Catholic school teachers in the Western Vicariate. Two of the Sisters were so moved that they sought and obtained permission from their Superiors and the Archbishop of Cambrai to go to Glasgow. *

On their arrival in the summer of 1847, shortly after Bishop Murdoch's breakdown in health, they found that no provision had been made for housing them, so for a time they lodged with a Catholic lady in Monteith Row. They started to learn English, and began to teach the girls in the Orphan Institute. Private tuition in French helped to support them.

The senior of the two Sisters, Adelaide Vaast, died during the cholera epidemic of 1849 and Bishop Murdoch urged her companion to return to France or to join a teaching community in England or Ireland, but she decided to remain in Glasgow, living alone with a young French lady, Mlle. Marchant, who had accompanied her to Scotland. Almost miraculously a new community came into being with the clothing as a novice of Mlle. Marchant, who took the religious name of Mary Francis. By 1851 the Franciscan Sisters had increased to eighteen. Most of the postulants came over from Ireland. Before long the school in Charlotte Street, between the Gallowgate and Glasgow Green, had seventy pupils and seven boarders. The Sisters attended other schools on weekdays and also taught in Sunday schools.†

In 1849 Bishop Murdoch arranged for some Sisters of Mercy at Limerick to come to Glasgow. He put them in charge of St Mary's School and the Girls' Orphanage, hitherto staffed by laywomen. Two years later Mère St Euphrasie, foundress of the Sisters of Our Lady of Charity of the Good Shepherd at Angers, sent some of her large community to Glasgow. Bishop Murdoch found them a house at Dalbeth outside the city, where they opened what was called a 'Home for the Reformation of Females', otherwise what in Victorian times was known as a 'Penitentiary'. Considering the abject poverty of the Irish Catholics in the hungry 'forties, it is not surprising that many Irish Catholic girls were driven to prostitution.

---

* There were no female communities in Glasgow previous to the Reformation and only two of men—Dominicans and Friars Minor Observant, founded respectively in 1246 and 1475-6.

† The Glasgow community, which started as a group of Tertiaries, adopted the constitutions of the Third Order Regular of St Francis in 1867 and became known as the Franciscans of the Immaculate Conception. The convent in Charlotte Street remained their mother-house until 1920, when it was transferred to Newlands. Several daughter-houses, some of brief duration, were opened in other parts of Scotland during the second half of the last century.

It was not only the poor Irish in the southern part of the vast Vicariate who were a constant responsibility to Bishop Murdoch. In 1846 a potato famine in the Highlands led to increased destitution and many families were evicted because they could not pay their rents. The Bishop made periodical Visitations of the missions in the North West, and these must have been made exhausting by the difficulties of transport. In 1849 he moved from St Andrew's to St Mary's, Abercromby Street, so great was the need of more priests. Later on he took over the Gorbals mission, where housing conditions could hardly have been worse. Here the houses were a veritable breeding ground for disease. It was not uncommon to find ten persons living together in one small room —men, women, youths and children, sleeping side by side on the floor, very often only with straw to serve as bedding. Whisky was cheap and drunkenness rampant. *

Shortly after Bishop Smith's consecration in 1847, he went with the Rev. John Gray on a begging tour of parts of the United States and did not return to Scotland until early in 1849. It was said that " his winning ways, his mild yet firm character, endeared him to all who came in contact with him." It was Bishop Smith, rather than Bishop Murdoch, who was responsible for the foundation of the Franciscan Sisters of the Immaculate Conception, and dealing with the many problems connected with them.

The Eastern District, 1843–1852

In the Eastern District, as much as in the Western District, the spread and even the conservation of Catholicism were prevented by the shortage of priests. During the eighteen-forties more and more Irish immigrants continued to arrive in Dundee, Perth, Arbroath, Dunfermline and other places. Mostly they became mill-workers but some also settled in mining villages. There were not nearly enough priests available to minister to these displaced persons.

At the same time there were several wealthy converts who wanted chaplains for their domestic chapels. Neither Bishop Carruthers nor Bishop Gillis cared to offend them by appearing to be indifferent to their spiritual welfare.

The most influential of the convert lairds was Sir William Drummond-Steuart of Grandtully in Perthshire, who had inherited

---

* In 1848 some of the ministers of the Church of Scotland Committee for the Suppression of Intemperance, in reply to questions, tended to blame the influence of the Irish Catholics as the cause of drunkenness in their parishes. One of them stated that the only remedy for the evil was to send back every Irishman and prohibit any more from coming to Scotland! (cf. Handley, op.cit. pp. 257-8).

the baronetcy in 1838 on the death of his elder brother in Paris. *
For eight years he wandered around the United States and
Canada. At one time he commanded an irregular troop of armed
men escorting the Oregon trail. At another he was collecting skins
for the fur trade. When he returned to Scotland and took up
residence at Murthly Castle, ten miles north of Perth, as the
seventh Baronet, his inseparable companion was a half-breed
Indian and French-Canadian, named Antoine Clément, with whom
his relations were not unlike those of Queen Victoria and John
Brown, from 1858 until his death in 1883.† The policies of the
Castle soon became famous as a Scottish Zoo, where roamed the
animals and birds brought back from North America by Sir
William. A herd of bison, i.e. buffaloes, was among the attractions. Lady Drummond-Steuart preferred to live at Grandtully
Castle, about ten miles north-west of this menagerie.‡ It is
difficult to understand why the wealthy, eccentric, convert laird
became on such intimate terms of friendship with Bishop Gillis.
Perhaps it was because the Bishop had been born and bred in the
French-speaking part of Canada.

Sir William's first appearance as one of the leading laymen of
the Eastern District was on July 14th, 1841, when he acted as
chairman of a meeting in Edinburgh where Bishop Gillis was
presented with a magnificent clock and 200 guineas to buy a
carriage. On the following Sunday the Bishop celebrated Mass
and administered Confirmation in a chapel fitted up within the
Castle. After this there was a close association between the titular
Bishop of Limyra and the Baronet of Grandtully.

The chapel did not satisfy Sir William, so he asked Gillespie
Graham to prepare designs for a new one and it was agreed that
the style should be what he described as "Saxon or Bysantyne"
[sic]. On the morning of November 1st, 1846, being the feast of
All Saints, Bishop Carruthers, Bishop Gillis and priests from Edinburgh, Perth, Dundee and Dunfermline took part in the opening
of this new chapel. There had never been quite such a spectacular
Catholic function in Scotland since the Reformation, other than

---

* Born in 1795, William Steuart became a cornet in the 6th Dragoon
Guards at the age of seventeen and as a lieutenant in the King's Hussars
he fought at the Battle of Waterloo. When he retired from the Army in
1821 he went off to North America, where he travelled as far west as the
Rocky Mountains and beyond, to Fort Vancouver on the Pacific coast.
Much of his time was spent living with Red Indians, hunting buffaloes and
having the most extraordinary adventures. In 1837 he was received into
the Catholic Church at St Louis, Missouri (Cf. W. J. Anderson, 'Sir
William Drummond-Steuart and the Chapel of St Anthony the Eremite,
Murthly', in *Innes Review*, Autumn 1964, pp. 151-70).

† The half-breed was transformed into a butler-valet, and on special
occasions wore "full Highland dress."

‡ The date of the marriage is not known, and her origins are obscure.

the Requiem Masses arranged by Bishop Gillis in Edinburgh.* If the convert Baronet did nothing else, he certainly provided a milieu for the exotic liturgical enthusiasms of the titular Bishop of Limyra.

The dedication of the Chapel of St Anthony the Eremite began with a procession of the Bishops and clergy, headed by the cross-bearer, acolytes and other officials, with much sprinkling of holy water and the chanting of psalms.† It is recorded that "The myriads of lighted lamps and tapers which irradiated the golden altar and which reflected their gleams on the richly-stained glass windows — the gorgeousness of the sacred vestments of the bishops and priests — the solemn tones of the organ, the chimes of the bell — the beautiful paintings with which the interior is decorated—all combined to produce the most thrilling effect . . . The altar surmounted by a most splendid tabernacle and crucifix, which is supported by columns of marble, and communicates with the old family chapel . . . Signor Paolo della Torre presided at the organ, and the choir of St John's, Perth, and other amateur per-formers sung their respective parts with admirable taste and effect.‡

The pontifical High Mass, celebrated by Bishop Gillis in the presence of Bishop Carruthers, must have been awe-inspiring to the majority of the congregation, for never in their lives could they have witnessed anything on the same scale, at least not in Scotland. We are told that "The Presiding Bishop descended from his throne, and knelt with the clergy at the foot of the altar—no one was standing in the sanctuary but the officiating prelate who was offering the sacrifice, and when he raised on high the consecrated elements clouds of incense arose from the thurible, the organ played its softest notes, and the glorious bell in the tower sent forth its most solemn peal! The effect was overwhelming".

During the afternoon vespers were followed by pontifical Benediction and at the end of the festivities the numerous guests were entertained to dinner "in the most princely style." §

* See pp. 256, 270.
  † One wonders if the choice of the dedication to St Anthony, the Egyptian hermit-monk, was connected with Antoine Clément, Sir William's half-breed butler-valet. So far no evidence of any medieval dedication seems available.
  ‡ *Scottish Catholic Directory*, 1847.
  § In 1847 the body of Sir William's younger brother, Thomas Stewart, was brought back to Scotland from Italy, and buried in the adjoining mortuary chapel after a solemn Requiem at which both Bishop Gillis and Bishop Kyle assisted. He had been at Christ Church, Oxford, as a con-temporary of Dr Pusey, and became a Catholic in 1829. Later on he joined the Cassinese Benedictine Congregation, taking the religious name of Sylvester, and was ordained priest at the Abbey of S. Martino delle Scale, near Monreale in Sicily. He was assassinated at Ancona on July 1845, at the time of a revolution against the temporal power of the papacy. Nearly 2,000 of Gregory XVI's subjects are said to have been in exile, prescribed, or in prison for political reasons.

Although the Eastern District was desperately short of priests, Bishop Gillis felt that Murthly Castle deserved a resident chaplain, its little chapel being quite the most magnificent place of worship under his jurisdiction.* Mr James Mackay was moved from Perth, where for many years he had ministered mainly to poor Irish labourers and their families.†

The expenditure on the Chapel of St Anthony the Eremite was prodigious, but the whole thing was in keeping with the dreams and visions of the titular Bishop of Limyra, which now included a grandiose cathedral in Edinburgh.‡

An epidemic of fever started in the summer of 1847 and by July 26 the Edinburgh Royal Infirmary, with accommodation for only 300 patients, had 600 cases. The majority were Catholics of Irish birth or descent. Tents were pitched outside, four buildings were requisitioned and another fever hospital opened. The priests were kept busy giving the Last Sacraments and burying the dead.

Before this outbreak of fever Bishop Gillis had set off for Germany to investigate the affairs of the Scots Monastery at Ratisbon. Unlike other Bavarian monasteries, it had not been suppressed in 1803, on the supposition that it was extra-territorial. But it was difficult to see what could be done to restore this venerable foundation to its former state of prosperity. Dom Benedict Arbuthnot, who was born in Aberdeenshire in 1737, joined the community at the age of eleven and was elected Abbot in 1776. When he died in 1820, Dom Benedict Deeson succeeded him as Prior. The novitiate, however, had been closed for many years. It was not re-opened until 1827 and three more years passed before

---

* It was only 60 ft long and 25 ft wide, inclusive of the sanctuary.

† After 1849 he also had to serve Lady Drummond-Steuart's private oratory at Grandtully Castle, near Aberfeldy. Then he took on the missions at Blairgowrie and Crieff, but retained his status of chaplain at Murthly until 1862. The chapel was closed after Sir William's death in 1871. It was finally dismantled in 1890.

‡ Probably his imagination had been stimulated by what the Episcopalians were doing. In 1846 a group of wealthy laymen, influenced by the Oxford Movement, among them Lord Forbes and the Hon. G. F. Boyle (later 6th Earl of Glasgow), gave their patronage to a project to erect a cathedral at Perth. Its chancel and transepts were designed by William Butterfield, and were dedicated in 1850. By the time the Murthly chapel was opened, Boyle had already begun to make plans too for the Collegiate Church of the Holy Spirit on the Isle of Cumbrae on the Firth of Clyde. He was prepared to defray the total cost, besides making provision for a resident body consisting of a Provost, five Canons, organist, clerical students, choristers and servitors, who would carry out daily choral services. The Church (designed by Butterfield) was opened in 1851. Only eight miles from Murthly was the College of the Holy and Undivided Trinity at Glenalmond, the foundation stone of which was laid on September 8, 1846. This Episcopalian establishment was envisaged both as a theological college on moderate High Church lines and as a school for the sons of gentlemen.

the first group of students for the seminary arrived from Scotland after a long interval. By 1835 all but two of the old monks were dead. The boys had no choice but to attend the public schools for lack of monastic professors. The Bavarian government insisted that more monks must be found but the Scottish Bishops contended that the seminary funds belonged to the Mission, not to the monastery, and they did not want the students to become monks. Eventually they agreed to allow a certain number to embrace the religious state if they felt called to do so. The situation went from bad to worse after 1839, when Dom Marianus Graham became Prior. With the deaths of more newly professed monks, the Government renewed its demands that the seminary must be re-organised. Dom Marianus died in 1844 and Dom Benedict resumed the priorship. Bishop Gillis appears to have felt that he must find Scottish secular priests to act as professors and that the Vicars-Apostolic should take over the direction of the former Benedictine seminary.

Having made a careful enquiry into the situation at Ratisbon, the Bishop went on to Rome. He failed to find any solution there for the problems affecting the Bavarian monastery, but he returned home with a papal brief, approving the project for a cathedral in Edinburgh. He revisited Germany in 1848 and on his way through London he preached at the opening of Pugin's church of St George's, Southwark, where he revelled in the gorgeous pontifical functions, enriched by the singing by Mario and Tamburini of the Italian Opera. But this second trip to Bavaria led to nothing. King Ludwig I's attachment to the adventuress known profession-ally as Lola Montez had reached the stage where his subjects could stand it no longer. He abdicated and because of the political crisis which followed, all the students at Ratisbon were sent back to Scotland. Since 1830 the King had restored several abbeys to the Bavarian Benedictines. As there were only two Scottish monks available, it was impossible to carry out the orders. So the Bishop submitted the case to Lord Palmerston, the British Foreign Secre-tary, and also the Holy See. Nothing resulted, because in November 1848 Pius IX fled from Rome to Gaeta, and he did not return until two years later.

Having got back to Scotland on March 31st 1849, Bishop Gillis persuaded Bishop Carruthers to write a pastoral letter, which was read in all the churches and chapels of the Eastern Vicariate on Easter Sunday, explaining that it was hoped to erect a cathedral in Edinburgh. * No time was wasted, for it was taken for granted that the money would drop down from heaven, once the ball was

---

* In 1844 Bishop Gillis acquired land to the south of Edinburgh, beyond the Meadows, on which he planned to erect a seminary in emulation of the English ones at Oscott, Ushaw, and Old Hall, Ware. His visions were always on a grandiose scale.

set rolling. At Bishop Gillis's request, Augustus Welby Pugin came north to inspect the site at Greenhill and discuss the sort of building that was required. *   Pugin returned to his home at Ramsgate, and set to work on the plans, sections and elevations of the Cathedral. It would be a fairly large and very lofty cruciform church, in which the choir and high altar would be surrounded by aisles, with a Lady Chapel beyond. Above the crossing of the transepts would rise a massive tower, crowned by a soaring spire. On either side of the nave of six bays at the west end there would be a tower, each with a spire. Unlike his churches at Southwark and Nottingham, there appeared to be no limits set on the total cost of this cathedral and he felt able to let his imagination run riot with fourteenth-century English Decorated Gothic.

He would provide Bishop Gillis with traceried windows filled with jewel-like stained glass by Mr Hardman of Birmingham, that would cast a dim religious light over the interior. There would be pavements of multi-coloured encaustic tiles with heraldic emblems, made by Mr Minton of Stafford; also a stone font, carved by Mr Myers, with a towering wooden cover, like those of the later Middle Ages. There would be some chantry-chapels, endowed by some of the richer Scottish Catholic families. Bishop Gillis had mentioned a seminary adjacent to the Cathedral and therefore at least two rows of choir-stalls were demanded, so that the students, vested in flowing surplices, could assist at High Mass and Vespers. A spacious sanctuary was essential to enable the Vicar-Apostolic of the Eastern District, or his Coadjutor, to pontificate with greater dignity than was possible in the confined space at St Mary's, Broughton Street. To add to the devotional effect of the interior there must be gorgeous polychromatic paintings on the walls and ceilings in the medieval manner, like those which in 1846 Lord Shrewsbury's munificence made possible at St Giles's, Cheadle, Staffordshire. By this time rood-screens had become almost an obsession with Pugin, so it was inevitable that his Edinburgh cathedral must be provide with one to create a sense of mystery.†
The Episcopalians had already set a good example to Scottish

---

* Pugin had already designed large churches at Birmingham, Nottingham, Southwark, and Newcastle-on-Tyne, which were intended for ultimate use as cathedrals. In 1849 he was working on the plans for the new Houses of Parliament at Westminster.

† His *Treatise on Chancel Screens and Rood Lofts, Their Antiquity and Symbolical Signification* was published in 1851. But Pugin's principles had already got as far north as Aberdeenshire a year before this. After Mr Charles Tochetti was appointed chaplain to the Leslies of Fetternear in 1849, he appealed on behalf of a new church at Inverurie, and stated: "Its architecture and furniture will be in *strict medieval style*, so far as circumstances permit; and in course of time, we may hope to see restored in Scotland, a Parish Church as it was in the *Good Olde Catholick Tymes*. A Rood Loft will not be forgotten", Tochetti died as the Rt. Rev. Mgr. Vicar-General of the Aberdeen Diocese in 1903.

Papists by inserting chancel screens into several new churches, including St Columba's, Edinburgh, consecrated in 1848. *

When critical persons pointed out to Bishop Gillis that his proposed Cathedral would be more than a mile from the centre of the city, he had merely to reply that the terraces and 'loans' between Grange Road and Morningside were fast becoming one of the most exclusive residential districts in Edinburgh; their stately mansions (mostly in the Scottish Baronial style) and pretty villas secluded in gardens were being bought up by members of the aristocracy, for whose daughters' education St Margaret's Convent in Whitehouse Loan made ample provision. There were, however, some more realistic-minded people who felt that the money to be spent on this grandiose Cathedral would be better devoted to erecting chapels for the impoverished Irish Catholics, scattered over the Vicariate, both in towns and in mining villages, where there were as yet no permanent places of worship.

For his part Bishop Gillis, like the seventeenth century Jesuits, believed that the re-conversion of Scotland would be brought about, not so much by the natural process of a steady increase in the birth-rate on the part of Irish immigrants, but by the nobility and landed gentry. To make up for many of the old Scottish Catholic families who had fallen into heresy and schism, a fair number of the upper classes had been reconciled with the Church during the eighteen-forties.

Among the first was Mrs Isabella Hutchison (1782-1866), the widow of Colonel Hutchison, a daughter of Lord Cunningham.† This "charming old--fashioned lady", as she has been described, was a convert from the Catholic Apostolic (Irvingite) Church. Bishop Gillis referred to her as "stiff as buckram", but until her death she was a leader in Edinburgh Catholic society. In 1842 Edward Douglas (1819-98), a cousin of the sixth Marquess of Queensberry, 'went over to Rome' and joined the Redemptionists. Two years later Charles Scott-Murray of Danesfield (1818-82), of Scots descent if not domicile, took the same step, and in 1846 he married the Hon. Amelia Fraser, the eldest daughter of the twelfth Baron Lovat. It was also in 1846 that Mrs Eleanor Leslie (1800-92),‡ wife of Archibald Leslie (1789-1851), last of Balnageith,

* Pugin's cathedral, although not so large in area, had it ever been built, would have rivalled St Mary's Cathedral, designed by Sir Gilbert Scott for the Episcopalians, the foundation stone of which was laid in 1874.

† After a pilgrimage to Rome in 1842 she returned to Scotland with the bones of an unknown Christian martyr, St Crescentia, presented to her by Gregory XVI. She had considerable difficulty in getting them out of Italy, and when she reached Edinburgh they were given to St Margaret's Convent. A. W. Pugin designed a reliquary, and the Sisters were allowed to expose these bones on the feast of St Crescentia, and during its octave.

‡ Cf. J. M. Stone, *Eleanor Leslie* (1898), pp. 95-6. In 1847 and 1848 four of her children became Catholics; and her husband, who was a kins-

Moray, made her submission to the Holy See at St Margaret's Convent, Edinburgh, at the hands of Bishop Gillis.

The following year Lucy, wife of Sir Alexander Duff-Gordon, of Halkin, Ayrshire, the third Baronet, and assistant Gentleman Usher to Queen Victoria, seceded to the Roman Church. So did Miss Charlotte Hay (1824-1903), daughter of Lord James Hay of Seaton, son of the seventh Marquess of Tweeddale.

More influential, however, was the conversion in 1847 of Robert Monteith of Carstairs (1810-84), and his wife, for they devoted their wealth to many charitable objects. * Among their neighbours in Lanarkshire was Colonel Archibald Gerard of Rocksoles (1812-80). He and his wife, a daughter of Sir John Grahame, were both confirmed by Bishop Gillis in 1847.†

Other members of the Noblesse of Scotland followed in 1850. The Lady Margaret Kennedy (1800-77), daughter of Archibald Earl of Cassilis (later first Marquess of Ailsa), widow of the seventh Earl of Newburgh, took the road to Rome.‡ David Erskine, twelfth Earl of Buchan (1783-1857), and his third wife, Caroline Rose Maxwell (1802-93), were the next of the Scottish aristocracy to abjure heresy and schism.§

But the great sensation of that year was the reception into the Church in August by Bishop Gillis of Rudolph, Viscount Fielding (1823-92), later eighth Earl of Denbigh, Count of the Holy Roman Empire, and his first wife, Louisa, daughter of David and Lady Emma Pennant. Lord Denbigh, accompanied by his Anglican chaplain, hurried north to Edinburgh, hoping to stop the 'perversion' of his eldest son and heir, but it was too late.**

Two months after this Bishop Gillis arranged for the exhibition of Pugin's plans for the proposed cathedral in Edinburgh, but they

---

man of the 12th Earl of Caithness, finally made up his mind "to become a Roman" shortly before his death in 1851 (op.cit. p. 124). Their only son Eric joined the Society of Jesus.

* It was his father, a rich merchant and owner of cotton mills, who in 1792 enabled Mr Alexander Macdonell to open the first permanent Catholic chapel in Glasgow. His second son Robert joined the Society of Jesus and four of his daughters became Religious of the Sacred Heart.

† Their son John became a Jesuit, edited *The Month*, and was Provincial for a time.

‡ In 1858 the House of Lords allowed the claim of Cecilia, Princess Giustiniani, to the earldom of Newburgh, and swept away the *soi-disant* 6th, 7th, and 8th Earls. For the rest of her long widowhood, the legal Mrs Eyre of Hassop, with the acquiescence of Queen Victoria, retained the courtesy title of Countess, and remained a devout Catholic, given to good works.

§ In 1862 the widowed Countess erected a Catholic chapel on her estates at Broxburn, West Lothian, for the benefit of the numerous Irish families who had settled in this shale-mining village.

** The chaplain, Mr Baylee, published his version of the stormy three hours' interview in the *Morning Herald*, which evoked a reply from Bishop Gillis in a printed pamphlet.

aroused little interest. Very few of the Catholic aristocracy offered to contribute towards its erection. Both the seminary and the cathedral remained visions that never materialised.

By Letters Apostolic, dated September 29th, 1850, Pius IX restored the English Hierarchy, and it was rumoured that similar measures were contemplated for Scotland. Four ultra-Protestant-minded out of the seven who made up the Episcopalian Hierarchy took fright, and between them they composed a message of sympathy to their brethren of the English Establishment—brimful of accusations against the "arrogant assumption of the Bishop of Rome", not to mention his "unexampled insolence". This intriguing document, which might well have been drawn up by some of the seventeenth-century Covenanters, ended with "an earnest repudiation of the errors of the Church of Rome " and its "intolerable aggression" in appointing schismatic bishops for England and Wales. *

What with the 'papal aggression' in England, and the alarming increase in the 'perversions' in Scotland, some hyper-sensitive Presbyterians also went into action. They founded the Scottish Reformation Society, its objects being "to resist the aggressions of Popery; to watch the designs and movements of its promoters and abettors; to diffuse sound and Scriptural information on the distinctive tenets of Protestantism and of Popery; and to promote the instruction of Roman Catholics in Bible Truth". At the same time an appeal was made to the general public, asking all who held Evangelical Protestant opinions to become members of the Society.

There was no need for all this renewed terror of the machinations of 'Mystery, Babylon the Great, the Mother of Harlots, and Abominations of the Earth' (as mentioned in the *Revelation of St John the Divine*), because *Pio Nono* made no attempt to restore the Scottish Hierarchy. It was not until twenty-eight years later that the Episcopal College of Bishops would have cause to protest against " the high crime " which had been committed by the Bishop of Rome, and to do so in even stronger language than that used in 1850.†

The Gorham Judgment of March 8th, 1850, gave great offence to High Church Anglicans, by leaving it a matter of private opinion whether the doctrine of Baptismal Regeneration was held in the Church of England. It also worried a fair number of Scottish Episcopalians, although Bishop Forbes of Brechin did his best to assure them that the ruling given by the Judicial Committee of the Privy Council did not affect the Episcopal Church, even if supported by the ninety-second successor of St Augustine as Archbishop of Canterbury, in the person of Dr Sumner.

---

* Bishop Forbes of Brechin refused to add his name to this militant anti-papal manifesto, having many Catholic friends, especially on the continent.

† See p. 337.

The Rev. J. C. Robertson, chaplain to the Duke of Buccleuch at Dalkeith Palace, had 'gone over to Rome' in 1848. He was a great friend of the Lady Cecil Chetwynd-Talbot (1808-1877) widow of the seventh Marquess of Lothian, who for many years had been a devout disciple of Bishop Forbes, and to whom he had dedicated a Short Commentary on the Penitential Psalms in 1847. Largely due to Mr Robertson's influence Lady Lothian was received into the Roman Church in 1850. *

Her neighbour at Dalkeith, the Lady Charlotte Thynne (1811-95), youngest daughter of the fifth Marquess of Bath and wife of the fifth Duke of Buccleuch, felt unable to become a Catholic until five years later. This step "brought her domestic trials which she probably reckoned as nothing in comparison with religious certainty and peace, but which were very real notwithstanding." But the 'perversion to Popery' in 1850 of Anne Colquhoun, third wife and widow of the seventh Duke of Argyll, aroused far more horror among pious Protestants than that of the Episcopalian Duchess of Buccleuch, because, taken as a whole, the Campbell clan had always been militantly Presbyterian.†

Another friend of Bishop Forbes whose faith in Anglicanism was shattered by the Gorham Judgment was James Hope (1812-73), third son of Sir Alexander Hope of Rankeilour and Luffness, who in 1847 had married Charlotte, only daughter of John Gibson Lockhart and granddaughter of Sir Walter Scott. With Archdeacon Manning, he was reconciled with the Holy See by Fr. Brownbill, S.J., at Easter, 1851. Mrs Hope followed her husband's example at Whitsuntide.‡

Bishop Gillis did all he could for Lady Lothian, her children and the Hopes, following their reception into the Catholic Church, and after attending a crowded meeting in Dublin at which the Catholic Defence Association was formed, he placed himself under

* Her two youngest sons, Lord Ralph and Lord Walter Kerr, followed her in 1853 and 1854. Her eldest daughter, Lady Cecil Kerr, became a Religious of the Sacred Heart.
The dowager Marchioness feared she was guilty of sacrilege by living at Newbattle Abbey, which had been occupied by Cistercian monks from 1140 to 1587. The last abbot, Mark Ker, having adopted the reformed religion, remained on as commendator, and married a daughter of the Earl of Rothes. Their son, Mark, became 1st Marquis of Lothian in 1606. It was not until the 7th Marchioness had obtained a document signed by Pius IX, authorising her to remain in possession of former monastic property that her scruples were removed.
† Sir David Hunter-Blair, O.S.B., A Medley of Memories (1919), p. 104. The Duchess helped to build the church at Selkirk (1866).
‡ In 1853, Mr Hope assumed the name of Hope-Scott on becoming Laird of Abbotsford. Besides building churches at Kelso (1855), Galashiels (1858) and Mingarry, Invernessshire (1859), he made it possible for Mass centres to be opened at St Andrews and Oban. He left large sums of money to St Margaret's Convent, Edinburgh, where he was buried in 1873, three years after the death of his second wife, the Lady Victoria Fitzalan-Howard, daughter of the 14th Duke of Norfolk.

the care of Dr Gully at Malvern Wells in October 1851. It is related that this then fashionable practitioner "subjected him, for several weeks, to a course of Hydropathic Treatment" and "declared that his ailments proceeded from threatened Congestion of the Brain, which, if allowed to make further progress, would end in paralysis." *

The Bishop, feeling the better for the hot and cold baths at this Worcestershire health-resort, returned to Edinburgh in January 1852 but until his death twelve years later he was frequently liable to attacks of severe illness. None of the many spas whose waters he tried effected a permanent cure.

Since 1849 Bishop Carruthers had been living at Dundee, keeping in the background and leaving his dynamic Coadjutor to make the public appearances. There was no question of him neglecting his duties as Vicar Apostolic of the Eastern District, however. He made visitations of the missions, administering Confirmation and promoting works of charity and mercy. He encouraged the Society of St Andrew, which had been established for the support of poor missions. The Wellburn Academy at Dundee, which provided secondary education for boys and girls, was another of his special interests; likewise the United Industrial School in Edinburgh, of which he was Vice-President.†

It may have been during one of the visitations of poor missions that he picked up a typhus germ. He died at Dundee after eleven days of fever on May 24th, 1852, having been a bishop for twenty years.

Bishop Gillis was in London, preaching the 'Mois de Marie' at the French Chapel in Portman Square. On hearing that the Vicar-Apostolic was seriously ill, he hurried north, and near Newcastle his train was involved in a collision, the shock of which is supposed to have affected his spine. He arrived, however, in time to arrange a magnificent obsequies for the deceased prelate, whose body was laid to rest in the vaults beneath St Mary's, Broughton Street. For the first time in Scotland since the Reformation, the 'Month's Mind' took place, i.e. a solemn Requiem Mass celebrated roughly on the thirtieth day after death or burial. Most of the clergy of the Vicariate attended this function on July 8th.‡

* Scotichronicon, p. 486.

† The lack of any reference to Bishop Carruthers in Miss J. M. Stone's memoir, Eleanor Leslie (1898), the greater part of which records Catholic life in Scotland between 1846 and 1892, suggests that he can have had few direct contacts with the aristocratic converts of the 'forties and 'fifties.

‡ During the 19 years that Bishop Carruthers ruled over the Eastern Vicariate, houses were bought and used as temporary missions at Annan (1839) Kirkcudbright (1846) and Forfar (1849). New chapels were erected at Perth (1834—enlarged 1849), St Andrew's, Dundee (1836), Stirling (1838), Falkirk (1839), Lochee, Dundee (1851), Arbroath (1848), Blairgowrie (1848), Dunfermline (1846), Hawick (1844), Linlithgow (1850), Peebles (1850), St Mary's, Dundee (1851).

CHAPTER NINE

EASTERN, WESTERN & NORTHERN DISTRICT 1852-1869

The Western District, 1852–65

SINCE THE ACHIEVEMENT of Catholic emancipation in 1829, Scottish priests had continued to provide schools for their missions, wherever the numbers and means made this possible. In most cases this involved strenuous efforts and much sacrifice, especially in the Western District. The Protestant majority was usually unhelpful and unsympathetic, so a system of Catholic 'voluntary schools' developed in all the larger towns and villages of the industrial Lowlands. *

The establishment of a school in every parish of the Church of Scotland had been made compulsory by an Act of Parliament of 1696. Such schools were supported by a tax, which local landowners could impose on themselves, aided by money collected from their tenants. But although the establishment of a school and the appointment of a schoolmaster for each parish was compulsory, nothing was said about the attendance of children. The parish system of education proved inadequate, and by degrees other schools were opened throughout Scotland, notably by corporations and individuals, some by Presbyterian societies.

After a series of government investigations into the conditions of education in Scotland, a committee of the Privy Council was appointed in 1839 to deal with annual grants voted by Parliament for the purpose of "promoting the education of children belonging to the classes who support themselves by manual labour." Rules and regulations were drawn up, and since all schools were excluded which were not directly connected with a religious denomination, or in which the Bible was not read daily in the Authorized Version, the reading of a Protestant version of the Scriptures had to be tolerated in the first Catholic schools opened in Glasgow.†

Catholics in the southern part of the Western District were almost invariably of "the classes who support themselves by manual labour". Although it was hard for them to spare money towards building schools, paying of teachers' salaries or providing books, desks and furniture, somehow or other this was done in most missions during the first forty-five years after the Catholic

---

* The term 'voluntary schools' means a state-aided school not provided by education authority.

† See p. 234.

Relief Act of 1829, with the help of the small Government grants for Catholic schools which were available. Again, it was not easy to get children to attend school, for they were still allowed to work from ten to eighteen hours daily. *

In 1845 an Act of Parliament required parents to send children to school for at least three hours daily.† That same year the Principal Secretary to the Home Department paid the following tribute to Catholic schools in Scotland:—"The influence of the priests, from their constant intercourse with their congregation, their knowledge of every one of them in sickness and in health, and their unremitting devotion to their wants and interests, both spiritual and temporal, is deservedly very great, and has been, it must in candour be allowed, most beneficial in promoting the cause of temperance and of education among those professing the same faith as themselves."‡ In a sense history was repeating itself, because it was monks from Ireland who had 'invaded' Scotland in the sixth century. The same thing was happening again, but in the nineteenth century the missionaries were poverty-stricken layfolk, driven from their country by famine and forced to settle in those parts of Scotland where unskilled labour was in demand.

It was from the grim man-made 'Black Country', roughly from Ayr in the south-west to Dundee in the north-east, that the Catholic religion was brought back to Scotland after the middle of the last century—not from the castles and mansions of the old Catholic families and the wealthy converts. So far as the Western District was concerned, there was no 'Catholic Crusade', no well-planned 'Forward Movement', no carefully thought-out publicity. It was a natural (more correctly supernatural), realistic and spontaneous re-birth of the Faith, resulting from the influx of cradle-Catholics from Ireland, following after the depopulation of the Highlands, and succeeded later on by immigration from certain continental countries. Those who at first regarded themselves as aliens took root in this uncongenial soil, where little was done for their material welfare. They were prepared to live in what was little better than squalor, but they would not do so without the Mass and the Sacraments. School-chapels were erected sooner or later, giving place as time went on to permanent and often stately churches.

* It was not until 1847 that Lord Ashley managed to get an Act passed which limited child-labour to ten hours a day, and the Act was so worded as to make evasion easy.

† The employers of child-labour were ordered to pay not less than 2d per week, this being deducted from the child's wages More than half the children in Glasgow at that date did not attend school. (Cf. Cathures op.cit. p. 67.

‡ Cf. Cathures, op.cit. p. 68.   There were eight Catholic schools in Glasgow by 1850, two conducted by the Franciscan Sisters, and two by the Sisters of Mercy.

T

Unfortunately some of the Irish immigrants did not appreciate what Bishop Murdoch and his priests were doing for their spiritual welfare. In 1851 the *Glasgow Free Press* (a newspaper which had been started as an organ of the Irish on Clydeside) began to attack him. For the next ten years the articles in this journal, with their abuse and lampoons, were more remarkable for their ready Irish wit than for respect for the priesthood or episcopal authority. "The Hielan Clique", as the Scottish clergy were termed, were exposed as a lazy incompetent set of men, hidebound by routine and ruling with obstinate tyranny. The few Irish priests in the Western District, however, were held up as models of every sacerdotal virtue, persecuted by their colleagues who came from outlandish glens, and brought up illiterate clannish caterans, i.e. Highland robbers or freebooters. The management of temporal matters was condemned above all, Bishop Murdoch and Bishop Smith "keeping Sentry" and "herding Paddy" at the doors of the chapels with collection plates. Particular missions and priests were singled out as being never free from debt and subjecting the poor Irish to ceaseless importunities. Other priests were denounced as "worldly-minded", just because they were methodical and business-like. What was described as 'Nepotism' came in for special attack, and one writer said: "With all its inherent evils, it has, for half-a-century, held undisputed sway in the Scottish Mission; where laziness, incompetence, routine, tyranny, are the leading features that characterise an alien usurpation of power and position in the Church." *

This controversy dragged on throughout the eighteen-fifties, but Bishop Murdoch accepted it as a trial sent by God, and made no attempt at first to refute the lies printed about him in the *Free Press*. On June 15th, 1861, he lost his coadjutor, Bishop Smith, who had been in poor health for a long time. He was given a stately funeral, although not on quite the same scale as those organised by Bishop Gillis in Edinburgh. All the Vicars-Apostolic were present at the requiem Mass in St Andrew's. It is recorded that "the music, which was very effective, was under the direction of the Rev. A. Reid." The service lasted over two hours, with the solemn strains of Handel's *Dead March in Saul*.

The relations between the Irish and Scots in the Western Vicariate were not improved by Propaganda's choice of yet another Banffshire priest as coadjutor to Bishop Murdoch, in the person of Mr John Gray. His consecration as titular Bishop of Hypsopolis in Phrygia (with right of succession) took place in St Andrew's, Glasgow, on October 19th, 1862. The consecrating prelate was Dr David Moriarty, Bishop of Kerry, assisted by Bishops Kyle and Murdoch.†

* Cf. *Scotichronicon*, p. 503.
† John Gray was born at Buckie, Banffshire, in 1817, and educated at Blairs and the Scots College, Rome, where he was ordained priest in 1841.

A few more religious orders and congregations had been brought into the Western District, the first being the Little Brothers of Mary (usually known as the Marist Brothers). Having opened a school at Dundee in 1855, they were put in charge of the boys' school in St Mungo's mission in 1858.* It was also in 1858 that Bishop Murdoch invited the Society of Jesus to Glasgow, and handed over to them St Joseph's, North Woodside Road, a dignified church in the Grecian style of architecture, opened in 1850. It served not only the slums of the Cowcaddens but also a wide area lying between Garnethill and Maryhill. The Jesuits established a boys' school in Charlotte Street, which, after its removal to Garnethill in 1866, became known as St Aloysius' College.†

After nearly two hundred and fifty years the Vincentians or Lazarists (officially known as the Congregation of the Mission) returned to Scotland from Ireland in 1859. Bishop Murdoch arranged for them to take over the stately Gothic Revival church at Lanark, erected at the cost of the wealthy convert, Robert Monteith of Carstairs.‡ The Sisters of Charity of St Vincent de Paul founded a boys' orphanage at Lanark that same year. Not long after this the French Little Sisters of the Poor, who already had a home for old men and women in Edinburgh, established a similar home in Glasgow.

The Congregation of Barefooted Clerks of the Most Holy Cross and Passion of Our Lord Jesus Christ—commonly known as the Passionists—were given charge of St Mungo's, Glasgow, in 1865§. Three years later a new mission was formed on the south side of the Clyde, cut off from St John's, Portugal Street (which had evolved from the original Gorbals school-chapel), and was handed over to Franciscan Recollect Fathers from Belgium. On July 11 1869 a Gothic Revival friary was opened. Provided with cloisters and a chapel-house, it was spacious enough to accommodate not only the community but also a limited number of retreatants.

Meanwhile the *Free Press* continued to attack Bishop Murdoch and the 'Hielan Clique'. Early in 1864 its editor, Mr A. H. Keane, published a pamphlet entitled *The Case of the Irish Catholics in*

On his return to Scotland he acted as curate to his uncle, Bishop Scott, at St Andrew's, Glasgow. In 1846 he was placed in charge of the Gorbals chapel. From there he moved to Airdrie, and after his return from the begging tour in North America with Bishop Smith in 1849, he resumed work in the Gorbals. In 1853 he was appointed senior priest at St Andrew's, and in 1860 Vicar General.

* The Brothers established a second school at Dundee in 1860, and made a third foundation at Dumfries in 1874.

† That same year a temporary church was opened adjacent to the College and, like it, dedicated to the patron of youth.

‡ See p. 284.

§ Cf. Louis Edmond, C.P., 'Fr. Austin Edgar, C.P., the first Scottish Passionist', in *Innes Review* (Autumn, 1965), pp. 159-64.

Scotland Stated: *Being a Memorial on the Present State of the Catholic Church in Scotland, addressed to His Eminence Cardinal Alex. Barnabò, Prefect of the Sacred Congregation of Propaganda Fide.* It was printed in English and Italian, and priced at 3d. On St Patrick's Day a Memorial, signed by twenty-four Irish priests of the Western Vicariate, was forwarded to Rome. They complained that, while more than nineteen-twentieths of the faithful and one-half of the priests of the Vicariate were Irish by birth or parentage, yet the Scots were, for the most part, trustees of all the ecclesiastical properties—lands, churches, chapels, houses, schools, colleges, convents, orphanages, reformatories, cemeteries, etc. They recommended, as a cure for these grievances, the appointment of mixed clerical and lay committees, and the restoration of the Hierarchy. Irish bishops should be chosen, so that the episcopate would not continue an exclusively Scots body as hitherto.

Cardinal Barnabò's reply must have been a shock to those twenty-four Irish priests, for there was a great deal to be said in favour of their petition. His Eminence forbade all further discussion of ecclesiastical affairs in the *Free Press*. In April 1864 Bishop Murdoch wrote a charitably worded protest to Mr Keane, pointing out that, in spite of the Cardinal's prohibition, his newspaper was still printing attacks on the Scots clergy.

A sign of the affection and respect with which the Bishop was regarded by some of his priests and people was the presentation of a carriage and pair of horses, which were ultimately given to a lottery on behalf of the Franciscan convent in Charlotte Street. Before this " a handsome brougham " had been presented to the Bishop by a Mrs Wallace, but he handed it over to the Sisters of the Good Shepherd at Dalbeth. His death took place at Glasgow on December 15th, 1865, and his body was laid to rest in the vaults beneath St Andrew's, a church with which he had been associated for forty-five years. *

* During his episcopate many new missions and churches were opened in the Western Vicariate, including: Laggan, Inverness-shire (1846); St Alphonsus, Glasgow (1846); St Joseph, Kilmarnock (1847); Rothesay, Isle of Bute (1849); St Patrick, Coatbridge (1848); Pollokshaws, Glasgow (1849); Campbeltown, Argyll (1850); St Joseph, Glasgow (1850); Rutherglen, Lanarkshire (1853); Maryhill, Glasgow (1850); Airdrie, Lanarkshire (1850); Dalry, Ayrshire (1848-51); Johnstone, Renfrewshire (1852); Duntocher, Dunbartonshire (1850); St Mungo, Glasgow (1850); Eastmuir (1851); Stranraer, Wigtownshire (1853); Port Glasgow, Renfrewshire (1854); St Laurence, Greenock (1855); Muirkirk, Ayrshire (1856); Springburn, Glasgow (1856); Saltcoats, Ayrshire (1853-6); Partick, Glasgow (1858); Carluke, Lanarkshire (1849-57); Craigston, Isle of Barra (1858); Irvine, Ayrshire (1862); Eaglesham, Renfrewshire (1857); Dalmellington, Ayrshire (1860); Alexandria, Dunbartonshire (1860); Neilston, Renfrewshire (1861); Girvan, Ayrshire (1850-60); Glenuig, Moidart, Inverness-shire (1861); St Mary, Greenock—new church (1862); Carluke, Lanarkshire (1859); Nitshill, Ayrshire (1862); Carfin, Lanarkshire (1862); Dornie, Ross-shire (1862); Dunoon, Argyll (1862); Strathaven, Lanarkshire (1853-63); St Ignatius, Wishaw (1859); Lanark (1859); Larkhall, Lanarkshire (1862).

Almost immediately after Bishop Murdoch's death the *Free Press* declared itself the organ of the Fenian Movement, which had just been launched in the United States and Ireland to overthrow British rule, and to establish an Irish Republic by force of arms. The paper was condemned by Cardinal Barnabò, and ceased publication. The Protestant press throughout Scotland, with a curious lack of logic, applauded the first definite act of papal interference in Scottish secular affairs since the Reformation. * Meanwhile Propaganda had awakened to the fact that steps must be taken to settle the differences between the Irish and the Scots in the Western Vicariate, and began to investigate the situation.

The Eastern District, 1852-1864.

During the twelve years that Bishop Gillis ruled over the Eastern District, he never stopped trying to bring Catholic life into line with continental countries—in ways that often alarmed the more conservative-minded of his clergy. One of his first acts was to organise the Vicariate into provostries to secure better discipline among the priests. Associations of the faithful for the exercise of some work of piety and charity (otherwise known as 'pious unions'), and sodalities and confraternities for the promotion of public worship, were strongly encouraged. The Bishop also tried to establish in every mission two organisations of French Jesuit origin—the Archconfraternity of the Sacred Heart and the Apostleship of Prayer.† After Pius IX had defined the doctrine of the Immaculate Conception in 1854, everything possible was done to foster greater devotion to Our Lady by forming groups of the Confraternity of the Living Rosary, and the Confraternity of the Immaculate Conception. To help people to prepare for a holy death the Bona Mors Confraternity, which had been founded by the seventh General of the Society of Jesus, was introduced into the Vicariate. Considering the Bishop's belief in the spiritual and moral values of magnificent requiem Masses, it is not surprising that he did his best to establish confraternities for the relief of the poor souls in purgatory. At the same time he encouraged the Society of St Vincent de Paul (founded at Paris in 1833 and launched in Scotland ten years later) in its work on behalf of the members of his flock who could be regarded as deserving objects of charity. There were plenty among the Irish.

But the rich as well as the poor had souls to be saved, hence the importance of keeping in touch with the nobility and landed gentry. This involved occasional visits to such people of influence

---

Nearly all these missions or churches were opened for the spiritual benefit of Catholics of Irish descent if not of birth; and they prove that the 'Hielan Clique' cannot have been quite such an incompetent set of men as the *Free Press* maintained they were from 1851 to 1865.

* A short-lived successor, the *Irish Catholic Banner*, did not catch on.
† See p. 328.

T¹

as Sir William Drummond-Steuart at Murthly Castle, the Hope-Scotts at Abbotsford and Lady Lothian at Newbattle Abbey. Neither could the Bishop ignore other members of the Noblesse of Scotland who had already 'gone over to Rome', or who showed signs of wavering in their Episcopalian or Presbyterian allegiances.

In May 1853 the Bishop nominated a Vicar General, with full powers of jurisdiction to deal with ecclesiastical business when he was absent from the Eastern District. Then he went off to Malvern Wells for a second course of hydropathic treatment by Dr Gully. Back in Edinburgh after two months, he presided over the first Clergy Retreat ever held in Scotland. * This gathering, which was a novelty for most of the priests, took place at the Wellburn Academy, Dundee. Shortly before the Retreat, a Pastoral Letter was issued ordering the erection of the Sodality of the Sacred Heart in every mission.†

The pious Lady Lothian wanted advice about the Early English Gothic church, designed by Joseph Hansom, which she was having built at Dalkeith. Dedicated to St David, it was blessed by Bishop Gillis in 1854. A priest had to be found to take charge of this new mission and another was required for Haddington, hitherto served from Portobello, where a small chapel had been opened in 1835. A pretty church, also in the Early English style, designed by Edward Pugin and dedicated to Our Lady Star of the Sea, had just been built at Leith, replacing the temporary chapel dating from 1833, which got its first resident priest in 1846. Most of the congregation was poor Irish.

Towards the end of Lent 1854 Bishop Gillis left Scotland for France, and pontificated in Amiens Cathedral at High Mass on Easter Sunday. He also preached an eloquent sermon there when the relics of the virgin-martyr St Theodosia, found in the cemetery of St Hermes at Rome in 1842, were solemnly translated. Among those who listened to this Scottish prelate, to whom French was a second language, were the Emperor Napoleon III and the Empress Eugénie, to whom he was presented. From Amiens he made his way south to Lyons, hoping to obtain an increase in the grant which had been made by the Association of the Propagation of the Faith for the Eastern Vicariate. On his arrival in Rome he heard rumours that Pius IX had decided to promulgate the doctrine of the Immaculate Conception of Our Lady.

Exhausted by the strain of business, the Bishop felt it would be

---

* Annual ecclesiastical retreats had been the rule in France and most continental countries since 1815. Bishop Gillis, as a former Sulpician student, had been accustomed to making the Spiritual Exercises of St Ignatius since he was a youth.

† This sodality, heavily enriched with indulgences, had been founded at Rome by Padre Felici, S.J., in 1797, and in 1803 Pius VII had raised it to the rank of an archconfraternity.

worth the long journey from Italy to the south of France, so that he could take the cure at Aix-les-Thermes. He had been told that the sulphurous waters of this fashionable spa in the Pyrenees were beneficial to diseases of the spine. He gave them a fair trial for about six weeks but with no apparent result, and it was not until the end of November that he got back to Edinburgh after an absence of eight months from the Vicariate.

He had intended to return to Rome, to assist with other prelates at the promulgation of the Bull defining the dogma of the Immaculate Conception on December 8, but we are told that "from some apprehension" he changed his mind at the last moment. His Christmas Pastoral Letter dealt with the recently defined dogma, and soon afterwards he issued another Pastoral on behalf of the spiritual and temporal needs of the British and French soldiers fighting side by side in the Crimean War.

A new church at Jedburgh, dedicated to the Immaculate Conception and built at the cost of Lady Lothian, had to be blessed and a resident priest appointed. On January 13, 1856, there was another pontifical function in Perthshire at the opening of a new church for the mission at Blairgowrie. Built through the efforts of the Rev. John Carmont, it was mainly for the benefit of the Irish employed in the cloth-mills, and for agricultural labourers scattered over a wide area in Strathmore. The Crimean War ended on April 19. This enabled the Bishop to pontificate at a solemn Requiem Mass in St Mary's, Broughton Street, when, as usual on these occasions, the interior was in semi-darkness, except for the artificial light provided by candelabra and torches. British and French flags were draped over shields, displaying the names of the chief battles which had been fought.

It was a consolation to the Bishop that there had been a steady trickle of converts from the upper classes since he became the third Vicar-Apostolic of the Eastern District. In 1852 the Rev. Lord Henry Kerr (1800-82) a son of the sixth Marquess of Lothian, seceded from the Church of England together with his wife Louisa, daughter of the Hon. Sir Alexander Hope and granddaughter of the second Earl of Hopetoun. They lived at Huntleyburn, near Melrose, where Bishop Gillis arranged for them to have a private oratory, the nearest church being at Galashiels. * Two years later the Rev. George Erskine (1802-60) of Dryburgh Abbey, a kinsman of the Earls of Mar and Buchan and of Baron Erskine, also gave up communion with Canterbury for that of Rome.

In 1855 Princess Marie, youngest daughter of Charles Louis,

* Most Catholic members of the peerage and landed gentry had their domestic oratories at this time, very often with reservation of the Blessed Sacrament. In some cases the chaplain was treated as a special kind of servant, with precedence over the butler and housekeeper. It was not only Bishop Gillis who found difficulty in providing chaplains for country mansions; more than one English bishop had the same problem to solve.

reigning Duke of Baden, and wife of the seventh Duke of Hamilton and eighth Duke of Brandon, became a Catholic.* The Scottish Reformation Society failed to check this slow but fairly constant succession of 'perversions to Popery' in the 'fifties and 'sixties. In 1856 a Perthshire laird, Charles Trotter of Woodhill, 'went over to Rome', and he had to be allowed a private oratory, at the opening of which Bishop Gillis officiated. Jane, wife of William Douglas Dick of Pitkerro, Angus, and daughter of Sir Williams-Drummond, second Baronet of Hawthornden, was received into the Church in 1854. When her husband followed her example five years later, he too expected a private chapel. In 1859 David Shaw Ramsay, son of David Ramsay, of Grimmet, Ayrshire, was another convert from the Scottish landed gentry.†

The titular Bishop of Limyra was in his element in such society. He dearly loved wearing richly embroidered stoles presented by noble ladies, like the Countess de Senfft-Pilsach, wife of the Austrian ambassador, or Elizabeth Gubbins who in 1839 became the second wife of William Aubrey de Vere, ninth Duke of St Albans.‡ In the luxurious, over-furnished, gas or lamp-lit boudoirs and drawing-rooms of the convert duchesses, marchionesses, countesses and other titled ladies, swaying languorously in their billowing crinolines, the *soigné*, ascetic-featured titular Bishop of Limyra was an ever welcome guest, partly because of his bad health and need of mothering. As Archbishop David Mathew pointed out when writing of the Catholic Revival in England: " In the whole situation there may have seemed something a little over-sugared; for the female element predominated in this convert circle with its wealth and enthusiasm, its warm devotional spirit, its absence of general literary interest and the close relationship with the 'black' or papal Roman aristocracy.§

Yet it would be utterly wrong to leave the impression that Bishop Gillis were merely a worldy-minded prelate who was most at home in the society of titled ladies. What must be remembered is that he differed from the other Scottish Vicars-Apostolic in having been brought up in a Catholic environment. His education with the Sulpicians in Montreal and Paris gave him a spiritual background unlike that of the clergy who had been trained in the Scots College abroad, or merely at Aquhorties and Blairs. He was

---

* A "magnificent and costly pew with elegant chairs and prie-dieu" was fitted up for the convert Duchess in St Mary's, Hamilton. She made many gifts to this church, built in 1843-6, including what was described as "a beautiful plaster statue of the Virgin and Child", and an immense oil-painting of the Adoration of the Shepherds (a copy of a Tibaldi), taken from the Hamilton Palace collection of *objets d'art*.

† He became a priest, and a domestic prelate to Leo XII, but spent his latter years on his estate in the Province of Quebec, Canada.

‡ After his death in 1849 she married Lucius, 10th Viscount Falkland, and died in 1893.

§ *Catholicism in England* (1936), p. 210.

St Peter's, Buckie, Banffshire (1857)

St Patrick's, Edinburgh (1858).

297

steeped in French mystical theology, and was in great demand as a spiritual director. He never neglected the poor members of his flock. The number of new missions he started and the new churches he had built proves this. *

In 1856 the Duc de Montpensier and his wife Luisa Fernanda, the Infanta of Spain, visited Edinburgh. Bishop Gillis organised a reception for them at St Margaret's Convent, which may well have been embarrassing for the French Sisters who were not Orléanist in their political sympathies, but either Bourbon or Bonapartist.†

It was during this year that the Bishop acquired possession of the Cowgate Chapel, which had been erected as a 'qualified' Episcopalian place of worship in 1774.‡ Rededicated to St Patrick, and re-orientated, it was first used for Catholic worship in 1858. It appears that the Bishop had the idea of enlarging the chapel as a sort of Roman basilica, and making it a pro-cathedral, for it was quite clear by this time that Pugin's grandiose Gothic Revival cathedral would never materialise.§

In the spring of 1857 the Bishop felt that it might benefit his health to sample the alkaline waters at Vichy, a spa in central France which had now become extremely fashionable as the result of imperial patronage. While taking the cure there, he received an invitation from his former Sulpician fellow-student, Mgr. Dupanloup (elected Bishop of Orléans in 1849) to preach the panegyric of Joan of Arc in his cathedral.** According to a report, the discourse was "magnificent in its power and eloquence", and it produced generous offerings for the poor Scottish Mission. The Mayor and Municipality of Orléans, as a token of their respect and appreciation of this panegyric, presented Bishop Gillis with the heart of King Henry II of England, Normandy, Aquitaine,

---

* See p. 302, note ‡.

† The Duke was a younger son of the deposed King Louis-Philippe, who had died an exile in England in 1850. He was hoping that Isabel II (his wife's elder sister) would be forced to abdicate, and that she would become Queen of Spain. The Comte de Paris regarded himself as the *de jure* King of France in succession to his father and, in conjunction with his brothers, was plotting behind the scenes against Napoleon III.

‡ Since the closing of the Chapel in Blackfriars Wynd (See p. 229), Catholics living in the 'Old Town' of Edinburgh had been obliged to attend St Mary's, until a chapel of ease, dedicated to St Patrick, had been opened in Lothian Street in 1834. It became a separate mission in 1849.

§ It is only fair to add that there were outspoken criticisms from his own Vicar-General, John Macpherson, who took the usual step of writing to Rome, accusing his own bishop of long absences from his vicariate, failure to maintain discipline among his clergy and, above all, of having accumulated a debt of £27,671 with small prospect of paying it off. The result of this action was Dr Macpherson's removal to the small and remote mission of New Abbey, in the Stewartry of Kirkcudbright.

** It was not until 1909 that the "Maid of Orléans' was beatified. Two years after her canonization in 1930 she was declared the second patron of France, St Louis IX being the first.

Anjou and Ireland, who had died at the Chateau de Chinon in 1189, having made himself overlord of Scotland in 1157.

There was a rumour about this time that the titular Bishop of Limyra might be nominated as coadjutor with right of succession to Cardinal Wiseman. Bishop Errington of Plymouth, who had been translated to the titular see of Trebizond in 1855, had been deprived of his status in the Westminster archdiocese.

The need for more priests to staff the increased number of missions had become urgent. Early in 1858—about the same time as Bishop Murdoch felt that he must have Jesuits in the Western District—Bishop Gillis wrote to Fr. Joseph Johnston, the English Provincial of the Society of Jesus, asking if any priests and co-adjutor-brothers could be spared for the Eastern Vicariate. * The following year the Jesuits were given a missionary district comprising the south and west parts of the city of Edinburgh, extending into the country as far as the Pentland Hills, inclusive of the villages of Colinton, Juniper Green, Balerno and Ratho, in which Irish Catholic families had settled. Premises recently used as a lodging house were acquired in Hunter's Close, off the Grassmarket, where the first Mass was celebrated on the feast of St Ignatius Loyola, July 31, 1859.

A spacious church in the Classic style was built in Lauriston Street, and was opened in 1860. It was the first in Scotland to be dedicated to the Sacred Heart of Jesus.† Before long the Sacred Heart, Lauriston Street, began to fulfil much the same position in Edinburgh Catholic life as the Jesuit church of the Immaculate Conception, Farm Street, did in London. It offered several weekday Masses, frequent Benedictions and Holy Hours, the devotion of the first Fridays, Confessions at Call, besides Confraternities, Guilds and Sodalities. Neither of the two other churches in Edinburgh could supply the same spiritual attractions in the sixties.‡

* Fr. James Macgillivray, the last of the old Jesuits who had served the Scottish Mission, died in Traquair House in 1811, three years before the Society was formally restored by Pius VII.

† In 1856 Pius IX had extended the feast of the Sacred Heart to the universal Church. The auditorium-shaped building, lighted by two cupolas, was designed by Fr. Richard Vaughan, S.J. The first rector was Fr. Albany Christie, who was of Scots descent, a close friend of J. H. Newman at Oxford. Both were received into the Church in 1845.

‡ It was not until 1860 that St Mary's began to advertise Benediction. So far as is known, Mr John Strain (the future Bishop) was the first priest in Scotland to start regular weekly Benediction. He did so at Dalbeattie in 1853. About 1960 Benediction was given at Blairs College after Vespers on the greater festivals; at St Andrew's, Dundee, at 8 p.m. on holidays of obligation; and occasionally at Chapeltown, Glenlivet, where a monstrance was acquired that year. At St Margaret's Convent, Edinburgh, there had been at least Sunday Benediction since 1853, and it was there that the Forty Hours Devotion was introduced in 1842 (See p. 269). Benediction too was certainly given by French clergy while Bourbons were at Holyrood.

By this time the choir at St Mary's, Broughton Street, had made a name for itself in the city. Under the direction of Mr Charles Hargitt, it performed not only elaborate Masses but also oratorios. If an opera company happened to be playing at the Theatre Royal next door, and remained in Edinburgh over the week-end, there was always the chance of hearing the principal singers rendering the solo parts in masses by such composers as Haydn, Mozart, Beethoven, Cherubini, and Schubert. *

In 1861 Lady Lothian managed to induce Bishop Gillis to hand over the Dalkeith mission to the Jesuits and Mr Hope-Scott also obtained their services later on, at Galashiels and Selkirk. The French Congregation of the Missionary Oblates of the Immaculate Conception, which had been brought to England by Cardinal Wiseman in 1852, was invited to Scotland by Bishop Gillis in 1859, when he put some of the priests in charge of the new church at Galashiels that had been opened the previous year. It was also in 1859 that the Oblates of Mary Immaculate was given the Leith mission, where the congregation was mainly composed of poor Irish families.†

It was about this time that Bishop Gillis obtained the services of the Sisters of Mercy from Limerick, for the Eastern Vicariate, and people became accustomed to the sight of nuns in the streets of Edinburgh. They were put in charge of two schools in Lothian Road, Edinburgh, and in 1861 the community moved to Lauriston Gardens, to the Convent of St Catherine of Siena, which Mrs Hutchison, a wealthy convert widow, erected for them.‡

By the early spring of 1862 Bishop Gillis was in such a bad state of health that, even with the help of his Vicar General, Mr John Strain, he was unable to attend properly to the affairs of the Eastern District. He intimated in a Pastoral Letter that he intended to ask Propaganda for permission to resign his office. With a view to achieving this he went off to Rome, after another trial of the chalybeate and bituminous waters at Malvern. At Pentecost he assisted with Cardinal Wiseman at the canonization of the twenty-six Japanese martyrs of 1597, but when he begged Propaganda to relieve him of his office he was bidden to carry on and was promised the help of a coadjutor.

Armed with a letter from Pius IX to Queen Isabel II, he made the very long train-journey from Rome to Madrid, with the hope of discovering some relics of St Margaret of Scotland, reputed to

---

* In 1866 the Jesuits persuaded Mr Hargitt to become organist and choirmaster at their fashionable church in Farm Street, London, where the same type of music was favoured.

† In 1863 the Sisters of the Immaculate Conception, whose mother-house was at Bordeaux, began to teach in the schools at Leith and to visit families in their own homes.

‡ See p. 283.

be enshrined in the church of the Palace of the Escorial.* The timing of this Iberian pilgrimage was unfortunate. Isabel was only three years of age when she became Queen of Spain in 1833 and since then her country had been in a state of turmoil, with frequent insurrections. In 1862 the virtual ruler was General Leopoldo O'Donnell but the real power behind the throne was a certain Sor Patrocinio, a nun of the Franciscan Order of the Immaculate Conception. If the titular Bishop of Limyra had consulted her, she would probably have told him at once where the relics of St Margaret were hidden, because she never ceased to have visions and revelations, even on political affairs, and was alleged to have received the Stigmata. No matter: the Queen gave the Bishop permission to ransack the Escorial, where eventually he discovered an authenticated portion of the body of St Margaret. Although he was allowed to take this away, he was not allowed to take two old paintings of Malcolm III of Scotland and his canonized wife.†

On his way home through France he made a détour to Sens in the départément of Yonne, and there the Bishop gave him permission to have a small portion of an altar in the former Cistercian Abbey of Pontigny sawn off. There St Thomas à Becket was said to have celebrated Mass during his exile in France between 1164 and 1167. Having got back to Edinburgh, Bishop Gillis handed over these relics to St Margaret's Convent, as an addition to the bones of St Crescentia.‡

Since the Bishop's visit to Ratisbon in 1848, negotiations about the Abbey of St James had dragged on between the Bavarian government, the Bishop of Ratisbon, the Scottish Vicars-Apostolic, the British Foreign Secretary and the Holy See. The last Prior, Dom Benedict Deeson, died in 1855, aged ninety-one, and in 1862 Pius IX suppressed the monastery. The buildings passed into the possession of the government, which in return paid a large sum of money to Propaganda, for use in enlarging the Scots College at Rome. The Ratisbon monastery became a diocesan seminary. The two surviving monks got nothing, except pensions on condition that they remained in Bavaria.§

* At the Reformation the head of St Margaret came into the possession of Queen Mary and was later acquired by the Scottish Jesuits at Douai, where it was lost during the French Revolution. Other relics of the Queen went to Spain.

† Queen Isabel's younger sister, Luisa Fernanda, had married the Duc de Montpensier in 1845, and had been entertained in Edinburgh by Bishop Gillis in 1856 (See p. 298).

‡ See p. 283, note †.

§ It is not known what became of Dom Placid Boehme, who had acted as Superior since 1855. Dom Anselm Robertson (1824-1900), professed in 1845, returned to Scotland. He founded a reformatory school for boys at West Thorn, near Glasgow, and hoped and prayed that there would be a revival of Scottish monasticism before he died. He was now the sole living representative of the *Schottenkloster*.

Bishop Gillis, who had always disliked Blairs College, even after nineteen years, had not given up hope of founding a junior seminary for the Eastern District. In February 1863, hearing that an Episcopalian institution at Crieff, known as St Margaret's College, was for sale, he borrowed the money and bought the property. * Most of the clergy regarded this as unwise and nothing materialised out of it, although a new chapel was opened there in 1871. The proposed seminary merely involved financial loss.

At the special request of Cardinal Wiseman, Bishop Gillis preached what proved to be his last sermon at the Italian Church in Clerkenwell, London, in April 1863. After his return to Edinburgh his health gave way completely and he died on February 24th, the following year.

His obsequies were quite as magnificent as those which he had devised for other people, as will be realised from a contemporary report: " St Mary's, Broughton Street, was crowded in every part by a sorrowing congregation. The gorgeous Coffin, on which were laid the Mitre and Crozier, rested upon a splendid Catafalque, surrounded by a blaze of light from huge silver Candelabra. At the corners of the Bier rose four alabaster Vases, with Spirit-lamps, which threw the changeful flickering of their flame fitfully on the rich purple velvet of the Coffin, and its heavy studding of gilt nails. The windows of the Church were darkened, so as almost to exclude the light of day. The Sanctuary and Galleries were draped with black. The scene was one of imposing grandeur, as, through this twilight gloom, the silence unbroken by a whisper, the voices of the Choir broke in with the solemn opening of Mozart's Requiem."†

After the Mass, Fr. Grant S.J., delivered an oration which was nothing if not eloquent. The Absolutions having been given, the coffin was removed amid the mournful music of the *Miserere* and the long funeral procession wended its way through the streets of Edinburgh to St Margaret's Convent, where the Sisters sang both the *Miserere* and the *Benedictus* before the body of the titular Bishop of Limyra was laid to rest in the vaults of the Chapel.‡

---

* The buildings had been erected by the Rev. Alexander Lendrum, first rector of St Michael's from 1847 to 1866

† *Scotichronicon,* p. 490.

‡ During the 12 years that Bishop Gillis ruled over the Eastern Vicariate the following new missions were opened and new churches built: *Missions*: Montrose, Angus (c. 1852); Linlithgow, West Lothian; Glencorse, Midlothian (1851); Blackburn, West Lothian; West Calder, Midlothian; Lochgelly, Fife (c. 1859); Broxburn, West Lothian (1860); Ratho, Midlothian (c. 1864); *Churches*: Leith (1852); Dalkeith, Midlothian (1854); Jedburgh, Roxburghshire (1855); Tullymet, Perthshire (1855); St Patrick, Edinburgh (1856); Blairgowrie, Perthshire (1856); Kelso, Roxburghshire (1858); Galashiels, Selkirkshire (1858); Peebles (1858); Sacred Heart, Edinburgh (1860); Cupar, Fife (1864).

The Northern Vicariate

Since the eighteen-thirties, life in the Northern Vicariate had drifted along without anything startling to disturb it. Bishop Kyle had been leading a quiet and studious existence at Preshome, remote from the world but very much in touch with it by correspondence. It was he who was mainly responsible for obtaining financial recompense from the Bavarian government for the property of the Scots Benedictines at Ratisbon. * The funds of the Vicariate were administered by him with scrupulous exactitude.

Moreover he was a great scholar, with an encyclopedic knowledge of most branches of learning. He was familiar with many foreign languages, ancient and modern. It was said at Rome that few prelates could write better Latin than the titular Bishop of Germanicia. He took an interest in art and archaeology. The Spalding Club, founded in 1839 to commemorate John Spalding, the seventeenth century Scottish historian of Aberdeen, elected him as one of the first members.† Except for making visitations of the Vicariate he seldom left his unpretentious house in the heart of the Enzie District, exposed to every wind. Yet nobody could be more friendly and hospitable when occasion demanded. It was often remarked that the hermit-Bishop had an almost uncanny power over the affection and loyalty of his priests. Most of them regarded him more as a father than as an ecclesiastical superior.

Until Bishop Scott's death in 1846, he and Bishop Kyle kept up a ceaseless correspondence. The gifts of the one supplemented those of the other—as Scott neatly put it on one occasion: "Your maxim of *cunctando constituit rem*—it is a very good and true one in certain occasions, but you must allow that the maxim 'Delays are dangerous' is equally true".‡ Scott, when dealing with the problems of the Western Vicariate, usually resorted to a quick and often painful operation. Kyle trusted in the healing hand of time.

The Northern Vicariate remained more or less a placid backwater in comparison with the Eastern and Western ones. There was no noticeable increase in the number of Catholics, except in Aberdeen and a few towns, and Bishop Kyle was spared troubles with poverty-stricken Irish immigrants. All his clergy were Scottish-born, the majority being natives of the North Eastern counties.

Several new churches were built, e.g. Elgin (1843), Beauly (1843), Peterhead (1851) and Inverurie (1852). The Bishop himself designed the imposing twin-spired church at Buckie, which was

---

* See p. 281.

† His ingenuity and perseverance discovered a key to a cypher in some of the letters of Mary Queen of Scots, which had hitherto baffled the greatest experts.

‡ Cf. J. K. Robertson, 'The Bishop looks at his Diocese', in *Innes Review*, Vol. III (1952), p. 31.

St Mary's, Aberdeen (1860).

opened on June 29th, 1857 * Not long after this he instructed Mr John Sutherland to start raising money for a large church to be erected in Aberdeen.

Evidently there was no objection to employing local talent, in spite of Bishop Kyle's disapproval of certain English Catholic architects, for the job was entrusted to a young Aberdonian, Alexander Ellis.† The foundation stone of St Mary's, Huntly Street, was laid on March 16th, 1859. While its walls were rising, thousands of young men from all over Europe, including England, Wales, Scotland and Ireland, were hurrying to Italy in response to the call from Pius IX to defend the Papal States from further invasion by Garibaldi's army, which was drawing nearer and nearer to Rome. Bishop Kyle dedicated the new church on December 21st, 1860, when Bishop Murdoch pontificated at the High Mass.

A contemporary writer described St Mary's as "one of the most noble and magnificent modern edifices of the kind in Scotland". The treatment of the local grey granite is worth comparing with the granite cathedrals in Brittany, e.g. Quimper and Saint-Pol-de-Léon.‡ Great praise was given to the high altar and tabernacle—"both magnificent in design and chaste in ornament". Above them was "a grand picture of the Assumption of Our Blessed Lady, executed *gratis* by a talented member of the congregation, Mr John Russell." So far as is known, St Mary's was the first post-Reformation Catholic Church in Scotland to be furnished with a rood beam across the chancel arch.§

The Huntly Street church, which became the cathedral of the Aberdeen Diocese in 1878, retained its Victorian character for nearly a hundred years, and was a remarkable period-piece in its furnishings. But even ecclesiastical fashions swing backwards and forwards all the time between austerity and opulence. After Bishop Walsh had completed the purging of his Cathedral to commemorate its first centenary, the words of the psalmist could have been applied to him: "For zeal for thy house has consumed me, and the insults of those who insult thee have fallen on me".**

---

* He seems to have mistrusted most architects, because in a letter dated March 1st, 1859, he wrote: "Why should not I be as sensitive as to my honour as an architect as Goldie or any other? I am sure I have planned and built as many churches, chapels and houses as he has, beginning with my first labour, one elegant 'Chateaubriand' (*sic*) at Aquhorties, down to the latest finished one, Buckie Cathedral." It had come to the Bishop's notice that George Goldie (1828-87), who designed St John's, Fetternear (also opened in 1859), had complained of the competition by this amateur episcopal architect.

† He also designed Catholic churches at Banff (1870) and Fraserburgh (1896). His Episcopalian churches include St Mary's, Carden Place, Aberdeen (1862), and St Magnus, Lerwick (1864).

‡ The 200 feet high tower and spire were not completed until 1878.

§ There had been talk of erecting one at Inverurie where a new church was opened in 1852 (See p. 303).

** Psalm 69, v. 9 (R.S.V.).

U

By 1960 the high altar and tabernacle had ceased to be regarded as "both magnificent in design and chaste in ornament". They were cast down, likewise the two side altars, the rood-beam, canopied pulpit, episcopal throne, statues, communion rails and almost everything else of the original furnishings.* Having been smashed to atoms, the carved angels and saints in the high altar reredos in St Mary's Cathedral were carted to Pluscarden Priory, Moray. The monks used most of the broken stones to make a rockery. Other bits were built into a wall, where they may puzzle antiquaries of some future generation.

One fears that both Bishop Kyle and his architect would have been distressed had they been granted a vision of what to them would have been 'Murder in the Cathedral', for they believed that nothing could be too rich and splendid in a House of God. After all, they lived in the days when fashionable ladies were still wearing billowing crinolines, and drawing rooms were overcrowded with furniture. They would hardly recognise the interior of the Huntly Street church if they could see it today, pruned, stream-lined and purified of lush symbols of Victorian piety. *Autres temps, autres moeurs*!

St Peter's, Justice Street, which had served the spiritual needs of Aberdonian Catholics since 1803, was turned into a boys' school in 1860. A small portion of it became a chapel-of-ease to St Mary's, and so it remained for many years. Also in 1860 the Franciscan Sisters of the Immaculate Conception at Glasgow established a small community in Aberdeen, replacing the Apostoline Sisters as teachers in St Mary's Schools. On February 14th, 1862, a group of the Poor Sisters of Nazareth from Hammersmith, London, took over the former chapel-house of St Peter's as a Home for the Aged and Infirm.

In 1861 Propaganda decided to relieve Bishop Kyle of the county of Caithness and the Islands of Orkney and Shetland. This considerable part of Great Britain was transferred to the jurisdiction of the recently appointed Prefect-Apostolic of the Arctic Missions, who had also been entrusted with the spiritual welfare of the Faroe Islands, Iceland, Greenland and Lapland, besides part of Hudson's Bay in Northern Canada. The Prefect was a Polish priest, Dr Stephen de Djunkowski, who was usually known as Mgr. Etienne.

The Catholic Directory for 1864 informed its readers that "at Wick, where for the last three years, the Prefect-Apostolic has fixed his residence, there is a modest chapel and a small chapel-house. At Lerwick in the Shetland Islands, where a priest has

---

* Curiously enough, in 1864 Dr Suther, Episcopalian Bishop of Aberdeen and Orkney, refused to dedicate St Mary's, Carden Place (designed by Alexander Ellis), until the figures on the rood-beam had been removed. He also insisted that the sanctuary-lamp and a crypt-altar must be taken out. At the same time he forbade the wearing of eucharistic vestments.

resided for the last three years, the Mission still remains without a chapel or house . . . After this Station, there is another in almost equal distress in Orkney, where there are several families".

The county of Caithness. in the extreme north-east of the mainland of Scotland, had been put under the care of a French priest, the abbé Bernard. Although when he arrived at Wick he could not speak English, six months later he was preaching in this language. He wrote out long and extremely dogmatic sermons, some of which have been preserved, but it is doubtful whether much of them was understood by his congregation which was mainly composed of vagrants, except during the summer herring-fishing season.

A pamphlet entitled *Rélation sur l'Etat des Missions du Pole Arctique,* written by the abbé Ciamberlini and published at Brussels in 1865, helped to arouse interest among continental Catholics. The Italian author conveyed the impression of intensive missionary activity. Hundreds of Scot-Irish bairns were being saved from the Limbo of Infants by indiscriminate baptism. Their parents for the most part were itinerant tinkers and the father very often unknown. At Wick the French priest offered Vespers, Rosary and Benediction on Sunday afternoons, after he had instructed his flock in the Catechism. He also opened a school.

How Propaganda imagined the Arctic Missions would be evangelised is an unsolved mystery. The cardinals and other officials at Rome must have had very vague ideas of geography; even less of the means of transport between the north-east of Scotland, Orkney, Shetland, the Faroes, Greenland, Iceland, Hudson's Bay and Lapland. The Polish Prefect-Apostolic needed first of all a seaworthy mission-ship to enable him to voyage round his immence 'diocese', extending from the Davis Strait and Cape Farewell in Greenland to North Cape in Norway. His visitations of Iceland, Jan Mayen Island, Spitzbergen and the Lofoten Islands would have been heroic undertakings—even shorter voyages to the islands of Orkney, Shetland and Faroe quite adventurous.

Launched with quixotic enthusiasm but with little foresight, the Apostolic-Prefecture of the Arctic Missions faded out within ten years. In 1870 the Scottish portion reverted to the Northern Vicariate and, after the restoration of the hierarchy in 1878, became part of the Aberdeen Diocese. *

By 1868 Bishop Kyle had reached the age of eighty and was more or less incapable of fulfilling his episcopal duties. Only then, however, did he apply to Propaganda for a coadjutor. Mr John Macdonald was appointed, but Bishop Kyle died at

---

* In 1863 a Dutch priest, the Rev. Thomas Verstraaten, who belonged to the *Missions du Pole Arctique,* bought land at Lerwick, the capital of Shetland, on which to erect a chapel, but after 1870 it was seldom visited more than two or three times a year. It was not until 1900 that a mission was established. In Orkney a chapel was opened at Kirkwall in 1877.

Preshome on February 23rd, 1869, only one day before the date fixed for his coadjutor's consecration at Aberdeen. *

Most of the clergy of the Northern District found their way to Preshome for the funeral of their father in God, which took place on February 26th. The newly consecrated Bishop Macdonald celebrated the Requiem Mass, at which Dr Strain, Vicar-Apostolic of the Eastern District, "addressed the people in a short impromptu Discourse, wherein he spoke concerning the talents and acquirements of the Deceased."† It is recorded that "the Solemn Service was relieved from time to time by the Choristers singing with fine effect". Within the chapel, erected in 1788 and served by Bishop Kyle since 1828, " the wall behind the altar was draped in sombre black, relieved with white figuring, which well harmonized with the mournful occasion. In a like manner, also, the Altar itself was clothed in black". While half-a-dozen priests were carrying the coffin to the opening in the floor of the chapel " the choir sang with marked effect the small motet, 'O Dulcis Passio', the fine tenor voice of Mr McDonald, Tombae, ringing out prominently from among the rest of the Choristers". Bishop Hay, whose discouragement of music in public worship was mentioned earlier, would have been shocked by all the singing that relieved the mournfulness of his successor's obsequies, for "after the Body had been deposited in the Sepulchre, the " Choristers " burst into the psalm 'Out of the depths have I cried to Thee, O Lord', concluding their efforts with the *Miserere*. We are told that—"according to the custom of the Church, Bishop Kyle was Buried in his full Pontifical Robes . . . The striking remark that 'no one would ever share the burden of the Episcopate with him' was verified . . . A striking incident happened to Bishop Macdonald the evening before the Funeral. He, in company with a Priest, went out to examine the Grave, 8 feet down, when, by a false step, both fell in."‡

Scottish Catholic authors and bookshops

Looking back more than a hundred years, it is surprising to find evidence of such a demand for reading matter. Scotland had at least three Catholic bookshops by 1850. Hugh Margey ran the Catholic Book Warehouse at 28 East Clyde Street, Glasgow, and

* See p. 325. Born in Strathglass in 1818, John Macdonald was educated at the Scots Monastery, Ratisbon, and the Scots College, Rome. After his ordination at Preshome by Bishop Kyle in 1841, he served several missions before being put in charge of Inverness in 1846. Three years later he returned to his native Strathglass, and remained there until he was raised to the episcopate. For details of his career as second Vicar-Apostolic of the Northern District, see p. 326.

† *Scotichronicon,* p. 644.

‡ ibid, p. 645. During the latter years of Bishop Kyle's rule over the Northern District new chapels were erected at Dornie, Ross-shire (1860); Nairn (1864); Marydale, Inverness-shire (1866). Then a small chapel at Stratherrick, Inverness-shire had been built in 1859.

James Marshall owned a similar establishment at 22 Leith Street, Edinburgh. * These shops acted as agents for Charles Dolman of London, whose publications were more numerous than those of Catholic publishers of our own time. Some of the *Directories* contain catalogues issued by March and Beattie at 13 South Hanover Street, Edinburgh. These are nothing if not comprehensive, and include a large selection of French works.

The literary activity in Scotland during the first quarter of a century following Catholic Emancipation was far greater than in the first half of the present century, and some of the forgotten authors deserve to be recalled.†

Mr William Wallace (1764-1854), born at Huntly, was a great writer of tracts, including *The Owl and the Bat, or the Infidel and his disciples, A Preacher in the wrong Box,* and *Who are Catholics?* Another priest author was Mr Evan MacEachan (1769-1849), who served the missions at Arisaig, Badenoch, Lismore and Strathglass, and who generally wrote in Gaelic.‡ Mr James Carruthers (1738-1832), brother of the second Vicar-Apostolic of the Eastern District, was the author of a *History of Scotland,* and *A Summary of the Catechetical Exposition of the Mass.* Mr James Bremner (1798-1847) somehow found time when in charge of the widely scattered mission of Paisley to write many pamphlets, addressed mainly to Presbyterians. Some were reprinted in book-form, and went into several editions.

No Scottish Catholic author of the first half of last century achieved such fame as Mr Stephen Keenan (1804-62), an Irish priest whose chief sphere of apostolate was Dundee. In 1846 he published his *Controversial Catechism, or Protestantism and Catholicism established by an appeal to the Holy Scriptures, the Testimony of the Holy Fathers, and the Dictates of Reason.* It was reprinted again and again.§ Mr Keenan believed in the value of arresting titles, and among his other books are *Hades unmasked, or the true Hades discovered, The Flowers of the Gaelic Kirk*

* Hugh Margey (1814-94) was a native of Co. Donegal. It was Bishop Scott who first encouraged him to start selling Catholic books in Glasgow. His first publication was a *Catechism of Christian Doctrine,* which was followed by a small *Bible History for Schools.* Catholic authors were most indebted to this one-time monitor-teacher in Boar Lane, Glasgow, for the publication of their books and pamphlets around the middle of last century. The name of Hugh Margey deserves to be remembered, for with little or no financial backing he carried on in his own humble way what the Catholic Truth Society has tried to do in later years.

† Cf. Cathures, "Scottish Catholic Literature 100 Years Ago", in *St Peter's College Magazine,* Vol. XVIII (1946), pp. 143-50.

‡ Among his works are *An Abridgement of Catholic Doctrine,* and translations of *The Imitation of Christ,* and *The Spiritual Combat.* In his later years he published a *Gaelic Dictionary,* compiled when he ministered at Ballogie and Tombae.

§ A revised edition was issued by Bishop Hedley, O.S.B., in 1914.

U¹

Fathers, and *The Catholic Faith Vindicated and Protestant Error Exposed.* *

An equally active priest-writer was Mr Paul Maclachlan, born at Dundee in 1805. As a missionary of Lennoxtown and Stirling (1834), Falkirk (1843), Stirling (1856) and Doune (1875), Mr Maclachlan kept up a continuous literary output until his death in 1885. Not only did he publish innumerable pamphlets, most of them directed against Protestants, but for some years he acted as Scottish correspondent to the Paris *Univers.* How he found time for all this writing is a mystery, because he is better known to fame as the nineteenth century apostle of Stirlingshire.

Mr John Stuart McCorry (1812-80), who served missions in many parts of Scotland, was a prolific writer for over thirty years. In 1846 Gregory XVI made him a Doctor of Divinity in recognition of his services to the Faith.†

Neither must James Augustine Stothert be forgotten, because he wrote the greater part of the fourth volume of the commonly called *Scotichronicon,* published at Glasgow in 1869, from which so many quotations have been made in this book.‡ Born near Dumfries in 1817, and brought up a Presbyterian, he was one of several advocates who joined the Episcopal Church, but in 1844 he became a Catholic. Two years later he was given the tonsure and minor orders by Bishop Gillis; the subdiaconate by Bishop Wiseman; and having gone to Rome, he was ordained priest there in 1848. On his return to Britain, he spent a year at Prior Park College, near Bath; came back to Scotland where, after a curacy at St Patrick's, Edinburgh, he was appointed chaplain to the Monteiths at Carstairs House. His name ceased to appear in the *Catholic Directory* after 1857. Little is known of his subsequent career except that he retired to Belgium, probably because of serious debts, some of which may have been paid by Dr Gordon. Stothert was an embittered man.§ He had hoped to publish the Life and Works of Bishop Hay, but only twelve Scottish Catholic clergy offered their names as subscribers. So it came about that

---

* This last named book was written as a reply to what he called *The Slanders of Various Free Kirk Ministers.*

† His activities were not confined to literature. In 1848 he formed the Association of St Margaret for the protection of the Catholic poor and labouring classes in Scotland, of which committees were set up in many parts of the country.

‡ J. F. S. Gordon (1821-1904), who compiled *Scotichronicon* and *Monasticon,* was an Episcopalian clergyman, for over forty years incumbent of St Andrew's-by-the-Green, Glasgow, and the author of other historical books. (Cf. W. J. Anderson, 'J. F. S. Gordon and his contribution to the history of Scottish Catholicism', in *Innes Review,* Spring, 1965, pp. 18-26).

§ It is uncertain if he ever functioned as a priest in Belgium. On September 29, 1871, he announced in *The Times* his marriage at Dover to Katherine Tanghe of Bruges. They lived at Clapham after this and had children. He died at Clapham on January 8, 1882. His widow survived him until October 22, 1914.

Dr Gordon got possession of the MS, and used it for the greater part of the fourth volume of *Scotichronicon,* the title of which is *The Catholic Church in Scotland from the Suppression of the Hierarchy till the Present Time.* *

Last but not least there was Bishop Gillis, who set an example to the other Vicars-Apostolic by his intensive output of sermons and pamphlets.†

The impression formed is that Scottish Catholics, in proportion to their numbers, were engaged in quite as much literary activity as their brethren in England and Wales during the first quarter of a century after they had gained their Emancipation. It will be noticed from the titles of the books and pamphlets published that most were of a controversial character, and not what would now be called 'ecumenical' in spirit. What must be stressed is that, although far and away the greater number of Catholics in Scotland by 1850 were poor illiterate men and women, Irish in origin if not in birth, there was a minority who bought and read books, not only in English, but in foreign languages, proved by the authors and titles advertised in the catalogues issued by the Edinburgh and Glasgow bookshops.

---

* The additional matter was partly written by Stothert, but some portions were obviously added by Gordon, who noted on page 15 that Stothert was then in Belgium.

† He published the following: (2) *A Letter to the Moderator of the General Assembly of the Church of Scotland, containing a refutation of certain statements made by the Revd. Frederick Mound* (Edinburgh, 1846); (2) *Letter to the Duke of Argyll on the subject of his speeches as Chairman of the late annual meeting of the Edinburgh Bible Society* (Edinburgh, 1849); (3) *A Discourse on the Mission and Influence of the Popes, delivered on the day of thanksgiving for the return to Rome of Pius IX* (London, 1850); (4) *Facts and Correspondence relating to the admission to the Catholic Church of Viscount and Viscountess Fielding* (Edinburgh, 1850); (5) *The new Penal Law considered in its bearing upon Scotland; or two Letters addressed to the Earl of Arundel and Surrey* (Edinburgh, 1851); (6) *Letter to Duncan Maclaren, Lord Provost of Edinburgh, on the proposed 'Voluntary' Amendment of the Lord Advocate's Educational Bill for Scotland* (Edinburgh, 1854); (7) *A Lecture on Education* (Edinburgh 1856); (8) *Panégyrique de Jeanne d'Arc, prononcé dans le Cathédrale d'Orléans à la fête du 9 mai. 1857* (3rd ed. London, 1857); (9) *A paper on the subjects of Burns's pistols*—read before the Society of Antiquaries of Scotland (Edinburgh, 1859).

CHAPTER TEN

END OF THE EASTERN,
WESTERN & NORTHERN VICARIATES

The Eastern Vicariate

Mr John Strain was the priest chosen by Propaganda to succeed Bishop Gillis as Vicar-Apostolic of the Eastern District. * His consecration as titular Bishop of Abila in Syria took place in the Vatican on September 25th, 1864, and was performed by Pius IX.

On his return from Rome Bishop Strain set to work to deal with the financial and other problems of his Vicariate.† His two predecessors had built many churches, presbyteries and schools, in most cases with borrowed money. He was faced not only with these liabilities but also with the need to open more missions, owing to the rapid increase of the Catholic population. He devoted the greater part of his personal income to founding new missions, and died a poor man nineteen years later. Between 1864 and 1877 the secular clergy of the Eastern District increased from forty-five to fifty-seven, and the regular clergy from nine to twenty-two, while the number of places where there were resident priests rose from sixty-nine to eighty-nine. Four more religious congregations made foundations.‡

Bishop Strain made several visits to Rome and took part in the Vatican Council of 1870, when he was given the rank of Assistant to the Pontifical Throne. He devoted himself assiduously to the affairs of his Vicariate and won the loyalty of his clergy by his readiness to supply for them, in cases of sickness or enforced absence from their missions for other reasons.§

* Born at Edinburgh in 1810, he was educated at Aquhorties, and the Scots College, Rome. After his ordination in 1833 he served at Dalbeattie and Dumfries until 1859, when he was appointed Rector of Blairs College. Three years later he was made Vicar General of the Eastern District.

† He appointed the Rev. George Rigg as the first Administrator of St Mary's, Broughton Street. Bishop Gillis had retained the position of parish priest throughout his episcopate.

‡ In 1870 the congregation of the Holy Redeemer, usually known as the Redemptorists, erected a Gothic Revival monastery on Kinnoull Hill, outside Perth, planned as a House of Retreat for priests and laymen. The Marist Brothers established St Joseph's College, Dumfries, in 1874.

§ Between 1864 and the restoration of the hierarchy in 1878 the following new missions were started or new chapels erected: Kilsyth, Stirlingshire (1866); Dunfermline, Fife (1867); Lochee, Dundee (1866); Selkirk (1866); Crofthead, West Lothian (1867); Kirkcaldy, Fife (1869); North Berwick, East Lothian (1869); Denny, Stirlingshire (1869); St Andrews,

312

During the last sixteen years of the Scottish Mission a good number of people whose names appeared in *Who's Who*, and in *Burke's Peerage*, or in the *Landed Gentry* took the road to Rome. In 1862, Caroline, daughter of General Sir William Clayton Bt., and wife of the seventh Marquess of Queensberry, caused no small stir by her submission to the Church. * The following year, Charles Cunninghame, of Lainshaw, Ayrshire (1841-88) took the same step, assuming the name of Edmundstone-Cranstoun on succeeding in 1869 to the estate of Corhouse, Lanarkshire.

The year 1868 witnessed several aristocratic conversions. Arthur Capel de Broke Pollard, third son of William Pollard, of Pollard, Co. Westmeath, and Craigston Castle, Aberdeenshire, became a Catholic.† A more romantic 'Romanising' was that of the Lady Alice Hay, third daughter of the eighteenth Earl of Errol. In 1874 she married Count Charles Edward d'Albanie who claimed descent from 'Bonnie Prince Charlie'. But an even greater sensation was caused by the 'perversion' (as the Scottish Reformation Society regarded it) of the twenty-one-year-old John Patrick Crichton-Stuart, third Marquess of Bute (1847-1900) who was 'seduced' by Mgr. Capel. This priest was caricatured by Disraeli in his novel *Lothair* (1870) as the "fascinating prelate who talked fluently on every subject except High Mass". He pursued his proselytism in the drawing-rooms of Belgravia and Mayfair— even their ballrooms! Bute's submission to *Pio nono*, not to mention his Confirmation by the Pope himself, meant to all intents —so pious Presbyterians feared—that several islands off the west coast of Scotland, besides large areas on the mainland, would henceforth be *de facto* if not *de jure* parts of the Papal States. The young Marquess was immensely rich (also owning coal mines and docks in South Wales), so it was a foregone conclusion that vast sums of money would be set aside for the propagation of Popery.

There were more 'goings over to Rome' that year, and among them was that of Caroline (1837-1895) daughter of Sir Albert de Hochpied Larpent, Bt., on her marriage with John Steuart of

---

Fife (1871); Dunbar, East Lothian (1871); Methven, Perthshire (1871); Crieff, Perthshire (1871); Pathhead, Midlothian (1872); Tranent, East Lothian (1873); Fauldhouse, West Lothian (1873); Kirkintilloch, Dunbartonshire (1874); St Joseph's, Dundee (1874); Doune, Perthshire (1875); Alloa, Clackmannanshire (1876); Lochgelly, Fife (1876); South Queensferry, West Lothian (1876); Linlithgow, West Lothian (1876); Ballechin, Perthshire (1876); Duns, Berwickshire (1877); Stonehaven, Kincardineshire (1877); Innerleithen, Peebles-shire (1877); and Bankfoot, Perthshire (1877).

* Her third son, Lord Archibald Douglas, was ordained priest by Cardinal Manning in 1876, and worked as a secular priest in Scotland until he retired as an Hon. Canon of the Galloway diocese in 1920. He died in 1938.

† He joined the Benedictine community at Fort Augustus, was ordained priest, and in 1892 succeeded his brother as 7th Earl of Craigston, when he assumed the name of Pollard-Urquhart. He died in 1916.

Ballechin, Perthshire. *   Another was the Hon. Colin Lindsay (1819-92), fourth son of the twenty-fourth Earl of Crawford, seventh Earl of Balcarres.†

In 1869 Colonel David Hunter-Blair of the Scots Fusilier Guards (1827-69), fourth son of the third Baronet of Dunskey, Wigtownshire, became a Catholic in France, a few months before his death in Rome. Six years later his nephew, Captain David Hunter-Blair (1853-1939) eldest son of Sir Edward Hunter-Blair, fourth Baronet, took the same step.‡   James Ogilvie-Fairlie of Myres Castle, Auchtermuchty, Fife, and his wife were received into the Church in 1874.§ His brother, Colonel Francis Fairlie, of Coodham, Ayrshire, followed his example a year later.

The Western Vicariate

After the death of Bishop Murdoch on December 15, 1865, his successor, Bishop Gray, continued to have trouble with the Irish. Reports of dissentions in the Western Vicariate had begun to alarm some of the English Hierarchy. On April 24, 1864, Cardinal Wiseman wrote: "In my judgment there is no room to doubt that a thorough change is required in the ecclesiastical organisation of Scotland. An increase in the number of vicars-apostolic would naturally appear to be advisable in the first place; and at the same time, many difficulties would be overcome were the existing form of Church government to be modified by the nomination of ordinary bishops."**

When consulted about the restoration of the Scottish hierarchy, Bishops Murdoch, Kyle and Gray expressed their unanimous opinion that the time was not yet ripe. They felt that the proposed change would merely intensify the prejudice against Catholics and hinder the development of the Mission.

---

* This branch of the royal family of Scotland claimed direct descent from one of the illegitimate sons of James II, who died in 1460. Two of the sons of the 12th Earl of Ballechin joined religious orders.   Robert became a Jesuit, Ronald a Benedictine of Fort Augustus, and a daughter Veronica a Carmelite nun.

† He was the first President of the English Church Union, founded in 1860 to defend and further the spread of High Church principles in the Church of England.

‡ He helped to defray the cost of new churches at Newton Stewart (1876), Maybole (1878), Wigtown (1878) and Kirkoswald (1879). In 1878 he joined the newly-founded Benedictine community at Fort Augustus, was ordained priest in 1886, succeeded his father as 5th Baronet in 1896, and was 2nd Abbot of Fort Augustus from 1913 to 1919. After his retirement he became titular Abbot of Dunfermline. He translated Bellesheim's *History of the Catholic Church in Scotland* and was the author of many books, including three *Medleys of Memories.*

§ He was a Privy Chamberlain to Popes Leo XIII and Pius X. His second son, Reginald Fairlie R.S.A. (1883-1952), was a famous Scottish architect; and his fourth son, the Very Rev. Canon Gilbert Fairlie, was ordained priest in 1922.

** Bellesheim, op.cit. Vol. IV, p. 296.

The strain of long years of unwearied labour in the over-crowded and poverty-stricken closes and tenements, the hours spent in the confessional and pulpit, the financial worries and the opposition of the Irish proved too much for Bishop Gray. He begged Propaganda to give him a coadjutor and by way of pouring oil on troubled waters an Irishman was chosen in the person of Dr James Lynch, who belonged to the Congregation of the Mission, i.e. the Vincentians. For the past eight years he had been Rector of the *Collège des Irlandais* in Paris, founded in 1578. * His con-secration as titular Bishop of Arcadiopolis (the modern town of Lüleburgaz in Turkey in Asia) took place in the College Chapel on November 4, 1866. The consecrating prelate was Dr Keane, Bishop of Cloyne, who was assisted by Dr Gillooly, Bishop of Elphin, and Dr O'Hea, Bishop of Ross. Fr Tom Burke, the famous Irish Dominican preacher, delivered a rousing sermon. None of the three Scottish Vicars-Apostolic was present.

No expense was spared to mark what was regarded as a victory for the Irish priests and layfolk in the Western District of Scotland and the downfall of the 'Hielan Clique'. It is recorded that the College Chapel "was ornamented with rich Hangings, in velvet and gold, and decorated with exquisite taste. A Canopy of the richest description overhung the High Altar, the folded Hangings just permitting the beautiful marble Statue of the Madonna to be visible. Two gorgeous Chandeliers, with sixteen Branches and numerous cut-glass Pendants, adorned each side, whilst two others of great beauty were hung in front. The varied hues of light, refracted and reflected, looked like an immense collection of Irish Diamonds.† About a hundred and sixty distinguished guests par-took of a sumptuous dinner at 6 p.m. and there were apparently no Scotsmen among them, judging from the names printed. Per-haps they declined invitations.

After these festivities—almost evocative of the receptions in the Palais des Tuileries or at the Château de Compiègne with the Emperor Napoleon III and the Empress Eugénie as host and hostess—the titular Bishop of Arcadiopolis travelled to Glasgow. He took with him a superb mitre and splendid crozier, presented by the professors and students of the College, as outward symbols of his status as coadjutor to Bishop Gray. He had found on his arrival in Scotland that many of his mainly Irish flock were unemployed owing to the collapse of the cotton mills, resulting partly from the American Civil War. There was still work for them, however, in the coal and iron mines. Some were helping to build the first dock on the Clyde, opened in 1867.

---

* Born at Dublin in 1807, James Lynch studied at Clongowes and May-nooth Colleges. Shortly after his ordination to the priesthood he joined the Vincentians, and for some years was a professor at Castlenock College, Dublin.

† *Scotichronicon*, p. 512.

All that resulted from uprooting the Rector of the Irish College in Paris and sending him to Glasgow as Coadjutor to the Vicar-Apostolic of the Western District was that soon they began to act as two equal and quasi-independent bishops, not as superior and assistant. Within a year Propaganda had received more than enough information about the chaotic state of affairs on Clydeside. It requested Archbishop Manning to report on the situation which had arisen. The Holy See seems to have feared a possible schism within the Scottish Mission. *

The Archbishop of Westminster arrived at Glasgow on October 2nd, 1867. There he spent five days, meeting Bishop Gray and his coadjutor Bishop Lynch, Bishop Strain of the Eastern District and certain priests, religious and layfolk. Having returned to London he wrote a very long letter in Italian to the Cardinal Prefect of Propaganda† and he did not mince his words. He said: "The present state of the Western District of Scotland is very much like the condition of England before the Restoration of the Hierarchy. The district is very extensive; the jurisdiction of the Bishop very weak; the missions do not have diocesan government; through the lack of synods the clergy lack the laws and guidance which are in many respects necessary. As a result of this there are certain disorders and dangers, of which I do not think it necessary to give any detailed account. Until the year 1800 the Catholics of Scotland were nearly all of Scottish birth, and the clergy entirely Scottish. After that, a sudden and numerous immigration of Irishmen came to Glasgow and other industrial centres. But the great majority of these settled in Glasgow and remain there to this day. They were different from the Scots not only by race and religious conviction but they were also separated from them because of mutual prejudices, and there was a good deal of racial antipathy; the Irish population remained isolated and perhaps in some way hostile to the Scots. Moreover the notorious *Free Press* and its adherents advised the Irish to maintain this isolation. On this basis they want to show the need for appointing an Irish bishop in Glasgow."‡

* Both Wiseman (who died in 1865) and Manning had visited Scotland. The former once stayed at Beaufort Castle with Lord Lovat. Neither of the two English prelates had any knowledge of the common people of the Sister Kingdom of Presbyterianism. Manning's contacts with life in Scotland had been confined almost entirely to house-parties in the castles and mansions of the Catholic lairds. As a convert from Anglicanism, he would have found it difficult to appreciate the fervour which led to the union in 1820 of the Burghers and Anti-burghers as the United Secession Church, the formation of the Free Church of Scotland in 1843, or the amalgamation of the Associate Synod (1742) and the Relief Presbytery (1761) as the United Presbyterian Church in 1847.

† Both the original text and a translation are given in an article by the Rev. James Walsh, 'Archbishop Manning's Visitation of the Western District of Scotland in 1867'. (*Innes Review*), Spring, 1967, pp. 3-18. See also A. Bellesheim, *History of the Catholic Church of Scotland* (1890), vol. IV, pp. 293-5.

‡ Walsh, op.cit. pp. 11-12.

But Manning wrote that he could not hide the conviction that the appointment of an Irish Coadjutor [Lynch] had "done much to hinder integration, to increase the exclusiveness mentioned above, and also to foster the notion of a kind of ecclesiastical supremacy." He explained to Propaganda that the Irish priests justified their discontent on three grounds: " (1) a certain national arrogance of the Scots and lack of fraternal charity . . . (2) A lack of fairness in the administration of correction and the inflicting of suspensions of the priests of the two nations . . . (3) In the appointment of priests to different missions, the more affluent missions are given to the Scots." Manning added that he did not believe this to be true, for he had found that "the majority of the Irish faithful" showed "complete trust, submission and charity towards their Scottish pastors." He went on to say: "I must add that the unhappy discord between the Irish and the Scottish clergy is fostered by the national character and the behaviour of the Scots. The reserve of the Scots does not react sympathetically to the Irish temperament, and the clergy of Scotland, being in their home country, have held themselves aloof as if affronted by the Irish invasion. The active, expansive, zealous and sometimes more heated than calm temperament of the Irish clergy has given some annoyance to the less active and perhaps less zealous Scottish clergy. Furthermore, the strong national sympathy existing between the Irish people and the Irish clergy has perhaps, on the whole, wounded the sensitivity of some of the Scottish priests. It would be impossible to give a fair assessment of the mutual accusations of calumnies, rumours and insults. Both sides believe themselves wronged and offended, perhaps with all too much reason. But these additional matters are not the causes but rather the consequences of the present situation." *

The long letter ended with the recommendation that Bishop Lynch should be translated "to his own country", for Manning feared that "his presence in Scotland might always revive the memory if not rekindle the fires of the quarrels that have been settled." He also told Propaganda that the "characters of both the Vicar Apostolic and his Coadjutor are quite irreconcilable . . . For this reason I do not hestitate to say that the continuance of the present state of affairs is impossible; and therefore there is no other solution than the removal of one or other or of both."

Finally came the suggestion: " After thinking over the matter many times and with the help of many wise people with experience of the conditions of Scotland, I remain completely convinced that the only adequate remedy for the very serious troubles of the present and the great dangers of the future is to be found in the division of Scotland into dioceses and in the restoration of the hierarchy . . . In the face of Protestant public opinion in Scotland

* ibid, pp. 14-15.

the establishment of the hierarchy, prudently carried out, would not bring any danger of opposition. The Presbyterians nowadays concede to others full freedom of conscience and religious observance. The Anglican bishops of Scotland are not only not recognised by Scotland, but are rather disparaged. The change would not be noticed by outsiders and I have no hesitation in saying that, with prudence in the mode of execution, the erection of the hierarchy would not give occasion for any danger." *

Manning recommended that Mgr. Errington, titular Archbishop of Trebizond, should be appointed Apostolic Visitor for Scotland, with the ultimate object of restoring the hierarchy. In 1862 Pius IX had deposed him from the coadjutorship with right of succession to the see of Westminster, a position he had held since 1855. He was now working as an ordinary parish priest in the Isle of Man.† Manning said of Errington: "Although English by birth, he has intimate connections with Ireland where his brother, whose wife is of a distinguished Irish family, has made his home. He enjoys the full trust of the Most Eminent Cardinal of Dublin and of the Irish clergy and laity. His personal and religious virtue is such, as well as his energy and steadfastness of character, that there is no point in my saying anything more. I do not doubt that such an appointment should be agreeable to the Vicars Apostolic and the Scottish clergy. His English birth would not give reason for opposition in Scotland. His reputation is so well known that the reason for the appointment would be clear. The future diocese of Glasgow will require, as I think I have shown clearly in this present report, a person not only of exemplary life but someone already well prepared with mature experience of ecclesiastical and episcopal administration; conditions that cannot be found in a bishop unless he be already experienced in the episcopal office. These qualities are admirably united in the person of the Archbishop of Trebizond."

By this time Manning was such a *persona grata* with the Roman Curia that it is not surprising that Propaganda requested him to

---

* ibid, pp. 17-18.

† George Errington (1804-86) belonged to a Northumbrian family with a lineage going back to the 12th century, and his mother was Irish. Ordained at Rome in 1827, he was president of St Mary's College, Oscott, from 1843 to 1847. After the restoration of the English hierarchy in 1850 he was made first Bishop of Plymouth. In 1855 he was appointed coadjutor to Cardinal Wiseman, having already been nominated provisional Administrator of the Clifton diocese. For various reasons the Holy See decided to sever his connection with Westminster, and so enabled Manning to become the second Archbishop in 1865. Errington declined the offer of the see of Trinidad in the West Indies, and retired to the Isle of Man, which was in the Liverpool diocese. Manning was correct in telling Propaganda that he was "already well prepared with mature experience of ecclesiastical and episcopal administration," but whether this would have been much use in Scotland is doubtful. He had the reputation for being a rigorous disciplinarian of a somewhat narrow type.

approach the Archbishop of Trebizond. In a letter dated March 3rd, 1868, he explained: "The Holy Father has decided to restore the Hierarchy in Scotland and directs that your willingness should be ascertained to go as Apostolic Administrator to carry out this very great purpose . . . I trust you will accept this for many reasons."* The future Cardinal even offered to go to the Isle of Man if the now sixty-four-year-old titular Archbishop of Trebizond felt unable to face the seventy mile sea voyage to Liverpool, followed by the 193-mile train journey to London and back again.

Having consulted Mgr. William Clifford, third Bishop of Clifton, like himself a member of the old Catholic aristocracy, Errington informed Manning that he feared his age and state of health would prevent him from discharging such difficult duties with satisfaction to the Holy Father. The prospect of having to travel occasionally from the Mull of Kintyre to the Outer Hebrides, when making visitations of remote missions, may well have determined him to keep away from the Western District. More correspondence followed, and the advice of Bishop William Turner (1790-1872) of Salford was sought. The latter replied to Errington on August 10th, 1868: " Your going to Scotland, as it appears to me, would not be to settle a Vicariate trouble; but to establish a Hierarchy when it was deemed advisable, meanwhile you holding the highest rank and office that the Holy See could confer on you, hence I thought your reasons for refusing were not good . . . When Manning and Talbot were in Salford, little was said about your affair.† Manning merely said that he was sending another pressing letter from Rome which I presume you received."

When it became clear that there was no hope of inducing the titular Archbishop of Trebizond to leave his mission in the Isle of Man, even with the prospect of sooner or later becoming Archbishop of Glasgow, somebody else had to be found as Apostolic Administrator for the Western District of Scotland. Manning looked around for a cleric who, in his opinion, would be able to pour oil on the troubled waters of the Clyde. Propaganda's eventual choice was Mgr. Charles Eyre, then acting as Vicar-General of the Hexham and Newcastle Diocese, who had missed his chance as its second bishop in 1866.‡ There was already talk

* Cf. Vincent A. MacLelland, 'Documents relating to the appointment of a Delegate Apostolic for Scotland', in *Innes Review* (Autumn 1957), pp. 93-9.

† The Hon. and Rt. Rev. Mgr. George Talbot (1816-86), son of James 3rd Lord Talbot of Malahide, was chamberlain to Pius IX, and a canon of St Peter's, Rome.

‡ Charles Eyre (1817-1902) belonged to the Catholic branch of an old Yorkshire family. Educated at Ushaw College, and the English College, Rome, he was ordained priest in 1842. After working as a curate in Newcastle-upon-Tyne, his health broke down, and he became domestic chaplain at Haggerston Castle, where he wrote his *History of St Cuthbert*

of his being made coadjutor with right of succession to John B. Polding, O.S.B. (1794-1877), first Archbishop of Sydney, New South Wales, who was visiting England at that time.

Eyre's consecration as titular Archbishop of Anazarba (in lesser Armenia) took place in the Church of S. Andrea della Valle at Rome on January 31st, 1869. The consecrating prelate was Cardinal Reisach, Bishop of Sabina, assisted by Archbishop Manning, and Archbishop de Mérode, a Belgian ecclesiastic, at that date Papal Almoner.

Bishop Lynch had already left Glasgow and on April 15th he was translated to the united see of Kildare and Leighlen as co-adjutor with right of succession. * His sojourn in Scotland had lasted less than three years.

On Archbishop Eyre's arrival on Clydeside, Bishop Gray formally resigned the Vicariate into his hands and retired to Rothesay on the Isle of Bute, where he resided until his death on January 14th, 1872. Since Bishop Murdoch's death in 1865, Bishop Gray had managed to open six new missions in the Western Vicariate.†

The nine years during which the titular Archbishop of Anazarba ruled over the Western District have been summed up by Mgr. David McRoberts: "He was a man of commanding presence, physically, intellectually, and spiritually. He refused to pay any heed to the petty national jealousies which had divided his flock. He worked exclusively for the spiritual and social welfare of his people on that basis, he re-organised the Catholic life of the Western Vicariate with urbane impartiality and energy. His first act was to publish an excellent code of regulations for the conduct of ecclesiastical affairs of the District. He then divided up the extensive and heterogeneous District into eight regions or deaneries (and one notes in passing that some of the missions in the first list of deaneries had not even a patron saint). Having made his people 'of one mind in the Lord', he directed their energies towards the building up of God's Church in their midst. New churches and schools were erected and—what is no doubt the most important act of this preliminary period of Eyre's episcopate—a seminary, St Peter's College, was established at Partickhill to ensure a steady supply of clergy, trained at home for the special circumstances of the Church in the West of Scotland.‡

(1849). Then he became senior priest at St Mary's Cathedral, later a Canon, and subsequently Vicar-General of the Hexham and Newcastle Diocese.

* He succeeded Bishop James Walshe in 1888, and died in 1896.

† Rothesay, Isle of Bute (1866); St Aloysius, Garnethill, Glasgow (1866); Old Cumnock, Ayrshire (1867); Daliburgh, South Uist (1868); Shotts, Lanarkshire (1868); and St Mungo, Glasgow (1869).

‡ 'Scottish Survey' (Glasgow Observer, 1955), p. xiii.

During the nine years that Archbishop Eyre administered the Western District fifteen new missions or churches were opened. *

The foundation of Fort Augustus Abbey

One of the most noteworthy events in the history of the Western Vicariate during its last years was the foundation of the first Benedictine monastery in Scotland since the Reformation. When the Scots Monastery at Ratisbon was suppressed in 1862, Dom Anselm Robertson retired to his native country. He never gave up hope of a revival of the monastic life but meantime he continued the direction of the boys' orphanage he had founded near Glasgow.†

Early in 1872 the third Marquess of Bute, whose reception into the Catholic Church in 1868 had caused such a sensation, made a retreat at Belmont Cathedral-Priory, near Hereford, before his marriage to the Hon. Gwendoline Mary Fitz-Alan-Howard, eldest daughter of the first Lord Howard of Glossop. The guestmaster, Dom Jerome Vaughan (1841-96), was the fourth son of John Vaughan, seventh of Courtfield, Herefordshire, whose eldest brother, Herbert, was consecrated Bishop of Salford on October 28, 1872.‡ Dom Jerome, with the approval of the Abbot-President of the English Benedictine Congregation, was already planning to revive the Abbey of SS. Adrian and Denis at Lambspring, in Hanover, founded for English monks in 1644.§ He visualised a foundation somewhere near London and obtained promises of donations from several wealthy benefactors. Lord Bute's interest was aroused by this project. He seems to have told Dom Jerome that he was prepared to make a first gift of £5,000, but only if the monastery was located in Scotland and the old line of Scottish monks, of whom Dom Anselm Robertson was now the sole survivor, was incorporated into the new community. Dom Jerome had no links with Scotland, and neither had the Lambspring community, but he could hardly turn down Lord Bute's generous offer, especially considering that this immensely wealthy and devout convert peer was more to be relied on than any other benefactors.

---

* Bridgeton, Glasgow (1872); Larkhall, Lanarkshire (1872); Motherwell, Lanarkshire (1873); Glenfinnan, Inverness-shire (1874); Whifflet, Lanarkshire (1874); Troon, Ayrshire (1874); Maybole, Ayrshire (1874-8); Irvine, Ayrshire (1875); Stepps, Lanarkshire (1875); Parkhead, Glasgow (1876); Kinning Park, Glasgow (1874-6); Cleland, Lanarkshire (1874-7); Blantyre, Lanarkshire (1877); St Anthony, Govan, Glasgow (1878); Cambuslang, Lanarkshire (1878).

† See p. 301, note §.

‡ He was translated to Westminster in 1892, and created a Cardinal the following year.

§ It was suppressed by the Hanoverian government in 1803. The community returned to England and, from 1828 to 1841, resumed conventual life at Broadway, Worcestershire, after which the few remaining monks were dispersed to missions of the English Congregation. The community was never formally disbanded.

v

Nothing happened for about a year, then Bute began to discuss a site for the new monastery. By that time the superiors of the Anglo-Benedictine Congregation had agreed that it could be in Scotland and they had also consented to Bute's stipulation that when two daughter-houses had been founded they should all become an independent Scottish congregation. The Marquess first offered part of his Loudoun estates in Ayrshire. Then he recommended St Andrews and in a letter dated October 24, 1874, he wrote: " I think you should bear in mind the probability, that when a hierarchy is again established in this country, the Primate may not improbably be re-established at St Andrews, and were the primatial see (like Newport and Menevia—*parva componere magna*) to be settled for ever on the Order of St Benedict, it would surely be a matter for sincere congratulation. Nor do I think you should forget the extreme healthiness of the place, with its sea-bathing, and the ground along the sea for three miles, where the respectable and invigorating game of golf is played."*

Neither the attractions of sea-bathing nor the prospects of monastic recreations on the golf links were sufficient to convince Dom Jerome that the ancient cathedral city beside the North Sea, with its university founded in 1411 and formally recognised by Pope Benedict XIII three years later, would be the ideal spot for his foundation. Yet it is surprising that he was not tempted by the possibility of becoming a Benedictine successor to David Cardinal Beaton (1494-1546) as Primate of Scotland, which was the bait held out to him.†

Various other sites were discussed and rejected in turn. Then came an offer from Simon, thirteenth Baron Lovat, to present the English Benedictine Congregation with the buildings of a dismantled barracks, built in 1729 for the suppression of the Highland Jacobites and known as Fort Augustus. The twelfth Lord Lovat had purchased the property from the Government in 1867.‡ Abbot-President Burchall and Dom Jerome went to stay with Lord Lovat at Beaufort Castle, near Beauly, and one morning they set

* Cf. 'A Monastic Autobiography' by the Very Rev. Dom Jerome Vaughan, O.S.B.—a Reply to an article 'A Modern Monastery' in the *Pall Mall Gazette*, April 17, 1894 (Salford, 1894).
  The existence of a Benedictine diocese in England and Wales (Newport and Menevia, created in 1850, with St Michael's Priory, Belmont, near Hereford, as its pro-cathedral) gave Bute the idea of a similar diocese being set up in Scotland.
  † His elder brother, Roger Bede Vaughan (1834-83), a monk of Downside, had been consecrated as coadjutor Archbishop of Sydney, N.S.W. in 1872. Herbert Vaughan (1832-1903) was consecrated Bishop of Salford seven months later.
  ‡ The fort derived its name from George Augustus, Duke of Cumberland, youngest son of George III, better known as 'The Butcher', because of his brutality towards the Highlanders after the Battle of Culloden in 1746. The original name of the village was Abertarf.

off on the thirty-two mile drive, spending the night at the inn at Invermoriston.   There is a story, which may well be true, that when Lovat, the Abbot and Dom Jerome got out of the carriage to lighten the burden of the horses on a steep hill within a mile of Fort Augustus, Dom Jerome was so entranced by the beauty of Loch Ness and the mountains on either side, that he knelt down on the rough road, and exclaimed in the words of the psalmist: *"Hic habitabo quoniam elegi eam"* ("Here for ever is my resting place, here is my destined home"). *

Romance got the better of realism.   The impetuous thirty-four-year-old monk had no doubt that God had chosen this idyllic spot for the first Benedictine monastery to be founded in Scotland since the Reformation.   In the 1870s Fort Augustus was less easy of access than it is today—very much at the back of beyond, and in the heart of the Highlands.†   The long-abandoned fort was thirty-four miles from Inverness, the nearest town, and as yet there was no regular steamer service through the Caledonian Canal and Loch Ness.   No matter: Dom Jerome's faith was so intense that he was quite sure, if he said to any mountain "Move hence to yonder place", it would do so by some mysterious means.   Like his eldest brother, Herbert (the future Cardinal), he had the utmost confidence in the prayers of St Joseph and he therefore vowed that the new monastery would be dedicated to him.‡

Having obtained permission from Archbishop Eyre for the foundation of a monastery within the Western Vicariate in accordance with Canon Law, Dom Jerome got busy with publicity. He issued a printed appeal, far and wide, and announced that "This spot will become the source of many spiritual, and even temporal blessings to the surrounding neighbourhood, but here also the old English Monastery of Lambspring, and the Scotch College of Benedictines, which formerly existed at Ratisbon, will be restored, and the old Scottish line of Monks perpetuated.   Of these there is still one venerable father surviving, destined to be the connecting link between the Monks of the past and those of the future, and whose life appears to have been preserved thus far, that he may at length see the day he has desired and prayed for so long.   Dunfermline and Melrose, Coldingham and Arbroath, Paisley and Dundrennan, Kelso and Iona, with some twenty other Abbeys observing the rule of St Benedict, will live again, and the old chants which have been silent for so many years, will be heard once more in the land.   How great and wide an influence the new

---

* Psalm 131 (A.V. 132), v. 14.
† The West Highland Railway was not opened until 1894 and so there was no direct link with Glasgow, except by Perth, Forres and Inverness, unless one went by a change of paddle-steamers to Fort William.
‡ Eventually it was dedicated to St Benedict.

monastery is destined to exercise over the people of Scotland we cannot venture to predict." *

Then began a hectic begging tour throughout the length and breadth of Britain, with impassioned sermons by this enthusiastic monk with such great ideals. He reckoned that the monastery would cost at least £70,000 — a vast sum in those days. Both the rich and the poor were urged to contribute generously. It would not have been difficult to convert the large quadrangular buildings into a monastery and school. Planned to accommodate a garrison of between two and three hundred soldiers, with quarters for the officers, they were solidly built in the Georgian style of architecture, simple and dignified. But in the 1870's it was inconceivable that monks could serve God except beneath pointed arches, so Joseph Hansom, the seventy-four-year-old Gothic Revival architect, was commissioned to supply designs for an abbey in the 'correct' style.†

Dom Jerome managed to persuade the first Marquess of Ripon to lay the foundation-stone on September 13, 1867.‡ Considering the difficulties of transport, the lack of local labour and the remoteness of the site, it was almost miraculous that the building advanced so rapidly.

In 1877 Dom Anselm Robertson joined Dom Jerome at Fort Augustus, bringing with him some relics of the Schottenkloster at Ratisbon. When the first two novices were 'clothed' the following year, he invested them with the monastic habit, thus forming a real canonical link between the new foundation and the old Scoto-Bavarian house. The college block was opened on October 16, 1878, in the presence of a distinguished company, including Lord and Lady Lovat, Bishop John Macdonald of Aberdeen (a former alumnus of Ratisbon), the titular Abbot of Westminster (President-general of the English Benedictine Congregation) and other prominent Catholics.§

The community remained under the jurisdiction of the English Benedictine Congregation until 1882, when as the result of a

---

* Cf. Dom Odo Blundell, O.S.B., *The Catholic Highlands of Scotland*: *The Western Highlands and Islands* (1917), pp. 190-1.

A chapel dedicated to St Peter had been opened here in 1842, taking the place of the chapel at Aberchalder, four miles distant, erected in 1820. Previous to this the surrounding district had been served by the mission priests at Invergarry, often mentioned in earlier chapters of this book.

† It was he who invented the patent safety 'Hansom Cabriolet. in 1833. He died in 1882. At Fort Augustus his work consists of the college and hospice blocks. Peter Paul Pugin (1851-1904) designed the monastery and the stone-vaulted cloisters.

‡ Having been Grand Master of the English Freemasons for three years, the Marquess was received into the Catholic Church at the London Oratory in 1874, while he was Lord President of the Council.

§ The greater part of the cost of the monastery block and cloisters, which were completed in August 1880, was defrayed by Sir David Hunter-Blair, Bt. Professed as a monk of the community that same year, he became its second abbot in 1913, resigning four years later.

petition from the Scottish hierarchy, and certain members of the Scottish peerage including Lords Bute and Lovat, Leo XIII erected the monastery into an independent abbey directly subject to the Holy See. Dom Jerome Vaughan ceased to be Prior in 1886. The community was not re-united with the English Congregation until 1909.

The Northern Vicariate, 1869–78

The consecration of Mr John Macdonald as titular Bishop of Nicopolis took place in St Mary's Chapel, Aberdeen, on February 24th, 1869. * The consecrator was Mgr. Chadwick, Bishop of Hexham and Newcastle, assisted by Bishops Gray and Strain. It is related that " Bishop Lynch, owing to some oversight, was omitted in the invitations."† Fashions in ritual and ceremonial are fickle and fleeting, so it is worth recording what was regarded as the *dernier cri* of liturgical good taste at Aberdeen ninety-nine years ago: " Through the exertions in particular of the Rev. John Sutherland, the arrangements made for the Ceremony were all that could have been wished. The various Altars were tastefully decorated; the High Altar, especially, was exceedingly tasteful. A choir of some 50, under the leadership of Mr Hay, conducted the music, which commenced with the Gregorian Chant, *'Veni Creator'* (then) the Pascal Mass, by Pierre L. Lambilotte—a magnificent Composition of a French Jesuit priest, well known in the musical world . . . The Choir was greatly augmented both by Instrumentalists and Vocalists. Nearly all the solos were sung by Mrs Prendergast (wife of Brigadier-General Prendergast, both of whom had recently arrived from Madrid on a visit to the General's sister, Mrs Gordon of Wardhouse). She had volunteered to give her most efficient aid on the occasion . . . During the rendering of the *Te Deum*, the Bishop was led Pontifically through the Church, blessing the people as he went. This was a very imposing part of the Ceremony. Dr Macdonald is a handsome and stately-looking man, in the prime of life, and as he proceeded up the centre passage in his Robes and Staff, attended by the assisting Bishop, the spectacular effect was certainly striking."‡

As the titular Bishop of Nicopolis was of a very shy and retiring disposition, one wonders if he enjoyed the long drawn-out function—even the efforts made by the chorus and orchestra, with Mrs Brigadier Prendergast as *prima donna*. We are told that her "offertory piece" was Quino's *Ave-Maria;* and the "Elevation Piece", *O Salutaris* by Hummel.

Bishop Macdonald, during the nine years that he ruled over the Northern Vicariate, took little or no part in public affairs. His

* See p. 308.
† *Scotichronicon,* p. 642. He had already left Glasgow for Ireland (See p. 320).
‡ ibid, p. 643.

obituary notice in the *Catholic Directory* for 1890 recorded: "Though the district over which he had been called to preside was extensive, the number of Catholics was small, and their means not very abundant; and there would not in the nature of things be such development as has been in some other places within the same period. The Bishop was content to pass his years in the unosten- tatious but scrupulously conscientious discharge of his various duties to his flock." *

Catholic life in Scotland during the last years of the Vicars-Apostolic

A few clergymen of the Episcopal Church 'went over to Rome' during the 'sixties and 'seventies of the last century, but their secessions did not arouse much publicity. The Rev. William Humphrey, rector of St Mary Magdalene, Dundee, and chaplain to Bishop Forbes of Brechin, became a Catholic in 1868, finding his vocation as a priest of the Society of Jesus. Four years later the Rev. Edward Fortescue (Provost of Perth Cathedral from 1851 to 1871) and his wife took the same step.†

In 1861 the main school system in Scotland was placed under Government control and the Scottish Education Department was established. In 1867 a Commission was appointed to carry out a thorough investigation, which led to a report advocating a national system as the only solution of the educational problems. Reference was made to both Episcopalian and Roman Catholic schools as " hardly to be considered as a contribution to the general education of the country."

In March 1869 the Vicars-Apostolic, priests and some of the leading laity submitted a petition against the bill which was to be discussed in the House of Commons. But in 1872 the Education Act (Scotland) became law. It enforced school attendance for children of five to thirteen years of age, and made provision for schools to receive grants from the Education Department.‡ The Catholics were left free to keep their own schools and to earn grants from the government as they had done before. In theory their position remained unchanged, but in practice they had to carry a heavier burden than before. Now they were obliged to contribute to local rates, to maintain and build new public schools which the school boards—compulsory in every parish since 1872— set up in all parts of Scotland. Catholics did not have a share in any of the public funds derived from these rates.

* New churches were built at Banff (1870), Aboyne (1874) and Kirkwall, Orkney (1877). The Sisters of Mercy made foundations at Elgin (1871), and Keith (1872). The Sisters of Nazareth at Aberdeen eventually moved from Justice Street to a new convent in Claremont Street.

† Their son, the Rev. Adrian Fortescue (1874-1913), made a name for himself as a writer on the Eastern Churches and liturgical subjects.

‡ It was not until 1878 that a law was passed banning child-labour under the age of ten.

This meant that from 1872 onwards large sums of money had to be raised to build and equip new Catholic schools or to improve existing ones. The work involved by the Vicars-Apostolic and their clergy was recognised in the *Report of the Committee on Education in Scotland 1874–5,* which referred to "the extraordinary efforts the Roman Church is making for the education of her own children, while Catholics like others are rated for public schools." *
It was a hard effort, and in 1874 the expenditure for Catholic schools exceeded their income by about £500 in one district of Lanarkshire alone. Catholic teachers were paid much less than those in the public schools. In many missions the parents paid nothing for the education of their bairns.†

The Catholic Directory for the Clergy and Laity in Scotland, published annually, helps us to recreate the background and atmosphere of the missions during the eighteen-seventies. The older secular priests were still proud to be addressed as 'Mister', and it was due to the Irish that the use of the term 'Father' eventually became the norm.‡ The fear of giving offence to Protestants could still be seen in the wording "Divine Service" or "Public Service" for Sunday morning Masses at such and such an hour.

A few churches advertised "Mass with Music", but none mentioned 'High Mass'.§ At Kilmarnock there was "Public Service at nine (at which the School children sing hymns and say Catechism), and at eleven o'clock with Sermon." What is surprising is to find how easy it was for the laity in some of the larger towns to assist at Vespers on Sunday afternoon or evening.** St Andrew's, Dundee, offered Compline, Lecture and Benediction at 7 p.m. every Sunday.

In the Northern Vicariate only four of the forty chapels had Benediction every Sunday. There were a few, however, which ventured to provide this extra-liturgical devotion on the greater

---

* p. 81.

† Cf. Sister Mary Bonaventure Dealey, O.S.B., *Catholic Schools in Scotland* (Washington, D.C., 1945), pp. 123-75. It was not until after 1872 that Catholic Secondary education began to develop slowly. It had been started in 1840 when Mr Stephen Keenan, an Irish priest in charge of the Dundee mission, bought the property of Welburn, and established what was known as 'The Female Yearly Society' for the education of older children.

‡ It did not start in England until after 1850.

§ A 'Mass with Music' consisted of the priest saying a more or less inaudible Low Mass in Latin, during which the choir sang bits of things from start to finish, except during the sermon and at the consecration. The music either took the form of hymns, or selections from masses by various composers which were not too difficult for the average choir, generally made up of men, women and girls.

** Edinburgh—St Mary's, St Patrick's and the Sacred Heart; Glasgow—St Aloysius's, St Joseph's and St Mungo's; Greenock—St Laurence's. It was also possible to attend Vespers at Blairs College, Campbeltown, Dumfries, Galashiels, Hawick and Inverness.

festivals.   Over familiarity with the divine mysteries was discouraged by Bishop Kyle and the majority of his clergy.   The laity were not recommended to attend weekday Masses lest their sense of awe should grow lukewarm or cold.   Even the most devout men and women dared not go to Confession or receive Holy Communion except on what were known as the 'Times of the Eight Great Indulgences.' *   Each Holy Communion involved careful preparation for a week or longer.   The general level of piety was remarkable.   For the greater part, the inhabitants of those 'Papist pockets' in parts of Aberdeenshire, Banffshire and the Highlands remained loyal to the faith of their fathers as it had been handed down by precept and practice from the Penal Times. They were conservative by temperament, and suspicious of devotional novelties.   On Sunday afternoons they were quite happy to attend a service consisting of Religious Instruction or a Lecture, sometimes followed by the recitation of the Rosary.

In the industrial towns and villages of the Eastern and Western Vicariates great emphasis was also made on what is described in the old *Directories* as "Christian Doctrine".   At Carluke, for example, the Catechism was taught immediately after Mass for one hour by members of the Christian Doctrine Society.   At Arisaig in Morar the eleven o'clock "Public Service" was followed by Catechism in English.   There was also catechetical instruction in Gaelic at 4 p.m. during the summer months.   What must be remembered is that, of the older Catholics, many could still not read.

Stations of the Cross were becoming popular in the central Lowlands on Friday evenings and during Lent.   Most of the larger missions had already formed Arch-Confraternities and Confraternities, such as those of the Living Rosary, the Holy Family, the Sacred Heart of Jesus, the Immaculate Heart of Mary, St Joseph, the Apostleship of Prayer and the *Bona Mors*.   We find occasional references to the Society of St Vincent de Paul, whose members

---

* The eight 'Plenary Indulgences' are still explained on two pages of *The Catholic Directory for Scotland*, published annually.   The wording is as follows:

"1.   From the Feast of St Thomas, Apostle, 21st December, to the first Sunday after the Epiphany, inclusively.
2.   From Ash-Wednesday to the second Sunday of Lent, inclusively.
3.   During the time appointed in each Diocese for complying with Easter duties.
4.   From Pentecost Sunday to Sunday after Corpus Christi.
5.   From Sunday before the Feast of SS. Peter and Paul to the Octave Day.
6.   From Sunday before the Feast of the Assumption to the Octave Day.
8.   On the Feast of St Andrew, and during the Octave."

Since the new rules of 1955 the only three remaining 'Octaves' are Easter, Pentecost and Christmas, so the wording of this paragraph might be brought up-to-date.

visited the poor and gave charitable relief where needed, also to the Children of Mary. Indicative of a change in devotional habits among the laity was the increasing number of chapels in the industrial Lowlands advertising weekday Masses, where the congregations were mainly composed of families of Irish birth or descent.

Neither the old Catholic families nor the wealthy converts had much direct effect on the changes in modes of worship. During the eighteen-seventies more and more English members of the peerage, a fair number of them Catholics, were buying or renting estates in the Highlands for sporting purposes. Although deer-stalking, grouse-shooting and salmon fishing were the primary reasons for their annual migrations to 'North Britain', after the strenuous London 'Season', some of these rich aliens had domestic chaplains to say Mass for their house-parties on Sundays and holydays of obligation, if there were no Catholic chapel within easy access. A few helped to defray the cost of new churches. *

The newspapers drew attention to members of the noble Catholic families of Maxwell, Gordon, Lennox, Hastings, Fraser, Douglas, etc., when they took part in a pilgrimage to Rome in 1877, under the leadership of Bishop Strain. It was the occasion of the episcopal jubilee of Pius IX. In the name of the Vicars-Apostolic, the titular Bishop of Abila read an address and presented the Pope with the sum of £2,000. At the close of his speech the Bishop said: "When your Holiness shall be pleased to establish among us the ecclesiastical Hierarchy, as You have already done in England, there will be given a fresh impetus to religion, and many will return to the Faith of their Fathers."

As a matter of fact there were comparatively few of the old noble Catholic families left in Scotland. During the past two centuries many of them had given up their religion, while some had faded out. Even by 1877 families with alien names, none of whose members belonged to the so-called 'Upper Classes', had begun to influence Catholic life as a whole far more than the nobility and landed gentry. In the future it would be such names as Boyle, Burke, Connolly, Duffy, Gallagher, Kelly, Lynch, McGhee, McLaughlin, Maguire, Murphy, O'Connell, O'Leary, O'Sullivan, Quinn, Sheridan and Walsh—to mention but a few of the Irish families—which would mould and shape Catholicism in Scotland, even if most of the Bishops of the restored Hierarchy continued to be of native birth and descent. Except in the Dioceses

---

* Among them was Louisa Caton, great-niece of John Carroll, first Archbishop of Baltimore. In 1828 she married Francis, Lord Carmarthen, who became 7th Duke of Leeds ten years later. Left a widow in 1859, she died in 1874. Throughout her long life the Duchess was a generous benefactress to more than one mission in the Highlands, especially Brae-mar. In 1860 she built the church, school and convent at Dornie, Ross-shire, designed by Joseph Hansom.

of Aberdeen and Argyll and the Isles, both the clergy and the laity were to be of predominantly Irish origin.*

* Reference to the list of clergy in the *Scottish Catholic Directory* proves this. More than half have Irish names.

CHAPTER ELEVEN

RESTORATION OF THE HIERARCHY
1878

IN SEPTEMBER 1877 it was reported that business had started in Rome for restoring the normal government of the Church in Scotland, twenty-seven years having elapsed since the restoration of the English Hierarchy. Many of the older clergy agreed with the objections to the proposal which had been drawn up by Bishop Kyle before his death on February 28th, 1869. He had pointed out: (1) The fewness of Scottish Catholics amid the overwhelming Protestant majority; (2) Many so-called Catholics were not practising their religion; (3) A large proportion, notably the Irish, had no fixed domicile, but roamed around the country, and often left it altogether; (4) The poverty of the greater number of the faithful who were manual labourers—so poor that they could not provide for the bare necessities of divine service; (5) It was only by dint of great effort that it was possible to maintain the existing ecclesiastical arrangements and to meet the heavy debts that weighed down missions; (6) It would probably weaken the ties uniting Scottish Catholics with the Holy See were independent bishops to be introduced; (7) Last, but not least, it would be unwise to ignore the legal penalties to which regular bishops would render themselves liable by the assumption of territorial titles. *

Cardinal Manning, however, had produced the following answers to Bishop Kyle's warnings. He explained that: (1) The restoration of the Hierarchy would be greatly to the benefit of the clergy; (2) Many converts, who wanted to join the secular clergy, preferred to be incardinated into English dioceses which were properly organised, and thus Scotland suffered from these defections; He quoted (3) what Cardinal Wiseman had written to Propaganda in 1864: " There is no doubt that the dominant Presbyterianism of the country has had its influence on the Catholics, who have consequently lost their fervour in many ways, and in particular who have little liking for episcopal rule. I am of the opinion that these Presbyterian leanings, which are not infrequently apparent in the attitude of the priests towards their bishops, would be effectually destroyed by the mere fact of once again having a regularly ordered hierarchy". Wiseman had also

---

* Cf. Bellesheim, op.cit. Vol. IV, pp. 299-300.

stressed (4) that "the overwhelming majority of Catholics in the great commercial and manufacturing towns are poor Irish". He pointed out that in Ireland they were held firm to the fulfilment of their religious duties by their parish priests, to whom they were bound by inseparable ties. These ties were wanting in e.g. Edinburgh and Glasgow, where the Irish aliens were lost among Protestants and unbelievers. "Without parish priests or bishops, the hold which religion has upon them is not sufficiently firm." (5) Manning himself felt that the position of the Episcopal Church in Scotland could not be ignored. He was certain that the erection of a true ecclesiastical hierarchy would impress the members of this small body, who numbered about 55,000. Nearly all belonged to the upper classes, and consequently were presumed to possess great influence. He explained to Propaganda that many Episcopalians approximated both in doctrine and ritual observances to those of the Catholic Church. There was, therefore, only one point of difference between Catholics and Episcopalians—the duty of being in communion with the Holy See. The arguments in favour of the immediate abolition of the Apostolic Vicariates in Scotland were thus summed up: "Under these circumstances the revival of a national hierarchy was greatly to be desired; and indeed, if they retained any longer than was absolutely necessary ecclesiastical designations borrowed from heathen countries, leaving Protestants to usurp the ancient titles, the effect on recent converts could not but be highly detrimental, and might lead to consequences whose extent it was impossible to foresee." *

It is difficult not to feel that Cardinal Manning's friends in Scotland, most of whom belonged to the peerage and landed gentry, and who had only a remote knowledge of middle and working-class mentality in the industrial areas, had been leading him up the garden path when it came to the influence wielded by the Episcopalians, and the importance of recent aristocratic converts. Had the Cardinal Archbishop of Westminster, and former Archdeacon of Chichester, investigated the services in Episcopalian churches more carefully he would have found very few signs of close affinity between their ritual and ceremonial observances and those of the Latin Church.†

---

* *Acta Romana*; Nota d'Archivio, 26-33.   Cf. Bellesheim, op.cit. Vol. IV, pp. 300-2.

† A strong 'Anglicanizing' movement had been going on since about 1860, the policy of which was to achieve complete identification of the Episcopal Church in Scotland with the Church of England. The first step in this direction was the attempted complete suppression of the 1764 Scottish Liturgy, which was regarded as 'Popish', though actually it was framed more on Eastern than on Western lines. Largely due to the intervention of Mr Gladstone, then Chancellor of the Exchequer and leader of the House of Commons, a new Code of Canons drawn up in 1863 allowed the retention of the Scottish Liturgy in congregations where it was already in

The only member of the hierarchy composed of seven bishops who had strong Catholic leanings was Bishop Forbes of Brechin, who died in 1875. Bishop Eden of Moray and Ross was a learned moderate High Churchman, but Bishop Charles Wordsworth of St Andrews, Dunkeld and Dunblane, had such a horror of even mild Tractarian ceremonial that he refused to take part in the services at his own cathedral in Perth from 1859 to 1872.

There is little doubt that Manning had formed a wrong impression of the religious outlook of the estimated 3,360,000 total population of Scotland in the early 'seventies. The Papists numbered about 300,000, and the Episcopalians only 55,000. This left a majority of roughly 3,000,000, the greater number of whom were at least nominal members of one or other Presbyterian body. The Episcopalians were virtually a small but select group of nonconformists, often referred to as 'The English Kirk'. *

In the autumn of 1877 both Archbishop Eyre and Bishop Strain were summoned to Rome, so that they could take part in the negotiations which had been started. Cardinal Manning arrived towards the end of December, having been held up in Paris for two months with a severe illness. There was already much talk in non-Catholic circles about the almost certain creation of a Scottish Hierarchy, and on September 6 the *Glasgow Herald* had stated: " Since it pleases the Pope to call the bishops, who hold spiritual sway over the Roman Catholics sojourning in her midst, by titles taken from her ancient cities, she (Scotland) will allow him to do so, since it gives him pleasure, and does her no harm. Scotland will not for a moment deem that her liberties, civil or religious, are endangered, if Archbishop Eyre calls himself Archbishop of Glasgow . . . If Pius XI re-establishes the Roman Catholic hierarchy in this country, he will only act in accordance with the principle which has always guided the Roman See."

A prominent Free Kirk minister, Dr James Begg, who was Moderator of their General Assembly in 1865, and had written what from their point of view was a standard "Handbook on

---

use, but for all official functions the 1662 English communion rite had to be used, also in all new congregations, unless a majority of applicants to the diocesan bishop desired the 1764 rite. This was a partial victory for the 'Low Church' or 'Anglicanizing' party, represented by Dr Ewing (Bishop of Argyll and the Isles from 1847 to 1874). He never failed to call himself a " Protestant'.

* Possibly more significant than the presumed approximation between Episcopalian and Papist ritual and ceremonial was the foundation in 1865 of the Church Service Society by a group of liturgically-minded Presbyterian ministers. Two years later they published a *Euchologion or a Book of Common Order*. It ran into several editions, and helped towards a gradual renascence of more liturgical worship in the Established Kirk. (Cf. W. H. Maxwell, *A History of Worship in the Church of Scotland*, 1955, pp. 176-81).

Popery", expressed his opinions in language that was almost libellous, and on November 23 he was rebuked by the *Scotsman.* This newspaper had already explained to its readers that the restoration of the hierarchy was a purely internal act on the part of the Church of Rome, and one which did not affect Protestants of any denomination. The London *Times* went so far as to state that the proposed change in ecclesiastical government was strictly in accordance with canon law, and said: "the Pope may do just what he likes in this matter." A writer in the *Pall Mall Gazette,* however, felt it worthwhile to warn Roman Catholics that they were mistaken in supposing the restoration of the hierarchy would be a triumph for their Church in the Sister Kingdom. The *Glasgow Herald* felt rather differently and expressed the opinion that the creation of normal church government in Scotland might well lead to more Protestants, of all classes of society, seceding to the Roman Church. The *Times* agreed with this, but felt there was no reason to be alarmed.

As to the various Presbyterian bodies, for the most part they were too pre-occupied with their own internal dissentions to spare the energy to protest against threatened papal aggression. As Dr Maclean pointed out in his *Counter Reformation in Scotland 1560-1930:* "This important event in the history of Romanism in Scotland was received by the mass of the people with singular unconcern. But this apparent listlessness should not be construed as sheer indifference on the claims and power involved in this new display of Roman aggression. Organised societies, as in the eighteenth century, gave unhesitating expression of slumbering suspicion and distrust of the Scottish people, and memorials and petitions against this new threat to their Reformation heritage."[*]

Pius IX died on February 7, 1878, after the longest pontificate in history: and Leo XIII restored the Hierarchy of Scotland on March 4, the day of his coronation, by the Bull *Ex Supremo Apostolatus Apice.*[†] Two hundred and seventy years had elapsed since the death of Archbishop James Beaton of Glasgow, the last surviving member of the pre-Reformation Scottish Hierarchy.[‡]

The Bull provided for two archbishoprics — St Andrews and Edinburgh, and Glasgow; four bishoprics — Aberdeen, Argyll and the Isles, Dunkeld, and Galloway or Whithorn. The four bishoprics were to be suffragan sees of St Andrews and Edinburgh. The following nominations were made:—Mgr. Strain (Vicar-Apostolic of the Eastern District) Archbishop of St Andrews and Edinburgh and Metropolitan; Mgr. Macdonald (Vicar Apostolic of the Northern District) Bishop of Aberdeen; the Rev. Angus Macdonald to be Bishop of Argyll and the Isles; and the Rev. George Rigg

[*] op.cit. p. 272.

[†] The greater part of the Bull in an English translation will be found in Appendix XIX of Bellesheim, op.cit. Vol. IV, pp. 414-21.

[‡] See p. 4.

to be Bishop of Dunkeld. Archbishop Eyre was translated to the see of Glasgow, from being Administrator of the Western District.

There had been much difficulty in the choice of the metropolitan see. Manning was strongly in favour of Glasgow, but Strain insisted on Edinburgh. Manning maintained that Glasgow was not only the chief centre of commerce, manufactures and navigation, but it also had by far the largest Catholic population. It began to look at one moment as if the dispute would never be amicably settled. Finally a compromise was proposed—to give St Andrews and Edinburgh precedence over Glasgow, but to raise the Glasgow see, as in pre-Reformation times, to archiepiscopal rank, directly subject to the Holy See, but without any suffragan bishops, at least for the time being. This plan was finally adopted and incorporated in the wording of the Bull.*

The geographical distribution of the diocese was profoundly influenced by Manning's conviction that it was important to stress continuity with pre-Reformation sees, the titles and areas of which had been retained by the Episcopal Church, although in some cases pre-Reformation dioceses had been united.† A completely unsentimental and realistic plan would have boldly chosen the four main centres of population—Glasgow, Edinburgh, Aberdeen and Dundee—and named the bishops accordingly, granted that Glasgow and Aberdeen were medieval titles.

In 1878, St Andrews—the medieval ecclesiastical heart of Scotland—had (possibly) two Catholic families, and no place of worship. The cathedral 'village' of Dunkeld, with a population of about 400, had no resident Catholics, and nearly half-a-century was to elapse before there was any need to provide a Mass-centre. Bishop Rigg chose to live at Perth. The ancient royal burgh of Whithorn, with about 1,500 inhabitants including a few Irish families, did not justify a permanent chapel, much less a cathedral. There were no Catholics on the islands of Iona and Lismore, where the cathedrals of the sees of the Isles and Argyll has been located in medieval times. Practical considerations in fact dictated the residence of the Bishops of the new Hierarchy. Only those of Aberdeen and Glasgow fixed their headquarters where there were medieval cathedrals, now used for Presbyterian worship.

Whoever was responsible for the arrangement of the new dioceses cannot have realised what needless waste of time and money was being created for most of the bishops when making visitations. In the eighteen-seventies public transport depended on

---

* Glasgow was first made an archiepiscopal see by Innocent VIII in 1492, Dunkeld, Dunblane, Galloway and Argyll becoming its suffragans. Dunblane was restored to St Andrews in 1500 and Dunkeld shortly afterwards.

† So there were St Andrews, Dunkeld and Dunblane; Moray, Ross and Caithness; Argyll and the Isles. The diocese of Edinburgh was founded by Charles I in 1633.

the services provided by the various railway and steamer companies. There were no motor-cars or motor buses—far less aeroplanes. Had Cardinal Manning and his advisers consulted *Bradshaw's Railway Guide* before they drew up the boundaries of the new dioceses on a map, they would have saved bishops many a long and weary journey during the next half-century. *

The Bull has a significance which appears to have escaped notice at the time. Since the Act of Union of 1707 Scotland had ceased to be an independent nation. The Roman authorities might very well have ignored ancient political boundaries and created instead a united Hierarchy for Great Britain, the reigning Archbishop of Westminster adding *'Scotiae'* to his style of *'Coaetus Episcopalis totius Angliae et Cambriae Praeses Perpetuus'*. It is rather surprising that the Holy See in 1878 should have recognised that Scotland was still legally a 'Sister Kingdom' and not merely N.B. (North Britain), as English people generally addressed letters when writing to people beyond Carlisle or Berwick-on-Tweed. The Scottish Nationalist movement had not even been thought of, and most Scotsmen were still satisfied with the *status quo* of their country, except for a small handful of romantics, who lived in a Jacobite past and dreamed of the restoration to the throne of Britain of a descendant of Henrietta, daughter of Charles I.

The method of electing bishops— not identical in all countries —was another point which had to be decided at Rome. Eventually after 1850 it became practically the same in Scotland as in England. Where there were no chapters, the election was to be in the hands of the bishops, who voted three times and transmitted the names of the candidates to Propaganda in the order corresponding to the number of votes given to each.†

* The following figures show the number of Catholics in the three Vicariates (1877) and in the six Dioceses (1878):

	1877		1878
Western	225,600	Argyll & the Isles	10,400
		Glasgow	222,300
		Galloway (Whithorn)	16,700
		St Andrews &	
Eastern	74,300	Edinburgh	43,200
		Dunkeld	27,500
Northern	12,500	Aberdeen	12,500
Total	312,400		332,600

In 1969 the estimated Catholic population of Scotland was 818,930. The Established Church (Presbyterian) had a total membership of 1,201,033. The Episcopal Church claimed 52,950 Communicants. Its Congregations mustered 364 in comparison with the 2,115 of the Established Kirk of Scotland.

† In some dioceses it was a long time before cathedral chapters were erected. The dates are as follows: Glasgow (1884); St Andrews & Edinburgh (1885); Aberdeen (1892); Dunkeld (1895); Galloway (1901); Argyll & the Isles (1907).

Chapters having been erected, the method of election was different. On a see falling vacant, the chapter would meet and nominate three candidates by secret votes. These names would be notified to the Metropolitan, or in the event of his see being vacant, to the senior suffragan bishop who, after deliberation with the other bishops, would submit the result to the Holy See. The Pope retained the right to pass over the individual name, and to appoint another cleric to the vacant see, by what is known as *motu proprio*. It took time to solve the problem of finding a satisfactory arrangement for supporting the episcopate in the new dioceses.

The Bull *Ex Supremo Apostolatus Apice* failed to arouse any remarkable public demonstrations against priestcraft and popery. Instead of exploding with a loud bang, it merely fizzled like a damp squib. There were a few isolated protests, mainly among Orangemen in the industrial Lowlands, and from some of the more bigoted Free Kirk ministers in the Highlands, but that was all. Actually the only serious opposition to the papal bull came from the College of Bishops of the Scottish Episcopal Church, in a joint letter published on April 13, 1878. This manifesto was worded as follows: "In the name of God, Amen. Whereas we, the undersigned bishops, occupy by Divine permission the ancient sees of the Church of Scotland, claiming none other authority and jurisdiction than such as were claimed and exercised by the bishops of the primitive Church, before any of the kingdoms of this world became the kingdoms of our God and His Christ; and teaching the faith once delivered to the Saints (and none other) as it is contained in the Holy Scripture, and defined by the ecumenical Synods of the undivided Church of Christ; and whereas the Bishop of Rome, who neither hath nor ought to have any authority or jurisdiction, ecclesiastical or spiritual, in this realm, hath, on the plea of a pretended universal supremacy over the Church of Christ, intruded prelates of his own appointment into sees occupied by us; and whereas it is the law of primitive episcopacy, as instituted by the apostles of our Lord Jesus Christ, that all bishops in the Church of Christ are of the same order and hold the same apostolic office, and that for any one of them to claim universal supremacy is to usurp the office of the Lord himself; and whereas, also it is according to canonical rule and the order of the Catholic Church that there should be but one bishop in the same see, so that the intrusion of a second bishop into a see already occupied is a violation of the law of unity, and a rending of the body of Christ: we, therefore, the bishops aforesaid, etc . . ." *

* This letter was printed in *The Times*, April 22, 1878. It was signed by the seven bishops: Suther (Aberdeen and Orkney); Jermyn (Brechin); Cotterill (Edinburgh); Wilson (Glasgow and Galloway); Eden (Moray and Ross); Mackarness (Argyll and the Isles); and Wordsworth (St Andrews, Dunkeld and Dunblane).

The wording of this manifesto did not convey the idea that the Episcopal Church approximated in doctrine as well as in ritual observance to the forms of the Catholic Church. It gave no encouragement to the hopes that Manning had expressed to Pius IX and Propaganda, that before long there "would be but one point of difference between Catholics and themselves—namely, the obedience which the former rendered, and the latter refused, to the Holy See." *

Scottish lawyers on their part were interested in the purely legal aspects of the Bull. Both the Dean of Faculty (Mr Fraser) and Mr Taylor Innes had stated in the *Scotsman* that, although the recent papal act was contrary to Scots Law, yet in their opinion no pains or penalties would be incurred by the prelates adopting titles conferred on them by the Pope. They said: "Though we are of the opinion that the Pope's jurisdiction is abolished in Scotland, yet no one can by process of interdict, declaration or otherwise, prevent the establishment of the proposed hierarchy, or the assumption of titles by the Pope's bishops. All that the law does is to refuse recognition of such titles. A court of law would dismiss an action brought in the name of a person calling himself a bishop in virtue of the Pope's letters, or at all events order such designation to be struck out of a summons or other legal writ."

Pope Leo XIII, in a consistory held on March 28, 1878, said to the assembled cardinals: " We rejoice, Venerable Brethren, that it fell to our lot to satisfy the fervent desires of our beloved children in Christ, the clergy and faithful of Scotland, whose devotion to the Chair of Peter, has been manifested by many and most signal proofs. And we firmly trust that this work, now accomplished by the Holy See, will be crowned by joyful fruits, and that, under the protecting care of the Patron Saints of Scotland, it will be the case more and more in that region, that her mountains will be clothed with peace, and her hills with righteousness for her people."†

So ended the long drawn-out story of the Catholic Mission in Scotland, with the foundation of a new Church. An indication of how Catholicism in Scotland has come up from underground since the restoration of the Hierarchy in 1878 is found in the diocesan statistics of Catholics for 1969‡:— St Andrews & Edinburgh, 126,000; Aberdeen, 11,620; Argyll & the Isles, 11,270; Dunkeld,

---

* Bellesheim, op.cit. Vol. IV, pp. 301-2.

† Reprinted in *The Tablet*, 1878 (Vol. I), p. 387. Bishops as such have no precedence in Scotland, although the Moderator of the General Assembly of the Church of Scotland takes legal rank between the Lord Chancellor of Great Britain and the Prime Minister.

‡ Cf. *The Tablet*, 1878, Vol. 1, p. 435.

53,000; Galloway, 42,430; Glasgow, 325,830; Motherwell, 169,890; Paisley, 80,496. In 1878 the total Catholic population of Scotland was estimated at 332,600; in 1969 it was said to be 818,930.

APPENDIX

'Regular' and 'Irregular' marriages in Scotland

There was no period after the Reformation when it was impossible for a Scottish Catholic to contract a *valid* marriage. What must be remembered is that although the State imposed heavy penalties on a priest who officiated at a marriage, the decrees of the Council of Trent (1564) affecting matrimony were not promulgated in Scotland until September 1st, 1908. It was only then that the presence of a priest became necessary for the *canonical* validity of a marriage in which one or both of the parties was a Catholic.

The Scottish law of marriage is based on the Canon Law of the Roman Church as administered in Church Courts before the Reformation. As the present Archbishop of Glasgow, Mgr. James Donald Scanlan, D.C.L., B.L., wrote in 1958: " Canon Law has a strong bias in favour of marriage and tries to make the contracting of it . . . as simple as its dissolution is difficult. Thus in its classical period Canon Law made marrying a matter of mere consent and for centuries upheld the validity of clandestine marriages." *

A valid marriage in Scots Law may be either *regular* or *irregular,* according to the way in which it is constituted. A regular marriage is a marriage celebrated by a minister of religion (originally a minister of the Established Church, either Episcopal or Presbyterian), after banns in a place of worship of the Establishment, or (since 1878) notice to the civil registrar, or (since 1940) licence from the sheriff. In penal times all regular marriages had to take place before an Established minister, except where an Episcopalian marriage was celebrated by virtue of the Toleration Act of 1712. It was not until the Marriage (Scotland) Act, 1834, that it became generally lawful for marriages to be celebrated by clergymen not belonging to the Established Kirk.

Up to 1940 there were three forms of *irregular* marriage: (1) declaration *de praesenti,* i.e. the exchange of consent to marriage there and then, neither witnesses nor writing being essential; (2)

* An *Introduction to Scottish Legal History* (The Stair Society, Edinburgh, 1958), p. 71.

promise *subsequente copula* (technically betrothal) converted into marriage as soon as intercourse occurred; and (3) marriage by habit and repute. *

In 1940 the first two forms were abolished and only 'habit and repute' remains. For this no formal contract was or is needed. The parties must live together for a considerable period, treating each other as man and wife, and being regarded as such by their neighbours, friends and acquaintances. Such a marriage is valid no longer in the Canon Law of the Roman Church, but it was so for Scottish Catholics until 1908, when St Pius X applied the 1564 Tridentine marriage regulations to all parts of the world.

Mgr. Scanlan observed in the paper read to the Stair Society: "The Church directed the faithful to exchange their matrimonial consent publicly—*in faci ecclesiae*—and have their nuptials blessed by the priest; but that was not under pain of nullity".

The hardship for Papists in penal times was that for *regular* marriages it was necessary to find a friendly minister willing to publish the banns and perform the ceremony. Further the man and woman had to associate themselves with the Established Kirk for the puprpose, and this was forbidden in the *Statute* drawn up by Bishop Nicolson in 1700, which laid down: "Catholics married by Protestant ministers are to do public penance".

If a man had property, it was important to be able to prove that the lady with whom he was cohabiting was his *legal* wife, and that the children were not bastards in the eyes of the law. So long as the Kirk remained a power in Scotland, it could try to discipline a man for 'fornication' unless his marriage could be proved. There were many advantages in a regular marriage for, while an irregular marriage was just as valid under Scots Law and Canon Law, the problem was how to prove it. Eventually a standard was evolved. A man arranged to be prosecuted before a friendly magistrate or justice of the peace for having contracted a clandestine and irregular marriage. Having been convicted and subjected to a nominal fine, e.g. 4s 6d, the law-breaker procured an extract of his conviction and this served as a marriage certificate. The document was retrospective in its effect, i.e. the possessor was treated as married from the time the 'offence' was committed, possibly years before.†

So it can be seen that Scottish Catholics during the penal times had no difficulty in *contracting* valid marriages (according to Canon Law). The difficulty lay in *proving* that they had been contracted under Scots Law. While it was naturally thought better to have a priest to bless the contract, his presence was purely 'devotional', for a Catholic marriage up to 1908 was just as *valid* without him.

---

* 'Gretna Green' marriages followed form (1).
† The Marriage (Scotland) Act, 1856, made it possible for marriage to be registered by declaration before the sheriff.

INDEX